Law for the builder

Stephanie E. Owen
Ll.B (Hons), Solicitor

SHEFFIELD HALLAM UNIVERSITY
LEARNING CENTRE
WITHDRAWN FROM STOCK

Longman
Scientific &
Technical

D0302456

Longman Scientific & Technical
Longman Group UK Limited
Longman House, Burnt Mill, Harlow
Essex CM20 2JE, England
Associated companies throughout the world

© Longman Group UK Limited 1987

All rights reserved; no part of this publication may be
reproduced, stored in a retrieval system, or transmitted
in any form or by any means, electronic, mechanical,
photocopying, recording, or otherwise, without the
prior written permission of the Publishers or a licence
permitting restricted copying in the United Kingdom
issued by the Copyright Licensing Agency Ltd, 33–34
Alfred Place, London WC1E 7DP.

First published 1987
Reprinted (twice) 1990

British Library Cataloguing in Publication Data

Owen, Stephanie E.
    Law for the builder.___(Longman technician series)
    1. Law___England 2. Building laws___England
I. Title
344/203'7869   KD665.C/

ISBN 0-582-41619-1

Produced by Longman Group (FE) Limited
Printed in Hong Kong

For Barry, Edward and Chloë

Contents

Preface

This book is not intended for lawyers. It has been written for the many thousands of builders who are faced with legal problems either in their daily work or when studying for their building examinations. After lecturing to building students for a number of years it became apparent that the average builder takes to the law like a duck to water, providing the information is shown to be relevant to the building industry and wherever possible plenty of diagrams are given. This book has been designed to convey the essential elements of English Law in a relatively simple way, providing as much information and practical suggestions as possible and there are over 50 diagrams to assist. The index is detailed and should be used in conjunction with the text as a glossary.

Preferably the book should be read from the beginning as many of the mysteries of English Law can be simply explained by reference to legal history.

In a book of this nature which covers so many areas of the law, I had to finally fix the law as best I could as at October 1985. I appreciate that there will be some areas in which there will be changes and I urge the reader to open a legal file into which he can start putting relevant cuttings, brief notes on radio programmes, articles from professional journals etc. so that he builds up a living picture of the English legal system as it affects him. I hope also that by the time he throws away this book (and buys a new edition) that it will be dog-eared with use, pencilled and underlined, which is how a law book should be especially for those studying for examinations. There is undoubtedly a correlation, in my experience, between high grades in examinations and 'dog-earedness' of books.

Finally I hope that my book will encourage all builders to share my enthusiasm for the law. No other discipline is so relevant to everyday life and a well informed person gets much more satisfaction from their work.

Stephanie Owen
Ashtead April 1986

Author's acknowledgements

I wish to express my grateful thanks to the following; my mother Barbara Owen who typed the bulk of the manuscript; Margaret and Russell Morris for their help with the index; Reginald Greenslade who provided the illustrations of a transfer and a conveyance, and read much of the manuscript; my former colleagues Margaret Hollins and Philip Williams who also read much of the manuscript and made many helpful suggestions; Margaret Palmer and the library staff at NESCOT and the Chartered Institute of Building for allowing me to use the photograph of the Institute's charter.

In addition I would like to thank Leslie Bell, Bobbie Bradford, Breda Dallimore, Sarah and Dick Jefferies, Valerie Leech, Richard and Edgar Owen, Diana Price, Deborah Spinks, the Start family and my long suffering husband Barry.

Any errors that remain are of course my sole responsibility.

Table of cases

Table of statutes

Table of statutory instruments

CHAPTER 1

The nature of law and its sources

'To begin at the beginning' DYLAN THOMAS/UNDER MILK WOOD

What is law?

The law

Laymen often have a jaundiced view of the law, and no wonder. To them the 'law' means big bills, policemen, red tape, divorce, prison and American movies. What they forget is that the more harrowing aspects should only play a small part in the life of the average man. In other respects however, the law can creep into every nook and cranny of his life. Nearly every important occasion is affected by legal considerations, whether it is registering a birth, celebrating a coming of age, marrying, buying a house, making a will or dying. Even the builder lives his life in this manner!

The law and the builder

At work, the builder is even more beset with the need to comply with legal requirements. Before he can build, he may have to buy land by the process known as conveyancing. He may enter into a contract to build on someone else's land and will have to enter into hundreds of contracts to buy all the necessary materials. He must make sure that he has planning permission and must deposit plans which satisfy the Building Regulations. He will have to enter into contracts of employment with his workers and may negotiate with trade unions. He may operate his business as a sole trader or in partnership or may form a limited company. He must build carefully to comply with the contract specifications, the Construction Regulations, the Defective Premises Act 1974, the Health and Safety at Work etc. Act 1974 and to avoid being sued for breach of contract or negligence. He must not cause nuisances to his neighbours whilst building. He should make satisfactory insurance arrangements to cover his liability for many occurrences. He must not trespass on the neighbour's land, build beyond building lines, cause obstructions of highways nor dismiss his workers without good reason. The list is endless!

Why do we need laws?

Even in the most primitive of societies, people live their lives by rules which they create. Some things they make compulsory, others they prohibit. Such rules are imposed to make people behave in a similar way, in order to provide a harmonious way of life. For example, it is undesirable to have uncontrolled violence or theft, and ancient British tribes would have had customary rules dealing with such matters, punishing those who transgressed.

Without such rules, each person would have to make individual choices concerning his behaviour, which, whilst being perfectly logical and moral for himself, would not benefit society as a whole. For example, it is logical and much more usual to drive on the right-hand side of the road, yet it is the law of England and Wales that we drive on the left. Anyone failing to do so, would cause chaos. And so it is for the bulk of our law – it is there to prevent chaos, to create an ordered way of life.

What sort of laws do we need?

Obviously, laws are needed which support popularly held ideals. Thus, in the early days of English law, people would have been most concerned with protecting themselves, their families, land and property, and the laws that developed reflected this.

As society became more complex, and people stopped manufacturing everything on their own, they began to buy and sell things, and to get others, such as builders, to work for them rather than do the work themselves. As a result of these business dealings, a large body of mercantile law developed.

Following the Industrial Revolution, the state increasingly began to take a protectionist attitude towards the people, far different from the old *laissez-faire*, caveat emptor approach of nineteenth century law. Much social and consumer legislation has been passed in the twentieth century, and today there is a high level of legal control in all walks of life.

Thus, the law has to a certain extent, mirrored the changes in society, getting more complex, and increasing in volume as society has grown more sophisticated. Similarly, the methods of law creation have grown more complicated. What originally would have been a mere customary rule, must now either be created by Parliament, or by judges making decisions on the finer points of law in court cases.

Who benefits from the law?

As stated before, the law is mainly needed to benefit society as a whole, but this should not be at the cost of the individual. A fine balance must be maintained. This is so in nearly every country.

However, sometimes the balance is tipped in favour of the state, as in communist countries. Even in this country, many people feel that the law is unfair to them individually.

Substantive and adjective law

The laws necessary to achieve a harmonious way of life are substantive laws, i.e. the very substance of the law itself such as a law against killing people. Such law on its own however, would fail through lack of procedure to follow the law through to prosecution and if necessary, punishment. Thus, adjective law, which is concerned with procedural law, court practice and rules of evidence, is needed to make substantive law actually work.

Good law and bad law

This is entirely subjective. What may be good for society, may be bad for the individual. What is good and what is bad? Once again, the law can only reflect society's wishes, and if society does not meet with our personal conception of right or goodness, then we dub it bad law. Nazi Germany or Idi Amin's Uganda had laws which were perfectly valid during those regimes. To change such law one needs to change the society that created it. This can be done peacefully by evolution as in most western states today, or forcefully, by revolution, for example, as in Iran, where a modern legal system has been replaced by traditional Islamic law.

Even with an evolutionary process such as we now have in England and Wales, we have good and bad law, depending on our particular point of view. The way we think depends on our upbringing, religion, education, politics and many other external influences. Such factors also affect one's private morals and for that reason, morality is generally not the concern of the law.

Because we are not all alike, the law will not suit everybody. It is merely the lowest common denominator which will satisfy most people's requirements of a legal system, and achieve maximum stability in the state.

The 'law' compared with other types of law

- The long arm of the *Law*
- The *Law* of Gravity
- Criminal *Law*
- French *Law*

The word 'Law' of course, is used in other contexts, and thus, it is important to define one's terms. Scientific laws, for example are totally different to legal ones, for they describe things which must necessarily happen, such as the Law of Gravity. Legal laws can only lay down rules for people to follow. Whether they do or not is up to them. To encourage adherence to the rules, most have some element of coercion behind them, whether it is a threat of loss of liberty or some other right, or a financial penalty.

Every country in the world has law of some sort, and within each legal system, there are many different areas covering all aspects of life. Fortunately, for the purposes of this book, we are 'only' going to examine English law, i.e. the law applying to England and Wales.

The composition of a legal rule

Every area of law is made up of many individual little laws. A complex example of this can be found in the law of contract, which has hundreds of thousands of legal rules.

Each legal rule consists of two parts: a **right** and a **duty**. Thus, there is a duty imposed on all people in this country – not to kill others. Conversely, everyone has a right to life, or a right not to be killed. If someone breaks this rule, or as we say **breaches** his duty, then the state, on behalf of the people for whom the rule was designed to protect, will punish the wrongdoer. Thus, all legal rules are rather like see-saws (*see* Fig. 1.1).

This book is therefore concerned with many rights and duties under the law with which the builder must concern himself, and it is hoped that this introduction to the concept of law will help the reader with his studies.

English law

Legal systems in the British Isles

English law is the law of England and Wales – not of the United Kingdom, for in the United Kingdom of Great Britain and Northern Ireland, there are three legal systems, Scotland and Northern Ireland having their own. The Channel Islands and the Isle of Man are merely direct dependencies of the Crown and have their own legal systems. The reason for there being no uniformity is purely historical. The Scottish legal system for example, developed in an entirely different way with much European influence, as it was a totally separate country until the Act of Union 1707. It would be foolish to imagine that two countries would ever develop in the same way through a period which knew no other forms of communication than that provided by horse or foot. Wales, on the other hand, was conquered by the English in the thirteenth century, at a time when English law was only in its infancy. The new overlords imposed the new developing law on the Welsh, and thus, the laws of Hywel Dda are now lost in the mists of antiquity.

Example 1 The rule against murder

| Duty not to kill | Right not to be killed |

If the balance is tipped by a murderer, then the murderer will be punished on behalf of the state as the breach 'activated' that right.

Right to punish the murderer

Man kills someone

Example 2 In a building contract, the builder and the employer enjoy many different rights and are under many duties. At its simplest, the main object of the contract is that the employer wants building work done and the builder wishes to be paid for that work.

| Employer's duty to pay for work done | Builder's right to be paid for work |

If the employer fails to pay, then this activates the right of the builder to sue for breach of contract.

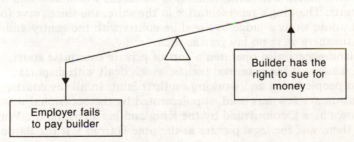

Builder has the right to sue for money

Employer fails to pay builder

A similar diagram relating to the builder's duty to carry out the work and the corresponding right of the employer to have the work done could be drawn.

Fig. 1.1 Diagram to illustrate the concepts of rights and duties

Common law

English law is a common-law system which is also found in many other countries in the world, mostly former British colonies. The words 'common law' have a number of different meanings. The first is of historical significance, and is the key to understanding what our law is all about. It is probably far easier to understand modern English Law, with all its peculiarities, if one first looks at its historical development.

The development of English common law

Before the Norman Conquest

Before 1066, England was not as we know it today. It was merely a collection of many different kingdoms, e.g. Mercia, Wessex and Kent. These kingdoms were in perpetual disruption, due to fighting between their respective leaders, and invasions from Europe of many warring tribes such as the Saxons.

Highly significant in the north-east, was the arrival of the Vikings, who established their own kingdom called the Danelaw. All these tribes settled and interbred, so that old and new customs were intermingled. Some of their customs would obviously have concerned 'legal' ideas, i.e. not killing people or stealing their sheep. As few people could read or write, and the dialects were different, most laws tended to be unwritten and customary.

In 924, Athelston was crowned on the Kings Stone at Kingston-upon-Thames having invaded Scotland, defeated many tribes in the North of England, and been paid homage by Welsh and Scottish kings. England was now united, but its laws remained much the same, and without an efficient system of communication, it would have continued but for the Norman Conquest.

For governmental purposes, it was divided into shires, each with its own courts. Shires were subdivided into hundreds which also had their own courts. The king's representative in the shire, the shire reeve (or sheriff) would sit as a judge in the shire courts with the gentry and clergy, for there were no lawyers as such.

The landowners also operated a sort of private enterprise court system, known as the manorial courts, which dealt with disputes between people living and working on their land. In all the courts, local customary law was used, supplemented by the occasional written law known as a Doom issued by the King and his advisors, the Witan.

This then, was the legal picture at the time Harold lost the Battle of Hastings.

After 1066

William of Normandy had been promised the throne of England by

Edward the Confessor, who had been brought up partly at the Court of the Duchy of Normandy. Unfortunately, Edward also named Harold II as his heir. To right this betrayal, William invaded England, and fought and won the Battle of Hastings.

Realising that to retain the throne of England would be a difficult task, he set out to overcome the Anglo-Saxon hatred of their Norman conquerors, and to establish himself as a strong ruler. In this seeking after complete power, he sowed the seeds of what was to become England's first unified legal system, or law – common to all men. However, he did not abolish the existing legal system based on custom, knowing that this would be too unpopular.

The development of modern English law occurred as a result of a number of innovations introduced by William and subsequent Norman kings.

The feudal system – a form of land holding

Firstly, the legal structure of society was completely changed by the introduction of the Norman *feudal system*. This was a system of land tenure or holding, whereby, the king confiscated all the land, declaring himself to be the only true **owner** of England. He then made grants of the land to those he wished to reward for past favours. These people merely held the land as tenants of the king. They in turn granted estates or interests in the land, and so on. All the tenants and sub-tenants owed their loyalty to their immediate landlord, and had to pay feudal dues to keep their land. In addition, all swore to be faithful to the king. This process of granting sub-tenancies was called *sub-infeudation (see* Fig. 1.2). By this means, William repaid past loyalty, and ensured continued obedience, as land could be forfeited to the landlord in certain situations.

The feudal system also produced a form of communication from the king, right down to the lowest of the low, the serfs. They were rather similar to slaves, in that they could be sold with the land, they could not hold an interest in land itself, and could not marry without their lord's permission.

In a time of poor communication, this system provided an adequate framework on which society in England could be unified. It also provided by means of the feudal dues, money and armies to strengthen the monarchy, which were needed to impose the embryonic King's law on the antiquated, inefficient and regional legal system already in existence.

The Curia Regis – a fore-runner of government departments, House of Lords and modern courts.   Secondly, the Norman kings reinforced their rule with the introduction of the Curia Regis or King's Council, which was an advisory body, consisting of the tenants-in-chief, or barons. Initially they met on only formal occasions, but as life became more

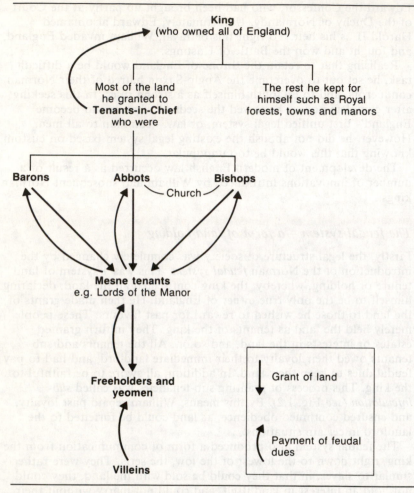

Fig. 1.2 Diagram to illustrate the process of sub-infeudation

complex, many of the advisors took on special responsibilities for various aspects of government, such as taxation. Later, they gathered around them, departments of suitably educated staff, to help with administration, and from these beginnings, Parliament and the courts as we know them, began to develop.

Circuit judges – unifying England by common legal rules. Thirdly, the kings started to send Royal judges around the counties, giving them specified tasks known as commissions, e.g. the Commission of the Assize. They went on circuit, and took with them 'central' policy from the King's Council. At first they had to use the old customary laws at the trials, as there was no other law. These, they applied, but on their return to the king, those customs of which they disapproved would be rejected, and those they liked would be incorporated into a new set of rules, to be used all over England, the common law.

Thus, the English people now had two court systems, the old pre-1066 courts, and those which were modified or introduced by the Norman kings. The Church continued to deal with matters relating to marriage and the family. Gradually, the people began to see the advantages of using the circuit courts of the king, for there was uniformity in treatment, little corruption and virtually no bias. The nobles who ran the manorial courts, and who derived a great income from them, were, of course, less than happy with Royal Law. Whenever a king was weak, the nobles would force him to do something which restricted his power in some way. This is well illustrated when the development of the writ system was hindered by the enactment of the Provisions of Oxford in 1258 (see p. 14).

At first, the new royal justice was concerned with law and order, so criminal law was important. Property, of course, was of extreme significance, and under the sole jurisdiction of the Crown and the royal judges would be asked to deal with disputes concerning property rights. In order to seek help from the new system, a plaintiff would have to obtain a document from one of the new government departments. This document was aptly called a writ. It was because of the writ administration system that the common law developed in a strange way. Eventually, because of the shortcomings of the common law, a parallel set of legal rules was developed known as equity (see p. 14). In addition to the common law created by the circuit judges, the king would also enact statutes on very important matters such as the Provisions of Oxford.

The writ system

Even today, if you wish to sue someone in the High Court, you need to issue a writ, a written document containing particulars of the claim you are making against the defendant (see Fig. 1.3). The modern writ is a printed form, which the plaintiff completes, to cover the circumstances involved. The old writs, on the other hand, were specially written by the clerks in Chancery which was one of the new government departments spawned by the Curia Regis. The head of the Chancery was the Lord Chancellor, who was one of the most important members of the Curia Regis. In the early days of common law, he was always a priest, and also the King's Confessor. This department was mostly made up of educated clergymen, as they were some of the few people who could read and write. The clerks drew up the writs, using a mixture of old English and Norman French. Each writ was unique, in that it only applied to the circumstances pleaded by

COURT FEES ONLY

Writ indorsed with Statement of Claim [Liquidated Demand] (O.8, r. 1)

IN THE HIGH COURT OF JUSTICE   19 84.—   .—No.

Queen's Bench **Division**

[Group   ]

[District Registry]

Between

BIGGLES BUILDING SUPPLIERS LIMITED   Plaintiff

AND

BORIS MOLE   Defendant

(1) Insert name.   **To the Defendant**(¹) Boris Mole

(2) Insert address.   of(²) 16 Chemical Road, London, N.W.1

This Writ of Summons has been issued against you by the above-named Plaintiff in respect of the claim set out overleaf.

Within 14 days after the service of the Writ on you, counting the day of service, you must either satisfy the claim or return to the Court Office mentioned below the accompanying **Acknowledgment of Service** stating therein whether you intend to contest these proceedings.

If you fail to satisfy the claim or to return the Acknowledgment within the time stated, or if you return the Acknowledgment without stating therein an intention to contest the proceedings the Plaintiff may proceed with the action and judgment may be entered against you forthwith without further notice.

(3) Complete and delete as necessary.

Issued from the(³) [Central Office] [District Registry]

of the High Court this   1st   day of August   19 84.

NOTE:—This Writ may not be served later than 12 calendar months beginning with that date unless renewed by order of the Court.

IMPORTANT

Directions for Acknowledgment of Service are given with the accompanying form.

Fig. 1.3   Writ endorsed with statement of claim for liquidated sum

```
                                        1984.—    .—No.
                        IN THE HIGH COURT OF JUSTICE

                            Queen's Bench Division

                        [Group        ]

                        [                      District Registry ]




                        BIGGLES BUILDING SUPPLIERS LIMITED

                                        V.

                                BORIS MOLE




                            Writ of Summons
                            [Liquidated Demand]
                        Date issued                    19
                        Acknowledgment of Service
                        lodged                         19




                            Fitch, Twitch and Snitch

                                    Plaintiffs Solicitor
```

Oyez Publishing Limited Norwich House, 11/13 Norwich Street, London EC4A 1AB, a subsidiary of The Solicitors' Law Stationery Society, Limited. ★ ★ ★ ★ F368—4-80

High Court A2B

Fig. 1.3 cont'd.

12

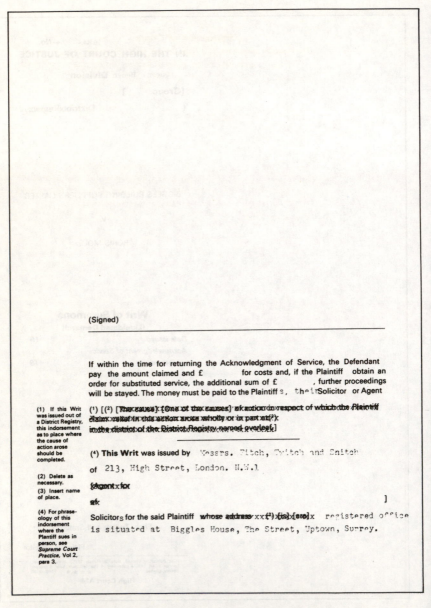

(Signed)
_____

If within the time for returning the Acknowledgment of Service, the Defendant pay the amount claimed and £   for costs and, if the Plaintiff obtain an order for substituted service, the additional sum of £   , further proceedings will be stayed. The money must be paid to the Plaintiffs, their Solicitor or Agent

(1) If this Writ was issued out of a District Registry, this indorsement as to place where the cause of action arose should be completed.

(¹) [(²) [The cause] [One of the causes] of action in respect of which the Plaintiff claim relief in this action arose wholly or in part at(³) in the district of the District Registry named overleaf]

(2) Delete as necessary.
(3) Insert name of place.

(⁴) **This Writ** was issued by   Messrs. Fitch, Twitch and Snitch

of 213, High Street, London. N.W.1

[Agent x for

x   ]

(4) For phraseology of this indorsement where the Plaintiff sues in person, see *Supreme Court Practice*, Vol 2, para 3.

Solicitors for the said Plaintiff whose address xxx(²) [is] [are] x registered office is situated at Biggles House, The Street, Uptown, Surrey.

Fig. 1.3   cont'd.

Statement of Claim

The Plaintiff's claim is for the sum of £8,966.75 being the price of goods sold and delivered to the Defendant by the Plaintiff company.

Particulars

1983	
April 27th	To goods comprising timber and bricks sold and delivered to the Defendant full particulars of which have been given to the Defendant.
to	
December 22nd	
	£8,966.75

Fig. 1.3 cont'd.

the plaintiff. One can understand the delight of those people, who had travelled, sometimes, hundreds of miles to obtain one of the new writs, for it meant that whatever their grievance, they would be able to take a private action in the modern king's courts.

This legal 'Shangri-La' was short-lived, for a side effect of allowing the issue of writs for every private legal grievance, was that the people flocked to use the king's courts. As a result, the manorial courts, run by the feudal lords, began to lose revenue to the Crown. Even today one must pay court fees before a civil action can be started.

In 1258, the Crown was comparatively weak. The lords pressurized King Henry III to enact a statute, called the Provisions of Oxford. This dealt with many matters, but one matter of great significance, was that the statute forbade the making of any **new writs**. This had a profound effect on the development of the common law, for unless you had a grievance already covered by the wording of an existing writ (which could be repeated, incorporating your name and other particulars) you had **no** remedy in the royal courts. The result of this, was that for many people, the only remedy, open to them, was to be found in the manorial courts – a retrograde step.

All was not lost, however. In 1285, King Edward I, a successful and strong king, enacted the Statute of Westminster II. Whilst he could not reverse the Provisions of Oxford, he could introduce a modification concerning the writ system. He decreed, that whilst no new writs could be issued, the wording of the old pre-1258 writs could be used to cover analogous situations. As a result, the civil side of common law continued to develop in an artificial fashion.

Equity

Development of equity

Thus, one of the main problems of the common law, was the lack of freedom to start a private action, unless there was a suitable writ, or one that could be adjusted to fit your grievance. No writ – no right! There were other problems which stemmed from this restriction. The wording of the writ became sacrosanct. Indeed it was called, the form of action, and had to be applied exactly in each subsequent case. One word wrong, could lose you your case, an early example of 'sticking to the letter of the law'.

So, for people who wanted to go to law, but who were unable to use the common law, because there was no writ available, there were two alternatives. Either, they went back to the manorial courts, or they applied directly to the king, who was the 'fountain of all justice'. The second method was excellent, as the king could grant whatever remedy he wished. But, it could involve following the king around, sometimes, even behind battle lines, until one got an audience. Even so, applying directly to the king for justice, became so popular, that eventually, the hearing of applications or petitions was taken on by the Lord

Chancellor. As we saw before, although he was in charge of the Chancery, originally, his main job was to be the king's spiritual advisor. As a priest, it is understandable that he viewed the problems presented to him in an entirely different light to that of the king and the judges. His was a moral and religious viewpoint, and he made his decisions, based on his own personal ideas of what was fair and just. He was not restricted by the writ system as, to start with, each appeal was made in person by the plaintiff. His remedies were based on concepts of conscience and fair play, and he would often order the defendant to perform his legal duty, which was fairer than requiring him to pay damages, which is all he would have got at common law.

Eventually, the Chancellor was given his own court, the Court of Chancery. Other judges were appointed, and a body of legal rules called **equity** developed, offering *not* an alternative system, but a supplement to 'stop the gaps' in the common law, relating to private legal matters.

The nature of equity

Remedies. Equity thus developed its own remedies, such as **injunctions**. These may order people, to stop doing something they should not be doing in the first place. Ignoring the order, may result in imprisonment. Also, the decree of **specific performance** is used to order a person to perform his part of a contract, such as for the sale of a house.

Unlike legal remedies, i.e. the common-law remedies, which are yours **as of right**, once you have proved your case, equitable remedies were, and still are, at the discretion of the judge.

Maxims (guiding principles) At first, there was no ordered way of coming to a decision in equity. Indeed, it was said 'Equity varied with the length of the Chancellor's foot'. Equity did not use precedents (*see* p. 27) but it did use **maxims,** which, even today, are at the root of equitable decisions. An example of one is, 'He who comes to Equity, must come with clean hands'. This means, that a plaintiff asking for an equitable remedy, or for relief in equity in some way, must have behaved fairly, throughout the affair, and not merely complied with his legal duties.

Other equitable maxims include 'Delay defeats Equity', meaning, that you cannot expect the court to help you in equity if you delayed seeking that help, as it may have adversely affected the opposition's position.

Jurisdiction. Because of the many deficiencies in the common law, equity developed its own jurisdiction in certain areas, totally separate from that of the common law. Thus, in some things, there were only rules in equity, and none at common law. One such area was that of

trusts. The concept of a trust was totally beyond the scope of common law. How could anyone give property to someone else, if that was not the end of the matter? Equity, however, acknowledged, that it was possible to give property to others, for the benefit of other people, even the donor or his family.

Equity also acknowledged, that as far as the law was concerned, the donees were the owners – in common law, but *not* in equity (*see* Fig. 1.4).

Fig. 1.4   Diagram to illustrate a trust

It must be stressed, therefore that in some areas of English law, equity never developed. Its main influence was and is, in *private* or *civil* law. It gave *individual* rights and remedies in such areas as contract, tort, mortgages and trusts. Nevertheless, equitable ideas and concepts have been taken into other areas of the law by analogy, in court decisions and statute.

The problems caused by common law and equity

By the nineteenth century, the English law system was in chaos. There were still many outdated anachronistic courts, dating back to pre-conquest times, using customary law, which had virtually fallen into disuse. Within the main court system, there were criminal courts, using mainly, common law and statute, such as the criminal assizes, (finally abolished in 1971); civil courts using common law and statute; and Chancery which used equity and statute.

Equity, of course, plugged the gaps in the common law, and was designed to achieve fairness within the total legal system. Unfortunately, one of the main problems with the system was, that the rules were applied totally separately in the different courts. As each type of law had its own remedies, a litigant, anxious to make sure of some remedy, would have to start his action in a common law court and in Chancery – a ludicrous state of affairs.

Reform

As a result of centuries of dispute, compromise and court decisions, the matter was finally resolved by Parliament in the Judicature Acts 1873–75. These acts were of inestimable importance, for they did many things:

1. They unified the court system, so that there were no longer, common law courts and equity courts.
2. The rules of equity and common law were applied in all courts, so that only one action was necessary.
3. If there was a conflict between a rule of common law and equity, then the equitable rule prevailed. As equity had developed to remedy the injustices in the common law, this was only right.
4. They reorganized the structure of the courts, by creating a hierarchical ladder system. This made it easier to determine to which courts appeals should be made.

It should be noted that the Acts did *not* combine the two sets of rules. Equity and common law remain like oil and water – they are present together in the same system, but they do not mix.

The court system has been altered greatly since 1875, but we still retain the courts in descending order of importance, as first introduced by the Judicature Acts, from the House of Lords, rights down to the magistrates' courts.

In conclusion if we examine how English law has developed **historically** we find that we have a legal system which consists of law derived from custom, the common law, equity, and statute.

(Note: if one is not talking in historical terms, lawyers tend to refer to common law as non-statute law, (*see* p. 27.)

Divisions of English law

If we examine the subject-matter of English law, we find that it falls into **two** broad categories – Public and private law (*see* Fig. 1.5).

Public law

This deals with matters which are of importance to the state, are for the well-being of society, and which give public rights and duties to the individual.

Criminal law

This encompasses, not only the crimes with which one is familiar, such as murder, rape, bigamy and theft, but also, matters which have been regarded by Parliament to be so detrimental to the state as to necessitate treatment by the criminal courts, e.g. breaches of the

Fig. 1.5 Divisions of English law

Construction Regulations, the Health and Safety at Work etc. Act or road traffic offences.

A person who fails to abide by a criminal rule will be prosecuted by the state or its agents, and will be punished accordingly, e.g. by imprisonment or fine. The most serious offences are prosecuted in the name of the Crown, and the law report will be headed *R* v. *Bloggs* – *R* standing for Rex (King) or Regina (Queen).

Constitutional law

This deals with the relationships between the individual as a citizen, and the state itself. It covers such matters as the roles of the Crown, Parliament, the government, the judiciary (judges) and the citizens. It gives the citizen certain public rights, e.g. the right to vote at elections, and imposes certain public duties on the elector, the duty to sit on a jury if so required. (Note: you must perform duties, but you need *not* exercise a right.)

Failure to perform one's duties may result in prosecution and punishment.

Revenue law

The state cannot be run without financial resources, and so taxes are levied on people and organizations. Failure to pay, may result in prosecution. There are many different taxes, e.g. income tax, capital transfer tax (combined death duties and gift tax), stamp duty (paid on transfer of land), value added tax and corporation tax (company income tax).

Administrative law

As society has become more sophisticated, and the state has played more of an interventionist role, a large body of law has had to grow to deal with the way in which government departments, such as the Department of Health and Social Security actually administer their statutory functions. Thus, not only are there many Acts and pieces of delegated legislation (*see* p. 25) relating to social security, the health services, land compensation, local government etc, but a large body of case law has also developed. It also deals with nationalized industries such as the National Coal Board.

Private law (civil law)

This deals with law relating to relationships between citizens. Whether a citizen has rights or duties, depends on which branch of private law he is concerned with. For example, only parties to a contract, will normally have rights, under that contract. Should there be a breach of duty, then the party suffering will be able to sue in the **civil** courts, i.e. in the non-criminal courts.

The following are some branches of English private law.

Contract

This deals with legally binding agreements between people, e.g. a contract for the sale of land, a contract of employment, a contract to buy a toothbrush, or a building contract.

Each party can only expect from the other what has been agreed between the parties, or what is implied into the agreement by Act of Parliament, or the common law, e.g. By S.14 of the Sale of Goods Act 1979, when buying materials from a builders' merchant, one expects, without having to express the wish, that the goods will be of merchantable quality. If they are not, then the party in breach could be sued for damages, or the goods could be returned on delivery.

Tort

A tort is a civil, and not a criminal wrong. It is not punishable by the state, unless the behaviour amounts to a crime as well. Each tort has grown up in a separate way, and has its own special requirements and remedies. Examples of torts, include, negligence, trespass, private nuisance and defamation (libel and slander) (*see* Ch. 8).

Law of property

This deals with the ownership or title to land and personal property, and the transfer of such property (*see* Chs. 5 and 6).

Family law

This deals with all matters relating to the family, such as adoption, legitimacy, divorce, marriage and nullity. Such law is derived, almost entirely, from statute law.

Succession

This concerns the transfer of property on death, whether the deceased died testate, having left a will containing directions, or intestate, having left no will, when a statutory order of transferring the property to the next of kin is applied.

Other types of law affecting us

One or two other types of law should also be noted, as we must remember that English law is merely one example of national or municipal law.

International law

Public international law. This deals with the interrelationships between countries, on a political level, and is not concerned with the internal or municipal legal systems. Thus, instead of talking about for example the law of England and Wales or Nevada, we are now concerned, with the general effect of international law on the United Kingdom and the United States of America.

Public international law is not all-embracing, but, covers legal problems of international significance, such as the law of the sea. This deals with international fishing rights, territorial waters, oilfields and piracy. The law of the air is concerned with, among other things, violations of air space (the cause of the crisis between the USA and the USSR in 1983) and hijacking.

Such law is created by political leaders signing treaties or conventions on behalf of their respective governments. Only the parties to the treaties, or subsequent signatories, become subject to the agreement thus created. Thereby hangs the problem. A country not signatory to a particular treaty or convention, cannot be politically punished by the other signatories, because they were never party to it in the first place. Such punishment as can be meted out, depends on the international standing of the signatory countries. If the recalcitrant country is a member of the United Nations, a complaint can be made there, or offensive action can be taken, as in the Falkland crisis in 1982, or economic sanctions can be taken. The content of a treaty or convention, may be incorporated into a state's internal law, using that state's legislative system, e.g. the Taking of Hostage Act 1982, ratified an international convention on that subject.

Private international law. This deals with the legal problems when two or more municipal (internal) legal systems are involved in one situation. Such a conflict between law, occurs frequently in the building industry, when an English or Scottish company contracts to build in another country such as Iran. If there is a legal dispute, then where is the action heard? It all depends on many factors. Often, where there is an American state involved, the party suing will try to have the case tried in that state as, on the whole, damages awarded in the United States are much higher than those awarded here.

On a more personal level, individuals often get involved in private international law, in divorce cases or on death, e.g. an Englishman marries a French girl and goes to live in Utah. She leaves him, and wants to get a divorce in California. Once again, the law is quite complex, and involves (in England) the principle of an individual's **domicile**. This is not his residence, but rather relates to the legal system to which the individual owes his allegiance. So, although the Englishman is British by nationality, as far as the divorce is concerned he may have changed his domicile to that of Utah, if he no longer felt bound to the English legal system. If he was living there temporarily, then this is unlikely.

N.B. When a person goes to a foreign state, he must abide by its laws, or face the consequences. There is no conflict of law in such a situation, and no choice in the matter. Furthermore, in most countries, ignorance of the law, is no defence.

European Community law

A new source of English Law see p. 23.

Origins. The European Economic Community was set up in 1957 by the first Treaty of Rome, which was signed by the original six member states. Two other communities were also set up, the European Coal and Steel Community (ECSC) by the Treaty of Paris 1951, and the European Atomic Energy Community (Euratom) by a second treaty of Rome 1957. The administrative aspects of the three communities, were merged in 1967, but they remain separate legal entities, the EEC being of the greatest importance.

Objects. The objects of the EEC are to create a huge Common Market for all member states, in which workers, capital, transport and goods can move about without restraint, thereby, encouraging prosperity in Western Europe.

Accession by the United Kingdom. In 1972, the United Kingdom, Ireland and Denmark signed the Brussels Treaty of Accession, by which they agreed to join the three communities. Like all treaties, this would have remained a mere political agreement had the United Kingdom's Parliament not passed the European Communities Act 1972. This came into effect on 1 January 1973. The Act ratified (confirmed) the treaty and incorporated the three treaties as part of the law of the **United Kingdom**, as well as all the case law from the European Court of Justice. At one fell swoop there was a new source of English, Scottish and Northern Irish law. Thus, the English courts must apply community law, if it is applicable, to a case before them.

Community institutions. The communities are run by four main institutions, the Council of Ministers, the European Parliament, the European Commission and the European Court of Justice. Each member state has voluntarily given up to these bodies some of its own rights to make law and decisions (sovereignty). This is because the communities are **supra-national**, having authority to make decisions for all the member states on certain community matters, e.g. the Common Agricultural Policy (CAP).

The member states. At present there are ten member states: Belgium, Italy, Germany (West), Greece, France, United Kingdom, Netherlands, Luxemburg, Ireland and Denmark (mnemonic: Bigg-fun-lid); Spain and Portugal have signed a new treaty of accession (mnemonic will then be Fling-big-spud).

Community law. The three community treaties are obviously the main source of community law, but the Commission and Council are allowed to make three types of law, called regulations, directives and decisions.

1. Regulations. These are rules, which once made, are immediately binding on all the member states, without reference to their legal systems.

    An example of this is the Council Regulation (EEC) No. 170/83 establishing a community system for conserving and managing fishing resources.

2. Directives. These are orders or requirements, directed to all or some of the member states, the results of which are binding, but the means to achieve them are left to each member state. This is useful because of the difficulties in translating legal ideas between different legal systems.

    An example of this is Directive No. 82/884/EEC which is a council directive on a limit value for lead in air. These two types of law and the treaties are binding on **all** the member states and their citizens – in effect it becomes new English law.

3. Decisions. These are decisions on some aspect of community life, which are binding on the person or body to whom they are addressed.

   Examples of these are Commission Decisions 83/151-7/EEC concerning the granting of financial assistance in favour of the following parts of the United Kingdom (North of England, North-West of England, South-West of England, Yorkshire, Humberside, Scotland, Wales and Northern Ireland).

European Court of Justice. This court, situated at Luxemburg, is a court specially set up to deal with problems of community law. Each state sends at least one judge. The court rules on the meaning of the treaties and, under the Treaty of Rome, a national case must be sent for clarification of the community law involved to the court, if there is any doubt as to the Treaties' meaning (Art. 177 EEC Treaty).

The court, also, has jurisdiction over disputes involving aspects of community law between states, corporations and even individuals.

The court, therefore, provides another source of English judicial precedent (*see* p. 27).

An example of a case brought before the ECJ is *Re Ultra Heat Treated Milk; EC Commission* v. *United Kingdom* No. 124/81 (1983). An application was made by the Commission under the European Treaty, for a declaration that the United Kingdom had breached the treaty by placing restrictions on the import and sale of UHT milk and cream. (This was to protect the British milk industry.) The ECJ held that the British Government had breached the treaty by imposing over-stringent requirements on health grounds and expecting that the processing should be done in the UK, which was unreasonable.

Sources of English law – creating the rules

We have already seen how English law developed historically. Also, we looked at the different categories of English law – but, how is English law created today?

There are two main methods (*see* Fig. 1.6): legislation and judicial precedent.

(Note: European community law is an external source of English law.)

Legislation

In England and Wales, legislation is law made by the Houses of Parliament (the Commons *and* the Lords). As Parliament fulfils two roles in the United Kingdom, governmental and legislative, much of the legislation covers all of the country and not just England and Wales.

Legislation can *create* new law completely from scratch. It may also

Fig. 1.6 Sources of English law

repeal old legislation when it is no longer relevant or useful, *amend* existing legislation to cover new situations or plug loopholes and it may *consolidate* piecemeal legislation into one comprehensive Act. Occasionally, an Act may be used to *codify* law which has been created by caselaw (mnemonic: Cracc).

Development

There has been legislation since Anglo-Saxon times, when the king, having sovereign power, issued laws called Dooms on something of importance. The Domesday Book of 1086 was the result of such a doom. Other types of legislation were also made, e.g. statutes, provisions and charters (Magna Carta). Today we still have charters (*see* Ch. 7) and the word statute is an alternative word for Act of Parliament.

Legislation, thus, is a most sophisticated form of law-making, relying on the wishes of Parliament, hopefully reflecting the needs of the people. Once, a piece of legislation has been made, it must be applied in all the courts and by judges and magistrates of whatever political persuasion. However, if a Bill has a political bias, then whether it goes through both Houses successfully will depend on the strength of the party in government. A governing party is the one with the majority of seats in the House of Commons.

Direct and indirect legislation

Legislation nowadays takes two basic forms – direct and indirect. But all legislation stems from an Act of Parliament in some way.

If we look at Fig. 1.7 we will see the first page of a typical Act, the Town and Country Planning Act 1971. After the Royal Coat of Arms, comes its year date and Chapter No. 78, i.e. the 78th Act of the year. Following this, is the preamble, which sets out briefly, what the intentions of the Act are. The reference to the Queen indicates that the Royal Assent has been given, and that the House of Lords *and* the Commons, have passed the bill. At the beginning of the Act, you will find the arrangement of the sections of the Act. Towards the end are miscellaneous and supplementary provisions, including definitions and an interpretation clause. For example, the expression, 'building operation' is defined **for the purposes of this Act**. Such a definition may then be adopted for other later Acts.

1. Direct legislation.   Here, the law is actually contained in the new Act itself. This means, that Parliament debated all the law found in the Act, and took it through the lengthy legislative process from Bill to final Royal Assent. Obviously, as Parliament has a limited amount of time to deal with all matters, pieces of direct legislation are usually going to be of vital importance to the country, or are considered to be so, by Parliament e.g. Finance Acts.

So, in the case of direct legislation, reference must be made to the Act to find out what Parliament enacted, and subsequent precedents, to see how the Act was applied in practice.

2. Indirect or delegated or subordinate legislation.   Sometimes Parliament sensibly acknowledges that it neither has the time, expertise, or even inclination, to deal with certain problems requiring legislation. It therefore solves the problem by passing what is known as an **enabling** Act, setting out the aims of the Act and giving to other people or bodies the power to make the necessay legislation. Legislation made in this way, is called **indirect** or **delegated** or **subordinate** legislation.

Despite these descriptions, however, such legislation has **all** the force of Parliament, because it could only be made following the transference of power from Parliament to the designated persons or bodies.

A classic example of an enabling Act, is the Health and Safety at

ELIZABETH II

1971 CHAPTER 78

An Act to consolidate certain enactments relating to
town and country planning in England and Wales
with amendments to give effect to recommendations of
the Law Commission.   [28th October 1971]

BE IT ENACTED by the Queen's most Excellent Majesty, by and
with the advice and consent of the Lords Spiritual and
Temporal, and Commons, in this present Parliament
assembled, and by the authority of the same, as follows:—

PART I

ADMINISTRATION

1.—(1) Subject to the provisions of this section, the council
of a county is the local planning authority for the county, and
the council of a county borough is the local planning authority
for the county borough.

(marginal note:) Local planning authorities.

(2) If it appears to the Secretary of State that it is expedient
that a joint board should be established as the local planning
authority for the areas of any two or more such councils as are
mentioned in subsection (1) of this section, or for any parts of
those areas, he may by order constitute those areas or parts as
a united district for the purposes of this Act, and constitute a
joint board (in this Act referred to as a " joint planning board ")
as the local planning authority for that district:

Provided that the Secretary of State shall not make such an
order except after holding a local inquiry unless all the councils
concerned have consented to the making of the order.

(3) The provisions of Schedule 1 to this Act shall have
effect with respect to the constitution of joint planning boards.

Fig. 1.7   First page of Town and Country Planning Act

Work etc. Act 1974. The Act itself is relatively short, because it transfers virtually all of the technical, policy-making and enforcement powers to others, mainly, the Health and Safety Commission, and the Health and Safety Executive.

Legislation made by such people as ministers of state or bodies such as the Health and Safety Commission are usually called **rules** or **regulations** and **orders**. In the case of local authorities who are empowered to make rules for their areas, these rules are called **byelaws**. Most forms of delegated legislation are published in a document called a **statutory instrument** (instrument meaning a document). Thus, the Building Regulations are published in Statutory Instrument reference S.I. 1985 No. 1065 and the relevant enabling Act is the Building Act 1984.

Judicial precedent (Case law or judge-made law)

If someone buys a round of drinks for his office colleagues because it is his birthday and no-one has done this before, then we might say that he has created a precedent. The others would then be expected to follow suit. It is this concept that is at the root of the legal doctrine of precedents. But, of course, it is not quite as simple as that.

The elements of a court case

When a civil or criminal case goes before a court, there are two elements involved in coming to a decision, the relevant *facts* and the relevant *law*.

The facts are relatively simple to determine on the evidence presented. (*See* the rules relating to evidence on p. 49). But, the law may be more difficult to apply and will even cover the acceptability of the evidence. This is due to the human element altering each factual situation, so that the law must be applied differently in each set of circumstances. This is so even if the facts of the case appear to be identical to those in another case.

Thus, in every court hearing, the judge or the magistrates must apply the appropriate legal rules which may have been created by statute or by judges in previous cases.

Precedents

A precedent (from the verb to precede) is a decision made by a judge on a point of law. There are four kinds of precedent (1) original; (2) declaratory; both of which may be (3) binding; and (4) persuasive, which cannot be binding.

Original precedents. If there is no relevant law applicable to a case being decided, because a particular aspect has not been considered judicially before or there is no relevant piece of legislation, then the judge must make a decision on what he thinks the law *should* be. He will come to his decision after listening to the arguments of the lawyers on both sides. Their arguments will be based on precedents gleaned from previous cases. For this reason, the judge cannot and should not come up with a startlingly unusual decision. He will take the other precedents and try to mould them to fit the case in hand. By doing this he is said to 'uncover' what the law is. His decision is called a precedent and if his decision appears to break new ground, even in the smallest way, then it is called an **original** precedent.

But, precedents cannot be plucked out of thin air. There must already be some law on the subject matter in existence. This was well illustrated by the case of the intruder who broke into Buckingham Palace in 1982. He was not prosecuted for trespass, as trespass is a tort (a civil wrong) for which the remedy is to sue in the civil courts (*see* p. 36). Although there are certain types of trespass which have been made crimes by Act of Parliament such as those on the railways or into diplomatic missions, trespass on royal premises had not been made a criminal offence. As there was thus no criminal law on the subject, and the Queen would not have wanted to sue the intruder for trespass, he was prosecuted for other minor offences. Significant and material changes in the law in a new direction can only be achieved by statute law.

Original precedents are of vital importance in the English legal system, as they create new laws to solve new problems posed in cases brought before the courts. This is an advantage over statute law as precedents can only be made to fit the facts of a case which have actually happened, however weird or fantastic. Statute on the other hand is made in a sort of vacuum and law may be created for situations which may never occur or which may never happen again.

Binding precedents. Precedents are even more important however, if they are made by judges in one of the superior courts e.g. the House of Lords, Court of Appeal or even the High Court, for their decisions **bind** the courts below. The lower courts, in cases dealing with the same legal situation at a later date, must apply the precedent, even if the judge privately disagrees with it. As the courts are operated as a hierarchy, it is relatively simple to determine which courts bind lower courts by their decisions (*see* Fig. 1.8). Neither the magistrates', nor the county courts make binding precedents, nor does the Crown Court, unless it is sitting as an appeal court. As a rule of thumb, only courts sitting as appeal courts make binding precedents, except for the High Court, even in cases heard **at first instance** (for the first time).

The House of Lords does not bind itself by its own decisions, although it will endeavour to follow them in most cases.

Generally, other courts are bound by the decisions of courts higher up the ladder. The Court of Appeal (Criminal Division) is not

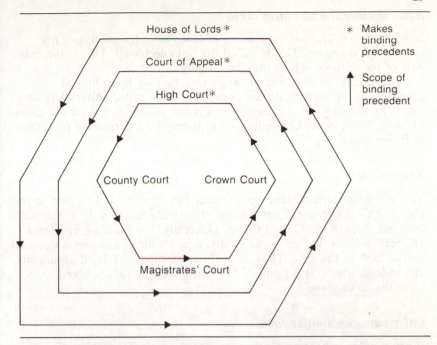

Fig. 1.8 The English court system with special reference to those courts which bind others by their decisions

necessarily bound by its own decisions unlike the Court of Appeal (Civil Division) which binds itself.

Persuasive precedents. Most cases, however, are not taken on appeal to other courts. Thus, if the judge, during the case, makes an original precedent, it may not be binding, but it will be a **persuasive** precedent. This means, that another judge, faced with the same legal problem, would undoubtedly be influenced by that decision. Unfortunately, not all such cases are reported in the law reports, and therefore, finding details of relevant decisions is difficult. This is why, one must keep abreast of the legal pages in professional journals, in which contributors give first hand reports of cases to readers.

Persuasive precedents are also made by courts in other countries which have common law systems, e.g. New Zealand, and most states in Canada and Australia, and by the Judicial Committee of the Privy Council. The JCPC hears appeals from certain Commonwealth countries.

Declaratory precedents. Where a judge is using a precedent that is already made, then he merely applies the precedent in a declaratory way, i.e. he declares how the law already stands.

Ratio decidendi and *obiter dicta*

In coming to a decision on a point of law, the judge must give his reasons for doing so. This is called the **ratio decidendi**. This is the only part of the decision which may be binding.

Occasionally, to illustrate his argument, he uses hypothetical examples to further explain his decision. This is called **obiter dicta** or words by the way. As the obiter dicta is not strictly based on the case in hand, it can never be binding – but it may be a **persuasive** precedent in future cases.

Judge v. *jury*

You will have noticed, that no reference has been made to a jury in the above. This is because, firstly, juries are usually found only in serious criminal cases in the Crown Court. Generally, few building problems are dealt with in that court. Secondly, a jury's duty is to give a decision on the **facts** of the case. Thus, it is not concerned with legal arguments, and indeed, wherever a point of law is argued, the jury is asked to leave the courtroom.

Later cases on similar facts

When a judge is hearing a new case, based on similar facts to those on which the binding precedent has been made, and that precedent is referred to him by one of the lawyers involved, he may do two things. He may agree with the precedent and **follow** it, or, he may say that the facts of the current case are different and that he will not follow the precedent, and will therefore **distinguish** it.

Appeals

If a case goes on appeal, and the appeal court agrees with the court below, it is said to **uphold** or **affirm** the decision.

If it wishes to go against the lower court's decision, then it **reverses** it.

A decision may, or may not, involve a precedent. If the appeal court is considering a precedent, set by the lower court, it may **approve** or **disapprove** it and **overrule** it. If the precedent referred to, was set by a higher court than the one being appealed to in the current case, then it cannot **overrule** the precedent.

The law reports

The proceedings of courts of record, i.e. those courts which can make binding precedents, are reported in special journals called law reports. There are many different types. The official law reports are published by the Incorporated Council of Law Reporting, representing the legal profession. These are either Appeal Cases (AC) or divisions of the Queen's Bench, Chancery or Family Divisions of the High Court (QB, Ch, Fam).

Other series of law reports are also published, e.g. the Weekly Law Reports (WLR), All England Law Reports (All ER), Times Law Reports (TLR) and Building Law Reports (Build LR).

The reports are prepared by qualified lawyers, usually barristers, who will have been present at the court hearing, and who will have access to the transcript of the case.

Reference to law reports is always made as in the following Fig. 1.9.

Without the law reports, finding out about relevant precedents would be extremely difficult. Sometimes, one sees advertisements in legal journals for information on unusual cases. However, the courts are reluctant to take notice of cases which have not appeared in the major law reports mentioned above.

Nearly all the cases mentioned in this book contain at least one important precedent. Some are known as *leading* cases as they contain original and binding precedents of such significance that the law has taken a completely new direction *see Anns* v. *London Borough of Merton* 1977 (p. 253) and *Saif Ali* v. *Sydney Mitchell & Co.* 1978 (p. 35).

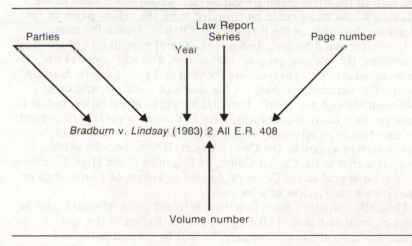

Fig. 1.9 How cases are referred to in law books

CHAPTER 2

The administration of English law

The legal profession

Barristers-at-law and solicitors of the Supreme Court

In England and Wales, the legal profession is divided into two
completely separate branches, that of **barristers** and **solicitors**, which
have developed in entirely different ways. Collectively, they and legal
academics are known as lawyers.

Generally

The man in the street seeking legal advice, would firstly need to see a
solicitor, whose name could be supplied from the yellow pages of the
telephone directory, or the lists kept at Citizens Advice Bureaux.

A solicitor could be described as the general practitioner of the legal
profession. He will give general legal advice, and will undertake to do
divorces, adoptions, conveyancing (buying and selling land), drawing
up of wills, obtaining probate on the death of someone, and debt
collection through the courts. Usually, he works at his office, but, if his
work involves court appearances, then a solicitor is entitled to present
the case (act as an **advocate**) in the magistrates' court, the county court,
and in certain situations the Crown Court. If however, the work
involves a trial at the Crown Court, or litigation in the High Court, or
there is an appeal to the Court of Appeal or House of Lords, then he
must obtain the services of a barrister.

Thus, the barrister's main function, is to act as an advocate, and he
has a right of audience in all English courts. Except in the magistrates'
court, where robing is unnecessary, he will be dressed in the old
fashioned wig with pigtail, winged collar, tabs and a gown. Etiquette
demands that his **instructing solicitor** be present at the same time in
court (and at any time, when the client is present), as he will be more
familiar with the client, due to frequent pre-trial meetings.

In addition to his function as an advocate, the barrister, who is
always referred to in the profession, as **counsel**, will often give specialist
advice to solicitors, called **counsel's opinion**. Suppose your company
wished to sue another organization, for something which turned on an

undecided legal point, your company's solicitor would hesitate before advising the board of directors to commit vast sums of money on a court case, the outcome of which was very much in doubt. He would therefore prepare a **brief** containing all the relevant details of the dispute. In particular he would specifically ask a number of questions, e.g. 'Would counsel give his opinion on the merits of the case, and in particular, estimate the possible **quantum** (amount) of damages that may be awarded'. The brief, tied with pink tape, would then be sent to a barrister having known specialist knowledge in that particular field. If counsel's opinion was favourable, the solicitor would then go ahead with the case. If it was not, he would have to decide whether the company should chance the outcome, or cut their losses without litigation.

This is where the analogy of general practitioner breaks down, for there are many barristers who could not be said to specialize in such work, and whose main tasks, are to do the everyday criminal court work. 'Rumpole of the Bailey', John Mortimer's brilliant creation comes to mind here. Other barristers however, specialize in certain areas, such as taxation, matrimonial law, building contracts, and you would be unlikely to find them doing any criminal work. Similarly, some solicitors, especially in London, tend to specialize in certain areas, e.g. shipping, theatrical contracts, and would not wish to handle your divorce.

Solicitors in more detail

Solicitors are governed by the Law Society, which regulates the entrance examinations, articles (apprenticeships), and admits them, on qualifying, onto the **rolls of solicitors**. The Law Society also issues **practising certificates**, without which, no solicitor is allowed to practise. Also, compulsory insurance cover must be obtained through the Law Society to cover against claims for professional negligence.

A client instructing a solicitor, will have a contract with him, and therefore can sue him for breach of contract, and can himself be sued for unpaid fees. Indeed, a solicitor who has not been paid by a client has a **lien** over his clients' papers, i.e. he will not release possession of them, until the bill has been settled.

Solicitors are not allowed to tout for business, nor advertise, except to announce that they have opened a new office, and to give a list of the sort of work they will undertake. Also, they are allowed to put a similar list on the outside of their premises. This is because it was discovered that people did not understand the variety of work a solicitor is able to do. Once again, American films, with their divorce and real estate lawyers, where the legal work is split up between types of law and not between professions as in this country, are to blame for such ignorance.

Solicitors have strict accounting rules, and must have two sets of
bank accounts, the **office** account and the **client** account. If money
from the client account is put into the office account, without
authority, whether deliberately, or not, serious penalties can occur –
the ultimate being **struck off** the rolls of solicitors.

As solicitors are court officers (unlike barristers), they are entitled, to
have oaths sworn before them. In the past, solicitors had to apply to
become commissioners for oaths, but nowadays, any solicitor with a
current practising certificate, is entitled to act as a commissioner. Most
people are aware of the oaths sworn in court, e.g. 'I swear to tell the
truth, the whole truth, and nothing but the truth' (not 'So help me
God' which is American). Swearing an oath before a solicitor, on
whatever religious book you require, has the same effect. So, you could
be prosecuted for perjury, if what you had sworn, was knowingly false.
If you are sent a form called an **affidavit** (a sworn statement), with a
request to get it sworn, you will need to go to any solicitor in practice,
(but not the one who prepared the affidavit). Holding the Bible, or
whatever religious book you adhere to, in your right hand, you say, 'I
swear that this is my name and handwriting, and the contents of this,
my affidavit are true'. If you have no religion, you may **affirm**, i.e.
promise that it is true. The solicitor signs his signature, and dates the
document.

Barristers

They are governed by the Senate of the Inns of Court and Bar, which
has under its control, a number of committees dealing with discipline
and professional etiquette. The Council for Legal Education deals with
the examinations and educational requirements of prospective
barristers.

All barristers must belong to one of the four Inns of Court, Gray's
Inn, Inner Temple, Middle Temple or Lincoln's Inn. They are all
situated close to the Royal Courts of Justice in the Strand in London.
However, there are groups of barristers working all round the country,
based not in offices, but in **chambers**, in which they 'rent' a room, and
share both the services of a **clerk** who runs the chambers, and the
expenses of maintaining the establishment. For convenience, all sets of
chambers tend to be very close to the town's courts.

After passing the required examinations, and eating a certain number
of meals at his Inn, the prospective barrister is called to the **Bar**. If he
intends to practise as a barrister, he must then do a years **pupillage**
(apprenticeship) with an experienced barrister.

There are a few aspects of the barrister's work, which must be
particularly noted.

Firstly, there is no contract between the client and the barrister, for
it is the solicitor who instructs him on behalf of the client. Strictly
speaking, there is no contract either between the lawyers. A barrister's

fees are called an **honorarium**, i.e. a voluntary payment for professional
services. Therefore, a barrister cannot sue for his fees. In practice, this
does not matter, for it is the solicitor who collects the fees with his bill,
and he can sue the client for breach of contract. Also, if the solicitor
does not pass on the fee, the barrister would not undertake any further
work for that solicitor, and would undoubtedly tell his colleagues to do
the same. Furthermore, the solicitor may be reported to the Law
Society for professional misconduct. If the solicitor remains unpaid, he
is professionally obliged to settle counsel's fee however.

Secondly, until recently, it was a hard and fast rule that no one
could sue a barrister for professional negligence. This has been slightly
modified since the case of *Saif Ali* v. *Sydney Mitchell (a firm) and
others* 1978, in which it was stated, that as a point of law only, it
should be possible to sue a barrister for pre-trial work, but not in
relation to his work at the trial itself. There has yet to be a case tried
on such facts however.

If you ever visit London, a worthwhile trip can be made to visit the
Law Courts in the Strand (*see* Fig. 2.1). Around the corner, in

Fig. 2.1   Sketch map of legal London

Chancery Lane, is the Law Society, the Public Record Office, and close by are the Inns of Court. Up Ludgate Hill, on the left, is the Old Bailey, London's Central Criminal Court which is a Class 1 Crown Court. Details of conducted walks around this area can be obtained, from the back page of *The Times* newspaper.

Queen's Counsel

Barristers who have been practising at the Bar, for at least ten years, may apply to the Lord Chancellor, for a recommendation, to be appointed a Queen's Counsel (QC). If his application is successful, he is said to **take silk**, because he exchanges his barrister's gown made of 'stuff' for a silk one. From then on, he takes fewer cases, and in many trials, may not appear without another barrister, called a **junior**. Most QC's specialize in some particular area of the law, and most have chambers in London.

The courts

Introduction

In England and Wales, the court system, unified since the Judicature Acts, is best studied in two parts, the criminal courts and the civil courts.

The criminal courts deal with pure crimes and behaviour treated by statute, as if it were criminal (*see* Fig. 2.3).

The civil courts deal with disputes or matters between private citizens, such as breaches of contract, tort, divorce, adoption, trusts, bankruptcy, winding up of companies, administration of estates on death, mortgages, land action and admiralty claims (*see* Fig. 2.2).

The civil courts

The magistrates' courts

Jurisdiction

(*authority, and extent of that authority to administer law*). More properly designated a criminal court, the magistrates' courts have a certain amount of civil jurisdiction.

1. Domestic proceedings   They can deal with domestic disputes between husband and wife, the custody of children, commit children into the care of a local authority, consent to the marriage of minors over sixteen, decide on the paternity of a child of an applicant and adoptions.
2. Licensing sessions   Licensed premises must have current licences issued by the magistrates at special sessions of the court.

Fig. 2.2 Diagram of the civil court system in England and Wales

3. **Civil debts** The magistrates can deal with the enforcement of tax arrears, national insurance arrears, and arrears of rates and gas and electricity supplied. All of these are called civil debts, as the debt is owed to an agency of the state, e.g. the Inland Revenue, or a nationalised industry, or local government. Because of the nature of the debt, the proceedings are to some extent criminal, and defaulters could be committed to prison.

Venue. Because of their great criminal jurisdiction, there are magistrates' courts in most towns in England and Wales. Whether a particular court has jurisdiction to hear a case, will depend on the wording of the Act of Parliament governing the circumstances.

'Judges' (magistrates; addressed as 'Your Worships').
The 'judges' are not proper judges at all, and are called magistrates. They may either be **Justices of the Peace**, (who are part-time) or **stipendiary magistrates.**
  Justices of the Peace (JPs) are laymen, who have been chosen, usually, because of their services to the community. They are appointed for a particular area, known as a **Commission** by the Crown on the advice of the Lord Chancellor. He chooses them from lists drawn up

by countrywide advisory committees. The JP's are not paid, but receive expenses. Because they are laymen, and have only received minimal training, they are advised in court by a **Clerk to the Justices** who sits in front of the **bench** (the collective term for JP's). The clerk is either a barrister or solicitor who has been qualified for at least five years. When sitting in court, the usual number of justices is three, although it is quite proper for any number between two to seven, to hear a case.

Stipendiary magistrates are professionally qualified magistrates, being either barristers or solicitors of at least seven years standing. They are appointed in cities where the amount of work warrants the need for a full-time magistrate. Only one is required to hear a case.

Procedure   The procedure is less formal than in the county court or High Court.

Civil proceedings are started by a **complaint** to a single magistrate. This is usually done by the complainant visiting the magistrate court office. The complaint may be written or verbal.

Practice   Details of jurisdiction, procedure and practice, may be found in *Stone's Justices' Manual* (the Blue Books) which is published annually. This is a vital book for those who have to appear regularly in magistrates' courts.

County courts

Jurisdiction

1. Types of law.   These courts, of which there are over 350 all over the country, are of great value to the builder, for it is here, that sums of money up to £5,000 can be recovered in actions for contract and tort excluding libel & slander. On p. 203 there is an outline of the methods used in the county court to collect debts.

Rather like a junior version of the High Court, the county court has jurisdiction over many other types of proceedings. All divorces have to be started there, and matters concerning adoptions and guardianship are also dealt with.

More importantly for builders, some county courts have jurisdiction over petitions for bankruptcy (*see* p. 206); the winding up of companies with a small amount of paid up capital (less than £120,000); equity matters such as trusts, mortgages and partnerships involving less than £30,000; and actions concerning land of a rateable value not exceeding £1,000 per annum.

It should be noted, therefore, that the county court has the above monetary limits on its jurisdiction. This should not lead you to think that the courts are of any less importance to the legal system. For example, approximately, three quarters of legally aided personal injury claims, and most of all debt and contract claims are for less than

£5,000, and they must therefore be taken to the county court and not to the Queens Bench Division.
2. Geographical jurisdiction. In order to start a case in a particular county court, one must first satisfy the court's officers that there is a good reason for this. On the request form, required to start the action (see p. 204) a number of questions have to be answered to indicate the reasons why that particular county court has jurisdiction, e.g. was the contract made in that court's district or is the defendant resident there or did the accident take place there?

Judges *(circuit judges; addressed as 'Your Honour').* Since the Courts Act 1971, England and Wales has been divided into six regions or circuits. Within each region there are a number of High Court judges, circuit judges and recorders. Circuit judges can sit both on less serious crown court criminal cases as well as in the county courts. To be appointed, they must have been practising barristers for 10 years, or have been recorders for five years. (Solicitors may be appointed as recorders, so may ultimately become circuit judges.)

Procedure. Actions in the county court are started by **plaint.** For an account of a default action, *see* p. 204.

Other types of proceedings called **matters**, e.g. adoptions, or windings up of companies or bankruptcies, are started either by **originating applications** or **petitions**, depending on the regulating Act and county court rules.

Practice. The 'bible' of the county court, is the *County Court Practice* (the 'Green Book') published in two volumes.

Other personnel. The administrative side is dealt with by a court staff headed by the **registrar** who has the powers of a judge for claims of less than £500. He also deals with applications and preliminary matters prior to the court hearing before the judge.
(Note: Both the magistrates' court and the county court are courts which have **original** jurisdiction only, i.e. they have no rights to hear appeals.)

The High Court

The High Court is split into three divisions – Queens Bench; Family; Chancery – each having original and **appellate** jurisdiction, i.e. can be sitting for the first time hearing a case, or it may be hearing appeals from the magistrates' court.

When sitting as an appeal court, it is called a **divisional** court (*see* p. 42).

Jurisdiction. See under each individual division.

Venue. Unlike the county and magistrates' court, the High Court has jurisdiction over the whole of England and Wales. The 'headquarters', however, are found at the Royal Courts of Justice in the Strand, London (*see* Fig. 2.1) where the administrative headquarters called the **Central Office** of the Supreme Court may be found. In the county, High Court cases will be usually heard in the Crown Court building, but, of course, the court will be convened as a High Court. The provincial administrative offices are called district registries.

Judges. (*High Court judges; addressed as 'Your Lordship'* – knighted on appointment). They must either have been circuit judges, or have been practising at the Bar for at least 10 years. They are called **puisne** (pronounced puny) judges, in that, they are of a lesser standing than the senior judicial officers, such as the Lord Chief Justice.

Procedure. See under each individual division.

Practice. High Court practice and procedure is set out in the *Supreme Court Practice* (the White Books).

Other personnel At the Central Office, administration is dealt with by masters and registrars. In the district registries, this is undertaken by district registrars.

The Queen's Bench Division (Head: Lord Chief Justice)

Jurisdiction. This is the big brother of the county court, and can deal, in theory, with any cases in contract and tort, including libel and slander. In practice, because of the county court's £5,000 limit, it will not deal with cases involving a lesser sum. Indeed, the High Court, of its own volition or on application, can now transfer cases brought before it to the county court, if the sum at issue is likely to be less than £5,000, or if the case does not involve an important question of law or fact.

There are three specialist sub-courts of the Queen's Bench Division; the Commercial Court, the Admiralty Court and the Patents Court (*see* p. 195).

The Commercial Court has judges with a commercial background hearing the case and using a simplified procedure. It deals with such matters as commercial contracts, including building contracts.

Commercial Court judges, because of their expertise, may also act as arbitrators or umpires in commercial arbitrations (e.g. under a building contract) (*see* p. 57).

The Admiralty Court deals with many other matters, salvage claims, and prize claims, (property captured from an enemy at sea, as for example, in the Falkland campaign). The judges are appropriately qualified.

Procedure. Actions are started by **writ**. For an account of an action begun by writ, *see* p. 204.

Other types of proceedings called matters may be started by **originating summons**.

Family Division (Head: President)

This is the most modern of the divisions, created in 1970 by the Administration of Justice Act 1970. Once again, it has similar jurisdiction to the matrimonial and family cases of the county court.

Jurisdiction. This deals with defended divorces and nullity actions, judicial separations, recognition of foreign decrees of divorce, ancillary financial matters relating to proceedings, custody and protection of children, protection from molestation and violence, wardship proceedings, etc.

Procedure. Divorces and certain other proceedings are commenced by **petition**, other proceedings may be started by originating application or originating summons.

A sub-division of the Family Division deals with the granting of probate, or letters of administration on death. These are obtained, either from the **Principal Probate Registry** in London's Somerset House, or at one of the district probate registries. Applications for a grant are done by filing an executor's or administrator's oath.

Chancery Division (Head: Lord Chancellor – in practice: the Vice Chancellor)

Jurisdiction. Obviously, this deals with predominantly equity matters, such as trusts, mortgages, rectification of deeds, specific performance of contracts, interpretation of documents, such as contracts and wills.

In addition, it deals with revenue cases and company law, as well as contentious probate (i.e. where there is a dispute).

Venue. Until recently, nearly all chancery cases, were heard in London, at the Royal Courts of Justice, which, whilst being convenient for the judges and the chancery barristers, was less convenient for the parties and their witnesses. Now, chancery cases can also be heard at certain designated regional centres (sitting in the local Crown Court building).

Judges. There are judges specially assigned to the Chancery Division created from the chancery Bar, which consists of barristers specializing in chancery matters.

Procedure. Originally, the Chancery Court used no writs. However, it is possible to use writs in certain circumstances in the Chancery Division nowadays. Other modes of starting cases are by such means as originating summonses and **motions**.

The Divisional Courts

1. *Queen's Bench Divisional Court.* This hears criminal appeals on points of law from the magistrates' court or the Crown Court **by way of case stated** (*see* p. 46).

    It also has jurisdiction of a supervisory nature over lower courts and tribunals if they have failed to exercise their own jurisdiction properly. The court exercises this supervisory jurisdiction by the use of **prerogative orders** of **mandamus, prohibition** and **certiorari**.

    Mandamus means 'we command'. It is used to order the performance of a public duty, e.g. where a local authority has failed to do something required of it by law.

    The order of prohibition is used to prevent a lower court from exceeding its jurisdiction, acting against the rules of natural justice, and to prevent a government minister or public corporation abusing their quasi-judicial functions, e.g. where a government minister refuses to hold a planning enquiry.

    The order of certiorari is used to command a lower court or tribunal to certify, as to some aspect of a judicial matter, that it should be investigated by the High Court.

    Most appeals are heard by two judges.
2. *Chancery Divisional Court.* This deals with appeals from the county courts on questions of bankruptcy and land registration. Also, it hears appeals from the Commissioner of Inland Revenue.
3. *Family Divisional Court.* This hears appeals on family matters from the magistrates', county court and Crown Court.

Court of Appeal – Civil Division (Head: Master of the Rolls)

Jurisdiction. As its name implies, this is a court with pure appellate jurisdiction. It can hear appeals from the High Court, the Queens Bench Divisional Court, county courts, the Admiralty Court, the Commercial Court and the Employment Appeals Tribunal, the Land Tribunal, the Patent Appeal Tribunal, the Restrictive Practices Court, the Social Security Commission Tribunal, and from arbitration appeals which have gone to the divisional court, or from commercial judges sitting as arbitrators.

Judges. These are called Lords Justices of Appeal, and are appointed from the ranks of High Court Judges.

They remain knights and do not become lords in the normal sense.

But, they are also made Privy Councillors on appointment.

The head of the civil division of the Court of Appeal is the Master of the Rolls.

Venue. Normally, the appeal is heard by two judges in the Royal Courts of Justice in London.

Procedure. Notices of appeal must be served on the other party within four weeks of the judgment in the lower court. The notice must contain sufficient details of the grounds for appeal.

The appeal is 'by way of rehearing' similar to that in the Crown Court (*see* p. 46), but the witnesses are not called, and transcripts of their evidence are read, and counsel for all parties put forward their arguments.

House of Lords

Jurisdiction. This is the highest court of appeal for all British courts in civil matters.

(Note: Its criminal jurisdiction is limited to England, Wales and Northern Ireland.)

It is part of the House of Lords, but when sitting in its judicial capacity, its lay peers, i.e. the hereditary life peers and bishops, are no longer allowed to sit as judges.

Generally, only cases which raise a point of law which is of public importance, may be taken to the House of Lords. A statement to this effect may be made, either in the Court of Appeal or the High Court. In the latter case, it is possible, in cases of great public importance, to by-pass or **leap frog** the Court of Appeal, and take the appeal straight to the House of Lords. In such cases, however, all the parties to the action must agree, as must the House of Lords Appeal Committee. Furthermore, in this situation, only certain aspects of the law may be the subject of an appeal to the House of Lords, e.g. concerning a binding precedent (*see* p. 28) of the House of Lords itself or the Court of Appeal.

Judges. In the House of Lords, the judges are called Lords of Appeal in Ordinary (to distinguish them from the Lords Spiritual, who are the bishops, and the Lords Temporal who are the lay peers).

A law lord must have been at the Bar for at least 13 years, or have been a senior judge for at least two years.

Venue. The appeal is heard in a committee room at the House of Lords at Westminster.

Procedure. At least three lords called an Appellate Committee listen to counsel arguing their case. Afterwards, they vote, whether to allow or dismiss the appeal. Their judgments take the form of written speeches, which often take some time to prepare.

Criminal cases

Introduction

All criminal cases begin in the magistrates' court. Whether it is actually tried there depends, on whether the offence is an **indictable** offence or a **summary** one. At its most basic, indictable offences are very serious crimes, summary being less so. But, unfortunately, there are some offences which are **hybrid**, which can be tried summarily or on indictment (triable either way), depending on certain circumstances. Indictable offences were originally created at common law, although nearly all of them are now statutory offences, and thus have the benefit of trial by jury. Summary and hybrid offences on the other hand, are purely the creation of Parliament, and this has increased the jurisdiction of the magistrates, especially in the twentieth century. Whether a trial is to be by magistrates or by jury in the Crown Court will depend on the wishes of the prosecution, and, if the defendant could possibly be sent to prison for more than three months, then he has the right to have a say in the matter.

Summary offences

Examples of summary offences

Failing to securely fence a dangerous part of machinery under the Factories Act; being drunk and disorderly; failing to pay national insurance contributions where liable to do so; obstructing the highway under the Highways Act 1980; using a television without a licence.

Magistrates' court

Procedure. Criminal proceedings are started by an **information** and not by complaint as in civil matters. The information is **laid** before the magistrates in court by the informant, whether it is the police, or a member of the public, or a private individual. If a warrant needs to be issued for the arrest of the defendant, then the information must be in writing on oath. A summons is then issued to summon the defendant to court to answer the charge (unless the charge is one where the defendant can plead guilty by post, e.g. for speeding). The information must contain sufficient particulars to deal with the case.

At the hearing, the clerk to the justices reads the charge, and asks for the accused's plea – guilty or not guilty.

1. *Plea of guilty*. If he pleads guilty, then there is, of course, no trial,

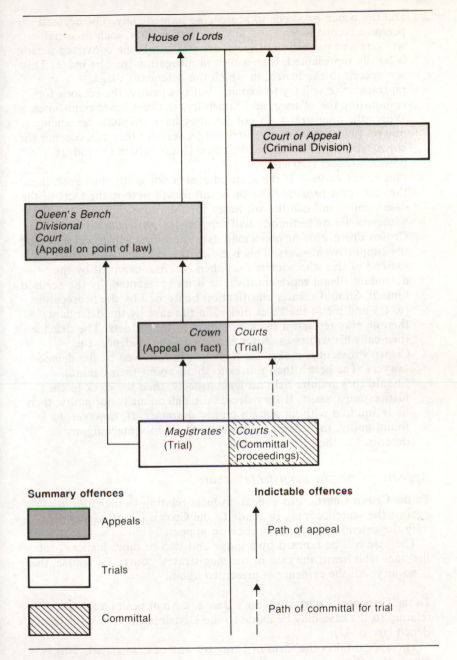

Summary offences

Indictable offences

Appeals — Path of appeal

Trials — Path of committal for trial

Committal

Fig. 2.3 Diagram to illustrate the criminal court system in England and Wales and the bench proceeds to sentencing immediately. The accused person's record is read and any relevant reports, such as social workers and probation officers, are studied. If the convicted person is legally represented, then a plea in mitigation may be made. This is a speech to the bench, in which the defendant's legal representative will try to explain, but not justify, the reasons for committing the offence, and hopefully, secure a lesser punishment. Where the magistrates do not feel they have adequate sentencing powers (which have been restricted by statute) they can commit the convicted person to the local Crown Court, where the judges' powers are less restricted.

2. *Plea of not guilty.*   If the accused pleads not guilty, however, then the case must proceed. The prosecution will outline the facts of the case briefly, and call the witnesses for the prosecution, i.e. all those witnesses whose testimony will support the *prosecution's* case. The Crown Prosecutor or policeman asks questions which will elucidate the supportive answers. This is called the **examination-in-chief**. At the end of this, the witness may then be cross-exmined by the defendant's legal representative, or if unrepresented, by the accused himself. Should greater clarification be needed by the prosecution (to try and mend the holes picked in the case by the defendant), then he may request a re-examination of the witness. The defence then calls his witnesses. After hearing all the evidence, the Crown Prosecutor makes his final speech followed by the defence lawyers. The bench then retires to think about their decision. Should they require help on legal aspects, then the clerk to the justices must assist. If they decide the defendant is not guilty, then he is aquitted without a stain on his character. If, however, he is found guilty, then the magistrates proceed to sentencing, as described in the previous section.

Appeals – *from the magistrates' court*

To the Crown Court.   An appeal on facts relating to the case, or against the sentence, may be made to the Crown Court. Generally, only the defendant may make such an appeal.

The case will be reheard by a judge and two or more justices (not the ones who heard the case in the magistrates' court). Of course, there is no jury. All the evidence is presented again.

To the Divisional Court of Queen's Bench.   An appeal, on a point of law relating to the case may be made to the Divisional Court of the Queen's Bench (*see* p. 42).

The appeal takes the form of being by way of case stated. This means that there is some legal aspect of the original trial which needs to be clarified. Either the defendant or prosecution may appeal, unlike appeals on fact or sentence in the Crown Court.

The case is actually stated by the magistrates' clerk, who sets out the points involved in writing.

There is no rehearing. Counsel for each side argue the points of law.

Appeal to the House of Lords

An appeal from the Divisional Court of Queen's Bench may be made to the House of Lords. But the court must first **certify** that a point of law of general public importance is involved. Either the Divisional Court or the House of Lords itself must give **leave** to appeal. Thus, the House of Lords only deals with the most important and significant cases.

Indictable offences

Committal proceedings in the magistrates' court

Before someone can be sent for trial in the Crown Court, he must first be **committed for trial** in the magistrates' court.

This involves the accused being summoned before magistrates, (sitting as **examining** magistrates), who decide whether or not, he should be sent for trial. In the majority of cases, nowadays, this is an automatic procedure, as long as the accused is aware, that he has the right to object to the quick form, and can ask for a long traditional type of committal. This is used where there is, perhaps some doubt, about the sufficiency and cogency of the evidence against the accused, and the chances of a trial producing a conviction. This does **not** mean that the committal proceedings are a form of 'pre-trial' trial. All the magistrates are trying to do, is prevent a waste of time and money on a prosecution in which the ultimate acquittal of the accused is predictable. The evidence is examined, and if there does seem to be a good case against the accused, he will be committed for trial.

Until the time of the actual committal for trial, the accused may be held in custody in jail. Each week he will have to be brought before the magistrates for a further period of being **remanded in custody**. In newsworthy criminal cases, such as the 'Yorkshire Ripper' case, television reporters may record such appearances.

In less serious cases, the accused will be allowed to remain at liberty, being **remanded on bail**. This means, that if he fails to turn up at court for any appearance, be it for remand, committal or trial, he will suffer serious penalties. If others had to stand as **sureties** for the accused, they will lose the money they promised to pay, if he lets the court down. If he stood as his own surety, then he loses his own money.

The trial at the Crown Court

Jurisdiction. The Crown Court has jurisdiction to hear cases in any part of England and Wales. There are Crown Court regional centres in most big towns. The Crown Court is divided into three tiers, the first, has both High Court and circuit judges, and acts as provincial court rooms for High Court civil actions as well as for criminal cases. The second tier has High Court and circuit judges, but deals only with criminal cases. The third tier only has circuit judges.

Offences are similarly divided into four groups, Class 1 being the most serious, which can only be tried by a High Court judge, down to Class IV, which can be tried by a circuit judge or recorder.

Judges

1. High Court judges, *see* p. 40.
2. Circuit judges, *see* p. 39.
3. Recorders – addressed as 'sir'. These are part-time judges in the Crown Court. Since the Courts Act 1971 he must be a barrister or solicitor of 10 years standing.

Procedure.   Indictable offences are brought before the court, by laying an information before the magistrates (*see* p. 44), or by arresting the accused, and then bringing the accused before magistrates for remand within 24 hours of arrest.

Practice.   The rules of the Supreme Court apply to the Crown Court (*see* p. 40), as the Crown Court, the High Court and the Court of Appeal together make up the Supreme Court.

The trial at the Crown Court.   The accused will be taken to court and put in the cells if he has been remanded in custody. If he is on bail, he must surrender to his bail, and wait in the cells to be called for trial, if he does not, a warrant for his arrest, may be made.

The arraignment.   The accused is asked to answer the indictment, i.e. plead, guilty or not guilty to the charges made.

If he pleads guilty, there will be no trial, and the judge will proceed to sentencing, in the same way as in the magistrates' court (*see* p. 44).

If he pleads not guilty, then the jurors will be summoned and sworn in. Under the Juries Act 1974, anyone on the electoral roll over 18, subject to certain exceptions, may be called to sit on a jury.

The course of the trial is much as described in the magistrates' court, except that the prosecution will be by Crown Prosecutors and the defence must be undertaken by barristers with instructing solicitors. Furthermore, it is of course, the jury's job to judge whether the accused is guilty 'beyond all reasonable doubt' which is the standard of proof required in criminal cases. Any submission concerning the law however, is heard by the judge in the absence of the jury.

The verdict. After the judge's summing up, addressed to the jury, the jury is sent out to the juryroom to consider its verdict. It is possible, where the jury has been out for a long period, that the judge will allow a majority verdict of either 11-1 or 10-2. But they must have been out for at least two hours.

The sentence. If the accused is found guilty, then the judge will then sentence him.

Types of punishment. The following are the types of punishment that may be meted out in the magistrates' and Crown Court.

- Imprisonment *The maximum sentence of life imprisonment is compulsory for murder and the maximum for manslaughter*
  For many offences, minimum and maximum sentences are laid down by statute
- Fines *There may be statutory upper and lower limits*
- Detention and attendance centres *These are appropriate where young persons are involved*
- Probation
- Absolute and conditional discharges
- Binding over to keep the peace
- Community service orders
- Compensation orders
- Restitution orders (to return stolen property)
- Order of criminal bankruptcy
- Deportation orders
- Care, supervision and guardianship orders of minors
- Deprivation of property
- Disqualification from holding licences
- Compulsory admission to hospital

Appeals. Appeals from the Crown Court go to either the Queens Bench Divisional Court on a point of law, or to the Court of Appeal, Criminal Division, and from there to the House of Lords. But, an appeal to the House of Lords is only permitted if the Court of Appeal has given its certificate, stating that the case involves a point of law of great public importance, and either the Court of Appeal or the House of Lords itself grants leave to appeal.

Essentials of the law of evidence

Need for evidence

No action can be satisfactorily presented in England or Wales, whether criminal or civil, without bringing sufficient evidence to support the case. If this were not so, then we would see the worst abuses of justice

that may be found in certain other countries, where trials are mere
farces and accusations of guilt are enough to put innocent people
behind bars, and even worse.

Innocence is presumed, guilt must be proved

In this country, we believe a person to be innocent until proved guilty.
Furthermore, it is for the plaintiff or the prosecution to substantiate
his case. The defendant does not have to prove his innocence. This
duty is called the **burden of proof**.

Standard of proof

The **standard of proof** refers to the amount of evidence needed to
support the plaintiff or prosecution's case.

In *civil cases*, the standard is sufficient, to prove liability **on a
preponderance of probability**. This means, that, after reviewing **all** the
evidence, the judge must decide, that in all probability, the defendant
did the act complained of.

In *criminal cases* the standard of proof is much greater. The
prosecution must prove to the jury or magistrates satisfaction, that the
accused committed the crime **beyond all reasonable doubt**.

Types of evidence

The law of evidence is a wide ranging and difficult branch of English
law, not least, because the vocabulary used by the courts and legal
writers, is diverse and contradictory. The following is thus a general
outline only.

First hand oral evidence of a witness

If a workman falls down a hole, and another sees him actually trip
over the ladder, which caused the fall, then this is highly desirable
evidence, and the witness should be summoned to court to give **oral
testimony**.

For this reason, accident reports should be properly kept, in
accordance with statutory requirements and company policy. (This will
of course be documentary evidence, *see* p. 51.) Full details of the
witness should be taken, such as, full name, address and job
description, so that, if the witness leaves his employment, he may be
recalled for the court case (which may take years to get to court).

Similarly, witnesses to documents should always put their address
and description next to their signature.

Attendance at court. Many witnesses are reluctant to offer their services at court. Because of this, some means of forcing them to attend is required.

In the magistrates' court and Crown Court, they can be compelled by witness order or summons, in the County Court by summons and in the High Court by subpoena (pronounced subpena) – under penalty. Failure to obey such orders, may amount to a contempt of court, and the witness could, at worst, be sent to prison.

Depositions and affidavits. Oral evidence at the court hearing is always desirable. But, evidence may have been given before the trial.

In criminal cases, at the committal proceedings, the witness could have given evidence in a written statement, called a **deposition**.

Occasionally, a witness may be examined before a magistrate, in the presence of the accused, and the deposition is then produced at the trial. This is useful, where the **deponent**, i.e. the witness, is too ill to attend, or abroad.

In civil cases, often, evidence is given by **affidavit**, i.e. sworn statements.

Evidence from previous criminal or civil proceedings, may be used as evidence in later **civil** actions, but not in criminal trials, unless precisely the same issues are involved.

First-hand documentary evidence

In some cases, documentary evidence is at the root of the legal action, e.g. in contract, land law, and contentious probate. So, it is important to be able to examine the actual written words, e.g. the contract, receipt, lease or conveyance, will or letter.

Because of their existence, evidence of external matters, i.e. not mentioned in the document, is only allowed in certain cases. After all, why bother to commit something into writing, if you do not expect to be bound by it.

Documents include, hand and typewritten documents, drawings, plans, maps, graphs, photographs, bank statements, discs, tape recordings, films and negatives. The list is growing.

What evidence should be produced. Obviously, the best evidence of a document is the **original**. Failing that, evidence of the contents of a missing document, could be by unsigned carbon. This would be treated as an original piece of evidence.

If original evidence is not available, then **secondary or inferior** evidence may be given of the contents of the document. (This is not admissible if the original is available). Examples of secondary evidence include photocopies, drafts, certified copies and oral evidence by witnesses of the contents.

Can such evidence be compelled? The production of documentary evidence can be enforced by the court, unless it is totally unconnected with the proceedings or the contents are protected by the rules relating to privilege (*see* below).

For the builder, documentary evidence is of the utmost importance and for this reason, all letters, contracts, receipts, reports, plans, drawings etc. should be properly filed. Documentary evidence is so persuasive in court that opportunities to rely on such should not be lost by sloppy office practice. This is especially important as oral evidence of their contents might not be believed.

As a further **caveat** (warning), it is always good practice to commit important matters into writing and indeed in some situations is essential. For example, written warnings will be needed to resist a claim for unfair dismissal (*see* p. 348).

Conversely, because of the strength of such evidence, care should be taken when writing anything, to make sure that what is written is accurate.

Extrinsic evidence

If a document is at the root of a case or even one aspect of the case, then no outside (extrinsic) evidence concerning the contents of the document is allowed.

Occasionally, extrinsic evidence will be permitted in specialized circumstances. For example, if a builder contracts with someone and the only written evidence is a letter containing the minimum of contract terms such as the date of commencement, details of the job involved and rate of pay, then extrinsic evidence may be used to prove additional terms which were agreed orally between the parties.

Also extrinsic evidence is allowed to show that there has been a later variation of the contract terms or even that the contract has been discharged by the parties.

Similarly, it may be allowed to explain local custom or trade usage or even foreign words, if used in a document.

Matters which do not have to be proved

Admissions

If a formal admission concerning a fact is made at or before a criminal trial, then that is conclusive evidence which may only be withdrawn with leave of the court. The admission may be made orally at court or elsewhere (such as at the police station) in writing. It may concern some minor aspect of the case such as being present at the scene of a crime or it may be an admission of guilt.

In civil proceedings, similar formal admissions may be made at various stages of the proceedings. If what is admitted is admission of liability then a party may proceed to ask for judgment.

Presumptions

Sometimes a party's behaviour allows the court to infer something from that behaviour. This is known as a **presumption**. If the presumption arises in a court case, then it may have two effects.

Firstly, it may dispense with the need to prove the underlying facts. Secondly, it may have the effect of moving the burden of proof from one party to the other.

Some presumptions are rebuttable. This means that they are not conclusive and may be shown by evidence not to be true e.g. that a person is sane, innocent, dead, validly married or legitimate. *Res ipsa loquitur* described on p. 266 is another example. These are presumptions of law and should be for the judge to decide whether or not they can be rebutted.

Presumptions of fact are the concern of the jury (at the judge's discretion) and are concerned with facts which would naturally lead one to infer something e.g. if someone would think to himself, that man must have meant to do that, otherwise why did he do this other thing? But of course, all the other evidence must be taken into account.

Matters which are not admissible in court

Privilege

There are certain situations in which the parties do not have to produce evidence or admit facts because of the existence of a privileged relationship. Examples of privilege are given below.

Communications headed 'without prejudice'.   Parties who are negotiating with each other prior to (and hopefully with the intention of avoiding) a court action, make statements 'without prejudice', either verbally or in writing. If they do, then these statements are usually not admissible in court. The **final** letter or statement containing the terms of a settlement following such negotiations, will not be able to claim this status, if one of the parties tries to avoid what was agreed. The rule is only designed to encourage a settlement and this would not be achieved if every letter offering a solution could then be used as evidence to bind the maker of the statement.

Privilege of lawyers.   Where a solicitor writes to or telephones his client, then such communications are privileged. The solicitor does not even have to admit that the client is a client.

As it is the client's privilege, he can waive it if he wishes.

It should be noted that doctors, nurses, journalists and priests do not have such privilege despite common belief.

Self-incrimination.   No person need answer questions or produce documents which could incriminate himself.

54

Privilege for reasons of public policy. Often disclosure will not be ordered if it is not in the public interest. This is usually for reasons of national security, the encouragement of crime detection (police informer protection), or matters relating to state secrets. Judges cannot be made to give evidence concerning cases they have tried. For the same reason, arbitrators cannot be ordered to give evidence concerning the reasons for making a particular award. (However, *see* p. 61).

Estoppel

From the old french root of word to stop, it is the rule of evidence that stops a person from making a statement or doing something and then later denying it. It can only be used in defence, as a 'shield and not a sword'.

It may be pleaded in a number of situations. A person may be estopped from denying a fact if he had agreed with the other party that it was or was not true. Thus, once a contractor takes lawful possession of a site in accordance with the contract, he cannot then deny that the employer is not the owner of the land, it that is the case.

Similarly, if a builder allows a company representative to think that his site agent has authority to make certain contracts on his behalf then he will be estopped from denying his liability on such contracts, even if the agent had no such authority (but the representative did not know this).

There may also be estoppel by record. This means that if a court has decided something then that decision cannot be raised as a point at issue in another case between the same parties.

In criminal cases a person may plead that he has already been acquitted of the offence with which he is currently being charged (autrefois acquit). Or he can plead he has already been convicted for that offence (autrefois convict). This is known as action estoppel.

If a deed is executed, then the parties to that deed cannot dispute the contents, unless there are grounds to show that the deed has been drawn up incorrectly.

Hearsay

The general rule is that hearsay is inadmissible evidence. As we have already seen, first-hand oral evidence is the most desirable evidence. Such evidence is on oath and can be tested by cross-examination. Hearsay has been defined by the Civil Evidence Act 1968 as a 'statement other than one made by a person giving oral evidence in those proceedings – as evidence of any facts stated herein'.

Does this mean therefore, that all hearsay is inadmissible? Of course not. Oral or documentary evidence falling within the definition above may be admissible under many exceptions to the general rule, especially in civil cases.

Alternative methods of settling disputes

Of course, court action should only be the last resort, after other ways of settling your problems have failed. Also, it must be remembered, that only **legal** problems can be solved in court. If there is no relevant law or legal rule, then the courts are no answer.

In some legal situations, there are alternatives or additional methods (*see* Fig. 2.4 and text).

Fig. 2.4 Methods of settling disputes

Do-it-yourself

The law has often encouraged self-help and in most situations, will prefer that the parties have tried to resolve their problems relatively amicably, *before* resorting to court. Indeed, occasionally, judges have been known to tell the parties to go away and to try to sort things out for themselves, as they feel that the courts are not the proper theatre for neighbour disputes and the like.

Some legal problems can be solved cheaply by one or more of the following methods.

- Reporting to the police, if a crime appears to have been committed.
- Reporting to local authorities for breaches of statute e.g. pollution, offensive trades, noise, unhygienic eating places, short weight, breach of byelaws, building regulations and town and country planning law. The appropriate department must be used (*see* Ch. 3 on local government).
- Seeking advice from citizens advice bureaux.
- Writing to consumer programmes on television and radio e.g. 'That's Life'.
- Reporting to the Director-General of Fair Trading, if an unfair trading practice appears to have been operated.
- Writing to the appropriate disciplinary bodies or governing bodies for trade, profession or industry e.g. the Law Society, the Chartered Institute of Building, the Association of British Travel Agents.
- Writing to the member of Parliament for your constituency.
- Seeking advice from your trade union.

In some situations, appropriate action can be taken by yourself to resolve a difficulty. This may be, for example, a problem concerning your tax affairs or a dispute over a small building project. A number of points should be noted.

(a) Avoid legal problems by thinking ahead

The crunch is always going to come at some time or another. So, it is far better to predict problems and by doing so, they may then be avoided. Whilst the following does not strictly relate to standard form building contracts, the principles are the same.

Important details of contracts/accounts should be committed to paper and copies kept and filed properly. Anything agreed by you and the other party should be evidenced in writing and copies kept by both parties. (Carbon copy books are useful for this purpose). An accurate record of expenditure and receipts relating thereto, should be maintained and a note of any moneys received from clients. Money should be paid into your account as soon as possible and into a deposit account for preference. Accounts should be rendered as quickly as you are able and followed up if unpaid. Maintaining friendly relations with others is essential. Pleasantness costs nothing and can often solve problems like magic.

(b) If a problem does occur

Either visit or telephone the other side (be it customer, electricity board or taxman) and try to resolve the matter before it gets worse and without undue delay. Keep a note of the date, time, the person to whom you spoke and what was said, for future reference (evidence if it goes to court).

If that fails, follow up soon after with a letter, keeping a copy referring to your previous conversation.

If there is still no reply or solution, send a recorded delivery letter referring to your previous visit, telephone call and letter and setting a time limit for a reply.

If there is still no reply or settlement then the usual courses are open to you in addition to the ones mentioned above. In some cases financial help with legal expenses is available. This is called legal aid and advice on whether or not you are entitled to it can be obtained from any solicitor's office with the legal aid symbol displayed. A list of legal aid solicitors can be supplied at your local citizens advice bureau.

Administrative tribunals

If you feel that you have been unfairly dismissed, your first reaction is not to take your employers to court, but to take them to an industrial tribunal (*see* p. 353).

Such a tribunal is one of many types which has been set up by Parliament to deal with such diverse matters as the discipline of the professions e.g. the General Medical Council, labour law matters by the industrial tribunals, rent disputes by the rent tribunals and land matters by the Lands Tribunal.

A tribunal as its name implies is composed usually of three people, one of whom is often a lawyer, the others representing certain aspects of the type of work/matter being dealt with.

The tribunal's procedure is less formal than that of the courts and a problem can be dealt with more quickly than in the over-burdened court system. The powers and remedies of the tribunal vary depending on the subject matter and the authority given to it by Parliament. Reference should thus be made to the appropriate Act.

Arbitration

Definition

This is the formal settlement of a dispute by a third person (or persons) chosen by the disputing parties. It is an alternative method to court action. But, it is impossible to avoid recourse to the courts by agreement, as any such agreement or contractual clause to that effect, is **void** at common law for being contrary to public policy. Thus, arbitration decisions, known as **awards** may be appealed against in the High Court, but only on a question of **law** (not fact) and the court may confirm, vary or set aside such an award or send the award for reconsideration back to the arbitrator.

Relevant law

The law governing arbitrations is found in the Arbitration Acts of 1950 and 1979, any particular Act relating to a special type of arbitration and in ordinary contract law. Contract law applies because the essence of an arbitration is that the parties agree to the dispute being decided by arbitration and agree to being bound by the arbitrator's award. Thus, agreement is essential at all stages of the proceedings.

When can you arbitrate?

Disputes may be settled by arbitration in a number of different situations.

Under a special Act of Parliament. Some Acts specifically provide for disputes to be referred to arbitration. Reference must therefore be made to the relevant Act for the scope of the arbitrator's powers and the conduct of the proceedings. If these matters are not dealt with then the Arbitration Acts apply.

In any legal dispute. Anyone with a legal dispute may decide to opt for arbitration instead of going to court. Both parties must agree to the arbitration either verbally or in writing, and must decide who is to be the arbitrator or who can choose if they cannot agree. They must also decide on the scope of the arbitrator's powers and that they will both abide by any decision he makes. The provisions of the Arbitration Acts apply to written agreements only.

(Note: The **small claims** system in the county courts is an arbitration procedure with the registrar acting as an arbitrator.)

Where court proceedings have already started. Sometimes a judge may decide that arbitration is better suited to the type of case being heard and he may order the case to be transferred for arbitration before a circuit judge who has the relevant expertise and who has been empowered to deal with Official Referee's business. Such cases usually require a detailed examination of documents or involve complex scientific or technological matters.

By prior agreement to arbitrate in the event of a dispute. Many contracting parties recognize that they may very well disagree at some stage of the contract. To avoid the necessity of going to court to settle their differences, a clause is inserted into the contract to submit the dispute to arbitration. Article 5 of the JCT Standard Form of Building Contract is such a clause. Such clauses do *not* oust the jurisdiction of the courts.

Advantages and disadvantages of arbitration

Arbitration is a very popular method of settling disputes in the commercial world and is frequently used in relation to building contracts.

Reasons for popularity

1. Privacy. Arbitrations are held in private, whereas court proceedings are open to the general public. Few people wish to wash their dirty linen in public, least of all commercial companies whose share prices may be adversely affected by bad publicity.
2. Expertise of the arbitrator. The arbitrator is chosen for his expertise on the subject matter of the dispute, be it ship-building or construction work. Often, valuable time is wasted in court proceedings whilst lengthy technical explanations are made for the benefit of the judge. However, as disputes get more complicated, involving many different disciplines, this may prove to be less of an advantage than it used to be.
3. Own choice of arbitrator. There can be no choice of judge in court actions. But, in arbitrations, the parties have the opportunity

of choosing someone they both trust and respect. If they cannot agree on the appointment, then they can refer the choice to someone else. Under Article 5 of the JCT form, either party may request that the President or Vice-President of the Royal Institute of British Architects choose on their behalf.

4. Convenience of parties.   Arbitrations can be conducted at any place and at any time, for the convenience of the parties and arbitrator. Whilst, a court may be convened somewhere other than a court house for special reasons, this is fairly unusual. (Such reasons have included holding the court in the court yard as the defendant had a contagious disease or at the house of a defendant who was a recluse and never went out.)

There is very little say in the timing of court cases, unless the matter is urgent, e.g. where an injunction is required.

5. Procedure more flexible than court proceedings.   Whilst arbitrations usually follow along the lines of ordinary court cases, the arbitrator, can, with the consent of the parties, deviate from the usual pattern in order to give an award more quickly, thereby reducing costs.

6. Exclusion of right to appeal: S.3 1979 Act.   Whilst a clause excluding the right to appeal to the courts, is void, it is now possible under S.3 to agree to this **after arbitration has commenced**.

The section only covers domestic arbitrations but this would apply to most building disputes in England and Wales.

This right of exclusion is an advantage, because the whole point of opting for arbitration is lost if the dispute can then be subjected to the courts' appeal machinery, thereby increasing the costs.

Disadvantages

1. Length of arbitration.   Once a court case has actually been listed for trial, the proceedings are quite swift and reluctant litigants can be brought to heel by the wide powers of the judge. For example, if the plaintiff does not proceed with any of the requirements of the case, the defendant can ask for it to be struck out for want of prosecution.

Arbitrations on the other hand have been known to 'drag on for ever' to quote Lord Denning (former Master of the Rolls). This is because, delaying tactics can be used to a party's advantage and the arbitrator has fewer powers than judges to force the delaying party to comply with his orders.

However, under the Arbitration Act 1979, extra powers may now be applied for and if such an order is made, the arbitrator may continue the proceedings **in default** of the attendance or otherwise of the other party. A Court of Appeal decision suggesting that arbitrations could be struck out for want of prosecution was reversed in the House of Lords.

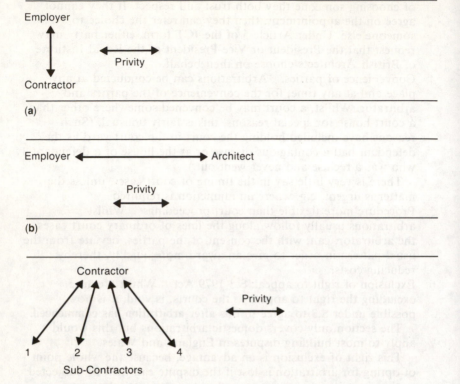

Fig. 2.5 Parties involved in a building contract situation illustrated separately

2. Only parties to agreement may arbitrate.   Only parties to a
   contract have rights and duties in relation to that contract. This is
   called **privity of contract** (*see* p. 111).

   It follows that only parties to an arbitration agreement can
   arbitrate, unless there is some clause contained in such an
   agreement, whereby other parties involved in the dispute, but not
   party to the agreement in question, may have their disputes settled
   at the same time.

   For example, a building contract is between a main contractor
   and an employer; the employer may also have a contract with an
   architect and in turn the contractor may also have contracts with
   sub-contractors, nominated or otherwise (*see* Fig. 2.5a, b & c).

   When one looks at the total building project, the contractual
   relationships are as shown in Fig. 2.6.   Parties who have no
   contract with each other such as the architect and sub-contractors,
   have no privity of contract. Any dispute between the employer and

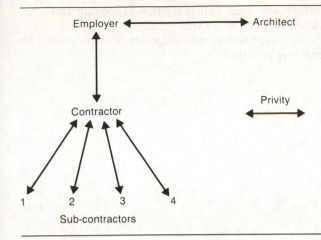

Fig. 2.6 Parties involved in a building contract situation illustrated together

contractor or employer and architect or contractor and sub-contractor must be arbitrated separately, unless their contracts are connected in some way and all parties have agreed that related disputes should be heard by the arbitrator at the same time.

Thus, the JCT form provides for the joining of separate disputes to be heard by the same arbitrator at the same time, provided the issues are substantially the same as or connected with issues raised in a related dispute between the employer and a nominated sub-contractor or the contractor and a nominated sub-contractor or between the contractor and/or the employer and a nominated supplier: Article 5. There are stringent conditions attached to this right.

In court actions however, even if the disputes are contractual, the judge has the power to have the separate proceedings consolidated and heard at the same time. If the disputes are tortious then any number of people may be joined as co-defendants, if they appear to share the blame.

3. Costs of hearing will usually be cheaper. Although it is well known that court proceedings are neither cheap nor necessarily quick, arbitration may sometimes be more expensive if there has been undue delay. Legal aid is never available for such proceedings and all the costs must be borne by the parties, whereas some element will already have been borne by the state in a court case.

4. Reasons are not necessarily given for the arbitrator's award. However, under the 1979 Act, if an appeal is made and one of the parties asks for reasons to be given, then the High Court may require the arbitrator to give his reasons for making his

decision. Arbitrators now must anticipate this happening and remember this when making an award.

In court cases, the judge will give full reasons for his decision in the **ratio decidendi** (*see* p. 30).

CHAPTER 3

Central and local government

Introduction

In every society, primitive or sophisticated, there must be some form of government which is needed to rule and control and to guide and regulate the people. A society without a government, it is argued, would lead to anarchy. Whatever the type of government, all have three aspects, an **executive**, a **legislature**, and a **judiciary**. In some regimes all or some of these functions will be vested in one person or a few people or many, depending on the politics of the country. Perhaps the most common should be mentioned briefly.

A **democracy** is government by the people or government by majority vote. A **dictatorship** is rule by one person. An **oligarchy** is government by a few people or families. A **monarchy** is rule by a monarch. A

Fig. 3.1   How the United Kingdom is governed

constitutional monarchy is a monarchy permitted by the state and thus having only limited powers. Therefore, this country is a democratic constitutional monarchy, with the monarch having limited powers.

We also refer frequently to the word **state**. This is extremely difficult to define but it can be said that it is composed of the executive, legislature and judiciary as well as the police and the armed forces in a particular geographic area. The 'state' carries on the politics of the 'government in power' which can change in a variety of circumstances e.g. revolution, coup d'états, or general elections. The executive consists of the policy and decision-makers and the action-takers.

The legislature, in the UK Parliament, makes laws for the state. The judiciary is necessary to enforce the carrying out of the executive's policies which have been made law by the legislature.

As we have already examined the roles of the legislature and judiciary in earlier chapters, we will now examine the position of the executive (*see* Fig. 3.1). This can best be divided into two parts: central government consisting of the Prime Minister, the Cabinet and the government departments, backed by the civil service and local government which is made up of all the local authorities in England and Wales.

Central government

The Prime Minister

The Prime Minister is appointed by the Queen. Party leaders are now chosen by special procedures by their respective parties. Thus once a party has a majority at a general election, there should be no doubt as to who will be appointed as Prime Minister.

Once appointed, the Prime Minister submits to the Queen the names of his or her Cabinet for the Queen's formal approval.

The Prime Minister acts as chairman of the Cabinet and draws up the agenda for each meeting. Where there is serious disagreement between the Prime Minister and a cabinet member, then his resignation will be called for. Occasionally, the member will resign of his own accord.

The Prime Minister is a major policy maker within the party. To what degree depends on his or her character. One has only to examine the role of the Right Honourable Mrs Margaret Thatcher to see that but for her, much of Conservative policy would take a completely different direction. Indeed, many parliamentary observers now consider that because of the strength of this Conservative Prime Minister, the executive role of Central Government is taking away power from the legislature i.e Parliament.

The Prime Minister also acts as an adviser to the Monarch in the appointment of officials and the giving of honours under the Royal

Prerogative. Thus people as diverse as the Church of England bishops or the Governor of the Bank of England, as well as the most important judges are appointed by the Monarch on the advice of the Prime Minister. In recent times, the degree of prime ministerial influence has been great.

Finally, the Prime Minister should play an active part in foreign and Commonwealth affairs, despite the fact that the Foreign Secretary has considerable powers in this field.

The Cabinet

This consists of approximately twenty members selected by the Prime Minister from the majority party. The members may be responsible for government departments and are called government ministers or they may have no department and they are then called ministers without portfolio. Cabinet members can be members of Parliament or members of the House of Lords.

The Cabinet's main function is to formulate government policy and decide which matters should be laid before Parliament for debate and subsequent legislation.

As much policy affects the government departments, discussion at Cabinet level is useful because the Cabinet will have among its members, the most important government department heads.

The Cabinet meets on average about once a week at 10 Downing Street and is co-ordinated by the Cabinet Office which is also situated there.

Government departments

Having decided in the Cabinet what policies the government wishes to pursue, these are put into effect by the government departments. These departments deal with all the important aspects of the state.

After the 1983 general election there were the following departments:

- Agriculture, Fisheries and Food
- Duchy of Lancaster
- Defence
- Education and Science
- Employment
- Energy
- Environment – this contains a Ministry for Housing and Construction
- Foreign and Commonwealth Affairs
- Health and Social Security
- Home Office

- Law Officers – Attorney General, Law Advocate and Solicitors General
- Management & Personnel Office
- Northern Ireland Office
- Privy Council Office
- Scottish Office
- Trade & Industry
- Transport
- Treasury
- Welsh Office
- Her Majesty's Household

The titles of the departments are not static, as each successive government puts a different emphasis on certain aspects of government.

Each department is headed by a secretary of state or occasionally a minister. There are also a number of ministers of state who act under the authority of the Secretary of State. The ministers of state are known as junior ministers. There may also be under secretaries of state appointed. All are political appointments and change with the fall of a government.

In addition to these political appointments, there are many permanent posts filled by **civil servants** who are there to run the government departments at a day-to-day level. The head of such officials is the permanent secretary e.g. Sir Humphrey in the television programme 'Yes Minister' gives a good idea of this role. The civil service is thus a very important aspect of central government, even where it operates at a local level e.g. in a DHSS local office.

Each department will have its own advisors who will research and provide information when and as required. Some ministers have to consult a standing committee or other body for advice before pursuing a particular policy if this is required by legislation.

Thus, the main functions of a department are, to draw up legislation which implements government policy and help steer it through parliament. It then implements the resulting legislation and administers all the relevant legislation.

The following government departments are of particular importance to the building industry.

Department of Employment

(Caxton House, Tothill Street, London SW1)
This deals with industrial relations and is responsible for the Advisory, Conciliation and Arbitration Service (ACAS) (*see* p. 353). It is also responsible for encouraging health and safety at work through the Health and Safety Commission to which many of the department's statutory

powers under the Health and Safety at Work etc. Act 1974 have been delegated. Job Centres are local DOE offices through which people can advertise for employees or seek employment. The department also runs many training schemes through its Manpower Services Commission. It is also responsible for matters concerning pay and redundancies.

Department of Environment

(2 Marsham Street, London S.W.1)
There are two ministers with special responsibilities for local government and housing and construction within the department. In addition the department deals with town and country planning, new towns, environmental protection and conservation areas and countryside affairs.

It also has responsibilities for the nation's royal palaces and parks, historic buildings and ancient monuments as well as for sport and recreation.

The Property Services Agency (PSA) a sort of modern ministry of works, deals with construction work, supplies and transport for all the government departments both at home and abroad.

Department of Health & Social Security

(Alexander Fleming House, Elephant & Castle, London S.E.1)
This oversees the administration of the National Health Service under the 1980 Health Services Act. The Secretary of State has introduced district health authorities to replace area health authorities at a local level and these are administered by regional health authorities.

Social services are administered by local authorities. Benefits such as disablement benefits etc (see p. 401) are administered by local DHSS offices.

Department of Trade & Industry

(1 Victoria Street, London S.W.1)
Within this department there is a separate minister for trade and minister for information technology.

The department is responsible for many aspects of Britain's economic life. It formulates policy and promotes international trade through many trade organisations such as the EEC or OECD (Organisation for Economic Co-operation and Development). It formulates industrial policy in the regions, promotes small firms and makes policy-making decisions for many of the nationalised industries such as the British Steel Corporation.

It is responsible for developing company legislation, the Companies Registration Office and the Patent Office. It oversees competition law and consumer protection with close relations with such bodies as the Office of Fair Trading.

It promotes research into science and technology and the development of standards and designs.

Department of Transport

This department is responsible for the construction and maintenance of motorways and trunk roads. It oversees transport planning in local authorities.

Local government

This is concerned with the provision of services and facilities in the country at a local level. This is necessary because it would be virtually impossible to centralize the administration of such matters as the provision of police, social services, fire services, cemeteries and crematoria, refuse collection, planning control, education, libraries, building regulation inspection, environmental health etc.

Finance

In order to provide these services, the local authorites levy rates on householders within their administrative areas. This is controlled by the Local Finance Act 1982. They also raise money in a more usual way by borrowing money from investors by mortgages of rates, which often gives a good rate of interest over a fixed period, and also leasing or renting council owned property. Central government also assists local authorities by providing grants called rate support grants. There are

Local Government

London	Conurbations in England
(1) 32 London Boroughs (12 Inner London) (20 Outer London) + City of London Corporation	(1) 36 Metropolitan Districts

Non-Conurbations in England	Wales
(1) 39 Counties (2) 296 Districts (3) Parishes	(1) 8 Counties (2) Districts (3) Community Councils

Fig. 3.2 The organization of local government in England and Wales

disadvantages attached to this latter method as central government can sometimes withhold all or part of the grant if a local authority fails to abide by central policy. Under the Rates Act 1984 Central Government can prevent by order rate rises beyond a specified limit. This may be seen as a fresh reduction in local authority power and an increase in central government intervention.

Organization

In England and Wales, there are two tiers of local authority, county and district authorities. There are slight differences, however, in the London area and in conurbations where there are metropolitan local authorities. The Local Government Act 1985 removed the metropolitan county status and abolished the Greater London Council.

London

London's local government was reorganised as a result of the Local Government Acts 1963, 1972 & 1985. Under these Acts there are now two types of local authority in London.

The City of London. The square mile of the City of London is administered by the ancient City of London Corporation.

London borough councils. There are 32 London Boroughs, 12 in Greater London and 20 in Outer London. They deal with all local government matters not undertaken by the City of London Corporation or other authorized bodies.

Metropolitan areas (in certain conurbations)

There are six metropolitan areas i.e. West Midlands, Greater Manchester, West Yorkshire, Merseyside, South Yorkshire, Tyne & Wear – all of which are heavily populated and built up areas. The Local Government Act 1985 abolished the metropolitan counties and transferred their jurisdiction to the 36 metropolitan districts, which thus have greater jurisdiction than non-metropolitan districts.

Non-metropolitan counties

The rest of England and Wales is divided up into non-metropolitan counties and districts. In England there are 39 counties with 296 district councils and there is also a lower level of parish councils which deal with such matters as bus shelters, car parking, and allotments, clocks, parochial charities, community centres, ponds and ditches, litter bins, village greens and war memorials. In Wales the lowest level is the community council.

Main Responsibilities of Local Government

Non-metropolitan Counties and Metropolitan Districts	All Counties
Libraries Social Services Education	Police Planning at County level Parks – Country and national Fire services Consumer protection Transport Refuse disposal

All Districts

Planning at local level
Environmental Health
Cemeteries
Allotments
Street cleaning

Fig.3.3 Main responsibilities of local authorities

County functions. They deal with education, social services, fire services, police, consumer protection, refuse disposal, libraries, museums, planning structure plans, national parks, highways and lighting, traffic and parking, smallholdings and some airports (shared with district councils).

District functions. These are responsible for: environmental health including building regulation control, clean air, control of disease, food hygiene, refuse collection, street cleaning, housing, town and country planning (local plans and development control), country parks, museums, recreational facilities, encouragement of tourism, cemeteries and crematoria, footpaths and off-street parking, allotments, airports with county councils, licensing and registration of local land charges.

Local government functions of importance to the building industry

Environmental health

This deals with such matters as statutory nuisances, air pollution, refuse collection and disposal, noise and building work control and sanitation.

Building regulation control

Under the Building Act 1984 local authorities are responsible for administering the Building Regulations 1985. Approved inspectors may be appointed by the Local Authority to supervise the works under the Building (Approved Inspectors etc.) Regulations 1985. These apply throughout England and Wales apart from Inner London which has its own byelaws but which will be eventually covered by the regulations. The regulations lay down standards of buildings in relation to their design and the way in which they are built, to achieve uniformity of standards of construction throughout the country (n.b. the Construction Regulations are chiefly designed to protect the building workers during the course of construction work).

The Act require the deposit of plans with the authority and if they conform with the regulation requirements, then the authority must pass the plans. They must reject the plans, however, in certain specified situations e.g. where the building work is going to be on ground filled with offensive material.

If the plans are rejected as being contrary to requirements then an appeal may be made to the magistrates' court of the Secretary of State. He may then appoint an inspector to hear the arguments for both sides.

Should the regulations be contravened, then the owner can be ordered to remove or alter the work. If he fails to do so, then the local authority can do this and charge the owner. Furthermore, the Attorney General, local authority or any interested party can apply for an injunction to get the work altered or removed.

The authority can also take the offender to the magistrates' court under S.35 Building Act 1984. The fines are limited to a maximum £2000 but there is a penalty for each day the offence is contravened after conviction.

Control of demolition

Under the Public Health Act 1961, a person wishing to demolish a building should first notify the local authority. If they authorize this, they may lay down requirements regarding shoring up other buildings, sealing up pipes etc. Appeals against such requirements are taken to the magistrates' court. It is an offence to ignore the requirements.

For Noise nuisances (see p. 294)

Prevention of infectious diseases

The relevant Act is the Public Health (Control of Disease) Act 1984.

Waste collection and disposal

Generally county councils are responsible for disposing of waste and district councils for collecting. The relevant Acts are the Control of Pollution Act 1974 and the Refuse Disposal (Amenity) Act 1978.

Rodent control

An occupier of land must under the Prevention of Damage by Pests Act 1969 inform the local authority if the land in question is infested with rats or mice. An infestation notice may be served requiring work to be carried out or in default the authority may carry out the work and charge it to the occupier. The local authority will carry out such work on request.

Sewage disposal

This is the responsibility of the water authorities. In some cases district councils are authorized to carry out some of the water authorities' functions.

Blocked drains

A local authority can order an owner or occupier to unblock a drain within 48 hours of the notice, failing which the authority can carry out the work and charge the owner – S.17 Public Health Act 1961.

Clean air (see p. 300)

Town and country planning

This subject is beyond the scope of this book and appropriate text books should be read.

Roads, footpaths etc.

See Ch. 9 on highways.

Local land charges

District councils, London borough councils and the Common Council of the City of London must, under the Local Land Charges Act 1975, keep a local land charge register. Searches may be made in this to reveal entries. A requisition in writing is made when purchasing land (*see* p. 161).

Housing

Local authorities with responsibility for housing must inspect their areas from time to time to check on housing provision and unsatisfactory conditions under the Housing Act 1957.

An authority may provide 'council' housing accommodation by, among other methods, building new houses, repairing or altering old and by buying such housing.

Certain tenants now have a right to buy their council houses under the Housing Act 1980 and the Housing and Building Control Act 1984. Also under the Housing Act 1957, Housing Act 1961 and Building Act 1984, local authorities must deal with unfit houses either individually if they can be made fit by spending a reasonable sum, or for those which cannot, then by dealing with them under a clearance area scheme.

Local authorities also have a duty to deal with overcrowding and may give house renovation grants to improve or convert homes.

The police

The police service should be familiar to you all and little need be said on their powers and duties. Most authorities cover either a county or an amalgamation of counties or parts of counties except for the metropolitan police district which covers all of London and the Greater London Council area. The regulating Act is the Police Act 1964.

The fire service

Similarly, you should be conversant with the duties of the fire services. They also may cover county areas or amalgamate.

The local fire authority also deals with the enforcement of the Fire Preventions Act 1971.

Water authorities

Reference to water authorities has been made elsewhere in the book (*see* p. 136).

Control of local authorities

This is achieved in a number of ways. It is desirable to avoid local authorities becoming too self-important, over-stretching their authority or not providing a standardized local government in England and Wales. Thus, anyone living in any part of the country will know that he will receive the same, or similar, treatment from his local authority to that of his neighbours in the next authority district.

Administrative control by government departments i.e. central government control

Informal control by departmental circular

Most departments issue circulars explaining new legislation and instructions on the way the legislation should be put into practice.

74

Whilst this is not law, most local authorities regard the circulars to be of the utmost importance and abide by their contents almost as if it were law.

Consultation between local authorities and government departments

Some statutes specifically require departmental ministers to consult with interested parties before making any regulations. Such interested parties may include local authorities, for as they have to put the law into practice, it is pointless to make rules that they will have difficulty enforcing.

Early consultation will thus help the minister reach a satisfactory approach to delegated legislation.

Financial control

A local authority's capital expenditure is now controlled by the Local Government Planning and Land Act 1980. The minister lays down a prescribed limit above which the local authority's expenditure is controlled. Should a particular scheme be of national or regional importance then the Act provides for specific approval to be given first.

The provision of grants by central government is also highly controlled under the Local Government Finance Act 1982. Some grants are for specific purposes like those given to the police. The threat of withholding such grants is usually sufficient to maintain central control.

General grants take the form of the rate support grant which consists of the domestic rate relief grant and the block grant and is designed to achieve parity between different areas of the country, thereby eliminating differences between poor and wealthy communities. The minister must consult with the local authorities to check the demands for servies, development needs and prices against cost levels. The way in which the rate suport grant is calculated is intended to prevent the local authorities from raising the rates beyond approved levels. This is reinforced by the Rates Act 1984.

All local authorities must have their accounts audited annually by the district auditor or an auditor approved by the Secretary of State. Whilst this does not produce a direct means of central control, the code of practice issued by the Secretary of State directs the auditor to check that an authority spends the money in a way authorized by law and that any financial limits are not exceeded.

Provision of information and enquiries

In some cases Acts require information to be provided for the minister or for the public and if necessary to hold inquiries into matters of concern e.g. Town and Country Planning Act 1971.

Inspection

Government inspectors are required to visit certain establishments to check on their efficiency and to provide advice and information and, in some cases, to see that there have been no breaches of the law. For example, Home Office inspectors visit laboratories where animal experiments are carried out. Department of Education and Science inspectors inspect educational establishments and there are also inspectors of Constabulary and Fire Services.

Complex legislation often needs complex regulation to enforce the law. Thus, regulations have been made for local authorities to abide by when carrying out their statutory duties for example under the Control of Pollution Act 1974, local authorities must use the Control of Noise (Measurement and Registers) Regulations 1976 when measuring noise levels in a noise abatement zone.

Default powers

If a local authority fails to carry out its duties, there are many Acts giving the minister the right to take over the proceedings himself or issue directions as to what is to be done in the circumstances.

Thus, under the Town and Country Planning Act 1971, if a local authority has not properly prepared its structure or local plans then the Secretary of State for the Environment may carry out these duties or transfer them to another authority.

Byelaws

The right to make general byelaws stems from the Local Government Act 1972 S.235. Byelaws must be confirmed by the appropriate minister, usually the Home Secretary. In order to achieve some level of uniformity, model byelaws have been issued by the government. This is because the laws have to pass strict tests of validity if challenged in the courts and the model byelaws are based on examples which have stood the test over the years.

Prior approval

Some Acts require local authorities to submit proposals for carrying out statutory duties to the appropriate minister. The minister may then alter or influence the proposals and may even receive representations from interested parties before finalizing the schemes. The proposals may then be approved or rejected.

In other cases, the local authority may have to seek prior approval of a scheme because they do not have the necessary powers without such approval.

Appeals to ministers

Under some Acts such as the Town and Country Planning Act 1971 a person may appeal against a local authority's decision directly to the minister or secretary of state, or somebody approved by the legislation, e.g. a local government planning officer.

Judicial control

Local authorities may only do what they are authorized to do by individual Acts of Parliament or those things which are incidental to their general powers under the Local Government Act 1972 S.111.

Acts which are totally outside the scope of their powers are said to be **ultra vires** (beyond their powers) and will be void. Such acts are, of course, unusual as no local authority sets out to break the law. However, where procedural requirements have been broken, which is more common, many Acts of Parliament allow such defects to be corrected by the local authority itself.

Where an Act is allegedly ultra vires, an interested party may apply for a **judicial review** of the local authority's decision. The court may grant the usual remedies such as an injunction or damages. Also, it can make a declaration as to the true meaning of the words or phrase in the Act or regulation. The court may also be asked to make one of the prerogative orders of mandamus, prohibition, and certiorari (see p. 42).

If the action concerns public rights then the Attorney General will have to be made a party to the action (although the real plaintiff will still have to pay the costs of the case). This is called a **relator** action (see p. 289). The person can sue in his own name if he can prove some special damage to himself which is over and above that suffered by the public or an additional interference with his private rights.

CHAPTER 4

Contract

Introduction – common misapprehensions

Many people think that a contract must be some complicated 'legal looking' document covered with red seals and full of complex clauses in small print. To some extent, those who deal with the standard forms of building contract may be forgiven for thinking this. But a standard form of any sort, be it a building contract or credit or hire agreement, is in fact in the minority. The majority of contracts are not even in writing. They are entered into in a seemingly casual way every day by millions of people when they buy things in shops, or petrol from a garage, use child minders, go to the cinema or buy a drink in a public house.

A contract is thus used in all transactions in which one person bargains with another, even if the subject matter seems to be trivial.

Why then, are people under the misapprehension that contracts *must* be in writing? This appears to have arisen for three reasons.

First, most important contracts such as buying a house, renting a television or car, buying goods on credit or hire purchase, take the form of complex printed documents. As the printed standard forms are prepared by central bodies or credit companies or even the company selling or hiring the goods or services, they are intended to cover all eventualities, and thus will contain a large number of terms, and regrettably and inexcusably, many which are not easily understood by the general public. Whilst a person in theory could ask to have a special one-off contract drawn up between the parties, in practice, the seller etc will merely refuse to do business with the 'individual'. Because these lengthy printed contracts are contracted at an important stage in the average person's life, the trouble and harassment caused by trying to understand the terms, will probably be vividly remembered and they assume that all contracts must be in writing. This is not so.

Secondly, time and time again, people are unable to take legal action against someone for breach of contract, because they cannot prove that what they are alleging is true. This is not simply because they had nothing in writing. This is because they cannot provide the evidence to support their case, be it written or verbal or any other sort. **Good sense** tells the businessman therefore, that he should commit his contracts into writing and preferably get the other side to sign the agreement.

Failing this, he must have witnesses to support any verbal dealings.

Thirdly, a small number of contracts have to be in writing or at least there must be a note or memorandum to record what was agreed. For example, a contract to transfer an estate or interest in land must be evidenced in writing. Others have to be in a **deed** (a document under seal). Such a contract is called a **specialty** contract and it gives the parties the advantage of being able to sue within **twelve** years of the breach of contract. This is one of the reasons why they are used in the building industry. Ordinary contracts called **simple** contracts allow the parties only **six** years in which to sue.

The absence of writing (or a deed in exceptional cases) is not necessarily fatal in contracts concerned with the transfer of land in which the doctrine of **part performance** may assist someone who has complied with his part of the contract, e.g. paid the purchase price. The court may at its discretion (as the doctrine is equitable) order specific performance of the contract, so that the other party must transfer the land as was agreed orally.

As these written contracts are concerned with important and expensive matters such as buying a house, transferring shares in registered companies, assigning copyrights and bills of exchange, they are extremely memorable.

The second major misapprehension is a development of the first. This is, that parties are not bound by what they have agreed unless the agreement is in writing. For some reason, many people appear to think that there are degrees of 'bindingness' and that oral agreements are less binding than written ones. Once again this is absolutely fallacious unless the contract happens to be one of the small proportion that must be in writing, and even then, as we have seen, equity may be used to help the party suffering from an unwilling contractual partner. Of course this misapprehension is again to do with lack of evidence. If there is no evidence, then the party wishing to enforce the contract may be in difficulties. Because so many people avoid their contractual liabilities through lack of evidence, the misapprehension grows daily. But, this is wrong, even in situations where there is going to be some formal written contract at a later date (which should merely confirm what was verbally agreed at an earlier stage).

Parties become contractually liable **immediately** there is an **agreement** between them, and the actual time of day may be of vital importance.

The is one of the most important elements of a contract, (*see* pp. 83–96). **No** agreement, **no** contract and **no** contractual liability (*see* Fig. 4.1).

Contract law

The law of contract is found mainly at common law and equity and in some legislation.

Definition

A contract is a bargain or agreement between persons giving them rights and duties in law. It does not usually have to be in writing but it must be the sort of agreement which would give rise to legal duties. The majority of contracts are verbal (*see* introduction).

Fig. 4.1   The importance of the timing of the agreement in contract

Examples

Buying a cup of tea in a canteen or a beer in a public house; travelling on a train having paid a fare; hiring a band to play at a rock concert; putting in central heating for a friend at less than the normal charge; building a garage based on a written estimate and a telephone conversation agreeing the rest of the terms; agreeing to build a multi-million pound development using a JCT standard form of contract; a contract of employment; a loan from a building society.

In each of the examples, there are a number of obvious common aspects. There is an agreement between the parties to give or do something in return for something given or done by the other side. There is an exchange of goods or services or something else of value between the parties. This is known as consideration. It would also seem that in the most trivial of situations, such as purchasing a cup of tea, the parties expect to be bound by their promises, and if they fail in some way, such as putting salt in the tea by mistake, that they will have to rectify the situation. This third element is absent for example in social arrangements which usually are not contracts as there is no intention to be legally bound by the terms and thus there is no legal redress if one party breaks a promise. So if you 'stand your girlfriend up' she can take no legal action against you.

Elements of a contract

Thus, the main elements for a valid binding contract are that there must be:

1. An agreement (*see* p. 83).
2. Consideration (*see* p. 80).
3. An intention to be bound by the agreement (*see* above).
   The main ingredients presuppose the existence of certain other requirements. These are:
4. That there is no fundamental mistake over the subject matter (*see* p. 96).
5. That the parties are capable of entering into that particular type of contract (*see* p. 101).
6. That the contract is for a legal purpose (*see* p. 102).
7. That if the contract is supposed to be in a particular form, e.g. writing or in a deed, that it is (*see* p. 106).
8. That the parties consented to the agreement of their own free will (*see* p. 108).

Validity of contracts

Validity means that the agreement takes effect as a contract, giving the parties rights and duties which are enforceable in the courts.

If any of the elements which are essential to the contract are missing, then the purported contract is **void** (not valid). This means that the agreement has no effect in law, gives no rights and duties to the parties and is unenforceable in the courts. **It never was a contract** right from its inception. This is called being **void ab initio**, void from the beginning. For example, consideration is essential on both sides. Thus, if I give £100 to X and ask for nothing in return, this is a gift and not a contract. I cannot later ask X to do something in consideration for giving him the £100 earlier.

Some matters make an otherwise valid contract **voidable**. This means that if a party wishes to avoid the contract, because of some important defect in the contract, the contract then becomes void (see Fig. 4.2).

Consideration

Definition

All simple contracts must have consideration given by each party to the other as the price of each other's promises. It may take the form of money, goods, services, promises not to sue, work etc. It may be positive or negative, but it must represent the **price of the promise** (see Fig. 4.3). If there is no consideration or consideration given only on one side (as in a gift) there is **no** valid contract. it is **void**.

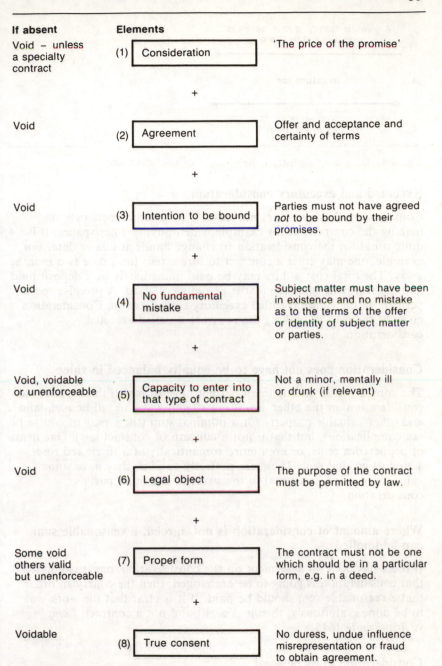

Fig. 4.2 Requirements of a valid contract

Fig. 4.3   Diagram to illustrate the concept of consideration

Executed and executory consideration

Consideration however does not have to be given immediately on making the contract, as for example, when buying a newspaper. It is quite usual for the consideration to change hands at a later date. For example, one may enter a contract to hire a tent for a date two months away. The total cost of hire may be paid immediately or a deposit paid and the rest paid when the tent is actually collected. A promise to perform in the future is called **executory** consideration. Consideration given at the time of making the contract is called **executed** consideration.

Consideration does not have to be equally balanced in value

The consideration on one side does **not** have to match the value of the consideration on the other. So, it is perfectly valid to sell houses, land and other valuable property for a nominal sum (there may of course be tax complications, but that is not a concern of contract law). One hears of peppercorn rents, or even more romantically of a single red rose acting as ground rent. These are perfectly valid as they have some value, even if it is not equal to the value of the other party's consideration.

Where amount of consideration is not agreed, a reasonable sum can be implied

If there has been no agreement on the consideration, but it is implicit that consideration is going to be exchanged, then the court can order that a reasonable sum should be paid. If it is clear that the work was to be done gratuitously, then it is a gift and not a contract: *Lampleigh* v. *Braithwaite* 1615.

Consideration must be legal

Any consideration given must be legal, otherwise the contract is **void** (*see* illegal contracts on p. 102).

Consideration must not be 'past'

You cannot make a contract in which one person promises to do something for another in exchange for a consideration which has already been performed (past consideration). So, Bill cannot say to Arthur 'Remember that fence I mended for you last week while you were on holiday, I'd like £50 for that'. When Bill had mended the fence, he had done so freely, or if he had intended to be paid for it, he had no way of contracting with Arthur because Arthur was away. If on the other hand, Arthur had been present at the time Bill mended the fence, it is possible that it could be implied that Arthur should pay a reasonable sum. It is clear therefore in contract that before work is started, the consideration must be clearly defined by reference to a fixed sum, or to rates, or some other agreed method: *Roscorla* v. *Thomas* 1842; *Re Mc.Ardle* 1951.

The agreement

The second important element of a contract is that there must be an **agreement** between the parties on the subject-matter and terms of the contract.

Most agreements can be broken down into two parts – an **offer** and an **acceptance** of that offer.

The offer

Anyone with legal capacity can make an offer, either verbally, in writing or by implication from conduct, such as gestures. A combination of any form is perfectly valid such as a telephone conversation, which is verbal plus a written estimate. Sellers or buyers may make offers, as may contractors or employers or indeed any type of contracting party. Who makes the offer has to be assessed in each set of circumstances in order to determine who may accept the offer.

Examples

'Will you buy my car for £2,000?'; 'Can I buy your car for £2,000?'; offering to pay for goods at the cash desk of the supermarket; 'Collect 5 tokens from side of packet and we will give you a free seed dibber'; Lost – Black kitten called Tiger, Reward £5.

The person making the offer is called the **offeror**, and the person to whom the offer is made is called the **offeree**.

Invitations to treat are **not** *offers*

Displays of goods in a shop or shop window or a 'for sale' board outside a house are **not** offers. They are called **invitation to treat** and are mere invitations to others to make an offer. This is why no-one can force shopkeepers to sell goods in their windows as they are not making an offer: *Fisher* v. *Bell* 1961.

Intentions only are not offers

An announcement of an intention to sell, or merely giving someone a piece of information concerning something is not an offer. So, if a person asked you, 'If you were going to sell your car, how much do you think you will get for it'. Your reply '£1,000' merely amounts to the giving of information, and there is no offer. Therefore, he cannot 'accept' your 'offer' as it is not an offer in law. If he then said, 'Alright, I'll give you £1,000 for it,' you are then in the position of being able to accept or reject the offer, as he is now making the offer to you: *Harris* v. *Nickerson* 1873; *Harvey* v. *Facey* 1893.

Offers to individuals or general public

Offers can be made to a particular person as in the example just given, or to a particular group e.g 'Members of the Sporran Football Club can have 20 per cent discount on football gear' or the offer can be to the general public as in the reward example: *Carlill* v. *Carbolic Smoke Ball Co.* 1893 (*see* Fig. 4.4).

Communications of offers essential

Offers must be **communicated** to the offerees. Otherwise, how can a person know of the existence of the offer and be capable of accepting it. Any method of communication is acceptable, from a letter to semaphore, telephone to telex, sign language to gestures: *Taylor* v. *Laird* 1856.

The offer must not be vague or couched in an indefinite way

Otherwise, even if there is an apparent acceptance, the courts may have difficulty in finding a binding contract (*see* p. 80): *Guthing* v. *Lynn* 1831.

Tenders

An invitation for tenders is an invitation to treat (*see* above). However, the tender itself is an **offer**, which, if accepted, forms the contract.

Auctions

Each bid at an auction is an offer which may or may not be accepted.

CARBOLIC SMOKE BALL

WILL POSITIVELY CURE

COUGHS	CATARRH	HOARSENESS	THROAT DEAFNESS	INFLUENZA	CROUP
COLD IN THE HEAD	ASTHMA	LOSS OF VOICE	SNORING	HAY FEVER	WHOOPING COUGH
COLD ON THE CHEST	BRONCHITIS	SORE THROAT	SORE EYES	HEADACHE	NEURALGIA

As all the Diseases mentioned above proceed from one cause, they can be Cured by this Remedy

£100 REWARD

WILL BE PAID BY THE

CARBOLIC SMOKE BALL CO.

to any Person who contracts the Increasing Epidemic

INFLUENZA,

Colds, or any Diseases caused by taking Cold, after having used the CARBOLIC SMOKE BALL according to the printed directions supplied with each Ball.

£1000 IS DEPOSITED

with the ALLIANCE BANK, Regent Street, showing our sincerity in the matter.

During the last epidemic of **INFLUENZA** many thousand **CARBOLIC SMOKE BALLS** were sold as preventives against this disease, and in no ascertained case was the disease contracted by those using the **CARBOLIC SMOKE BALL**.

THE CARBOLIC SMOKE BALL,

TESTIMONIALS.

The DUKE OF PORTLAND writes : "I am much obliged for the Carbolic Smoke Ball which you have sent me, and which I find most efficacious."

SIR FREDERICK MILNER, Bart., M.P., writes from Nice, March 7, 1890 : "Lady Milner and my children have derived much benefit from the Carbolic Smoke Ball."

Lady MOSTYN writes from Carshalton, Cary Crescent, Torquay, Jan. 10, 1890 : "Lady Mostyn believes the Carbolic Smoke Ball to be a certain check and a cure for a cold, and will have great pleasure in recommending it to her friends. Lady Mostyn hopes the Carbolic Smoke Ball will have all the success its merits deserve."

Lady ERSKINE writes from Spratton Hall, Northampton, Jan. 1, 1890 : "Lady Erskine is pleased to say that the Carbolic Smoke Ball has given every satisfaction : she considers it a very good invention."

Mrs. GLADSTONE writes : "She finds the Carbolic Smoke Ball has done her a great deal of good."

Madame ADELINA PATTI writes : "Madame Patti has found the Carbolic Smoke Ball very beneficial, and the only thing that would enable her to rest well at night when having a severe cold."

AS PRESCRIBED BY
SIR MORELL MACKENZIE, M.D.,
HAS BEEN SUPPLIED TO
H.I.M. THE GERMAN EMPRESS.

H.R.H. The Duke of Edinburgh, K.G.
H.R.H. The Duke of Connaught, K.G.
The Duke of Fife, K.T.
The Marquis of Salisbury, K.G.
The Duke of Argyll, K.T.
The Duke of Westminster, K.G.
The Duke of Richmond and Gordon, K.G.
The Duke of Manchester.
The Duke of Newcastle.
The Duke of Norfolk.
The Duke of Rutland, K.G.
The Duke of Wellington.
The Marquis of Ripon, K.G.
The Earl of Derby, K.G.
Earl Spencer, K.G.
The Lord Chancellor.
The Lord Chief Justice.
Lord Tennyson.

TESTIMONIALS.

The BISHOP OF LONDON writes : "The Carbolic Smoke Ball has benefited me greatly."

The MARCHIONESS DE SAIN writes from Padworth House, Reading, Jan. 13, 1890 : "The Marchioness de Sain has daily used the Smoke Ball since the commencement of the epidemic of Influenza, and has not taken the Influenza, although surrounded by those suffering from it."

Dr. J. RUSSELL HARRIS M.D. writes from 6, Adam Street Adelphi, Sept. 24, 1891 : "Many obstinate cases of post-nasal catarrh, which have resisted other treatment, have yielded to your Carbolic Smoke Ball.".

A. GIBBONS, Esq., Editor of the *Lady's Pictorial*, writes from 172, Strand, W.C., Feb. 14, 1890 : "During a recent sharp attack of the prevailing epidemic I had none of the unpleasant and dangerous catarrh and bronchial symptoms I attribute this entirely to the use of the Carbolic Smoke Ball."

The Rev. Dr. CHICHESTER A. W. READE, LL.D., D.C.L. writes from Rustead Downs, Surrey, May 1890 : "My duties in a large public institution have brought me daily during the recent epidemic of influenza, in close contact with the disease. I have been perfectly free from any symptom by having the Smoke Ball always handy. It has also wonderfully improved my voice for speaking and singing."

The Originals of these Testimonials may be seen at our Consulting Rooms, with hundreds of others.

One **CARBOLIC SMOKE BALL** will last a family several months, making it the cheapest remedy in the world at the price –10s., post free.

The **CARBOLIC SMOKE BALL** can be refilled, when empty, at a cost of 5s., post free. Address:

CARBOLIC SMOKE BALL CO., 27, PRINCES ST., HANOVER SQ., LONDON, W.

Fig. 4.4 An advertisement for the carbolic smoke ball (by kind permission of the Illustrated News London Picture Library)

Termination of offers

An offer, once made, does not go on for ever. It may be brought to an end in a number of ways.

Revocation

Here the offeror retracts his offer and communicates this to the offeree **before** a valid acceptance can be made. If the offeree hears from another source that the offer no longer stands because, for example, the goods have been sold, he cannot then accept the offer: *Byrne* v. *Van Tienhoven* 1880; *Dickinson* v. *Dodds* 1876.

Lapse

An offer will lapse if not accepted within a reasonable time or if a time is specified within the time limit. Reasonableness depends on the subject matter of the contract. For example, offers concerning perishable goods such as ready mixed concrete must be accepted without delay: *Ramsgate Hotel* v. *Montefiore* 1866.

Rejection

This may be a flat rejection or it may be a **counter offer**, e.g. 'Yes, but I'll only pay £950'.

A **conditional acceptance** also amounts to a rejection e.g. 'Yes, but you'll have to put new tyres on the car'.

Death

If either party dies **before** acceptance, the offer ends. This is obvious. Occasionally, however, it is possible for there to be a valid acceptance, despite the death of the offeror. For this to be valid, the contract must obviously not be of a personal nature. Nor must the offeree have known of the other party's death. Selling a car is not a contract of a personal nature, so it is possible for a contract to be valid and binding on the deceased's personal representatives, who must then pass the car to the purchaser. The purchase price will then form part of the deceased's estate. The death of a customer who wanted a decorator to decorate her house, is a contract of a personal nature, and her death would terminate the offer.

Acceptance of the offer

Once again this can be in many forms, oral, in writing, or implied from conduct.

In the five examples of offers given previously, what sort of acceptances can be made? In the fourth example, merely collecting the tokens and sending them to the company would be enough. There is no need to tell them that you are now going to start collecting and will contact them in due course. Similarly, finding the kitten (in the fifth example) and returning it to its owner, is sufficient to claim the reward (provided the finder has notice of the offer).

Who can accept?

If the offer is 'particular' i.e. it is made to one person or a particular number of persons, then only that person or one from the group may accept. If the offer is made to the general public, then anyone who has notice of the offer may accept the offer.

Communication is essential

The offeree must take some positive step to accept the offer. He cannot do nothing and then claim that there is a contract. So an offeror must not say 'If I don't hear from you, then I will assume the deal is on' and cannot rely on the lack of response amounting to an acceptance. The offeree might be on holiday, or even dead: *Felthouse* v. *Bindley* 1862.

If the offeror specified a particular method of acceptance such as first-class post or by hand, then that method must be complied with. It is a condition of the offer.

There are a number of exceptions to the rule that the acceptance must be communicated.

Firstly, communication may be **waived** either expressly or impliedly: *Carlill* v. *Carbolic Smoke Ball Co* 1893. Also acceptance can be implied from conduct. The token and reward contracts are examples of this: *Williams* v. *Carwardine* 1833.

Thirdly, where acceptance is by **post** (and no particular method of acceptance has been specified) a valid acceptance is made immediately the letter is stamped, addressed and posted as the Post Office is the agent of the recipient.

As the rule strictly applied, could lead to ridiculous situations, the courts may find that there was no agreement until the acceptance was actually communicated, depending on the facts of the case: *Household Fire Insurance Co* v. *Grant* 1879; *Entores* v. *Miles Far East Corporation* 1955.

Acceptance must be of all the terms offered

(*see* conditional acceptance and counter offers above).

Auctions

An offer (bid) is accepted at the time the auctioneer brings his hammer down. At that time he can sign the contract on behalf of both parties, despite originally only being the agent of the vendor.

If there is an offer and an acceptance of that offer, is there always an agreement which is binding on the parties?

Generally, the answer is yes. However, as we have already seen, all the rules must have been adhered to, otherwise there will probably be no agreement. Two further points need to be discussed.

Agreements made 'subject to contract'

It is common in conveyancing (*see* pp. 158–67) to agree to buy and sell land 'subject to contract'. Thus, the solicitors' letters on behalf of vendor and purchaser will contain those words, so that the parties will not be bound by their agreement, until there has been a proper formal contract agreed, signed and exchanged between them. However, those words are not magic, and if the court finds that there was a definite agreement to buy and sell between the parties, and that they had regarded the formal contract merely as written confirmation of what had already been agreed, then they will be liable under that contract. The court thus strips away all the words and writing to find the parties true intention at the time of the alleged 'contract'.

Lack of certainty of terms

If there appears to be such a lack of definition over what had been agreed by the parties, the court may take the view that there is no contract, either because there is a lack of consensus ad idem (meeting of minds) or because the parties were still at the negotiating stage, whereby they had agreed that a contract of a certain type was going to be entered into, but that they had not defined the terms.

Nevertheless, the court may still find that the parties had agreed in contract, even if they had not agreed on all minor terms, which could perhaps be safely ignored.

Also, where the parties have not agreed on all terms, it may be implied that a **previous course of dealings** will control some (though not all) of the matters not expressly agreed in the present case, e.g. the amount of pay which could be the same as that paid on a prior occasion.

Terms of the agreement – Express or implied

Of course, most contracts are not like the simple examples used above. Take for example a building contract. In addition to the basic elements of the bargain, i.e. building work for money, there are a myriad other details which must be settled as part of the agreement. For example, when work is to be started, what materials must be used, allowances for delay, etc. It is far easier at the outset, to agree to all these terms **expressly**, either orally or in writing, to cover all eventualities. But, often terms will be agreed in a slightly different way. For example, standard forms of contract such as the JCT building contract may be used. This contains standard clauses with which the building industry is familiar. Parts of the contract may be altered by agreement. The terms of such an agreement are still **express** however.

Contractual terms may also be **implied**, i.e. not specifically stated. They may be implied by the courts as being present in the contract, by virtue of past dealings between the parties, trade usage or custom, or because of an Act of Parliament such as the Sale of Goods Acts 1979 or the Supply of Goods and Services Act 1982 (*see* below).

Also, the courts will imply a term if it is obvious that the parties must have intended it to be present in their agreement. The leading case is *The Moorcock* 1889. To quote Scrutton L J in *Reigate* v. *Union Manufacturing Co (Ramsbottom)* 1918, such a term will be implied in situations where, if the parties had been asked whether such and such a term should be implied, they would have answered 'Of course, so and so will happen; we did not trouble to say that; it is too clear'.

Terms implied into contracts for work and materials (e.g. building contracts), by the Supply of Goods & Services Act 1982

Part II of the Supply of Goods & Services Act 1982 deals with the supply of services. Part II covers contracts relating to pure services where no goods are transferred such as for hairdressing, drycleaning, professional services of accountants, solicitors, etc. and carriage of goods, as well as contracts where goods are transferred in conjunction with a service such as building, repairs, etc. This second category is thus covered not only by this part of the Act but also by Part I of the Act covering the transfer of goods (*see* p. 182). Also, by Part II of the Act contracts of hire are also covered if the contract provides a service in addition to the hire of goods such as hiring a television set (*see* p. 185).

Definition By S.12 a contract for the supply of a service is 'a contract under which a person ('the supplier') agrees to carry out a service ... whether or not goods are also –
i) transferred or to be transferred; or
ii) bailed or to be bailed by way or hire
under the contract, and whatever is the nature of the consideration for which the service is to be carried out'.

Thus, Part II only applies if there is a **contract** between the parties. In such cases, where there is no contract, the rules of common law have to be relied on. If there is a contract then the party suing can choose to sue either in contract or in tort (*see* p. 243).

It should be noted that the Act specifically excludes contracts of employment (of service) or apprenticeships.

Section 13 – care and skill   This section imposes an implied term on suppliers of services in the course of a business, that the supplier will carry out the service with **reasonable care and skill**.

The standard of care required would, it seems, be that of the average, competent builder; dry-cleaner; plumber; architect, etc., performing his usual job and would probably be approached in the same way as the standard care in negligence (*see* p. 251). However, it would appear that no guarantee of success at something would ever be implied as a result of this term (such a term would have to be expressed). However, as a result of certain express terms in a contract, a term may be implied by common law that the result of the contract should be, for example, fit for a particular use, e.g. in *Greaves & Co (Contractors) Ltd* v. *Baynham Meikle & Partners* 1975. In this case a firm of consultant structural engineers (BM) designed a warehouse under a sub-contract for G Ltd, the main contractors employed by Duckhams Oil. BM were made aware of the use to which the warehouse would be put including the fact that forklift trucks would be crossing the floors carrying and stacking oil drums. After the building had been completed, the floors began to crack due to vibrations from the trucks. G Ltd, accepted liability, under the main contract and paid damages but then claimed an indemnity from BM. The Court of Appeal held that they were liable because the 'package deal' contract had specified the type of building, the purpose to which it would be put and thus there could be an implied term in the sub-contract that the engineers would design a building that would be reasonably fit for that purpose.

Section 14 – time for performance   By S.14(1) a supplier acting in the course of a business must carry out the service within a reasonable time, if the time has not been fixed by the contract or has not been fixed by prior dealings between the parties or in some other manner agreed by the parties. What is reasonable is a question of fact: S.14 (2). If the supplier does not perform his contract within a prescribed time, then this is a breach of contract even if time was **not** made of the essence and the party suing may claim damages as it is a breach of warranty. If time is of the essence and the supplier has failed to complete within the specified period, the other party may repudiate the contract. If time is not of the essence (i.e. time for performance is not a condition) the customer can then give reasonable notice making it so, e.g. 'If you do not repair my window within seven days, I shall go elsewhere'. If the repair has still not been done within that period, the customer can regard the contract as at an end.

It would appear that if a mercantile contract contains a clause relating to time, then time for performance is of the essence and thus such clauses are conditions. For time of payment to be of the essence however, it would have to be the subject of an express term. Of course in most building contracts, time is always of the essence as dates for completion are expressly stipulated.

Are all statements referring to the agreement, actually part of the contract?

Not necessarily. One has to differentiate between the **terms**, which are part of the contract, and **representations** which are not. A representation is a statement of fact made before the contract is made, and which is not intended to become part of the contract. Some representations become terms by undergoing a metamorphosis. Those that do not, remain in their original state, and if they are incorrect, give the misled party no rights to sue for breach **of the contract** itself. This is because the representation did not become part of the contract. However, there are alternative remedies which are available for **misrepresentation** (*see* p. 109).

It is obviously difficult to differentiate between representations and terms, especially if the contract is not in writing. The following tests may be applied, which whilst not wholly conclusive may indicate whether a statement made regarding a contract is a term of that contract or a mere representation.

- Statements made by an expert, relied on by the other party, who is a layman, are more likely to be contractual terms, e.g. 'This car has got a new engine', stated the garage proprietor.
- Statements made some time before the contract is agreed upon are less likely to be terms, unless reaffirmed at the time of making the contract.
- Oral statements which are not incorporated into later written contracts are less likely to be contractual terms, unless the court views the contract as consisting of both the document and a prior oral statement.

What happens if the parties later disagree over what was agreed in the contract?

Where the contract is in writing, then the general rule is that **only** the written contract should be evidence of what was agreed, (the parol evidence rule). However, as we have seen before, many contracts are in writing **and** in conversation, e.g. a builder's estimate and telephoned instructions verbally agreed. Thus, evidence of what was agreed orally must, of course, be admitted in a dispute, e.g. a letter confirming the contents of the telephone conversation which was not challenged at the time of receipt.

Where the written document appears to cover all the matters in dispute, then it is unlikely that any orally agreed terms will override the written agreement, unless exceptions to the rule can be applied.

Exceptions. Evidence that a word in a written document was used in a customary or trade way will be admissible.

Evidence may be admitted to show that there was an orally agreed pre-condition that the contract was not to come into being until that pre-condition had been met.

If the written document was executed in a mistaken way by the parties, then an application in equity may be made for **rectification** of the document. Rectification can be ordered only of the *written* agreement and not of the **actual** agreement between the parties. Thus, if a building contractor agreed to build a house and swimming pool for a client, then if the formal contract under seal has been mistakenly executed, omitting to mention the pool, the contract may be rectified at a later date. Obviously, evidence of a cogent nature must be put forward by the party wishing to have the deed rectified. (Plans and drawings of the building and pool and estimates would probably be good evidence). Also, it must be proved that at the time the written contract was executed, the parties were **still in agreement** over all the terms, and it was only afterwards, that one of the parties tried to stick to the letter of the written agreement.

(Note: Had the parties been in agreement **after** the mistake was discovered, they could remake the contract by a new deed (*see* termination of contracts p. 116).

Categories of terms

Terms, whether express or implied may be either **conditions** or **warranties**.

A condition is a term of the utmost importance to the contract, which, if breached, allows the other party to repudiate (end) the contract.

A warranty is a term of less importance to the contract concerning some subsidiary matter, breach of which allows the other party to merely claim damages.

Unfortunately, the words 'condition' and 'warranty' are used haphazardly in practice and often the court has to decide whether a term is one or the other. If it is found that a term, labelled warranty, is in law a condition, then, the right to repudiate the contract will arise.

Exclusion terms

As a person can virtually agree to anything (within the law) in a contract, can a party exclude or exempt his liability under a contract? In other words, can he restrict his contractual duties in some way, so that he will only be liable for breach of contract in a limited number of situations? The answer is, yes, but subject to certain restrictions imposed at common law and by statute.

Statutory restrictions on limiting contractual liability.

- The Sale of Goods Act 1979 (*see* p. 173).
- The Supply of Goods (Implied Terms) Act 1973 (*see* p. 180).
- The Supply of Goods and Services Act 1982 (*see* p. 89).
- The Unfair Contract Terms Act 1977. 'A person cannot by reference to any contract term ... exclude or restrict his liability for **death or personal injury** resulting from **negligence**': S.2(1) of the Unfair Contract Terms Act 1977.

By S.2(2) 'In the case of other loss or damage, a person cannot so exclude or restrict his liability for negligence, except in so far as the term ... satisfies the requirement of reasonableness.'

The above sections only apply to persons who may be liable in the course of a business, or from the occupation of premises used for business purposes of the occupier. It should be noted that by the Occupiers' Liability Act 1984 amendment to the Unfair Contract Terms Act 1977 the term business purposes is not to include places used for educational or recreational purposes unless they are used to fulfill a business function e.g. a private college.

Where one contracting party is a **consumer,** or one contracts by reference to the other's **written standard terms** of business, then by S.3, as against that party, the other cannot by reference to any contract terms, exclude or restrict any liability of his in respect of his breach of contract. Nor can he claim to be entitled to render a contractual performance substantially different from that which was reasonably expected of him or to render no performance at all, unless such clauses satisfy the test of reasonableness.

(Note: by Sched. 1 of the Act, the above sections do not apply to insurance contracts, contracts for the transfer of land, patents, trademarks, copyrights, registered designs, technical or commercial information or other intellectual property, contracts concerning the formation or dissolution of a company or to its constitution or rights or duties of its members or securities. Section 2 does not apply to contracts of employment.)

By S.13 the Act prevents making the liability or its enforcement, subject to restrictive or onerous conditions. It also prevents excluding or restricting any right or remedy in respect of the liability or subjecting a person to any prejudice in consequence of his pursuing any such right or remedy.

(Note: by S.13(2), an agreement in writing to submit present or future differences to arbitration does not amount to excluding or restricting liability.)

Section 8 Unfair Contract Terms Act 1977   If a contract contains a term purporting to exclude or restrict liability for a misrepresentation or a remedy available as a result of a misrepresentation, then that term is **void** unless it is reasonable in the circumstances.

Exclusion clauses in standard form contracts.   The building industry is particularly conversant with standard form contracts. Unfortunately, familiarity breeds contempt and many a person when trying to pursue a remedy for breach of a contract is caught by an exclusion term which they had not bothered to read or had merely overlooked at the time of making the contract.

Standard form contracts are subject to the statutory restrictions above.

In addition, the common law has developed a systematic approach to the treatment of exclusion clauses in written (and standard form) contracts. The courts and Parliament recognise that exclusion clauses between parties who are in a relatively equal bargaining position, such as between parties in business, are in need of less protection than the consumer contracting with a businessman. This is illustrated by the different levels of protection under the Acts above. The following rules must also be noted.

Notice of the term.   Reasonable notice of the exclusion terms must be given **at the same time** or **before** a contract is made. This is obvious, as otherwise, the party adversely affected may possibly not have otherwise entered into the contract.

In *Olley* v. *Marlborough Court Ltd* 1949, guests at an hotel had their property stolen, unaware, until they had entered their hotel bedroom where a notice was displayed, that the hotel only took responsibility for property handed to the manageress for safe custody. The court held that the notice was not valid. The notice should have been exhibited at the reception desk, where it ought to have been specifically brought to their attention.

Notice of such terms could however be inferred from previous dealings between the parties. This is particularly so in business, where valuable time would be lost, drawing a party's attention to contractual terms of which he should already have knowledge.

Is the term really part of the contract if it is only displayed in a receipt or ticket?   Many of us have received tickets or receipt, which to our surprise contains reference to 'company conditions' or an exclusion clause, of which we were not aware before we had entered into the contract. The courts take the view, that if such receipts or tickets are merely receipts and no more, then the party adversely affected by the term is not bound by the term, as the ticket is not part of the contract. The exclusion should have been brought to their notice when or before the contract was made: *Chapelton* v. *Barry UDC* 1940 (man injured by collapsed deckchair).

What if the document containing the exclusion term has been signed by the affected party? A person signs documents at his own peril, for the courts always believe that they must have intended to be bound by agreements, to which they had affixed their signatures. The golden rule is thus, never sign something which you have not read and understood. Only in exceptional circumstances will someone be able to avoid the consequences of signing such an agreement.

These are:

1. Fraud.   Where he was induced to enter into the contract by the other party acting fraudulently.
2. Misrepresentation.   Where the other party innocently or negligently (or fraudulently) made a statement of fact, which caused the other party to enter into the contract. e.g. *Curtis* v. *Chemical Cleaning & Dyeing Co* 1951, where a dry cleaning shop assistant misled a customer, by telling her that the receipt which had to be signed, excluded liability for damage to sequins and beads only. This was untrue.
3. Pleading non est factum (it is not my deed).   Very occasionally, there occurs a situation, in which the party signing a document is under a total misapprehension as to the nature of the document. If it turns out that the document is totally different in nature to what he intended to sign, e.g. an IOU and not a will, then when someone attempts to enforce it against him, he may plead, Non est factum – It was not my deed. A party who is careless in signing, cannot use this defence.

Contra proferentum rule.   Where there is an ambiguity concerning the exclusion clause, then the courts will construe the clause against the party who inserted it into the contract, e.g 'Cars are parked at the owner's risk'. This is ambiguous, therefore the car park owner cannot rely on such an exclusion clause in contract. It may thus happen that he is liable in both contract and tort.

Can an exclusion clause avoid all liability under the contract?   This is possible, but each case must be viewed in the light of the Unfair Contract Terms Act 1977 (*see* above) and *Photo Production Ltd* v. *Securicor Transport* 1980 (HL). In this case, (a pre-Unfair Contract Terms Act case), the plaintiff company employed the security company to patrol their property for a relatively small fee. One of the security company's employees set alight to the plaintiff's premises. The plaintiff company sued Securicor for damages, who then relied on an exemption clause which stated that under no circumstances would the defendant company be liable for **any injurious act or default** by **any employee** of Securicor.

The House of Lords held that the parties were in an equal bargaining position, and therefore the exemption clause was valid and reasonable in the circumstances. If the security company had not inserted the exclusion clause and thus laid themselves open to liability, the amount they would have had to charge would have been much greater. The plaintiffs would be covered by insurance and their original bargaining positions would have taken these factors into account. The 'reasonableness' tests of the Unfair Contract Terms Act 1977 would thus be applied to any future cases tried, since the Act came into effect.

Intention to be bound in law by the agreement

Generally, where there has been an agreement between parties with consideration on both sides, a contract will automatically arise, the presence of consideration, indicating that it is not a gratuitous arrangement. Thus, in the majority of cases, parties do not have to set out to create contracts, they arise naturally from their behaviour.

Nevertheless, as we have already seen, in certain situations, a contract will not be found, either because of the nature of the agreement or because the parties specifically state that the agreement is not legally binding. Thus, mere social arrangements are generally not contractual.

Domestic agreements, such as an arrangement to pay a regular sum for housekeeping to a wife, while the husband is abroad, may not be held to be contractual, but then again the opposite may also be shown.

Commercial agreements are generally presumed to be contractual. However, the parties may agree that their arrangements should not be binding at law, in which case, the courts may very well refuse to go against the wishes of the parties. The words used to achieve this however must be clear and unambiguous. The burden of proving the meaning of ambiguous words intended to exclude legal relations falls on to the shoulders of the party who wishes to rely on them.

Summary

The three vital elements of a contract are thus: consideration; intention to create legal relations; agreement (mnemonic, CIA) (see Fig. 4.5).

If any one is not present, then the contract is void, and therefore unenforceable in the courts.

If they are all present, the parties can seek to enforce the contract in the courts.

Nevertheless, in certain circumstances, the courts will not enforce the seemingly valid agreement.

What follows is an outline of the factors which may make a contract unenforceable.

Mistake – Can a mistake affect the validity of a contract?

In most situations, a mistake concerning some aspect of a contract will

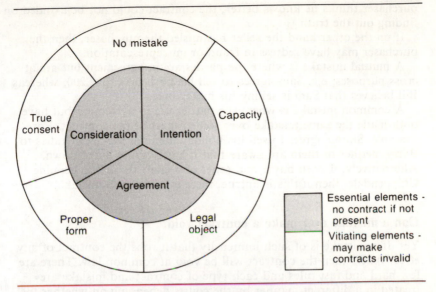

Fig. 4.5 Essential elements and vitiating factors in a contract

Key:

Essential elements - no contract if not present

Vitiating elements - may make contracts invalid

have **no** affect on its validity and the parties will be bound by the terms of their agreement. Thus, parties must make sure that they have understood, in every sense, the terms of their agreement otherwise, they may be forced to perform a contract which they would prefer to avoid.

The following are typical examples of such mistakes.

1. *Mistakes over price.* If both parties agree to buy and sell an article for a particular price, neither party can later avoid his contractual responsibilities if it turns out that the price is incorrect and that the article is too cheap or too expensive.
2. *Mistakes over quality.* Similarly, agreements over an article based on the mistaken belief that it is an antique or a reproduction or has some special quality cannot be avoided (unless the seller had deliberately misled the buyer to believe that it was genuine or there was a misrepresentation) (*see* p. 109).

Types of mistakes

Mistakes can thus be divided into three categories: unilateral; mutual; common.

A unilateral mistake is where only **one** party is mistaken over some aspect of the contract, e.g. a purchaser thinks he is buying a guitar which he mistakenly believes belonged to John Lennon and the other party knows this.

(Note: if the seller has told the purchaser that this is not so, but the purchaser thinks he knows better, the contract could not be avoided on finding out the truth.)

If on the other hand the seller has misled the purchaser, then the purchaser may have redress in fraud or misrepresentation.

A mutual mistake is where the parties are in agreement but are at cross purposes, e.g. Sam agrees to sell his push bike for £200, whereas Bill believes that Sam is selling his motor bike.

A common mistake is where the parties are in agreement but have both made the same mistake over some aspect of the contract. For example, Simon agrees to sell his holiday home in the West Indies to Barry, neither of them are aware that it has recently burnt down. Alternatively, if both buyer and seller of a chair think it is genuine Chippendale, then if this is untrue, there is a common mistake.

Can a mistake ever make a contract void?

Yes. If a mistake is of such immensity that it robs the contract of any effectiveness then the contract will be void at common law. There are few hard and fast rules and each type of contract and mistake are treated in a different manner by the courts depending on whether the mistake is unilateral, mutual or common. If a mistake makes a contract void, it is said to be **operative**.

Unilateral mistake – at common law

An error of judgment as illustrated above in the guitar example, would amount to a unilateral mistake and would generally not be a ground for avoiding the contract.

Occasionally, unilateral mistakes may be operative if the mistake is of fundamental importance to the contract and one party knew of the other party's mistake, e.g. where a con-man had tricked someone. Such mistakes have occurred in relation to someone's identity.

Mistakes over the identity of the other contracting party

If someone believes that he is making a contract with a **particular** person but they make the contract in each other's company, as for example in a shop, then, the contract generally cannot be avoided on finding out the truth of the matter.

Occasionally, however, the mistaken identity of someone will be of such importance that on finding out the truth the contract could be declared void for mistake. Contracts in which the importance of dealing with a particular person are such a rarity that the courts apply stringent pre-conditions before declaring such a contract to be void. The court would have to be satisfied that:

- The mistaken party intended to contract with another person and not the person with whom he made the contract (who was aware of the other's intention).

- He considered the identity of the other party to be of fundamental importance **at the time he entered into the contract**. In other words had he known of the true identity of that person he would not have entered into the contract.

- He checked the identity of the person, e.g by asking to see his bank cards or other means of identification. *See Ingram* v. *Little* 1961; *Lewis* v. *Averay* 1972. *See* also unilateral mistakes as to nature of document (*see* p. 95).

Unilateral mistake in equity

Strictly speaking, if a contract is void ab initio, no declaration of this is necessary and in most cases, the fact that the contract was void ab initio would be pleaded as a defence in an action for damages or specific performance.

Equity however may assist further by: refusing to award a decree of specific performance; or formally setting aside the contract by declaring it to be void; or allowing rectification of a valid contract provided the mistaken party can prove that the document should have contained a term of benefit to him and the other party knew of this omission, e.g. in *A Roberts & Co Ltd* v. *Leicestershire CC* 1961, the plaintiffs tendered to build a school over a period of eighteen months. The defendant council drafted a contract for execution by the plaintiffs in which the work would be completed over thirty months. The plaintiffs failed to notice the mistake and the defendant council officers, knowing of the builders mistake, failed to have the agreement altered before execution by the council. The court allowed rectification for a unilateral mistake and the clause was altered to the shorter period (*see* p. 92).

Mutual mistakes at common law

A mutual mistake will only operate to avoid the contract if the mistake is such as to remove the real basis of the contract, i.e. the mistake is of fundamental importance as for example was the mistake over the sale of the bikes above. Obviously there is no agreement between them as there has been a mistake over the offer or the identity of the subject matter. Thus, in *Raffles* v. *Wichelhaus* 1864, a seller contracted to sell a ship's cargo aboard the *Peerless* sailing out of Bombay. The buyer was under the misapprehension that he was buying the cargo of another ship which was also called the *Peerless* and also in Bombay. Neither knew of the existence of the other ship. The contract was held to be void for **mutual** mistake.

If, on the other hand, a seller agrees to sell facing bricks by sample at a special bargain price, when he later discovers that the sample shown was of a brick of much higher quality, he will be forced to sell at the bargain price. Here both parties are mistaken. The seller thinks he is selling 'X' bricks at 'Y' price. In fact he is selling 'Z' bricks at 'Y' price. The purchaser thinks he is buying 'Z' bricks at 'Y' price therefore the parties are at cross purposes over the type of bricks. There is thus a mutual mistake but not one which is so fundamental as to avoid the contract. The parties would be bound. A reasonable man viewing the contract would have inferred that there was an agreement between the parties, albeit based on a mistake.

Mutual mistake in equity

Once again equity follows the law and in the exceptional circumstances in which a contract is void, it will be void in equity and no equitable relief may be given.

If it is valid however, equity also follows the law and will generally refuse equitable relief and the mistaken party will be forced to perform the contract as agreed. Occasionally however, a court will use its equitable discretion and may refuse a decree of specific performance.

Common mistake at common law

A common mistake will only make a contract void at common law if the common mistake is concerned with the existence of the subject-matter or other fundamental basis of the contract **at the time the agreement** was entered into. Thus, for example, if the goods to be bought already belong to the purchaser, the contract is void. Also, if the property to be sold has been destroyed or never existed, then the contract is void.

So in *Scott* v. *Coulson* 1903, an insurance agreement was entered into on the life of someone who was already dead. Obviously, the contract was void for **common** mistake, as both parties were under the same misapprehension over the existence of the subject matter.

Thus, where parties contract on the basis of a common mistake, which is not concerned with the above matters, the mistake is not operative, e.g. if Simon agrees to sell what he thinks to be a genuine antique to Bill who is also under the same misapprehension, despite the existence of a common mistake, the contract is not void at common law.

Common mistake in equity

Where the contract is void at common law, equity will follow the law and equitable remedies would therefore be refused as no rights and duties would flow from a void contract.

However, if the contract is valid at common law the court may use its equitable discretion and may award the following remedies
1. *Rectification of written contracts See p. 92.*

2. *Set aside agreements on terms fair and just to both parties.* Whilst the court will admit that the contract is valid at common law, the judge may nevertheless be unwilling to grant a decree of specific performance and may even go so far as to set the contract aside on terms favourable to both parties. The parties may even be sent away to remake their contract.

Mistakes over type of document signed

See p. 95.

Who can make contracts? Capacity

Generally anyone, i.e. any legal person can enter into a contract. This is called **capacity to contract**.

However, there are certain people, who because of their age or mental state are restricted in the types of contracts that they may enter into.

Minors

Fortunately, the law has set out to protect minors from unscrupulous people trying to take advantage of their youth, by forcing them to perform contracts which perhaps they should never have entered into in the first place.

Unfortunately, the degree of protection varies depending on the type of contract. Thus, some contracts are **void** under the Infants' Relief Act 1874, some contracts are **voidable** i.e. valid at common law unless repudiated by the minor when he reaches 18 years of age. Certain contracts are valid and binding on the minor. These are contracts for necessaries and beneficial contracts of service.

Contracts under the Infants' Relief Act 1874 – void

By S.1 any contract entered into by a minor for the repayment of a loan or for the supply of goods or for an account stated is absolutely void. An account stated is a document admitting indebtedness, such as an IOU.

Thus, a lender of money to a minor cannot recover this money. However, the minor would not be granted an order for specific performance against the lender as it would be inequitable to grant; if such an order could not be obtained against the minor. Strangely however, any money paid by the minor in such a contract is not recoverable, should things go awry, unless there is a total failure of consideration, e.g. where the goods were not delivered.

Thus, it appears that such contracts are not absolutely 'void' in the accepted sense as some rights and duties do flow from such contracts. Adults, therefore, should be wary of doing business with minors.

Voidable contracts

These contracts are valid, unless avoided by the **minor** before or within a reasonable time of becoming 18 years of age. Thus, a minor is bound by its terms, unless he avoids the contract.

Examples
1. Interests in land.   By S.1 of the Law of Property Act 1925 no minor may hold a legal estate in land. Nevertheless if someone attempts to grant a lease to a minor he will then hold an equitable interest in the land and will have to pay the rent and comply with the covenants contained in the lease.
2. Shares in a company.   Similarly he is bound by any obligations imposed on owners of shares unless he repudiates.
3. Shares in a partnership.   Whilst no creditor of the partnership may sue the minor partner personally for a debt, he can still pursue his claim against the joint assets of the partnership.

Valid contracts

Contracts for necessaries.   Necessaries are food, clothing and things which one would expect a minor to require having regard to his status, profession, income, etc. e.g. a bicycle, watch, radio but not antique goblets, very expensive watches, etc. In such cases the minor must pay for these goods unless the contract contains terms which are not for the minor's benefit.

Contracts of service.   Provided a contract of apprenticeship or service is beneficial to the minor, the courts will regard the contract as valid. Thus, in *Dunk* v. *George Waller & Son Ltd* 1970, where a master broke an apprenticeship agreement, the apprentice could sue on the contract.

Corporations

See p. 218.

Mentally disordered persons

These have varying rights depending on the degree of understanding of the contract.

The contract must be legal or if legal not void

Generally, the law of contract allows parties to make contracts for whatever purpose they wish even if they are not to their best advantage.

However, the contract must be of a type that is permitted by law nor must it be void, otherwise the parties will be unable to enforce the contract in the courts.

Illegal contracts

Contracts may be illegal at common law and by virtue of statute law. In both cases, such contracts are generally **void** ab initio. Thus, no rights and duties will flow from the contract at all. Money paid over under such a contract will usually be irrecoverable except in certain situations. These effects are due to the fact that the law never allows someone to be able to benefit from a wrong to which he was a party. This is encapsulated in the latin maxim *Ex turpi causa non oritur actio* – there can be no action arising from an evil cause. Also, because of this principle, any collateral contract or contract arising out of or as a result of the illegal contract will also be illegal and therefore void.

Contracts illegal in common law on the grounds on public policy

- sexually immoral contracts;
- contracts to commit crimes or torts, e.g. Rentakilla;
- contracts detrimental to the state, e.g. trading with the enemy;
- contracts for the sale of public honours such as knighthoods;
- contracts to impede the administration of justice;
- contracts to avoid paying taxes.

Contracts illegal by virtue of statute law

It is unusual for legislation to expressly forbid contracts. If it does so, then it is usually for the protection of the public. Most illegal contracts however would fall under the previous heading as being contrary to public policy in common law.

Nevertheless, certain pieces of legislation do expressly make some types of contracts illegal.

Thus, contracts designed to collectively enforce the maintenance of prices within a trade or industry are prohibited under the Resale Prices Act 1976, so that in general, sellers can sell goods at whatever price they wish. There are two exceptions to this, e.g. ethical and proprietary drugs and books which must normally be sold at fixed prices throughout the country.

More often, legislation makes only certain terms of contracts illegal or imposes conditions on the way in which contracts should be carried out, e.g. by requiring a licence to be obtained before operating. In such cases, the contracts will be unenforceable on the part of the person behaving illegally but will be enforceable by the innocent party. If the illegality is only a peripheral matter, then the courts may allow the person who committed the wrong to be able to enforce it (this shall not be presumed in every situation).

Void (but not illegal) contracts

At common law on grounds of public policy

The following are examples of such contracts:

- contracts restricting the freedom of marriage or otherwise contrary to the estate of marriage;
- contracts intended to oust the jurisdiction of the courts (*see* p. 58);
- contracts in restraint of trade (*see* post).

As such contracts are void, they are unenforceable in the courts. However, if a term can be severed from the contract so as to leave the rest of the contract untainted, the courts will allow the contract to be enforced minus the offensive term. Of course, sometimes, it is impossible to sever the objectionable term, and if this is not possible the whole contract will be void.

As such contracts are only void, and not illegal, it is probable that money or property paid over under the void contract could be recovered. (Cf illegal contracts on p. 103).

Finally, unlike illegal contracts, subsequent or collateral contracts arising as a result of the void contract will not necessarily be void.

Special mention must be made of the third type of void contract – contracts in restraint of trade.

Contracts in restraint of trade. Such contracts attempt to restrict parties from carrying on their business or profession in any way they wish. Whilst such contracts are prima facie void, they may be regarded as valid, provided they are **reasonable** as between the parties, and are in the **interest** of the **general public**.

Builders may encounter restrictive terms in contracts of employment. For example, a builder may employ a person to work for him under a contract containing a term, that if the employee should leave that employment, he would not attempt to compete with his former employer. Other terms in contracts of employment which have been held to be reasonable are that the employee should not divulge trade secrets. As the courts do not like such terms, they will only allow them to stand if the following requirements are met:

- the employee must be in a position whereby the customer/client would prefer to deal with him rather than his employer **or**
- the employee must have access to trade secrets *and*
- the area of restraint must be reasonable, e.g. a builder could possibly impose a limit on his employee carrying on a business within five miles of his former employment. Each case must be

judged on its merits however. Restrictions have been allowed to cover the whole of the United Kingdom.

- the duration of the restraint must be reasonable. A lifetime ban would probably be unreasonable.
- the term must not merely restrict competition as this is unreasonable
- the term will probably be invalid if the person imposing it was in a superior bargaining position to that of the other party (this is usually the position in the case of employers).

If a builder sold his business with the **goodwill**, then the courts are very ready to allow the validity of a term in the contract prohibiting the seller from soliciting his former customers' business or using the firm's name (if the name was sold as part of the goodwill). A restriction on carrying on a similar business in a particular area will be subject to the same test of reasonableness as before. It should be noted however, that such restrictive terms, must be of benefit to the business only.

Similarly, the courts are less likely to interfere with terms in restraint of trade between parties on an equal footing, such as businessmen.

Contracts void under statute law

Certain specified contracts may be made void under statute law. This means that the legislation, direct or indirect, has not made the contract illegal, but the contract will be void ab initio. Thus, whilst we are permitted to place bets with bookmakers, by virtue of various gaming and wagering acts, the contracts are legal but unenforceable.

Certain contracts which offend against the Restrictive Trade Practices Act 1976 are held to be void as being contrary to public interest, unless on investigation by the Restrictive Practices Court, they are found not to be so. A restrictive trade agreement is a contract by which manufacturers, suppliers or exporters, limit the supply or distribution of goods in some way. This may be so as to keep prices high or orders constant, for example, and thus may be detrimental to the interest of the public. Such contracts have to be registered with the Director General of Fair Trading. These contracts deal with such matters as recommended prices, terms on which goods are to be supplied, quantities in which they are available or the classes of people to or area in which they may be sold.

A customer protection scheme proposed by the Building Employers' Confederation has recently been approved by the Restrictive Practices Court and is now operational. It provides a guarantee that unsatisfactory work will be remedied in exchange for a charge of 1 per cent of the contract price. The scheme is compulsory for all members of the Confederation.

Finally, by virtue of the European Communities Act 1972 which ratified the Treaty of Accession by which the UK went into the EEC,

106

Art. 85 (1) of the Treaty of Rome is now part of English law. This makes certain contracts void if they attempt to impede competition within the European Communities. It only applies to trading agreements between the nationals of different EEC states. It does not affect domestic UK agreements.

Form of contract

Simple contracts

This may be in any form. They may be in writing, they may be oral (verbal) or implied from conduct or they may be a combination of any form, e.g. partly in writing and/or partly oral and/or partly implied from conduct. However, there must be consideration given by each party to the other.

Contracts which must be in writing

There are a certain number of contracts which must be in writing. (Note, 'in writing' does *not* mean being in a deed which is a document, signed sealed and delivered. *See* below). Thus the contract itself must be in a written form although it can be on any type of paper.

The following are examples: bills of exchange (*see* p. 198); agreements to which the Hire Purchase Act 1965 or Consumer Credit Act 1974 apply; transfers of shares in registered companies; transfers of debts (*see* p. 189); contracts of marine insurance.

The above contracts are **void** if not in writing.

Contracts which must be evidenced in writing

This does **not** mean that the contract must be in writing. There must however be some written evidence of the existence of the contract in order to be able to sue under the agreement.

Land

The most important contract under this heading is the contract for the sale or other disposition of **land**. It is governed by S.40(1) of the Law of Property Act 1925 which states that 'no action may be brought upon any contract for the sale or other disposition of land or any interest in land, unless the agreement upon which such action is brought, or some memorandum or note thereof, is in writing and signed by the party to be charged or by some other person thereunto by him lawfully authorised.'

This means that if an estate or interest in land is to be sold or disposed of in some other way then there must be a note or memorandum signed by the person against whom it is sought to enforce the agreement (or his agents). Thus if Vince agrees to sell 'Dunrobbin' to Pamela, and he alone signs a piece of paper setting out the gist of the agreement, then the contract can only be enforced against Vince and not vice versa.

What if there is no evidence in writing?   Section 40(2) of the Law of Property Act 1925 may assist a party who is suffering through lack of written evidence under the equitable doctrine of part performance.

For this to apply there must be:

* evidence of agreement between the parties
* the plaintiff must have performed some act of part performance in relation to the contract
* the part performance must relate to the alleged contract. Thus, if a builder builds a house on his own land which he claims to be subject to an oral contract for the sale of the completed house to a purchaser, this will not be a suitable act of part performance. The inference may be drawn from his behaviour that he is building the house for himself. However, if he allowed the purchaser to visit the site and issue instructions, e.g. as to the colour of the bathroom suite, etc., this may be a sufficient act of part performance.
* the contract must be one which can be enforced by specific performance in equity (*see* p. 122).

It should be noted that even if the doctrine of part performance can be used to help the party enforcing the oral contract, it is only enforceable in equity. Thus damages may not be awarded as of right as this is a legal remedy. Damages may be awarded but only in lieu of an injunction or a decree of specific performance. The courts equitable discretion is used in deciding whether to enforce the contract by injunction or specific performance (or to award damages in lieu).

Guarantees

A guarantee is where one person agrees to pay a debt for another if the debtor should default. Such contracts must be evidenced in writing: S.4 Statute of Frauds 1677.

Contracts of employment

See p. 332.

Contracts which must be in a deed

'Contracts' which have consideration on only one side must be contained in a deed. So, if your great aunt promises to give you £5,000 on your 21st birthday and asks you to do nothing in return (love and affection is not good consideration), then if you are going to be able to

108

enforce her promise to you, the promise must be contained in a deed, otherwise her promise is unenforceable. If she gives you the money it is a mere gift.

Certain other matters must be contained in deeds. Strictly speaking, they cannot be called true contracts although they are usually the result of contracts. These are: transfers of British ships; transfers of estates or interests in land (*see* p. 158).

A contract which is under seal is said to be a **specialty** contract and it has the advantage of extending the limitation period during which one may sue, from the normal six years to twelve years. This is one reason why many building contracts are under seal (i.e. in a deed).

A deed is a document signed, sealed and delivered. The seal is either a small red wafer for an individual or for corporations a large red seal with serrated edge on top of which is impressed the corporate seal. Delivery is no longer required in the normal sense. Merely regarding the deed as binding on the person executing (signing and sealing) a deed is enough.

Occasionally, a person will execute a deed but will deliver it **in escrow**. This means that despite execution and delivery to the other party they do not regard it as binding until some pre-condition is fulfilled. This is very common in conveyancing (see pp. 158–67).

True consent

The parties must enter into the contract freely, without force or undue influence. Nor must they have been duped into entering into the agreement by lies or misled by untrue statements.

Duress – common law

Threatening someone with violence or actually harming them will render a contract **voidable** at the option of the threatened party. It may even be void but there are few cases on this point.

Undue influence – equity

Undue influence is where someone exerts his influence over another in order to obtain a benefit from that person. Such influence may be presumed where a **fiduciary** (of good faith) relationship exists between the parties, e.g. as between a doctor and patient, solicitor and client, trustee and benficiary, parent and child, minister of religion and disciple, etc. This presumption is of course rebuttable in certain circumstances, e.g. where the giver of the benefit had independent advice in relation to the intended contract or where there is other cogent evidence of that party's free will. Also in *National Westminster Bank plc* v. *Morgan* 1983, it was made clear that the relationship between bank manager and customer is not presumed to be fiduciary – although in the facts of that case, there was such a relationship.

Undue influence may also arise where there is **no** fiduciary relationship but there is evidence that undue pressure was brought to bear on someone to gain advantage. This has occurred where that person is not very clever or who has delusions.

If there has been undue influence then the person on whom undue pressure has been brought, may set aside the contract and recover any property transferred. If there is no fiduciary relationship between the parties then undue influence must be proved to have been brought on the party wishing to rescind the contract.

Once a contract has been affirmed, rescission is impossible. Thus, if a person in a position to rescind, has acted in such a way as to lead one to believe that he is not going to rescind, then the courts may refuse to set the contract aside. An action to recover money or property should be taken therefore as soon as possible after the contract has been made otherwise the courts may view a delay in pursuing a claim as amounting to implied affirmation.

Where third parties have bought the subject matter of the contract, having had no notice of the undue influence, rescission of the original contract is then impossible. However, rescission may be allowed where purchasers have had notice of the undue influence or where the transferee gave no consideration for the gift.

Misrepresentation – common law, equity & statute

For a definition of misrepresentation and a comparison with terms of contracts *see* pp. 91 & 95.

It must be remembered that a misrepresentation must be a

- statement of fact not of opinion or of law
- untrue
- it must have induced the other party to enter into that particular contract with the maker of the statement (representor) (or his principal)
- the statement must have been relied on by the other party (representee) e.g. in *Attwood* v. *Small* 1838 a purchaser of a mine chose to have independent mining experts to check whether the claims of the vendor of the mines' production capacity were true. The experts confirmed the statement and the contract went ahead. Later the purchaser went to court for an order to rescind claiming that the statement was a misrepresentation. The House of Lords refused the order as it was clear the purchaser had not relied on the vendor's statement.

However, the courts would allow rescission if the misrepresentation was part of the reason for entering the contract. A plaintiff who knew the misrepresentation was untrue cannot then claim rescission.

However, the burden of proving that he did know the truth is placed firmly on the shoulders of the defendant.

There are three types of misrepresentation:

1. Fraudulent

Here the false statement is made 'knowingly, or without belief in its truth, or recklessly, careless whether it be true or false' per Lord Herschell in *Derry* v. *Peek* 1889. It must therefore have been made dishonestly.

Remedies

1. A plaintiff may sue under the tort of deceit (also called fraud) under which he can claim damages for the loss he has suffered as a result of the tort (whether or not he also claims rescission of the contract).
2. **And/or** rescission by the representee at common law (*see* below). It should be noted that the representee could, if he wished, claim damages in deceit but still affirm the contract i.e. go through with the contract but claim damages.

2. Negligent misrepresentation

The usual rules of negligence apply and an action in tort for negligence could possibly be brought where a person makes a statement, negligently hoping to induce the other to enter into a contract.

Remedies

1. A possible action for negligence (*see* above).
2. **And/or** rescission by the representee (*see* below).
3. Under the Misrepresentation Act 1967. By S.2 (1) (expressed in an extremely roundabout way), where someone makes a misrepresentation in a negligent manner, he will be liable to pay damages '**unless** he proves that he has reasonable ground to believe and did believe up to the time the contract was made that the facts represented were true.'

   Thus, unlike in fraudulent misrepresentation where the plaintiff has to prove the existence of fraud, the burden of proof is shifted to the shoulders of the defendant and he has to show that he reasonably assumed the statement to be true.

   Whilst this section gives a slightly easier method of claiming damages under the Act, this method can only be used where the misrepresentation was made prior to a contract. Thus, where no contract was entered into, for some reason, a common law action for negligence is the only method that can be used.

3. Innocent misrepresentation

Here the misrepresentation is made innocently without any element of negligence.

Remedies
1. Rescission – *see* below.
2. Under the Misrepresentation Act 1967. Damages in lieu of rescission under S.2(2). For damages to be awarded, S.2(2) requires that the opportunity to rescind must be still available. If it has been lost then the right to damages will be lost also (under this head). The damages will be awarded at the discretion of the court.

Rescission generally

Contracts brought about by misrepresentations are voidable. This means that they are valid until the representee rescinds the contract on discovering the truth of the matter. If he does not rescind when he realises he has been misled, he is said to affirm the contract.

Rescission is possible at common law when the representee's action of, for example, informing the police or returning the property or otherwise informing the representor of the rescission, makes the contract void ab initio. At common law however this is purely a practical matter, there is no action for rescission as in equity. Such court action may be advantageous, if the representor refuses to admit that the contract is void and tries to enforce it in some way.

Rescission is no longer possible if

- the contract has been affirmed after finding out the truth (*see* p. 109)
- restitution in *integrum* is possible to achieve. This means that it is impossible to put the parties back into the positions they were in prior to the contract – e.g. if the goods have been consumed
- if an innocent third party has obtained property rights over the subject matter of the contract to be rescinded (*see* p. 109).

Summary

If the basic elements of a contract are present and none of the factors which are grounds for making the contract void or voidable can be applied, the contract is valid (*see* Fig. 4.2).

The Doctrine of privity

The doctrine of privity is that only the parties to the contract have rights and duties thereunder. This has been illustrated by reference to building main and sub-contracts (*see* p. 60), under which employers and sub-contractors cannot generally sue each other.

However, it has always been possible to obtain a collateral warranty from the sub-contractor. This is a promise by the sub-contractor that his work will be of the quality required by the main contract. As this is a contractual promise, it must either be contained in a deed (unlikely) or there must be consideration. This may take the form of a promise in consideration for being made the nominated sub-contractor or it could be a separate fee for some element not found in the main contract, e.g. for design work.

It should not be forgotten that the doctrine only applies to contract. It is usually irrelevant in tort. See *Junior Books* v. *Veitchi* 1982 (*see* p. 254).

Some aspects which are exceptions to the doctrine are found in the doctrine of the undisclosed principal in agency (*see* p. 128); the transfer of contractual rights such as debts (*see* p. 189); third party rights in motor insurance (*see* p. 388); restrictive covenants (*see* p. 156); a beneficiary's right to sue under the trust created by other people (*see* p. 133); and the transfer of rights of action to the trustee in bankruptcy (*see* p. 212).

How do contractual rights and duties end?

A contract does not go on for ever, with the parties owing each other contractual duties ad infinitum. Contracts end in a number of different ways. These are by performance, agreement, frustration and by breach of contract.

Performance

Most contracts end by the parties performing their part of the bargain. This might have occurred quickly, e.g buying a cup of tea for 15p, or it may take some time as in a building contract. Once there has been performance the parties do not have to perform any more duties, although there is a residual right to sue, if it turns out at a later date that there has been a breach of the contract during the contractual stage, even if the damage shows up later.

This is of course subject to the limitation periods (*see* p. 122) and to anything agreed by the parties in the contract itself. For example, the final certificate under a JCT contract does not prevent the employer from suing at a later date, as such an action will probably relate to hidden defects which would not have been obvious during the defects liability period. Even though the contract states that the certificate is conclusive as far as the contractor's claims are concerned, this will be no bar to a claim for breach of contract within the limitation periods.

The major rule relating to performance

Performance has to be complete, anything less than what was agreed will not do. Thus, if a builder enters into a lump sum contract, e.g. to build X a house for £50,000 and for some reason the builder fails to complete the house, abandoning it before substantial performance, he cannot claim anything under the contract, nor can he claim on a **quantum meruit** (*see* below) as it is his fault that the contract has not been performed. A number of exceptions to this rule have been developed however.

Exceptions

Substantial performance.   If there has been substantial performance of the contract then this will discharge the liability of the parties. What is substantial performance? This amounts to performance as close as a reasonable man would expect. Obviously, in building contracts even with variations, the final building cannot be exactly as specified down to the last nut and bolt. Whether it is substantial will depend on the circumstances of the case.

Where one party accepts partial performance by the other.   This must have occurred voluntarily and if this is so, the other party can then claim to be paid on a **quantum meruit** basis, that is, be paid a reasonable sum for the work he has completed.
(Note: this is only so where the acceptance of the part performance was freely undertaken.)

Divisible contracts.   These are difficult to define. Suffice it to say that where a contract is made up of separate instalments of work to be done at different times, such as a maintenance contract, then, payment is not conditional on completion of the whole contract. Whether this is true or not however, will depend on what was agreed between the parties. If payment (or other consideration) cannot be recovered without complete performance on the other side then such a contract is said to be an **entire** contract and will not be divisible.

Complete performance prevented by the other party.   If one party, who is ready and willing to perform his part of the contract is prevented from completion by the other from doing so, then he cannot sue on the contract because it has not been completed, but he can claim a **quantum meruit**.

When can performance be expected?   This is normally up to the parties to agree. In building contracts this is usually strictly laid down because of the importance of getting the job done as soon as possible to avoid additional expense or liquidated damages. Under S.14 of the Supply of Goods and Services Act 1982 however 'where, under a contract for the supply of a service by a supplier acting in the course of a business, the time for the service to be carried out is not fixed by the contract, left to be fixed in a manner agreed by the contract or determined by the course of dealings between the parties, there is an implied term that the supplier will carry out the service within a reasonable time. S. 14 (2) what is a reasonable time is a question of fact'.

In all other contracts if no date is agreed then usually none will be implied by the law. Time is **not of the essence**. Many people are caught by this rule and if performance is necessary by a certain date then they should make this a condition of the contract, preferably by setting a date in writing, e.g. when hiring a wedding suit or getting household insurance before leaving on holiday. Such a clause makes time of the essence.

If performance does not seem to be likely in the near future, and no date was set for performance in the contract, a party can later make it a condition by giving notice that if the work is not complied within X days (a reasonable time) he will regard the contract as at an end. This is useful when dealing with delivery of goods (*see* p. 174).

The same rules apply if performance amounts to being paid. Time is usually not of the essence unless it is made a condition of the contract or there are statutory rules.

What if a party is willing to perform his duties but this is refused? If performance amounts to paying for something, if this is refused, he need not offer to pay again. However he is still liable to pay under the contract. He should pay the correct amount of money in legal tender. The other party is under no obligation to give change (*see* Fig. 4.6).

	Maximum
Gold coins	Any amount
Bank of England notes	Any amount
Silver and cupro-nickel coins of more than 10p	£10
Silver and cupro-nickel coins up to 10p and less	£5
Bronze coins	20p

Fig. 4.6 Legal tender

If performance is not to do with payment, but is concerned with goods or services, then offering to perform, which is then refused, cancels out any further liability under the contract and indeed it gives the offeror the right to sue for breach of contract. Thus, for example, if Jim takes a week's holiday to put up new guttering on Mrs Smith's house, when he arrives on the Monday as agreed and she turns him away, he can then sue her for breach of contract as he is ready and willing to perform his part of the contract, if he wishes he can of course waive the contract (*see* p. 116).

After a contract has been agreed, can one side satisfy the contract requirements by giving less consideration than was agreed? Generally the answer at common law is no, unless the contract is brought to an end in some way, thereby discharging the parties from their contractual liabilities.

Thus, unless equity helps out, someone must always pay the price agreed, even if a creditor agrees to accept a smaller sum in satisfaction of the contract terms. This is obvious because the original contract has not been performed and any subsequent agreement is not contractual as it is unsupported by consideration and therefore **not a valid contract**. Thus, in *D & C Builders Ltd* v. *Rees* 1966, Mrs Rees knowing of the builders' financial difficulties offered them a lesser sum than was agreed for building work done. Knowing they might get nothing if they waited, they accepted the offer. At a later date they sued for the balance. The court took the view that she could not rely on an old rule that payment in a different form to that originally intended is good consideration for the promise to accept a smaller sum in satisfaction of the original contract.

This rule is known as the rule in *Pinnel's Case* (1602).

Exceptions

Accepting a substitute consideration – common law. Mrs Rees tried to rely on the rule in *Pinnel's case* that a creditor may, if he wishes, accept something entirely different in the place of the original debt, even if the substitute, such as a car, is worth less than the debt. This is perfectly valid in common law and will bind the creditor, who may **not** then go back on his promise. Even an early payment of a smaller sum will fall within this category. Mrs Rees failed in her defence as the court took the view that a cheque was not sufficiently different. Nowadays it is virtually the same as cash.

Promissory Estoppel – equity. Occasionally equity will help out by stopping (estopping) a creditor from going back on his promise to accept a smaller sum in satisfaction of a debt, provided the debtor has relied on that promise and has changed his circumstances accordingly.

Example (*see Fig. 4.7*) Alan borrows £10,000 from Bill repayable on 31 December 1986 with interest at 10 per cent p.a.
Alan realises he will not have the money to pay the debt and asks Bill to settle for less. Bill will not be bound by any promise he makes unless:
(a) He agreed to accept a smaller sum at an earlier date; (b) He agreed to accept a ring in satisfaction of the debt; (c) Equitable estoppel bars him from suing Alan.
(Note: the parties could of course agree to bring the contract completely to an end but it would have to comply with the requirements below.)

Contract for loan	Alan asks Bill to settle for less	Date loan due
1 Jan. 1984	1 Jan. 1985	31 Dec. 1986

Interest and repayment
31 Dec. 1986

Alan   Bill

Loan of £1,000
on 1st Jan. 1984

What consideration for this new
promise? If none, Bill can still
sue, despite promise

Alan   Bill

Agrees to accept
smaller sum

Fig. 4.7 Diagram to illustrate the example on p. 115

Agreement

If neither of the parties have performed their part of the bargain, then they can of course agree by another exchange of promises to end the contract. (*See* Fig. 4.8.) They will have then made a new contract to end the old. This is called a **waiver**.

Contracts ended by deed are of course always valid as consideration is not necessary on both sides.

It is also common for parties to provide in the contract itself for a date for the contract to end automatically, e.g. as in a fixed term contract of employment (*see* p. 341), or for a procedure for either party to terminate the contract, usually by notice, again as in contracts of employment. (These are, of course, subject to statutory rules concerning compensation and periods of notice. *See* pp. 344–7).

If one party has completely performed his part of the bargain, the parties cannot waive the agreement as in Fig. 4.8. This is because the promise not to sue for complete performance would not correspond with having already performed a part of the agreement. *See* Fig. 4.9.

As we can see from the second balance in Fig. 4.9 Fred's consideration, the car, far outweighs Jim's £1,500. Does he have to accept the sum? The answer is NO, because Jim is already bound by the contract. (*See* p. 79). But, if he wishes for some reason to be kind then he must make a new contract in one of two ways.

He can execute a **deed of release**. Remember a deed does not have to have consideration from the recipient of a gift. Or, he can make a new contract with some new consideration element which is different to that already agreed. This is called **accord and satisfaction**. So, Jim could

Monday

Fred ──────── agrees to sell ────────▶ Jim

his car to

◀────────────────

for £2,000

On Tuesday, they both realise that they do not wish to go through with the contract.

Tuesday

Fred ──── agrees not to force Jim ────▶ Jim

to pay him the £2,000
and Jim agrees not to force

◀────────────────

Fred to sell him the car

Fig. 4.8 Waiver

Monday

Car ──────────▶

Fred   Jim

◀──────────────

£2,000

Car   £2,000

Fred   Jim

Tuesday Fred gives car to Jim who can only raise £1,500

£1,500

Fred

Car

Jim

Fig. 4.9 Diagram to illustrate the example on p. 116

offer him £1,500 and a ring (even if only worth a small sum). Had the situation involved the repayment of a loan, Jim could offer to pay the sum at an earlier date (which is considered to be new consideration). (Note: also that equitable estoppel may also apply (*see* p. 115)).

Frustration

A party cannot avoid his contractual obligations merely because costs have risen or circumstances have changed to make the contract difficult to perform. At the pre-contractual stage, the parties should have thought through the consequences of their contract and taken into account the possibility of changes in circumstances. They should insert, if necessary, terms in the contract to cover such eventualities, e.g. fluctuation clauses in a building contract. If the parties agree to end contractual obligations as shown previously, all well and good. Otherwise, these continue unless the contract can be shown to have been **frustrated**.

Frustration will only terminate the contract where some outside happening occurs, which is the fault of neither party and which has had such a dramatic and fundamental effect on the performance of the contract, that it is either impossible to perform or its performance is substantially different to that originally envisaged.

The following are examples where frustration has occurred.

Illegality after the contract is entered into

Trading with an enemy after war has broken out would make a previously legal contract frustrated.

Death or severe illness in personal contracts

Whether the illness frustrates the contract will depend on the facts of the case and take into account the position of the employee in the organisation. For example a drummer with the Barron Knights pop group was held to have been lawfully dismissed after his illness made it impossible to work on more than four nights a week: *Condor* v. *Barron Knights Ltd* 1966.

State intervention

The compulsory purchase of land for example or requisitioning of property during a war frustrates a contract in relation thereto.

Destruction of subject matter of contract

See sale of goods p. 179 and mistake p. 96.

Fundamental change in surrounding circumstances uncontrolled by either party

In *Metropolitan Water Board* v. *Dick Kerr & Co Ltd* 1918, D K Ltd contracted in 1914 with the board to build a reservoir over six years. The contract contained an extension of time clause, but owing to the war, the board, after two years work on the reservoir, ordered D K Ltd to stop work.

D K Ltd claimed that this order frustrated and therefore terminated any further obligations to build the reservoir. The court agreed as at the end of the war the contract to build the reservoir would have been entirely different to what was originally envisaged. It should be noted that the outbreak of war does not frustrate a contract automatically, unless the contract amounts to trading with the enemy, which is illegal. The surrounding events must be viewed to determine the effect of the war and the date on which frustration may or may not occur. See *Finelvet A G* v. *Vinaya Shipping Co Ltd, the Chrysalis* 1983 which was concerned with the outbreak of the Iran/Iraq war.

Effect of frustration   Under the Law Reform (Frustrated Contracts) Act 1943 a contract is automatically terminated by frustration from the date of the frustrating event.

By S.1 (2), money paid before the frustrating event is recoverable and money due to be paid will no longer have to be paid. However, if the party who had been paid or was due to be paid had incurred contractual expenses prior to the date of discharge, then the court may if it considers it fair, allow that party to keep or recover the whole or part of the money paid or payable. The amount cannot exceed the amount of expenses actually incurred. Any expenses after the date of discharge cannot be reimbursed.

In addition to the protection given by S.1 (2), S.1 (3) protects a party who has already performed part of his contract before the discharge by frustration.

Under S.1 (3) if one party has obtained a valuable benefit before the date of discharge as a result of anything done by the other party to the contract, then he must pay a sum, being no more than the value of the benefit he has received. Such a sum will be as much as the court thinks just. Thus, if a building contract is frustrated, then if the builder has already built a proportion of the works he should be paid for the work done. The wording of the section, however, is a little difficult to explain and there are few cases on the effect of frustration in such situations.

The Act does not apply to contracts of insurance and certain contracts for sales of goods (*see* p. 179) concerned with agreements for the sale of specific goods which have perished.

Breach

If one party refuses to perform the contract at all, i.e. he repudiates the contract without good reason, he commits an anticipatory breach. Alternatively, during performance of the contract if he fails to comply with all his duties he is also in breach of contract.

Remedies for breach of contract

If there has been a breach of contract, the breach may be such as to allow the innocent party to be able to treat the contract as discharged as where there has been a breach of a condition or it may be such as to allow the party only to claim damages as where there has been a breach of warranty.

Obviously there may be situations in which, despite there having been a substantial breach, the injured party will still choose to continue with the contract but will be allowed to claim damages. If the other party does not wish to perform his part of the contract at all, then a decree of specific performance may be asked for in the Chancery Division of the High Court.

Finally, if the innocent party wishes, he may claim to be paid on a quantum meruit for the work he has actually done, if the breach is such as to prevent him finishing the contract or if the contract is invalid (and thus a claim under the contract is impossible).

Treating the contract as discharged

The innocent party will not have to do anything further under the contract. If he chooses he may ask the court for a declaration to this effect. He will also be able to resist a claim for specific performance by the other party by raising the breach as a defence.

Damages

The rule in Hadley v. Baxendale 1854 – remoteness of damage. The actual damage for which the court awards compensation (damages) in contract must be: 'either arising naturally, i.e. according to the actual course of things, from such breach of contract itself or such as may reasonably be supposed to have been in the contemplation of both parties, **at the time they made the contract**, as the probable result of the breach of it', per Alderson B in *Hadley* v. *Baxendale* 1854.

This means that the courts will only award damages for damage which is not too remote from the breach in fact and in law.
(Note: the use of the two different words. Damage means what one usually means by damage. Damages means compensation.)
Hadley v. *Baxendale* concerned a millowner who sent a broken crankshaft for repair. He arranged for the defendant carrier to deliver it to the repairers. Due to the defendant's negligence, there was considerable delay in transporting the shaft and the mill had to close down for much longer than was expected by the millowner. The

millowner therefore sued the carrier for damages. As he had failed to inform the carrier that he had no spare crankshaft and that he would be forced to close for the period of repair, the court only awarded damages for the delay. It did not give damages for the loss of profits occasioned while the mill was closed. This would have been too 'remote' from the actual breach. The carrier would have realised that he was inconveniencing the millowner and would have to pay damages for this breach of contract. However, as he did not know the mill was closed, there was no way he could have reasonably contemplated the additional loss.

In *Victoria Laundry (Windsor) Ltd* v. *Newman Industries Ltd* 1949, a claim for loss of profits was allowed by the court as it would have been reasonable to contemplate such loss. The laundry had ordered a new boiler which arrived much later than expected. The laundry company sued for damages for normal loss of profit plus damages for the loss of new dyeing contracts which they had had to turn away. The court awarded damages for the first loss but not the second, using the principles of *Hadley* v. *Baxendale*.

Plaintiff must mitigate his loss. If there has been a breach of contract the plaintiff must not make the most of it. He should attempt to alleviate his position by reducing any financial loss he may suffer. If he fails to make a reasonable attempt the court will not award all the damages he was expecting. Thus, if a purchaser of goods has refused to take delivery, the seller must try to sell those goods elsewhere.

Prior agreement on quantum of damages. It is very common for businessmen to include a term in their contracts so that if certain breaches occur, a specified amount of damages will be paid by the party in breach. This is designed to avoid (but not prevent) litigation. Such damages are called **liquidated** damages as the amount is **fixed** by the contract. Normal unknown damages are unliquidated and are only determined by the court at the end of the action.

It should be noted that such clauses are sometimes referred to as penalty clauses. However, a penalty clause is a liquidated damage clause which is designed to punish the party in breach. Such clauses are prima facie void. Whatever words are used to describe such clauses, the courts will strip their description away and decide whether they are valid liquidated damage clauses or void as penalties. If the clause is invalid because the sum specified is so huge that it is obviously intended to punish the party in breach, then damage will be awarded but only to compensate for the true loss. Where a valid liquidated damage clause is inserted in a contract, then even if the actual loss is greater than allowed for by the clause, the court will not award greater damages than agreed in the contract.

Specific performance – in equity

A decree of specific performance will be awarded at the discretion of the court if it considers that the legal remedies are inadequate. Such a decree requires the party in breach to perform his part of the contract.

Decrees will thus be awarded in situations where the subject matter is unique, e.g. a Ming vase or a particular piece of land as in such cases damages will hardly compensate the plaintiff.

As the remedy is equitable, equitable principles are applied. Thus, if a plaintiff has behaved inequitably or he has not performed his part of the contract, then a decree will not be awarded. He who comes to equity must come with clean hands; he who seeks equity must do equity.

Specific performance will not be awarded in contracts for personal services, e.g. contracts of employment as it would be inequitable to force someone to work for another.

Nor will a decree be granted if the court would have to provide a constant monitor to see that it was carried out, e.g. as in a building contract.

Damages in lieu of specific performance. If the High Court is of the opinion that the plaintiff has a case in law and is entitled to a decree of specific performance in equity but for some reason refuses to award a decree, then they can award damages in lieu. Damages may also be awarded in addition to a decree.

Injunctions – in equity

Some contracts require performance in a negative way, e.g. a promise not to do something in exchange for money. Thus, a request for an prohibitory injunction might be a more suitable method of enforcing such a contract.

Mandatory injunctions are also available but they are less usual. Mandatory injunctions order a party to do something in order to remedy a breach. Thus, for example in *Charrington* v. *Simons & Co* 1970 the defendants were ordered by injunction to remove a road they had built in contravention of a contract.

Damages in lieu of an injunction

Once again, the court may, if it prefers, order damages in lieu of or in addition to an injunction.

Limitation of actions

It is unfair on a defendant and unreasonable of a plaintiff, if he (the plaintiff) fails to take action within a reasonable period of his right to do so. The Limitation Act 1980 (a consolidating Act) lays down strict periods after which the plaintiff will be unable to sue in court.

In *contract*, the limitation periods are: for simple contract – six years after the date the contract should have been completed; for specialty contracts – Twelve years.

If there has been an express defects liability clause inserted into the contract as is usual in building contracts, then time is said to run from the end of that period. If a defect has been deliberately concealed by fraud then the limitation period may be extended to take account of such fraud: S.32.

(Note: for limitation periods and date of accrual of action in tort (*see* p. 262) and in particular *Pirelli General Cable Works Ltd* v. *Oscar Faber & Partners* 1983.)

It must be noted that limitation is a defence and if not pleaded, an action which is statute-barred can still be taken.

It is possible for time to run afresh, if there has been an acknowledgement in writing by one party that he still owes a fixed sum or liquidated amount under a contract or if there has been a payment made in relation thereto.

In conclusion the stages of a contract are shown in Fig. 4.10.

Agents

Definition and examples

An agent is someone who is appointed to act on behalf of another person called a **principal**. Agents represent their principals in many ways. See Fig. 4.11. For example, a solicitor undertakes legal proceedings on our behalf. An estate agent undertakes to find prospective purchasers for someone selling his house. Sales representatives sell goods on behalf of their companies. Architects and consulting engineers act on the employer's behalf in relation to building contract work undertaken by a contractor. Site agents act as their employer's representative on site.

For our purposes however, we are most interested in a common aspect of most types of agency. This is the agent's ability to enter into a contract with a third party on behalf of his principal. A number of points emerge from this.

First, the principal must have capacity to enter into the contract, even if the agent does not. Thus, it is quite possible that an agent could be a minor.

Secondly, once the contract has been set up between the third party and the principal, the agent drops out of the contractual situation altogether, so that there is privity of contract between the other two parties only. The agent is therefore not liable at all under the contract (but *see* p. 128).

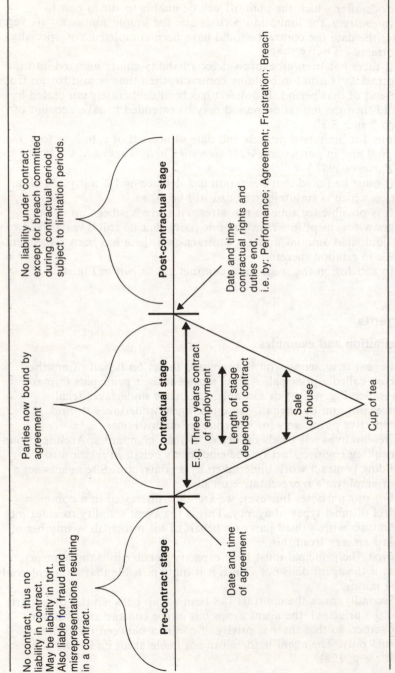

Pre-contract stage

No contract, thus no liability in contract.
May be liability in tort.
Also liable for fraud and misrepresentations resulting in a contract.

Date and time of agreement

Contractual stage

Parties now bound by agreement

E.g. Three years contract of employment

Length of stage depends on contract

Sale of house

Cup of tea

Date and time contractual rights and duties end,
i.e. by: Performance; Agreement; Frustration; Breach

Post-contractual stage

No liability under contract except for breach committed during contractual period subject to limitation periods.

Fig. 4.10 Stages in a contract

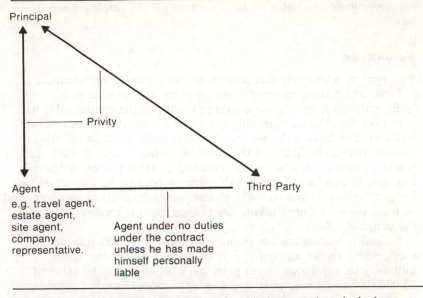

Fig. 4.11 Diagram to illustrate the relationship between the principal, agent and third party in agency

Thirdly, if the relationship between principal and agent is of a contractual nature, then in consideration for arranging the contract between the third party and the principal, the agent will be paid a fee known as 'commission'.

How does one become an agent?

An agent may be appointed in a number of different ways, be it implied from behaviour, by ratification, express appointment, out of necessity or by estoppel (mnemonic – IRENE).

Occasionally, agents may be appointed by deed called a **power of attorney** which gives the agent the right to do anything on behalf of the principal e.g. sign a conveyance, collect the principal's rents and even take out a grant of letters of administration to a person's estate. Powers of attorney are often used where the principal is going to be out of the country on business or is severely incapacitated. Note: a power of attorney is essential if the agent is to sign a deed.

Implied appointment

Becoming an agent by implied appointment is very common and particularly occurs in employment situations, where it is implicitly part of the employee's job that they may, for example, buy things on behalf of their employer. This sort of agency is essential otherwise the employee would be liable on such contracts if the employer failed to pay.

Ratification

This type of retrospective appointment can occur in two situations.

First, where someone who is not an agent acts as if he is, his 'principal' can if he so chooses, ratify (confirm) the contract. He will then take over the responsibility for the contract. If he does not ratify however, and he is under no compunction to do so, then the 'agent' remains personally liable on that contract. This situation could occur where an employee, who had never acted as agent before, suddenly attempts to contract on his behalf, perhaps because he was offered a bargain while his employer was absent, which he thought was too good to miss. He is of course taking the chance that his employer will ratify the contract.

Secondly, ratification can occur where the agent acts outside the scope of his known authority. For example, a buyer may have authority to buy goods on his principal's behalf up to the value of £5,000. If he wishes to purchase goods for more than that amount, prior permission must be given. The third party must know of this restriction. If he fails to ask for permission and agrees to purchase goods for £8,000, he will be personally liable on that contract if the third party was not aware of the limitation to the agent's authority. This is so unless the principal ratifies the contract.

(Note: Ratification is only permitted if the agent told the third party that he was acting as an agent for a named principal or one who could be identified. The principal must have had capacity to enter into the contract at the time of making the contract.)

Thirdly, the contract must be capable of ratification. Thus, a void contract cannot be ratified.

Express

Express appointments may be made in any way e.g. orally or in writing. If the agent has to enter into a contract under seal however, he must be appointed by deed also (a power of attorney).

Necessity

There are a few unusual situations in which someone may act as an agent and bind a 'principal' even though that person has no authority to do so.

For the acts of the agent to be binding:

● There must be a genuine emergency
● It must be impracticable to get the 'principal's instructions before the act is done. This has made the agency of necessity less important

nowadays with easy forms of communication.
- The act must be done in good faith.
- The act must be done for the benefit of the 'principal' and not merely for the convenience of the agent.
- The agent must already be acting on behalf of the principal as an agent.

It would be unusual for a builder to find himself acting as an agent of necessity. It is possible to imagine that such a situation could occur in relation to the supply of ready-mixed concrete. If the driver was sent to the incorrect address, through no fault of his own he could attempt to sell it elsewhere in order to prevent it solidifying. Although, he may not have authority to do this, he may come within the ambit of the agency of necessity if the above pre-conditions are met.

Agency by estoppel

This occurs where a 'principal' allows third parties to believe that someone is acting as his authorised agent. In such cases he will be estopped from denying the agency (even if in fact that person had no authority at all), if such third parties rely on such a representation to their detriment. This rule applies even if the principal had no intention of creating an agency.

Thus, if husbands, partners or employers allow their wives, co-partners or employees to act as their agents, they cannot later avoid responsibility for the agents' acts, unless they had previously expressly notified third parties with whom the agent has been dealing of their refusal to be bound by the agent's acts.

How wide is the agent's authority?

Is the principal always bound by the acts of his agent?

The courts regard an agent's authority to be **actual** or **apparent** (or ostensible).

Actual authority means the authority which the agent actually has by agreement (express) or by implication of the job or as implied by the law or what is usual in a particular business.

A principal will always be bound by the contracts made by his agent, which he authorised.

Apparent (or ostensible) authority is the authority which outsiders such as third parties assume the agent to have. This authority may be implied or what is usual in those particular circumstances or the authority which occurs in situations where the principal represented someone to be his agent – as in agency by estoppel.

Thus a person will be responsible for contracts which have been entered into by their agents in accordance with what is **usual** for a particular job. Thus, if it is normal for a site agent to make certain types of purchases, it is immaterial if that particular site agent has no such authority (unless the third party knew of such a restriction). The principal will therefore be liable on that contract.

Therefore an agents' authority depends on the type of agency, what has been agreed between the agent and principal, and on what the law implies into the agency situation.

Exceptions to a principal's liability for an agent's contracts

An agent will be personally liable on contracts made on behalf of his principal in the following situations.

Agreement to be personally liable.   If for some reason the agent agrees to be personally liable, then he can sue or be sued on the contract, whether or not the principal is joined with him. This could occur where the third party thinks the principal may not pay and asks for the agent's assurance that he (the agent) will be responsible.

Contracts signed in the agent's own name.   An agent signs contracts in his own name, without any qualification, at his own peril. This is because the courts will need strong evidence to the contrary that there was no intention that the agent should be bound by the contract. Thus, agents should always sign documents or letters with their name only if accompanied by words such as 'for and on behalf of'; 'pp Joe Bloggs' (pp – per pro, latin 'for and on behalf'); 'as agent for Joe Bloggs': *Plant Engineers Ltd* v. *Davies* 1969.

Similarly, if an agent signs a cheque in his own name and not on behalf of his principal, he will make himself personally liable for that cheque. Thus, personal cheques should always be avoided in business.

What is the extent of an agent's liability if he appears to be acting on his own?

In such cases, if he has not revealed that he is an agent, then a third party, who is of course, under the misapprehension that the agent is a principal, can enforce the contract against the agent. If he finds out about the agency, he can if he wishes, claim against the principal (provided he knows his identity). He must elect to sue one or the other. He cannot sue both. Conversely, the principal can take over the contract and claim any rights under it.

If the agent has revealed that he *is* an agent, but not the identity of the principal e.g. as at international art auctions, then the agent is not liable under the contract unless it falls within one of the exceptions above.

If a person pretends to be an agent, then he is obviously personally liable on any contracts he makes.

Duties of an agent

During the course of an agency, an agent owes his principal a number of duties, many similar to those owed by an employee to his employer. These are:

- A duty to use such care and skill as he possesses in performing his functions as an agent.
- A duty of obedience. He should do what is required of the agent, unless the act is illegal. If he fails in a contractual duty he will be in breach of contract.
- A duty to perform his contract in person, unless it is usual in a particular kind of agency to delegate certain duties. The agency itself cannot be delegated.
- A duty not to deny that his principal has title to the principal's property.
- A duty to account for any money received by him as an agent on behalf of his principal and must hand this over to the principal.
- Finally and probably most importantly he must act in good faith, i.e., he must not compete with his principal, nor make secret profits such as a discount allowed by the third party (*see* p. 337).

Termination of agency

This occurs by operation of law or as a result of the parties' actions.

Operation of law

Agencies are automatically terminated on the:

- death of the principal or agent.
- insanity of the principal or agent.
- bankruptcy of the principal or agent.
  Also, agencies may be terminated by:
- frustration (*see* p. 118).
- performance of the contract (*see* p. 112).
- effluxion of time (*see* p. 116).

Acts of the parties

The parties may terminate their agency by mutual agreement either under the terms of their contract or by subsequent agreement. The principal may revoke the agency at any time for a good reason. If the revocation was unjustified, then the agent may sue the principal.

CHAPTER 5

Law of property

Introduction

What does property mean?

What sort of property do you own? Make a list. The word property comes from the french word 'propre', meaning one's own, and, thus property in law is anything capable of **ownership**.

Your list should, therefore, include 'things' such as motor cars, clothes, jewellery, furniture, household goods, animals, food, cheques, copyright, patents, money and debts, as well as your house and land. You cannot own people or corporations.

You will notice that out of this list some property is **tangible**, that is it can be touched or is physical. Other types of property are **intangible** and cannot be touched, such as copyright, patents, shares in a company, or goodwill.

Possession and ownership

Property can be possessed or owned. What is the legal difference?

Possession

This was recognised much earlier in history, as it is relatively easy to determine who is the possessor of something. It is a question of **fact** and needs no law to determine it. Because of the ease of proving possession, it is often said that 'possession is nine tenths of the law'. Indeed, the person in possession of property has a better right to it than anyone else, **except for the true owner**. Thus, a squatter **has** rights, but only **possessory** rights, and they can never be better than those of the owner. If he remains on the land long enough, however, he may acquire ownership of the land by adverse possession. Similarly, if a person finds a lost ring he may have it returned to him by the police, but, if the true owner seeks its return within the limitation period, then the finder may be sued for the ring itself or its value. 'Finders, keepers' is only partly true.

Ownership

This concept encompasses all the legal rights that can attach to property, so that the owner can do with the property whatever he wishes, including, giving up possession. Ownership, is therefore better than mere possession as the owner is entitled to possession as well, and can claim any property back that has been wrongly taken out of his possession.

Can ownership be separated from possession?

It is usual for the owner of something to keep it in his possession. Sometimes, however, the possessor may not be the owner of the property. The building contractor, for example, takes possession of the employer's site. He often hires (leases) equipment, such as cars, lorries or compressors. He sends his equipment for repair, and the repairer takes possession of the equipment temporarily. The thief has unlawful possession of any goods he steals from the site.

Legal categories of property in English law

English law categorises property in a number of different ways, such as tangible and intangible property. The most important legal classification however, is historical and rather outdated – real and personal property (see Fig. 5.1).

Fig. 5.1 Categories of property in English law

Real property

This consists of **freehold** interests in land (*see* below).

Personal property

This consists of **leasehold** interests in land, which are called **chattels real**, as well as **pure personalty**, which consist of **chattels personal** e.g. things such as jewellery, bricks, lorries etc., as well as intangible things such as shares, patents, debts etc (*see* p. 168).

For our purposes however, it is far easier to divide property into two areas, **land and all other property**.

Land

Introduction

You will remember, from the history at the beginning of the book, that under the Norman feudal system, only the king could actually **own** land. Although, the feudal system gradually died out, this principle in theory still holds true today. Thus, only the Crown can own land. All other persons merely own **estates** or **interests** in the land. The words estates and interests are difficult to explain and reference should be made to the leading textbooks on land law for a full explanation. Suffice it to say that, for our purposes, 'estates' are interests in land, which continue either indefinitely or for fixed or determinable periods and which are capable of being owned. Interests are, as their name implies, interests which can be owned in relation to *other* legal estates in land.

Estates and interests

Estates

Before 1925 there were many different types of estates that could be owned in land. However, under S.1 of the Law of Property Act 1925 only **two** estates are now permitted at common law. All others must now exist in **equity** as *interests* behind a trust (*see* Fig. 5.2).

Uncle Fred leaves his house 'Dunworkin' in his will to Biggles, the banker and Seth, the solicitor, to hold on trust, for the benefit of his sister, Phoebe, for her life, after which it is to be sold and the proceeds given to Uncle Fred's favourite charity, Brian's Home for Sick Parrots. Biggles and Seth, as trustees under Uncle Fred's will, are the owners of the legal estate and their names will appear on the title deeds as legal owners. In equity, however, Phoebe, as the beneficiary under the trust actually owns the property.

On Phoebe's death, the purchaser is not concerned with the equitable interest in the house. He merely wishes to acquire the legal estate from Biggles and Seth, free from the equitable interest, with vacant possession (if there was a breach of trust, then the charity or Phoebe, if she was still alive, could sue the trustees).

Interests

Section 1 of the Law of Property Act 1925 also stated that in future, only **five** legal interests could exist in someone else's land. All other

Fig. 5.2   Diagram to illustrate an equitable interest existing behind a trust

interests from then on, had to be equitable.

The reason why the number of estates and interests was reduced, was to simplify the transfer of land. As there is now a smaller number of legal estates and interests fewer enquiries need to be made during conveyancing (*see* pp. 158–67).

What is meant by land

Subject to the restrictions in **use** of land, which we will examine later, a landowner will, in addition to owning the 'crust' or 'surface' of the land, also own the airspace above the land and the earth below.

Over the centuries this has been steadily whittled away. Gold and silver in a mine belong to the Crown. Articles of gold or silver found hidden also belong to the Crown as treasure trove, if the true owner of them is unknown. Any other chattels found on land may be judged to belong to the owner of the land rather than to the finder, as in *City of London Corporation* v. *Appleyard* 1963, in which a safe containing banknotes was discovered by two workmen in the basement wall of a house they were demolishing. The lessee of the house was held to have priority over the finders.

Coal and petroleum which is discovered on land now belongs either to the state, or to public corporations, such as the National Coal Board, by virtue of Acts of Parliament.

In addition to the land any buildings or things which have become attached to the land then become part of the land. Therefore, when a purchaser wishes to buy a house, his solicitor is just as concerned with the land because the house and land represents the property purchased. If the house were pulled down, what would the householder own? Attachments, which originally were chattels are known as **fixtures** and may include such things as fitted kitchens, toilet-roll holders, rose bushes and machines bolted to a factory floor.

However, machines standing by their own weight have been held *not* to be fixtures. Similarly, builder's materials, stacked for convenience to form a wall, were also found not to be fixtures. Fitted carpets are probably not fixtures. Removal of such fixtures, on sale, without prior agreement, gives the purchaser the right to sue for breach of contract. So if you are moving and wish to remove some fixtures you must make sure that this is made clear in the contract.

If a river runs through land, then the bed belongs to the owner of the land. If his land merely adjoins the river, then he and the owner of the land on the opposite bank will each own up to the middle line of the river, unless the contrary is shown from the title deeds.

Similarly, an owner of land adjacent to the sea will own up to the highwater mark (from the highwater mark to the low water mark belongs to the Crown).

The landowner also owns the crops on the land and may catch and kill wild animals – but he cannot own them till they are dead, as wild animals are free creatures, incapable of ownership.

Additional rights relating to the land

At common law the landowner, in addition to owning the land, will own certain rights, some of which have been reduced by statute (*see* p. 135).

One such right which is of importance to builders is that of **support**. A landowner is entitled to have his land supported from underneath and from the sides. Thus, if someone quarries under land, with the owner's permission, he must make sure that the surface does not collapse. If subsidence occurs he may be sued. Should there be a building on the land which collapses as a result of removing the support, damages may only be awarded in relation to the building, if the land would have collapsed whether or not there had been something built on it. Thus, there is **no** natural right of support for **buildings**.

A right of support for a building may however be acquired as an **easement** (*see* p. 147).

If the damage was caused by natural processes such as wind or rain, there can be no right of action.

Limitations of the use of land

Unfortunately for the land owner, whatever type of estate he owns, the idea that the Englishman's home, is still his castle has been considerably eroded in the twentieth century.

For the good of society, restrictions have been placed on the landowner's use of his land. Some are common law creations but most have been created by statute.

The following are merely some examples which should be familiar to the builder.

Development – statute

No 'development' of land as defined by S.22 Town and Country Planning Act 1971, can be undertaken, unless planning permission has been expressly granted by the local planning authority, or is permitted under a development order.

Nuisance – a tort (see Ch. 8)

A landowner should not commit a nuisance on his land which affects another occupier of land, otherwise, he may be sued for damages or an injunction. Actionable nuisances include creating dust, noise, smoke, smells and vibrations and permitting tree roots to undermine neighbours walls.

The commission of a public nuisance could lead to a criminal prosecution.

Dumping of rubbish and toxic waste – statute and tort

Not only could this amount to a nuisance, but also indiscriminate dumping of rubbish is controlled by statute, principally the Control of Pollution Act 1974. Under this Act there are regulations concerning toxic or dangerous waste which must be complied with. Infringement of these is punishable in the criminal courts.

Compulsory purchase – statute

There are over 70 Acts under which local authorities, government departments, and public corporations, such as the Central Electricity Generating Board, are authorised to compulsorily purchase private land for such varied uses as motorways, road widening schemes, slum clearance and public buildings. The Acquisition of Land Act 1981 governs the procedure for compulsory purchase.

Compensation is paid at open market value, with extra for removal expenses, and where the valuation is disputed, appeals may be made to the Lands Tribunal.

Preservation orders – statute

Under town and country planning legislation, trees may be subject to tree preservation orders, and buildings of architectural or historic interest may become listed buildings. If this is so, the trees may not be cut down or lopped, nor the buildings demolished or altered without consent from the local planning authority i.e. the district council.

The rule in Rylands v. Fletcher – tort

Where a landowner brings on his land something dangerous, which he allows to escape, he will be strictly liable for damage caused. Such dangerous things include water in a reservoir, fire, explosives and animals (*see* p. 285).

Negligence – a tort

Similarly, a landowner should not use his land in a negligent manner, which may result in damage to another person or property (*see* p. 251).

Occupier's liability – tort and statute

An occupier should see that his visitors are safe when entering his property. Thus he should make sure that it is not in disrepair and warn the visitors of potential dangers (*see* p. 275).

Rights of entry of public officials – statute

There are many public officials who have statutory rights to enter another's land. Normally, that entry would amount to trespass, unless the official is a police officer who is trying to prevent a breach of the peace or a serious crime being committed. Such officials include inland revenue officials, building inspectors, planning health and safety inspectors, environmental health officers, gas, electricity and water authority officials, bailiffs and police. Written authority to enter should be produced, for the landowner's inspection.

Withdrawal of natural rights – tort

If the landowner interferes with certain natural rights enjoyed by his neighbour, such as undermining the support to his land, he can be sued in tort.

Water – statute

The Water Resources Acts 1963 to 1971: the Water Act 1973 and the Control of Pollution Act 1974 Part II restrict the abstraction of water, without first obtaining a licence subject to exceptions, and make it an offence to pollute river water, springs or lakes.

Restrictive covenants – common law

These are terms written into deeds of transfer of land, which restrict the use of the land **being sold** in some way for the benefit of the land **being retained**. Typical examples are the prohibition of businesses or having caravans or livestock in the gardens (*see* p. 156).

Easements – common law

These are private rights over the land of another, e.g. a right of way. Where an easement exists, the owner of the land subject to the easement must allow the owner of the easement to exercise it (*see* p. 147).

Trespass – tort

A trespass to land takes the form of an unauthorised interference with the possession of another person's land in a direct way, e.g. walking on the land, swinging a crane through the airspace, or dumping rubbish (*see* p. 301).

Civil Aviation Act 1949 – statute

By S.40 no-one can sue merely for trespass or nuisance caused by aircraft flying over one's land, provided the height at which it is flying is reasonable, taking account of wind and weather and other circumstances and provided flying regulations are complied with.

The two legal estates: S.1 Law of Property Act 1925

These are (i) The fee simple absolute in possession
(ii) The term of years absolute.

The fee simple absolute in possession

This estate is the only *legal freehold* estate and is the nearest to true ownership that ordinary people can get. No-one has a better right to the land than the owner of the fee simple. There can only be one fee simple estate in a piece of land at a time.
   This estate
- lasts indefinitely
- can be sold, given away, split up, leased and inherited by will or on intestacy.
- is in possession, therefore the owner has exclusive rights to remain on the land.

Other freehold estates

(Note: **not** legal estates, now only equitable interests.)

Before 1926 there were other freehold estates e.g. Phoebe's estate on p. 133 was a freehold estate for life and lasted until her death. This could have been sold, but as it would have ended on Phoebe's death, any purchaser would have merely bought an interest **pur autre vie** (during the life of another).

Similarly there were freehold estates called fee tails i.e. the estate was inherited by a person within a limited category or class of people consisting of the donee's descendants. It was designed to ensure that the land was transferred in one piece from generation to generation.

These estates since 1925 are now only **equitable** and must exist as **interests** behind a trust.

Terms of years absolute (leases)

There can only be one fee simple owner at a time of a piece of land, but there may be many leases.

The owner of a lease is therefore an estate owner just as much as the fee simple owner. But his estate is limited in time to a fixed or determinable period, e.g. 99 years or a weekly tenancy. He must be given exclusive possession of the property (even if he later gives exclusive possession to a sub-lessee).

So, if the person owning the fee simple grants a lease the lessee gets exclusive possession and the fee simple owner loses it. The part of the fee simple that he retains is called the **freehold reversion**.

It is the same legal freehold estate, but minus his right to possession (*see* Fig. 5.3). He is then called the **freeholder** or **lessor** and the person holding the lease the **leaseholder** or **lessee**.

Leases are sometimes called **tenancies** especially where the period of leasing is quite short. In that case, the lessor is called the **landord** and the lessee the **tenant**. This is once again an indication of how history has influenced English land law, as it embodies the concept of land holding or tenure.

A lessee can **assign** his lease, i.e. sell it or transfer it by gift or will, in which case he transfers **all** that is left to run of the lease. Alternatively, he can **sublet** by creating a lease for a period shorter than his own lease. This is very common in business, where there may be a chain of leases.

The freeholder may also transfer his freehold reversion, and the person to whom it is transferred will then have all the reversionary rights, as well as the right to receive **ground rent** (*see* Fig. 5.4).

The essential elements of a lease

(i) The lessee/tenant must have *exclusive right to possession of the*

Fig. 5.3 Diagram to illustrate a lease

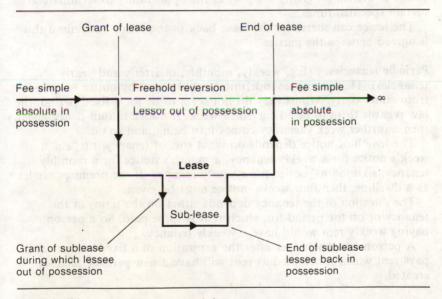

Fig. 5.4 Diagram to illustrate a sub-lease

property. Thus, lodgers and persons in service apartments are not tenants but mere **licensees** *(see* p. 157).

The description used in the lease or agreement to describe the relationship is not conclusive, and the court may strip away the description and examine the true relationship beneath.

(ii) The duration of the lease must be **fixed** or it must be capable of being **determined**.

The intention of the parties is very important. If a relative comes to live in your holiday cottage until he buys somewhere, he is probably not a tenant. He is more likely to have a **licence** to occupy the land (*see* p. 157).

If there is a dispute however, the court would look at all the relevant circumstances, and even if you swore that there had been no intention to create a lease, only a licence, they may still say a lease has been created.

Types of leases

Fixed period leases. These are common in business and domestic land ownership, e.g. 1, 3, 7, 99 or 999 years. At the end of the period the right to exclusive possession reverts back to the lessor. The lease cannot be ended by mere **notice to quit**, but if the lessee is in breach of a covenant then the lessor can take steps to remove the tenant.

Similarly, the lessee cannot give notice to end the lease unless a clause is written in, giving the parties the opportunity to terminate at certain specified times.

The lessee can surrender the lease back to the lessor but only if this is agreed between the parties.

Periodic tenancies. (E.g. weekly, monthly, quarterly and yearly tenancies). These continue indefinitely until ended by notice to quit from either party. Whilst they do not seem to be for a fixed period, the law regards them to be so e.g. for a week. If notice to quit is not given, then a further week's tenancy comes into being, and so on.

The length of notice depends on what sort of tenancy it is, e.g. a week's notice for a weekly tenancy, a month's notice for a monthly tenancy, six months' notice for a yearly tenancy. If the premises are let as a dwelling, then four weeks' notice must be given.

The duration of the tenancy depends either on the terms of the tenancy or on the period for which rent is to be paid. So a person paying weekly rent would have a weekly tenancy.

A person who **holds over** after the expiration of a fixed tenancy and pays rent which is accepted as rent will have a new **periodic** tenancy created.

The following are not leases

Tenancies-at-will. It is uncertain whether a tenancy-at-will is within the definition of a term of years absolute, though it seems to be more than a licence.

Here, the tenant occupies the land **with the landlord's permission**, but the tenancy may be ended at **any time** by either party. Thus, there is **no** certainty over the duration of the tenancy.

It may occur on holding over after a fixed lease had ended. If the landlord starts accepting rent in relation to a fixed period, e.g. a week or month, however, then a periodic tenancy will be created by implication. If either party dies, the tenancy-at-will ends.

Payment should be made by the occupier for his period of occupation. If it is a regular payment at periodic intervals, once again it becomes a periodic tenancy.

Tenancies-at-sufferance. If a lease ends, and the tenant holds over **without the landlords' permission** and **without the landlord accepting rent**, then the tenant is a tenant-at-sufferance.

It is *not* a true tenancy and the landlord may take legal steps to remove him at any time.

(Note: It is important to determine whether a tenancy/lease exists, because owners of such a legal estate are given many statutory rights. For example, a leaseholder with a long lease at a low rent may seek the compulsory purchase of his freehold reversion from the landlord or the grant of a new lease at a limited rent under the Leasehold Reform Act 1967. Tenants may also be protected; under the Rent Acts, the Protection from Eviction Act 1977 and the Housing Act 1980, from eviction or unreasonable increase in rent.)

Creation of leases as legal estates

Leases for less than three years. These may be created orally, or in writing or by deed. If the lease or tenancy agreement is not by **deed** i.e. a document signed, sealed and delivered, then, although no formalities are required, S.54(2) of the Law of Property Act 1925 must be complied with, i.e. the lease must take 'effect in possession for a term not exceeding three years ... at the best rent which can be reasonably obtained without taking a fine'.

A lease takes effect in possession if the lessee can take possession immediately. A fine is a lump sum or premium, which is sometimes paid in return for a lower rent.

Leases for more than three years. These must be created by **deed** in order to create a legal estate (S.52 Law of Property Act 1925).

Leases which do not come within the above categories, and are not legal estates, may nevertheless be treated as leases, either by virtue of equity or statute, and acquire many of the rights and duties associated with leases held as legal estates.

Rights and duties of lessors and lessees under a lease

As we have already seen, the lessee has virtually the same rights as the fee simple owner, except that the lease does not go on indefinitely. He is also subject to the same restrictions on the use of the leased property.

What is different, however, is that, the lease itself, whether written or oral, will contain provisions regulating the behaviour of both the lessor and the lessee. These regulations of behaviour are called **covenants** (promises). They may be **express**, i.e. actually written or spoken, or they may be **implied** by the common law or by statute, or the lease may talk of the **usual** covenants applying. Usual covenants are those which have become accepted over the centuries as being the '**usual**' ones found in a lease.

Thus, express covenants are those spoken about or written into the lease, which have been expressly drafted and tailor-made for that particular lease. Implied covenants do not appear at all in the lease, and the usual covenants will only apply if that expression is used in the lease.

Covenants normally found in leases. Whatever the type of lease and whether the covenants are express, implied, or usual, there will of course, always be covenants by the lessee to pay rent and rates, and by the lessor not to interfere with the lessee's 'quiet enjoyment' of the land, i.e. he will not physically prevent the lessee from enjoying the premises leased, e.g. by removing the doors or windows.

Also, the lessor impliedly promises not to '**derogate** from his grant'. This means, that if the premises were let for a particular purpose, then the lessor will not prevent its use for that purpose.

There is also an implied covenant that the property is fit for human habitation at the beginning of the tenancy, but this depends on whether the property is a house or furnished accommodation.

Covenants concerning repairs. The responsibility for doing repairs depends very much on the type of lease, and what sort of covenants are mentioned in the lease.

Lessor's implied obligations. If nothing is mentioned in the lease then at common law, there is no duty on the part of the lessor to repair or maintain property he has leased. Under the Housing Act 1961 however, if a dwelling house is let for less than seven years the lessor must keep the exterior and structure of the premises in repair. He must also repair, and keep in working order installations for the supply of water, gas and electricity, but not appliances using the supplies, such as cookers or fires, sanitation and water heating.

The lessor should be given notice of the disrepair by the lessee, unless the property to be repaired is within the control of the lessor e.g. a common staircase, where the lessor shares the premises with the lessee.

The courts are quite willing to imply covenants relating to repairs, taking into account all the circumstances. Any lease which is silent on a point, can be dealt with in this way.

Lessee's implied obligations. The extent of this implied duty to repair depends on the type of lease/tenancy he holds.

1. *Periodic tenancies*. A periodic tenant need not carry out repairs and maintenance, but he must take proper care of the property such as unblocking drains or turning off the water during winter holidays. This is called acting in a tenantlike manner. He is also liable for voluntary waste.

   (Note: **Waste** is the term used for something done, or not done, which alters the nature of land, for better or worse.

   In relation to a lease it is important that the lessor receives his property back in more or less the same state as he leased it.

   There are four types of waste, **permissive, voluntary, equitable** and **ameliorating.** Permissive waste amounts to allowing the property to fall into disrepair. Voluntary waste involves altering the land in a detrimental way, e.g. chopping down trees or demolishing buildings. Equitable waste consists of acts of wanton destruction, i.e. voluntary waste done maliciously and ameliorating waste involves acts which improve the land).

2. *Fixed term leases*. A lessee for a fixed term is liable for repairs and must keep the property in the same condition as he took it over at the beginning of the lease. He is liable, for voluntary and permissive waste.

The 'usual' covenants relating to repairs. When the lease states that the usual covenants apply, the lessee must keep the property in repair and allow the lessor to enter and inspect the state of repair. If the lessor is under an express duty to do some repairs, then the lessee *must* allow him to enter the premises for that purpose.

Leases of special types of property may have slightly different 'usual' covenants.

Express covenants. These are specially drawn up for the particular lease, and can cover whatever the parties wish. However, express covenants tend to be similar, depending on the type of lease and property.

Generally, long leases normally impose duties on the lessee to repair. This duty may include replacing the whole building if it is destroyed. This indicates the need to make sure the property is adequately insured to cover such an eventuality.

If the lease is short, then the lessor will usually agree to do all external and structural repairs.

At the expiration of a lease, with an express covenant to repair imposed on the tenant the lessor may inspect the property to view the state of repair and serve a **schedule of dilapidations** on the lessee itemising the work required to be done and the value of it.

By S.4 of the Defective Premises Act 1972 where the lessor has expressly agreed to do repairs then he owes a duty to those persons who might be affected by the state of the premises, such as visitors. This duty is to see that they are reasonably safe from personal injury or damage to their property, caused by a defect, of which he knows or ought to have known. Thus, although he is not in occupation, and therefore not within the scope of the Occupiers Liability Act 1957 he is under a similar duty to that owed by occupiers to visitors (*see* p. 275). The Act specifically restricts the lessor from excluding his liability.

Covenants against assigning and sub-letting. Assigning a lease is the transferring of all that is left of a lease. Sub-letting means that whilst retaining the lease, the lessee sub-lets, and allows into possession a tenant for a period less than his own lease.

If the lease says nothing against either of these, then the lessee is entitled to assign or sub-let his lease.

Most lessors expressly stipulate in the lease that there should be no assignment, sub-letting or mere parting with possession without consent. Statute has enacted that such a covenant is qualified by a proviso that the consent must **not** be unreasonably witheld.

Remedies for breaches of covenants. Both lessors and lessees can enforce the covenants by suing for damages at common law or seeking the equitable remedies of a decree of specific performance or an injunction.

The lessor may also seek forfeiture of the lease (see termination of leases below) or **distrain** against the goods of the lessee for rent arrears. This means that the lessee's goods may be seized.

Termination of leases

It should be noted that leases do not end on the death of either party and that the remainder of the lease or reversion will be transferred to the beneficiaries under the deceased's will, or on intestacy.

Leases may be terminated in the following ways

Expiry of a fixed term lease. This occurs automatically by effluxion of time.

Notice. Here the lessee or lessor gives notice to the other to terminate the lease. The length of notice and whether it is allowed depends on the type of lease.

Forfeiture i.e. taking the lease away, 'eviction', repossession. If the lease contains an express forfeiture clause, or one giving the lessor the right to re-enter the land if the lessee commits a breach of covenant, or the lease is granted on certain conditions, then the landlord will have a right to forfeit on application to court.

The law no longer encourages forfeiture without good reason and, therefore, there are many statutory requirements that must be complied with, before forfeiture can be allowed.

Surrender. It is possible that the lessee may no longer be able to afford the rent, especially on a short lease, which tends to be expensive. He may ask to surrender the lease back to the lessor. If it is accepted, then the lease comes to an end. There is no obligation on the lessor to accept surrender.

Merger. This arises when the lessee acquires the freehold reversion. The two interests then merge (*see* Fig. 5.5).

Fig. 5.5 Diagram to illustrate the merger of freehold and leasehold

Disclaimer on bankruptcy. A trustee in bankruptcy can disclaim responsibility for a lease which is a burden to the bankrupt. This does not end the lease. It merely terminates the bankrupt's liability under it.

Frustration. If circumstances surrounding the lease change so dramatically as to destroy the effectiveness of the lease, then the lease may be ended by frustration: *National Carriers Ltd* v. *Panalpina Ltd* (1981).
(Note: there are many Acts of Parliament which protect lessees from eviction, or even give them the right to claim new leases. One such example is that of business leases.)

Business leases

It is more usual for the businessman to lease his business premises. This is because freehold premises are very expensive, as they are usually in the most sought after parts of the country, e.g. in town centres.

Business lessees are given some statutory protection under the Landlord and Tenant Act 1954 Part II.

Compliance with the Act is essential. The lease can only be ended if the provisions of the Act are complied with.

This means that if there is a fixed period lease and the tenant holds over, having received only a normal notice to quit, then the lease will continue quite validly.

Notice to quit. A proper notice to quit must contain the following elements: (i) The lessor must give between 6 and 12 months notice in a form laid down by the Act; (ii) The period of notice must not expire earlier than the lease would have expired normally, i.e. regardless of the Act.

On receipt of the notice the lessee has two months to inform the lessor that he will not give up the premises and may apply to court for it to grant a new lease.

If the tenant has a fixed period lease, he may request the landlord to grant a new tenancy under the Act, and, having given such a request must then apply to court for confirmation.

Granting a new lease. The court **must** grant such a lease, unless the landlord is able to prove that one of seven grounds apply to the lease. These include the tenant's failure to repair the premises as requested, failure to pay rent, substantial breaches of covenants, the provision of alternative accommodation, that the lessor wishes to demolish or reconstruct the premises, and that the lessor wishes to occupy the premises for his own domestic or business purposes.

The rent to be charged on the new tenancy is controlled by the court. Should the lessee not be granted a new lease, then, unless any of the three grounds, which were for the benefit of the landlord applies, no compensation for loss of possession is paid.

Improvements. The tenant may have made improvements to the premises which have enhanced the letting value. Providing he gave the landlord notice of the carrying-out of the improvements, he may claim compensation under the Landlord and Tenant Act 1927.

Co-ownership of estates

It is perfectly usual for two or more people to own an estate in the same piece of land. Indeed, it is very common for husbands and wives to buy their matrimonial home and own it together. On the death of one of the spouses the whole of the estate then belongs to the survivor. This right of survivorship is the most important aspect of one type of co-ownership, a **joint tenancy**.

It would be inappropriate to have a right of survivorship in a business relationship, so there is another type of co-ownership in equity called a **tenancy-in-common**. Thus, if partners own property as tenants-in-common, if one partner dies, his share in the property goes to his next-of-kin or beneficiaries under his will.

There are some important differences between the two types of co-ownership which must be noted.

1. *Legal estates can only be co-owned by joint tenants, with a maximum of 4.*
As equitable interests can only exist behind a trust, if in our partnership example above there were 20 partners, four of them will have to own the legal estate as joint tenants, but they will hold it on trust for all 20 of them, as tenants-in-common. If someone wanted to buy the land, he will only be concerned with buying the legal estate from the four joint tenants. The trust is of no consequence to the purchaser.

2. *Joint tenants own the property, as if they were one person.*
Joint tenants own the whole estate as if they were one for the same length of time, and are entitled to have possession of the whole of the property. It is rather like when a husband and wife buy a suite of furniture out of their pooled income and refer to it as 'our suite'. Both of them enjoy the furniture, and neither would point to a particular part of it and say that it was their own.

Interests in other people's land

Section 1 of the Law of Property Act not only restricted the number of legal estates to two, the fee simple absolute in possession and the terms of years absolute, it also reduced the number of legal interests or charges which can exist over someone else's land to five. We are concerned with only two, easements and a charge by way of legal mortgage. We are also concerned with *equitable* interests, such as restrictive covenants and licences.

Easements

An easement is a legal interest, which one landowner has over another's land, such as a right of light, a right of way, a right to take water, or a right of support, a right to have a sign on a neighbour's building, or to use a clothes line on a neighbour's land.

These are very important, because without such easements, some pieces of land would be virtually useless and without value.

In theory, other sorts of easements may be recognised by the courts as the use of land changes over the years, but in practice they are reluctant to extend the types.

(Note: these are not public or private rights. They are particular rights attached to particular pieces of land. They only belong to the landowner, because of his ownership of that piece of land.)

There are certain essential requirements.

Dominant and servient tenements

There must be a **dominant and a servient tenement** of nearby land. In Fig. 5.6 below if the owner of Blackacre grants a right of way across

Fig. 5.6 Diagram to illustrate dominant and servient tenements necessary for easements

his land to the owner of Whiteacre, then Blackacre is the servient tenement and Whiteacre the dominant. The servient tenement is the land burdened by the easement, and the dominant tenement is the land benefiting from the easement.

The position would be the opposite, if the owner of Whiteacre granted a right of way over his land to the owner of Blackacre.

When the land is sold, or transferred in any way, e.g. by gift, or on death, the easements will pass at the same time.

The easement must benefit the dominant tenement

The easement is for the benefit of the **land** and not merely the owner of that piece of land. Thus, in the example, there is no doubt that Blackacre and Whiteacre are more valuable if they each have a right of way to both roads.

In the example, dominant and servient tenements are close together. It is possible however, for easements to exist where they are not so close but they should not be too far apart. So, a farmer down the High Road may have an easement across both Whiteacre and Blackacre, to get to Main Road. As this is a short cut for his animals, it will benefit his land. The dominant and servient tenements must be owned by different persons otherwise the landowner has rights of possession and ownership over his own land.

The easement could still exist, however if one person were the tenant of the other, as there are then two legal estates.

Types of easements

1. Rights of way. These may be limited to a particular time of day or a particular type of use, e.g. for cattle or pedestrians, or they may be totally unlimited.

There must be a definite path or route to be used, and the person who benefits from the easement must construct and maintain the right of way. The person exercising the easement must not then deviate from the defined route, unless he has been obstructed for some reason. (Note: this is actionable in nuisance, see p. 290).

2. Rights of light. These can only relate to a particular window or aperture, and not to the building, as there is no normal or natural right to have light.

3. Rights of support. These may relate only to a particular building, such as a semi-detached house (for natural rights of support see p. 134).

4. Rights to water. These can relate to a pond, lake, or river.

5. Miscellaneous. See above, also rights to use a letterbox or lavatory or a coal shed.

Acquisition of easements

These may be acquired in a number of ways.

(i) Statutes may indirectly create easements.
(ii) On the transfer of land an easement may be expressly granted by the transferor, or expressly reserved by him to benefit land he has retained.

(iii) Easements not expressly mentioned may be implied to give effect to the intentions of the parties if the land transferred is useless or less valuable without the easement. This would include easements of necessity. Thus if someone sells Pinkacre as in Fig. 5.7, without granting a right of way, then the shortest possible right of way will be implied between 'Pinkacre' and the bottom road.

(iv) By the rule in *Wheeldon* v. *Burrows* if **part** of a piece of land is transferred the transferee will receive all the quasi-easements which already exist over the retained land, providing they have been enjoyed continuously without interruption before transfer, were obvious on inspection, were necessary for the reasonable enjoyment of the land, and had been used by the transferor. The quasi-easements would then become proper easements. (They were quasi-easements because, before transfer, the transferor owned **all** the land and the rights were merely normal rights of ownership).

(v) By S.62 Law of Property Act 1925 a **conveyance** of land passes all **existing** easements to the transferee without the use of special words being used in the conveyance.

(vi) By presumed grant or prescription. This amounts to long use, i.e. exercising the 'easement' for a long period, as of right.

Prescriptive rights amounting to easements may be acquired in three ways. The oldest method is at common law. The claimant must prove that the easement has been in continuous use since time immemorial (1189) and has been exercised *nec vi, nec clam, nec precario*, i.e. without force, without secrecy or without permission from the landowner. Twenty years continuous use raises a rebuttable presumption that it has been in use since 1189.

The second method is by **lost modern grant** and has been described as 'that revolting fiction' by Lush L J in *Dalton* v. *Angus & Co* (1877). Here the court pretends that an easement was actually granted by a landowner but that the document has since been lost.

Fig. 5.7 An easement of necessity

The third method is under the Prescription Act 1832 and the Rights of Light Act 1959. They are rather like Limitation Acts, but in reverse, as they lay down periods of use, which will give rise to easements. An easement, other than that of light, enjoyed for 20 years as of right and without interruption, is absolute and indefeasable (unless oral consent was given).

Where the right was enjoyed for 40 years, then if written permission is granted, this will defeat the right to an easement.

Rights to light must be enjoyed for 20 years to create an easement, and only written permission will defeat it.

A recent Esther Rantzen 'That's Life' programme on BBC television gave an account of a man who was charged a very nominal fee by British Rail for his light. British Rail owned the land next door. Whilst he never paid the bill, nor was it ever enforced, the purpose behind it was to amount to a written permission to enjoy the light. At any time, therefore, British Rail could build something to restrict this light to a particular window, and he would not then be able to claim an easement of light.

Termination of easements

By statute. An Act of Parliament may enact law which will at the same time extinguish certain easements e.g. if an Act was passed to build a nuclear reactor on a piece of land which was subjected to easements, then these would be extinguished by the Act.

By release. Here the owner of the dominant tenement, either expressly or impliedly, releases the owner of the servient tenement from being burdened by the easement.

If this is done expressly it must be done by writing in a deed. This would be the appropriate method for a building developer, who wishes to buy out the easements on his land, in which case the dominant owner must execute a deed of release.

An implied release occurs where the dominant owner indicated by his behaviour that he regarded the easement as at an end. Merely stopping using the easement would not be enough, unless it was for a long time e.g. 20 years. Thus, the dominant owner should show some intention to release the servient owner e.g. by altering his land, so as to make the exercise of the easement impossible, such as demolishing a house benefiting from a right of light.

By merging ownership and possession of the dominant and servient tenements. As indicated earlier, there can be no easement unless, there is a dominant and a servient tenement. So, if one person acquires both pieces of land the easement must cease. It should be noted however that it is the fee simple that must be owned of both pieces, and not a mere lease.

Breach of an easement

If someone infringes an easement, this amounts to a nuisance and the dominant owner may sue for damages, or more importantly for an injunction.

Technically, he could also use the remedy of abatement (but *see* p. 293).

Mortages

Introduction

People often remark, when they are going to buy a house, that the building society has given them a mortgage. This is not legally correct. What has actually occurred is that in order to pay for the house the building society has loaned money to the borrower, who, immediately after the purchase, grants a mortgage of the property to the society as security for the loan. Because it is the borrower who grants the mortgage it is he who is the **mortgagor** and the lender is the **mortgagee**, and not the other way round (*see* Fig. 5.8).

Why?

Why does the building society, or indeed, any other lender of money, want a mortgage? Because it gives them security, which puts them in a better position than other creditors. If the debt is not paid the mortgagee can sell the mortgaged property and satisfy the debt. An

Lender gives **Loan** to **Borrower**

The **borrower** is the **mortgagor** as he gives a **mortgage** of his land to the **lender** who is the **mortgagee**.
(in law, 'or's always give to 'ee's, e.g. donor to donee)

Borrower gives **Mortgage** to **Lender**

Fig. 5.8 Diagram to illustrate a mortgage

ordinary unsecured creditor who has no security, like the milkman, can only claim in the borrower's bankruptcy. He may not even get the full amount owed, if there is not enough money to pay all the creditors.

Definition

A mortgage is therefore an interest in another's land, which secures a debt.

Mortgages may be either legal or equitable, which determines the rights and remedies of both parties.

Creation of legal mortgages

Since the Law of Property Act 1925 a freehold estate may only be legally mortgaged by either:

1. A **demise** (transfer by lease) for a term of years absolute, subject to a provision for cesser on redemption, i.e. the land is leased for a fixed period, usually 3,000 years, which will come to an end when the debt is repaid, *or*

2. A charge by deed, expressed to be by way of legal mortae.
(This is a short document containing the above expression, which by virtue of the Act, is 'legal shorthand' for the concept in (1) above).
By S.87 (1) of the Act, a mortgage created by a legal charge carries the same protection and remedies as if a lease for 3,000 years had been created.

Similarly, leases can be legally mortgaged either by sub-demise (sub-lease) subject to a provision for cesser on redemption, the sub-lease being at least one day less than the mortgagor's lease, or by method (2) above.

Creation of equitable mortgages

1. Of equitable interests – *equitable mortgages.* If a person has only an equitable interest in land, such as an interest under a trust, then any mortgage he grants appertaining to that interest must be equitable. It should be in writing and be signed by the transferor or his agent, Law of Property Act 1925 S.53(1)(C).

2. Equitable mortgages of legal estates. Where the requirements of the Law of Property Act 1925 are not met, as in (1) above, then any purported mortgage must be equitable.

An informal mortgage, such as depositing title deeds with the lender to prevent the sale of the mortgaged property, creates an equitable mortgage.

How does a mortgagee prevent the mortgagor selling the mortgaged property without the mortgagee knowing and therefore defeating the purpose of taking security

This is done in two ways:

1. By depositing the title deeds with the mortgagee. After the purchase of the property has been completed, the purchaser's solicitors will have to send the title deeds to the building society, or other mortgagee. The society will not release the title deeds until the debt has been paid, i.e. they have a lien over the deeds. If the property is going to be sold the solicitors will have to promise to hold the deeds for the society and not the mortgagor, and promise also to pay off the debt out of the proceeds of sale.

2. Registration. Where the property is the subject of a registered title, the fact that the property is mortgaged must be registered at the Land Registry (*see* p. 159).

Registration protects the lender's interest in the property, as anyone wishing to buy will search the registry records to discover the existence of any such interests.

Where the property is the subject of an unregistered title, mortgagees who do not have the title deeds, because their mortgage is a second or subsequent mortgage, must register their mortgage at the Land Charges department as their mortgage will otherwise be void against a purchaser.

The mortgagor's right to redeem the mortgage

The mortgagor must have the right to redeem the mortgage, otherwise the mortgagee's interest would be the more important. The mortgagee, therefore, is not allowed to impose any restrictions so as to prevent redemption. He may wish to do this, because the longer the loan continues the more interest he earns.

The mortgagee's rights if the mortgagor fails to pay the debt

1. Sue. He may sue for the money, as it is an ordinary debt. In practice, this is usually useless, as the debt would have been repaid if the borrower had any money.

2. Foreclosure. Once the date for redemption has been passed, or there has been a breach in the terms of the mortgage, which gives rise to full repayment being required, then the mortgagee may demand repayment in full. If, after a reasonable time has elapsed, no payment is forthcoming, the mortgagee can apply to the court for a foreclosure order.

If this is granted and the order is made absolute, the mortgagor's estate becomes vested in the mortgagee.

This is useful if the land is more valuable than the loan, and the lender would like to keep the land for some reason. In practice, however foreclosure is not often used as the lender really wants his money back, and not land in lieu.

3. Sale of the property. If the mortgage is by deed and if there has been a breach of covenant *or* no interest has been paid for at least two months *or* notice has been served on the mortgagor who has still failed to pay after three months, then the mortgagee can put the land up for sale.

This is quite usual for building societies, as they need the money and not a transfer of land, as under foreclosure.

On the sale the purchaser gets the mortgagor's interest in the property, freed from the right to redeem.

The mortgagee must act in good faith, when selling the property. Unless it is a building society, however, the mortgagee does **not** have to get the best price for the land. Building societies are under a statutory duty to get the best price reasonably obtainable.

Any money left over after paying the debt and expenses should be paid to the mortgagor. If there are other mortgages on the property then they should receive the rest to cover their debts. The order in which they are paid depends on the order of registration.

The advantage of this remedy is that, unlike foreclosure, there are no preliminary court proceedings.

4. Taking possession of the land. Proceedings must be taken in the Chancery Division first. The mortgagee's right to possession arises immediately a legal mortgage is created, as the mortgagee either has a lease or is treated as if he has one and is therefore entitled to possession. Thus, strictly speaking, the mortgagee can enter the mortgagor's land, even if there has been **no** breach of the mortgage.

In practice, this is unusual, unless the property is agricultural or commercial, where, by letting it or managing it better than the mortgagor, the mortgagee can raise more money on the property and thereby get paid the money owed.

The mortgagee must account strictly for the income which he has or should have received, e.g. rents from tenants. He must also keep the property in reasonable repair.

5. Appointing a receiver under S.101 Law of Property Act 1925. In any mortgage created by deed there is a statutory power to appoint a receiver. A receiver must be appointed in writing and can be appointed in the same circumstances as under a power of sale. The receiver should pay interest due under the mortgage to the mortgagee and pay any rents, rates, taxes and insurance premiums due on the land. He may, if the mortgagee tells him to, pay the cost of any repairs and pay off the principal sum outstanding.

In effect, the mortgagee, without taking possession, has appointed a manager to try to run the property better than the mortgagor or channel the funds in the proper direction.

Rights of mortgagees with equitable mortgages

These are very similar to the rights above, although in some respects they have been cut down or are limited because of the equitable nature of the interest or mortgage itself.

Restrictive covenants – equitable interests in land

Whereas an easement gives the owner of the dominant tenement the right to do something on the servient tenement, a restrictive covenant prevents the owner of the servient tenement from using his land in a particular way for the benefit of the dominant tenement e.g. preventing building or carrying on a business there.

Creation

Restrictive covenants can only be created by deed (cf. easements).

Essential requirements

1. A dominant and servient tenement (see p. 148).
2. The covenant must be restrictive or negative in nature.
3. The covenant must 'touch and concern' the dominant tenement e.g. a restrictive covenant to stop a business or trade being carried on 'touches and concerns' the dominant tenement, as it could affect its value.

Termination of restrictive covenants

1. Release (see p. 151).
2. Joining of ownership and possession of the dominant and servient tenements (see p. 151).
3. Statute.
   Apart from individual statutes which may extinguish restrictive covenants, there is a general right under the Law of Property Acts 1925 and 1969 for the servient owner to be able to apply to the Lands Tribunal for the termination or modification on a number of grounds. In particular, it may be granted if the restrictive covenant is now of no practical use, as the surrounding neighbourhood has changed in character since the restrictive covenant was originally made.
   As restrictive covenants can affect the value of land for development building contractors must be sure that either there are none which affect their building work or try to get them terminated by one of the above methods.

In appropriate cases where a restrictive covenant was imposed a long time ago, it may be possible to take out a restrictive covenant indemnity policy with an insurance company.

Breach of a restrictive covenant

Should a breach occur, an injunction may be sought. Damages, which are a legal and not an equitable remedy, may only be awarded if an injunction is an inadequate remedy. As only equitable remedies are available, the judges use their discretion in awarding an injunction or damages in lieu and will proceed on an equitable basis, e.g. 'delay defeats equity'. Thus, if you have failed to seek an injunction immediately your next door neighbour opened his whippet kennels, or soon after, the courts may decline an injunction.

Licences

A licence is a right given by an occupier of land to permit a person to do something, which would otherwise be a trespass on the occupier's land, e.g. the right to be a lodger, to watch a film at his cinema, or to swing a crane through his airspace.

The granting of a licence does not give the licensee any property rights, nor does it give him the right of exclusive possession of the property.

There are a number of different types of licences.

A bare licence

This occurs where no consideration is given by the grantee for the licence. So, if Albert allows Bertha to cross his land while Bertha's road is being dug up, and Bertha gives Albert nothing for the right, when he withdraws his permission, Bertha must stop using his land, or she will become a trespasser. The grantor may withdraw his permission at any time.

Contractual licences

These are rather like bare licences, except that they have been created by a contract, which stated they would not be revoked. So, when you buy a ticket for a football match or pop concert you are buying a contractual licence to be on the occupier's property for a particular purpose.

Equity regards such licences as irrevocable for that particular time and purpose.

Contractual licences are obtained by construction companies to operate cranes across another person's land.

Also, under clause 23 of the JCT standard form of contract a contractor is given a licence to occupy the site until the date of practical completion. It is implied that the employer will not revoke the licence, unless there is good reason to do so under clause 27, when the employer may end the contract.

Licences coupled with an interest

In addition to being allowed to enter the occupier's land, the licensee has the right to take something away, such as fish. The right to fish or take turf are two types of a category of interests called **profits à prendre**, and are similar to easements, in that they must be created by deed or prescription.

These licences are therefore irrevocable, and, indeed, can be sold or given to another.

Licences arising out of estoppel

Where an owner of land behaves in such a way as to lead another person to believe that he has granted or is in the process of granting him a licence over that land, then the owner shall be estopped (stopped or prevented) from denying that there is such a licence in existence.

Conveyancing – transferring ownership of land

Introduction

This is the legal term used for the transfer of ownership in land from one person to another. For most people the conveyancing transaction will be the one important legal transaction that they will remember, as they will usually employ the services of a solicitor when they buy their home.

For the lawyer the most important aspect of the transaction, is to make sure that the vendor transfers to the purchaser all that he owns in the property. This is called transferring the **title**. He may, of course, have agreed to sell less than he owns, e.g., where he leases the property and retains the freehold reversion.

Because there can be different estates and interests in the same piece of land, conveyancing is not as simple as say, selling a book, which can be done by merely delivering it into the possession of the purchaser. A certain procedure must be gone through, with numerous checks and searches made, to make sure that the property belongs to the vendor, that all matters that affect the land are disclosed, such as mortgages, and that the transferee gets what he is paying for. Proving ownership, (**proving title**) is done by producing documents of title and not producing the thing itself as in the case of the book, as this is impossible in relation to land.

Methods of conveyancing – Is the land registered?

In England and Wales there are two systems of conveyancing – one where the title to the land is **unregistered**, the other where it is **registered**.

A national system of land registration was introduced by the Land Registration Act 1925. In this system, once title to the land has been proved to the satisfaction of the Chief Land Registrar, the Land Registry issues a document of title, which guarantees that the estate owner mentioned in it is the true owner. Subsequent purchasers of the land merely have to check the land registry records to discover the identity of the estate owner and whether he has encumbered the property with mortgages, etc.

Not all land is registered yet, but approximately three quarters of all conveyancing transactions concern registered land.

Where title to land is unregistered then proving title, i.e., proving the vendor is the estate owner, has to be done by examining the title deeds.

In unregistered conveyancing, title to land must be proved through a chain of ownership bank to a 'good root' of title for at least 15 years. This means that if the vendor has owned the estate for over 15 years then all that is necessary is to prove back to his own conveyance i.e. the deed which transferred all the estate to the vendor. Otherwise, one needs to go back further to the next conveyance which transferred the land. If there is a break in the title, then one must find out why, otherwise there could be a defect, which could mean, at worst, that the vendor does not own the property, and cannot pass on a good title to the purchaser.

The following outline will indicate the differences between the two systems as and where necessary.

Basically, the transaction falls into **three** stages – before contract, contract to completion and post-completion. To simplify matters we will take a normal domestic conveyancing transaction.

Before contract

1. What can he afford and which house will he buy? The purchaser usually sorts out his finances first and finds out how much a building society or bank will lend him, based on his salary. Once he knows his price range he can then look for a suitable house. He may register himself with estate agents, whose job it is to find purchasers for vendors, or he may look at 'property for sale' columns in the newspapers.

2. Borrowing the purchase price. On finding a house he likes he will complete the building society or bank loan application forms and send them off with a survey fee.

3. Why is a survey needed? The survey fee is payable, as the society will send their own surveyor to look at the house, to see whether it is

valuable enough to act as security for the loan. If what you are borrowing is close to the purchase price, e.g. a 100% or 95% mortgage loan then the society's approval should indicate that all is well and that there are no serious defects. If you are borrowing a smaller amount, however, approval of the loan is no real indication of the state of the premises.

A recent case illustrates this point, and has led to changes in building society practice regarding surveys.

In *Yianni* v. *Edwin Evans & Sons* 1981, Mr Y wanted to buy a £15,000 house, borrowing £12,000 from his building society. Their surveyors, an independent firm, inspected the property and indicated to the society (whose agents they were) that it was good security for the loan. Mr Y did not get an independent survey, and went ahead with the purchase despite the building society's exclusion of liability attached in the loan offer. The exclusion stated that the society took no responsibility for the condition of the property, that they were not saying the price was reasonable, and that the survey report was confidential.

Almost a year later after buying the house the foundations were found to be defective and repairs would be needed costing £18,000.

The surveyors admitted that they had been negligent in failing to notice the defects and saying that the house was adequate security for the loan. As a result of their admission, Mr Y won his case against them, as the court decided that it was common practice for borrowers to rely on the report from the building society's surveyor (*see* requirements for negligence, p. 251).

As a result of this case, most building societies are now offering a number of different types of surveys. As the minimum survey has been shown to be inadequate for the borrower the basic survey fee has been increased, but the survey report is now available to the borrower. For an additional payment most societies will arrange a full structural survey which will be the same as that done by an independent surveyor.

In practice most people will probably still opt for the minimum survey, so that if their loan application is turned down they will not proceed with the purchase. A full survey would then have been a waste of money.

(Note: chartered surveyors have to take out professional indemnity insurance against claims for negligence.)

4. If the loan is agreed, the purchaser can tell his solicitor to proceed with the purchase.

5. Preparation of the draft contract. The vendor's estate agents will have informed the vendor's solicitors of the prospective sale and the solicitor's will have prepared a **draft contract**, either by looking at the title deeds if unregistered or by examining the land certificate if registered.

If the land is already mortgaged then the vendor's solicitors will have first had to borrow the title deeds from the building society. If the land is registered they can prepare the contract by obtaining copies of the land registry entries called **office copy entries,** which contain details of the property, the vendor and mortgagee(s) or other interests in the property.

6. The draft contract, and office copy entries are sent to the purchaser's solicitors.

7. If the land is unregistered the vendor's solicitors will send, instead of office copy entries, either an **abstract of title** or an **epitome of title.** An abstract is a document written in a sort of legal shorthand, containing a summary of all the title deeds and events which link each deed, such as the death of an owner and the transfer after a grant of probate to the widow.

8. An epitome, which is a more modern version of the abstract, is a collection of photocopies of the relevant deeds, topped with a summary of dates and events and description of the deeds. In both cases, they need only go back to a good root of title of at least fifteen years. A 'good root' is a deed which deals with the whole of the legal and equitable estate, such as a conveyance, and describes them in detail.

9. The purchaser's solicitors check the draft contract, to see that it contains all the particulars that they expect, e.g., that the price is the same as instructed, and that the fixtures are included or not (*see* p. 134).

They also check the office copy entries or the abstract or epitome, to see that what they are buying is what they expect, e.g a fee simple estate and not a lease, and that all mortgages have been disclosed. The vendor must undertake to redeem mortgages from the purchase moneys, so that the purchaser takes free of them.

10. The purchaser's solicitors also send a standard form called **inquiries before contract** to the vendor's solicitors. These contain questions on matters within the knowledge of the vendor and which the vendor is under no legal obligation to disclose, such as neighbour disputes, ownership of walls etc., availability of gas or electricity, shared facilities and outgoings. Additional questions not included on the printed form can be inserted, such as details of rewiring, or whether the central heating has been paid for. In the case of leases there are further questions concerning such matters as breach of covenant, details of the lessor, service charges and insurance cover.

11. In addition to the above forms, which are sent to the vendor's solicitors, the purchaser's solicitors send two forms to the district council for the area in which the house is situated. The first is a **search** of the local land charges register, which is kept by the council. This search is made against the address of the house and not the owner. It deals with matters which are registered by local authorities under the

Local Land Charges Act 1975, and various pieces of legislation. The charges may be financial, similar to a mortgage benefiting the council, when, for example, the council had to execute works on the property at their own expense, which has not been reimbursed by the owner. This could occur as a result of breaches of planning law or work contravening building regulations where the owner failed to comply with an order to demolish the work. Other charges are concerned with town and country planning, listed buildings, drainage schemes, civil aviation, land compensation etc. The registration of such charges acts as notice to the prospective purchaser, who then, if he continues with the purchase, takes the property, subject to the charge.

The second form sent to the council is called **inquiries of district councils**. The matters dealt with in this are, *inter alia,* whether the roadway is maintained by the council, whether the property is drained into a sewer, whether there has been a breach of the building regulations or town and country planning rules, if the area is going to be redeveloped, or if the house is in a conservation, slum clearance or smoke control area.

12. If the land is unregistered, a **land charges search** is sent to the Land Charges Department, at Plymouth, to check that there are no encumbrances registered against the property, such as second mortgages, which have not been revealed by the vendor.

These encumbrances belong to other people who have some interest in the land being sold. In order to protect themselves, they should (but it is not obligatory) register their interests at the Land Charges Department. If they do not register, a purchaser who buys the land will usually take the land **free** from the encumbrance.

Examples of such interests, include the following: pending actions, e.g., where the land to be sold is subject to a dispute pending in court, and this includes a petition for the bankruptcy of the vendor, or a claim for transferring the property in a pending divorce. Where there has already been a court case concerning the land and judgment has been made involving the land, e.g. appointing a receiver, the writ or order enforcing judgment can be registered.

There are also six classes of land charges, which may be registered and are identified by the letters A,B,C,D,E and F. Class C includes legal and equitable mortgages not protected by the deposit of title deeds with the mortgagees, such as a second mortgage to a bank. This class also includes **estate contracts**, i.e. where the legal owner has contracted to convey the legal estate to another. This would include **options to purchase**, which can be very important in the building industry.

Class D land charges include restrictive covenants and equitable easements.

A class F land charge is a deserted spouse's right to occupy the matrimonial home, which is extremely important in recent years with the increase in divorces. Anyone, buying from a separated couple must search, in case a class F charge is revealed.

The search is made not against the land but against owners of the legal estates in the land.

N.B. These interests would be noted in the office copy entries if the land were registered (and the interests had been registered).

13. If the purchaser's solicitors are satisfied as to the result of their searches and enquiries and have agreed the contents of the draft contract, they can **engross** it, i.e. make a proper final copy. Conveyancing contracts are always engrossed in two identical parts. One is sent for signature to the purchaser the other to the vendor's solicitors for their client's signature.

14. *Exchange of contracts* Until contracts are 'exchanged', there has been no binding contract. It is a mere gentleman's agreement, which can be broken at any time by 'gazumping' (accepting another better offer) or varying the original offer, or withdrawing the property from the market. To emphasize that there is, as yet, no binding contract, most people are wise to make an offer 'subject to contract', so that they will only enter into a binding contract if the searches, enquiries, survey and mortgage offer are satisfactory. Even if the parties make a verbal agreement, which is 'subject to contract', then the court may decide, in certain circumstances, that there was a binding contract and will enforce it. So, caution is important at the pre-contract stage.

Usually 10% of the contract price is paid on exchange of contract by the purchaser as a sign of good faith and this will be forfeit if he fails to go through with the transaction.

The purchaser's signed contract is sent to the vendor's solicitors, and the vendor's to the purchaser's solicitors.

On exchange of contracts, there is a **binding contract** – and *not* before.

At this point, equity regards the purchasers as the landowners and thus insurance cover must be arranged on the property by the purchaser's solicitors.

Contract to completion

1. The date for completion is usually entered in the contract, otherwise most standard forms of contract automatically have a completion date of 28 days following the date of exchange of contracts.

2. If the title was not proved before contract it must be done now. A form called **requisitions on title** is sent by the purchaser's solicitors to the vendor's solicitors. If the answers are not satisfactory, then the purchaser may terminate the contract. Nowadays, most solicitors prove title before contract, to save time.

3. If the title to the land is registered, the vendor's solicitors send the purchaser an **authority to inspect** the register to **search** for encumbrances which may have been entered since the date of the office copy entries. The purchaser's solicitors therefore sends a **search** form to the Land Registry.

   If the land is unregistered, a search is made at the Land Charges Department against the vendor.

4. Each certificate is dated and provides protection for the purchaser against further entries being made, by which he would be bound, provided he completed within a certain number of days of the date of the certificate.

5. The vendor's solicitors prepare a completion statement, showing the amount due on completion. This will not necessarily be only the 90 per cent balance of the purchase price, but will also include sums for carpets etc., apportioned rates, ground rent etc.

6. The purchaser's solicitors will have drafted, either a document called a **conveyance** if the land is unregistered, or a **transfer** if the land is registered (*see* Figs 5.9 & 5.10). This is sent to the vendor's solicitors for approval.

7. On approval, the purchaser's solicitors engross the deed. This deed, on completion, operates, to pass all the legal estate from the vendor to the purchaser.

   The deed is sent to the vendor for his signature (execution). The deed may have already been signed by the purchaser, but this is only necessary if the purchaser has to be bound by restrictive covenants.

8. Provided the searches come back clear from the Land Registry or the Land Charges Department, the purchaser's solicitors can then proceed to complete the transaction.

9. (i) It is usual for completion to take place in person at the vendor's solicitors office, but if the vendor is paying off a mortgage then completion is arranged at his mortgagee's solicitors' office. Nowadays, completion can be done by post, with the money being transferred by telephone through the banking system. This calls for split second timing, as the purchaser's money cannot be sent, unless it is absolutely certain that the land will be conveyed to him that day.

   (ii) on completion the money is handed over in return for the transfer or conveyance, plus any other old title deeds, together with the keys to the property (the deeds represent legal ownership, the keys to possession).

Example of a conveyance of land the title to which is unregistered

Stamps
(1) Duty £600.00
(2) P. D.

T H I S   C O N V E Y A N C E   dated 1st August 1984 is made BETWEEN

(1) URIAH HEAP of Bleak House Lawyers Lane Leatherbottom Blistershire (the Vendor) (2) PERCY PUMBLECHOOK and LIZA PUMBLECHOOK both of "Drowsy Cottage" Sleepers Lane Slumberwick Snoreshire (the Purchasers).

W H E R E A S

(1) The Vendor is seised of the property hereby conveyed for an estate in fee simple absolute in possession subject as hereinafter mentioned but otherwise free from encumbrances.

(2) The Vendor has agreed to sell his freehold estate in the said property to the Purchasers for the sum of sixty thousand pounds.

NOW THIS DEED WITNESSETH

1. The Vendor as Beneficial Owner conveys to the Purchasers his freehold estate in the property described in the Schedule (the Property) to hold unto the Purchasers in fee simple as joint tenants at law and in equity.

2. The Vendor acknowledges receipt from the Purchasers of sixty thousand pounds (£60,000.00) the purchase price of the Property.

3. The Property is conveyed with the benefit of and subject to the matters contained in the Conveyance dated 21st May 1936 and made between (1) ABEL MAGWITCH (2) JOE GARGERY (the 1936 Conveyance)

S C H E D U L E

The land together with the dwellinghouse stables and outbuildings erected thereon known as Bleak House Lawyers Lane Leatherbottom Blistershire described in and coloured pink on the Plan annexed to the 1936 Conveyance.

Signed sealed and delivered
by URIAH HEAP in the presence of

Name ....

Address ....

....

Occupation ....

Fig. 5.9 Example of a conveyance of land

Example of a transfer of land the title to which is registered

Stamps

(1) Duty
£600.00
(2) P. D.

H. M. LAND REGISTRY

LAND REGISTRATION ACTS 1925 TO 1971

County of Blistershire - Leatherbottom District

Title No. BL.5678910

Property: Bleak House Lawyers Lane Leatherbottom

Date: 1st August 1984

In consideration of sixty thousand pounds (£60,000.00) the receipt of which
is hereby acknowledged I URIAH HEAP of Bleak House Lawyers Lane Leatherbottom
Blistershire as Beneficial Owner hereby transfer to PERCY PUMBLECHOOK and
LIZA PUMBLECHOOK both of "Drowsy Cottage" Sleepers Lane Slumberwick Snoreshire
as joint tenants at law and in equity the land comprised in the title above
referred to.

Signed sealed and delivered   *Uriah Heap*
by URIAH HEAP in the presence of

Name   ....

Address   ....

           ....

Occupation ....

Fig. 5.10 Example of a transfer of land

Post-completion

1. The purchaser's solicitors must get the transfer or conveyance **stamped** with evidence of payment of **stamp duty** or tax, payable on certain legal documents. In effect, it is a tax paid on certain legal transactions, e.g., at present, a purchaser buying a house costing £60,000 will have to pay £600 stamp duty.
2. Particulars of the transaction must also be given to the Inland Revenue. This will be scrutinized by the **district valuer**, to check that the purchase price is not too low, in which case there may be a gift element, which would involve the payment of **capital transfer tax**.
3. If the land is registered, certain documents have to be completed and submitted to the Land Registry, together with the transfer and any mortgage. The Land Registry then issues a **land certificate** if the land is unmortgaged and a **charge certificate** if the land is mortgaged.
4. Finally, if the property is mortgaged all the deeds must be sent to the mortgagee to protect his security.

CHAPTER 6

Pure personalty

Introduction – Types of personal property

As we have already seen, pure personalty are **things** as opposed to land. They can be tangible or intangible, i.e. they can be things we can actually feel and touch, such as a brick or a lorry, i.e. chattels personal, or they can be things which we cannot touch, but will, nevertheless, have value, such as a patent, or a debt (*see* Fig. 6.1).

Tangible things are also known as **choses** (things) **in possession**, as they are capable of being possessed, and if they are taken away from their owner, he can physically take repossession. Intangible things are called **choses in action** as the only way an owner can enforce his rights in relation to them is to take court action.

Chattels personal – choses in possession – tangible property – moveables – goods

Transfer of ownership

Ownership of chattels can be transferred very simply by merely

Pure personality

Choses in possession
(tangible goods i.e. things which can be touched and the court can order repossession of the thing itself, e.g.: bricks; lorries; tools; animals; timber; furniture; jewelry, etc.)

Choses in action
(intangible goods i.e. things which represent value but which have no intrinsic value themselves. A court can only award damages in a court action, e.g.: bills of exchange; life insurance policies; debts; patents; trademarks; copyright; company shares; goodwill in a business

Fig. 6.1 Categories and examples of pure personalty

delivering the goods into the hands of the transferee. There must however, be an intention to transfer ownership, and not mere possession.

So, if I give you a present of a book, then that is sufficient to transfer ownership from me to you. If I lend you my book, I have no intention of transferring ownership. Therefore, despite delivery, I still own the book.

Contracts for the sale of goods

Because of the frequency of such transactions, the common law developed many rules relating to contracts for the sale of goods (chattels). In 1873, Parliament codified the law in the first Sale of Goods Act and this has now been updated and consolidated in the Sale of Goods Act 1979. However, the Act specifically states that the common law rules of contract still apply, unless they are inconsistent with the Act.

The builder should be fully aware of the main principles of the Act, as all building materials, tools of trade, plant and equipment bought and sold will come under the ambit of this Act.

What are goods?

Goods include all chattels personal (*see* p. 168), but not choses in action or money. Also, ships and things attached to the land, but which it was agreed would be detached before contract, are goods, e.g., timber.

The goods may be **specified** i.e. identified and agreed upon at the time of the contract e.g. my red Ford Sierra, registration number A123 XYZ. The goods may be **unascertained** such as a ten ton truck or 3,000 bricks, or even goods which have not yet been manufactured (*future goods*) e.g. a cement mixer, type No. 64C. **Ascertained** goods are goods identified and agreed upon after the contract, i.e. they were unascertained at the time of the contract, but became fixed or ascertained before delivery.

This Act does not apply to barter unless there is some element of part exchange. Nor does it apply to contracts for the supply of work and materials (the Supply of Goods and Services Act 1982 applies to these types of contract, *see* p. 89).

Forming the contract

All the usual elements apply and any form can be employed (*see* Ch. 4). But, by S.1 a contract for the sale of goods is one 'Whereby the seller transfers or agrees to transfer the property in goods to a buyer for a money consideration called the price'. Thus, the consideration is money in exchange for goods.

The price should preferably be fixed by the parties, although it can be fixed by reference to past dealings, or a stipulated method or even left up to a third party to decide. If no price or method of fixing is agreed, a reasonable sum should be paid (if it was obviously a contract but not if it was a gift.)

The effect of breach of terms in a contract for the sale of goods

For general discussion of terms, *see* p. 88. The terms will be those expressed between the parties plus those implied by the Act (if not expressed by the parties).

Breach of warranty.   A warranty is a contractual term which is of minor significance. Under S.62, damages only can be recovered.

Breach of condition.   A condition is a term of vital importance. If there is a breach, then the contract can be repudiated (set aside) under the Act, the goods can be rejected and the purchase price recovered.

By S.11 a plaintiff can choose whether to treat a breach of condition as a breach of warranty. This means he can keep the goods, but sue for damages. He has no choice in the matter however if he has accepted the goods or part of them and can only sue for damages, unless the contrary was agreed between the parties in the contract.

The most important terms implied by the Act and to be performed by the seller

Title (ownership): S.12(1)a: implied condition

This section *cannot* be excluded by agreement in any contract.

In the case of a **sale**, the seller must have a right to sell and in the case of an **agreement** to sell, the seller must have a right to sell at the time the property (the right of ownership) passes to the buyer. Thus, if John agrees to buy a lorry from Lorry Suppliers plc, then, without having to mention anything concerning ownership, he can assume that either the company already owns the lorry or they have a right to sell it in some other capacity (e.g. as an agent) or they will have a right to sell it when the time comes to transfer ownership. Obviously, if there is a breach of such a term, John would have no rights in the lorry and when it is recovered by the true owner, he can sue for the total purchase price of the lorry, even though he has been using it for some time and even though normally, depreciation would be taken into account.

Sales by description: S.13: implied condition

A sale by description is one where the article is referred to by a description such as a Ford Sierra or a tin of Heinz Baked Beans

selected by a buyer in a supermarket or half-inch thick staves or suit
No. 123 in a mail order catalogue. A sale can be a sale by description,
even if the purchaser has seen the goods, but is still expecting that they
are of a certain type, e.g. your 1980 Porsche reg. No. ABC 123Y.

Section 13 implies a condition into such contracts that the goods
must comply with the description. If they do not, the buyer can
repudiate or sue for damages. This is so, even if the goods are
otherwise of merchantable quality. If for example the Porsche turns out
to be a 1978 model, it is not what you had intended to buy. In *Arcos* v.
Ronaason (1933) for example, a buyer ordered 'half-inch thick' staves.
When they were delivered, the majority were between 'a half and nine-
sixteenths of an inch thick.' There was nothing wrong with them, but
they were not as specified. Therefore they could be rejected. This is
very important in building work, where measurements are of crucial
importance.

The word 'description' also covers the mode of packing, e.g. in
Christmas wrapping; quantity, e.g. in boxes of a dozen; and the date of
shipment, which can be very important for perishable goods.

If the sale is by sample and description, then the goods must
correspond with both.

Merchantable quality: S.14

Section 14 (1) restates the common law rule 'caveat emptor,' i.e. the
buyer should be careful when purchasing goods, examining them for
obvious defects etc.

The following terms are only implied into sales made in the course
of a business and do *not* apply to private sales.

Implied condition: S.14 (2). Goods sold must be of a merchantable
quality which is defined under S.62 as: 'fit for the purpose(s) for which
goods of that kind are commonly bought as it is reasonable to expect,
having regard to any description applied to them, the price and all
other relevant circumstances.'

Thus, while sale goods may be reduced in price, this does not mean
that they should be of any less 'merchantable quality' unless they have
descriptions like 'seconds' or they are so cheap for example in a
closing-down sale that no-one could expect them to be of top quality.
Each case may be different because of the use of the words 'reasonable
to expect' etc.

However, if one pays the normal price for such goods, then they
must not fall apart immediately or even within a reasonable time and
they must do the job they were designed for. Buttons falling off on the
first wearing would not make the clothes unmerchantable for example.

As this is a condition, if the goods are not of merchantable quality,
the contract can be repudiated and the purchase price must be
refunded by the seller. No-one is under any duty to accept a credit note

in lieu. Signs saying 'no refunds' are contrary to fair trading legislation and have no effect. It should be noted that because of privity of contract, only the seller is liable for breach of this condition. There is no contractual link whatsoever with the manufacturer of the article (unless he also sold it to the buyer). Thus, a shopkeeper who fobs a customer off with the words 'We'll send it back to the manufacturer' is trying to avoid his responsibilities, unless he believes that the article has not undergone reasonable use and suspects that the buyer is trying to defraud him.

Once again, evidence is all important to support one's case, especially if it eventually goes to court. Receipts with the date of purchase should be kept, and if possible, evidence of the amount of use should be produced.

Exceptions. Section 14(2), conditions as to merchantable quality are not implied into contracts where the defects were specifically drawn to the attention of the buyer **before** the contract was made.

Nor is the condition implied into a contract where the buyer examines the goods **before** the contract was entered into, and the examination should have revealed those defects.

Thus, goods sold 'as seen', 'with all faults' or even 'seconds' should be approached with care. 'You get what you pay for' really applies here.

Fitness for a particular purpose: S.14 (3): implied condition. Once again, this condition is only implied into a contract made in the course of a business and does not apply to a private sale.

Thus, if the buyer makes known to the seller either by telling him or by writing to him or even by implication, the purpose for which he wants to buy the goods, then S.14(3) implies a condition into that contract that the goods must be **fit for that purpose**.

This purpose would not have to be explained or implied if it was obvious what one was going to use the article for, e.g. a hot water bottle is designed to hold hot (but not boiling) water.

So for example in *McAlpine & Sons Ltd* v. *Minimax Ltd* (1970). McAlpines bought four carbon dioxide fire extinguishers from Minimax Ltd. A fire in a timber site hut in which there were 2 extinguishers was seriously worsened when the extinguishers were used. The extinguishers exploded causing far greater damage than if they had not been used. Obviously, the court held that they were not fit for the particular purpose for which they had been bought.

In building, contractors will often rely on the skill and judgment of manufacturers selling goods to them. It must be made quite clear in the contract therefore, that the buyer is relying on their skill in choosing a product for the particular job. Sometimes there will be joint reliance, i.e. the builder will use his judgment in relation to choice of goods in one area but relies on the seller in another. There may nevertheless be a breach by the seller if this judgment appears to be wrong, even if the goods are otherwise of merchantable quality, i.e. fit for the general purpose, but not for the particular purpose (*see* also p. 183).

Sale by sample: S.15: implied condition

Where goods are ordered by reference to a sample, then S.15 implies that the bulk must correspond with the sample in quality. A reasonable opportunity must be given to the buyer to check this and the goods must not be unmerchantable in a way which an examination would not reveal.

A sale by sample usually occurs where one is buying something which can vary in quality, such as facing bricks or wood or top soil. The buyer only wants to buy the goods if the goods delivered are all the same quality as that shown to him by the seller or the sales representative. Thus, when the goods are delivered, the buyer must (as soon as possible) examine the goods and check that they are of the quality he expects. If not he can reject the goods and recover the purchase price or keep them, but ask for damages, (in practice a discount or refund) unless the matter goes to court, in which case, damages will be assessed.

Can the above conditions be excluded?   Section 12, the condition as to title can **never** be excluded by agreement, or in any other way.

In consumer sales, Ss. 13–15 can not be excluded by the seller. A consumer sale is a sale made by a seller who is selling goods as a business to someone else for private use who is not buying in the course of a business. Thus, to a certain extent, it pays to buy from people selling goods as their trade, even if they have only just started.

When buying from private individuals, e.g. where a student buys a motor bike from another, or where a building contractor (who is in business and thus not a consumer) buys from a supplier, Ss. 13–15 **can be excluded**. The exclusion may be by express agreement between the parties, or it may be inferred from previous dealings between them. To be valid, the exclusion must be reasonable. Thus, the buyer must have known about the exclusion and it must have been possible for him to have bought the goods elsewhere without such an exclusion, e.g. from the seller or from some other source. Also, an exclusion clause is more likely to be reasonable where the goods were manufactured to the buyers specification. Nor must the buyer have been induced to agree to the exclusion, e.g. by giving him a discount.

Whether the exclusion of any other type of liability is valid, will depend on whether it satisfies S.3 of the Unfair Contract Terms Act 1977 (*see* p. 93).

Other duties of the seller

When must the goods be delivered?

Time for performance is not of the essence, unless the parties make it
so, either by express agreement or by implication. Thus the order of a
suit for a wedding should be made conditional on receiving the suit by
a particular date. If payment is to be required on a particular date,
then this must be expressly stated in the contract, S.10.

If the goods have not been delivered within a reasonable time, then
the buyer can introduce a new term making time of the essence e.g. by
giving the seller 14 days in which to produce the goods, failing which
the contract will be set aside. The length of notice must be reasonable.

Must the seller deliver the right quantity of goods?

Yes, by S.30, if the seller delivers a larger or smaller amount than was
ordered, then the buyer can reject all the goods, accept all the goods or
accept the right amount and reject the rest. But, if the buyer accepts
the larger amount, he must pay for the extra amount at the contract
rate.

Section 30 does not apply if the differences are so tiny as to be
inconsequential.

Duties of the buyer

Paying for the goods

He should normally pay on delivery unless the contrary has been
agreed.

Taking delivery

If he fails to take delivery of the goods, he is in breach of contract.

Remedies

If the seller has suffered loss through non-acceptance or late payment,
he can sue for damages. He can also sell the goods (even though
strictly speaking they are already sold) if the goods are perishable, such
as ready mixed concrete. If the goods have been accepted, but not paid
for, there is a breach of condition and the buyer can recover the goods
and claim damages if he has suffered loss.

Transferring ownership of goods from seller to buyer

On Monday Sam agrees to sell his car to Bill for £2,000, which he pays
for by cheque. Bill says he will pick it up on Saturday as he is away all

week on business. On Wednesday the cheque is cleared. On Thursday the car develops some electrical problem and catches fire. Whose responsibility is it? Who suffers the loss? (see Fig. 6.2).
There is no easy answer.

The answer in any event depends on the question, when does the property (title or ownership) in the goods, pass to the buyer. This is because, by S.20, the **risk** (responsibility for the goods) passes to the buyer at the same time as property passes **unless otherwise agreed**.

We are also helped by the fact, that the car is classified as 'specific' goods (*see* p. 169), for the Act lays down rules which are applied depending on whether the goods are specific or unascertained.

Thus to answer the question, we would have to know what the parties agreed about the passing of property, because by S.17, property passes in specific goods **when the parties intend** it to pass. So Sam and Bill could agree that property would pass on Wednesday or when the cheque was cleared or when he was going to pick it up on Saturday. The risk would pass at the same time unless the contrary was agreed. If there is a delay in delivery (or collection), responsibility falls on the one who was at fault.

The rules

Unascertained goods: S.16. For example 10 tonnes of slag, sand, potatoes, etc. Property cannot pass until the goods become earmarked or set aside for the particular contract, when they then become ascertained.

Specific or ascertained goods: S.17. For example my brown Metro reg. A456 BRO. The property passes when the parties intend it to pass, i.e. there must be an agreement, either express or one implied from previous dealings. So S.17 could be applied to the example involving Sam and Bill.

Fig. 6.2 Why it is important to determine when property passes

If there is no agreement or contrary intention shown, then the following rules must be applied: S.18

Rule 1.

Unconditional contracts for the sale of specific goods in a deliverable state. Here, the property passes when the contract is made, even though time for delivery or payment is postponed.

Thus, this could have occurred in our example, in which case, the car would have become the property of Bill at the time of the agreement to buy. He should have therefore taken out insurance immediately, even though he wasn't picking up the car until Saturday (see Fig. 6.3).

Fig. 6.3 Rule 1

Rule 2.

Sales of specific goods, where the seller must do something to put them into a deliverable state. In this case, the property in the goods cannot pass until the goods have been put into a deliverable state and he must then give the buyer notice of this.

So Sam may have agreed to put new tyres on the car and property would not pass until he had done this and told Bill. (see Fig. 6.4)

Fig. 6.4 Rule 2

Rule 3.

Sales of specific goods where the seller has to do something to ascertain the price, such as weighing, testing, measuring them etc   The seller must do this and give notice, and property will then pass to the buyer. (see Fig. 6.5)

Contract to sell all the apples in an orchard at £5 per ton

Fig. 6.5   Rule 3

Rule 4.

Goods sold on approval, or on a sale or return basis.   Property will only pass to the buyer when either of the following occurs.
   First, if he signifies that he has accepted the goods, such as, by telling the seller, or adopts the goods, such as, by using them, (or selling them to a third party). (see Fig. 6.6)
   Secondly, if he keeps the goods beyond the time laid down, or if no time was specified, after a reasonable period without signifying that he is not going to accept them. (see Fig. 6.6)

Rule 5.

Unascertained or future goods sold by description.   For example 10 tonnes next harvest's corn. Property passes when the goods in a deliverable state are unconditionally appropriated to that contract with the consent of the other and notice is given of that fact. (see Fig. 6.7). (Note: the above rules are only applied in the absence of agreement on such matters.)

Reservation of title under S.19

Under S.19 of the Sale of Goods Act 1979, in a contract for the sale of

Fig. 6.6 Rule 4

Fig. 6.7 Rule 5

specific goods or where the goods have been subsequently appropriated to the contract, the seller may either by an express term of the contract or at the time of appropriation, reserve title to the goods until certain conditions are fulfilled. Thus, despite delivery to the buyer or to a carrier, the ownership of the goods **does not pass** until the conditions are met by the seller. A common condition imposed is that the goods must be paid for in order for the property to pass.

A term of this nature was included in the leading case *Aluminium Industrie Vaassen BV* v. *Romalpa Ltd* (1976) under which property was

not to pass until the purchaser, R Ltd. had paid **all** the debts owed to
the seller ABV. Until the sums had been paid, R Ltd. was to hold the
goods for ABV in a fiduciary position. The contract permitted such
goods to be sold but unfortunately did not expressly deal with
what was to happen to the proceeds. R Ltd. sold some of the goods
and then went into liquidation. A sum of £35,000 was held in a
separate bank account by R Ltd's liquidator as representing the
proceeds of sale of the goods belonging to ABV. ABV asked for a
tracing order to recover the money from this account. The Court of
Appeal allowed this as it was said that the duty to account for moneys
acquired by such a sub-sale was part and parcel of the fiduciary
relationship. (Tracing is an equitable right of persons in such situations
as above to recover from the holder assets to which they are entitled or
other assets which have been bought using the proceeds of sale of the
original assets).

Thus, a builder may have to buy building materials subject to such
terms. How does this fit into a building contract situation?

It should be noted that once goods become incorporated into the
building works they become fixtures and thus property in the materials
passes to the owner of the land (*see* p. 134). Also by Cl. 16.1 of the JCT
contract, property passes to the employer if the builder has unfixed
materials on site and has been paid for them under an interim
certificate. Furthermore, by Cl. 16.2, if the value of materials stored
off-site has been included in an interim certificate by virtue of Cl. 30.3
(*see* post), such materials become the property of the employer.

By Cl. 30.3 of the JCT contract, an amount in an interim certificate
may include the value of goods not yet delivered to site, provided the
goods have been ordered in writing by the contractor or sub-contractor
and the contract expressly provides that the property (ownership) in
the goods shall pass unconditionally to the contractor or the sub-
contractor, as the case may be, not later than the event set out in Cl.
30.3.2 and 30.3.3. These clauses state that nothing must remain to be
done to the materials prior to incorporation into the works and they
should have been set aside as ready for the works marked with the
name of the employer and the works, destination.

Such reservation of title terms under S.19 may thus give the supplier
of the materials a form of security, so that on bankruptcy or
liquidation of a building firm, the suppliers may claim priority over
other creditors.

Destruction of specific goods

If the goods are destroyed **before** the contract is entered into, the
contract is **void**.

If the goods are destroyed **after** the contract is made but **before** the
risk has passed, then the contract becomes **void**.

If the goods are destroyed **after** the risk has passed, the buyer bears
the loss.

Conclusions

Thus, building contractors' main concerns with contracts for the sale of goods, are the following.

Time: S.10

Date of delivery must be specified or agreed between the parties (*see* p. 174). Date for payment must also be agreed.

Quality of correspondence with description or sample Ss. 13–15

As a building contractor's contract is not a consumer contract, these implied conditions can be excluded. This should be checked by reading the small print before agreement, otherwise it would be difficult to prove that there had not been an agreement on the exclusion.

On delivery of the goods, they should be checked immediately, preferably while the delivery men are still there, so that if they are not as required, the goods can be returned.

Sometimes the supplier inserts a clause giving a time in which goods can be returned e.g with 24 hours of delivery, so there must be no delay, otherwise there will be no chance of rejection and only damages can be claimed. In a building contract, it is more important to have the correct supplies at the right time than to have the chance of money compensation at a later date. Immediate rejection gives the building contractor a chance to get supplies elsewhere.

Transfer of ownership under hire purchase and consumer credit agreements

Not everyone is in the fortunate position of being able to buy goods outright for cash. Many people choose to buy their goods by paying in instalments. There are three different ways of buying goods in this way.

By hire purchase

Under this arrangement, the seller of goods **hires** them to the purchaser and the contract of hire gives the purchaser the option to buy after a certain number of instalments have been paid (usually the last). If the purchaser exercises the option there is a transfer of ownership of the goods to him. Thus, in a hire purchase agreement, the ownership of the goods remains with the seller unless and until the hirer exercises his option to purchase (*see* Fig. 6.8).

Under the Supply of Goods (Implied Terms) Act 1973, as substituted by the Consumer Credit Act 1974, there are terms implied into a hire purchase agreement similar to those contained in Ss. 12–15 of the Sale of Goods Act 1979. Thus, by S.8, there is an implied condition that the seller will have a right to sell the goods at the time property is to pass

Fig. 6.8   Diagram to illustrate a hire purchase agreement

to the hire-purchaser. Also by S.8, there are implied warranties concerning freedom from encumbrances and enjoyment of quiet possession. By S.9, goods bailed or hired by description must correspond to their description. By S.10 there are implied conditions as to merchantable quality and fitness for a particular purpose. By S.11, there is an implied condition concerning sales by sample that the goods must correspond with the sample in quality (*see* pp. 171–3).

Credit sale agreements

Here the purchaser contracts to buy the goods but he is to pay for them in instalments. The Sale of Goods Act 1979 covers such transactions, and the ownership of the property passes to the purchaser in accordance with S.18.

The Sale of Goods Act 1979 sections concerning implied terms as to title, sales by description and merchantable quality and sales by sample therefore also apply (*see* pp. 171–3).

Conditional sale agreements

Here there is a contract to buy the goods but it contains a term by which the ownership of the goods does not pass until all the instalments are paid. Whilst the Sale of Goods Act 1979 applies as to the implied terms of quality, etc., because of this conditional aspect, as to the passing of ownership, S.18 does not apply.

Protection of consumers who buy goods on credit

Traditionally, contracts for the sale of goods on credit have been weighted against the consumer who is generally in a weaker position for a number of reasons. This is largely due to the fact that the suppliers have drawn up standard contracts protecting their own interests and the consumer has little choice in using that standard contract (*see* p. 77).

The Consumer Credit Act 1974 has introduced a number of statutory protections for the consumer. For example, agreements must be in a particular form clearly setting out important terms; where an agreement is entered into at some other place than the supplier's place of business, then the purchaser has an opportunity to change his mind, etc.

Unfortunately this Act only applies to agreements with consumers and a consumer cannot be a corporation nor must they be buying in connection with business. Thus, builders who are buying goods for their business will generally be unaffected by these rules.

Contracts for the exchange or barter of goods

It is not uncommon nowadays to find that someone is offered goods in exchange for other goods or services, especially in times of high unemployment. The Sale of Goods Act 1979 only applies to goods in exchange for money. However, the Supply of Goods & Services Act 1982 now applies to contracts of exchange or barter.

Thus, terms as to title (S.2); compliance with description (S.3); quality & fitness (S.4) and sales by sample (S.5) are implied by the Act (*see* below).

As far as part exchange is concerned, it seems from the few decisions made that part exchange contracts are covered by the 1979 Act, especially in relation to the new or more expensive item. As for the traded-in old goods, it also appears that the 1979 Act applies.

Contracts for the supply of work & materials

We saw earlier that the 1979 Act did not apply to contracts for work and materials. Thus, building contracts are not covered by that Act despite the fact that a large part of the contract's performance depends on the incorporation of goods belonging to the builder. The rest of the contract is to supply work and labour.

The new Act, however, does apply to such contracts.

By S.2 there is an implied condition that the transferor of goods (repairer, builder, etc.) has the right to transfer **ownership** of goods. If there is a breach then the contract may be repudiated and a full refund may be claimed. This is so even if the goods have been incorporated into the building already. Extra damages may be claimed if, for example, someone else has to carry out the job at a higher cost. S.2 applies to all such transfers in business or in private.

Section 2 also implies warranties regarding freedom from encumbrances and quiet possession (*see* p. 142).

There is no equivalent to S.18 of the Sale of Goods Act 1979 and thus normally property will pass on completion of the contract. However, in the case of building work, once materials have been incorporated as fixtures, property then usually passes to the land owner.

Section 3 implies a condition that where the goods are transferred by description, then the goods will correspond with the description. Perhaps this will end the days of paying the book price for a motor part which has been 'modified' to fit.

If goods are transferred in the course of a business, then under S.4 there is an implied condition that the goods must be of merchantable quality and they must also be fit for any particular purpose for which these goods have been supplied. Thus, a builder in supplying materials for building work must make sure that they are of merchantable quality. If particular materials have been specified in the contract, then the builder must still make sure that the materials are of merchantable quality but does not have to ascertain that they are fit for a particular purpose as the contract specifications have overriden this requirement. It is still possible, however that he could be found to be negligent if he failed to point out to the client that the materials were not suitable for the particular purpose. To cover himself he should disclaim liability for the materials, keeping evidence of the client's knowledge of the disclaimer trusting that the disclaimer would be regarded as reasonable under the Unfair Contract Terms Act 1977. Otherwise he should probably refuse to take on the contract in the first place. In *Young & Martin Ltd* v. *McManus Childs Ltd* (1969) M Ltd., a building contractor, sub-contracted roofing work to Y Ltd., specifying a particular type of tile. Y Ltd. then sub-contracted the work to another firm B. B bought the tiles direct from the manufacturers S. The tiles had not been made properly and they were defective. As a result the roofs of seventeen houses needed replacing. M Ltd. sued Y Ltd., who were held to be in breach of an implied term (at common law) that these tiles should have been of merchantable quality. Y Ltd. would, of course, have then been able to recover the damages paid from B under an indemnity in the sub-sub-contract and B could have claimed for breach of S.14 of the Sale of Goods Act against the manufacturers. (*see* Fig. 6.9).

See Cl. 8 of the JCT contract as to work & materials and Cl. 36 where the supplier of goods is a nominated supplier. In the latter case the building contractor is not liable for special purposes of specified materials supplied by a nominated supplier. He is, of course, still liable if they are of unmerchantable quality for general purposes as in *Young & Martin Ltd* v. *McManus Childs Ltd* (1969).

If goods are referred to by sample then under S.5, there is an implied condition that the bulk must correspond with the sample. The transferee must have a reasonable opportunity of comparing the bulk with the sample and the goods must be free from any defect rendering them unmerchantable which would not be apparent on reasonable examination of the sample. If a supply is by both sample and description then the transferor must comply with S.5 and S.3.

We have only dealt here with the goods element of a building contract under the Supply of Goods & Services Act 1982. The part

M. Ltd.

Sub-contract specifying a
particular type of roofing tile

Y. Ltd.

Sub-sub-contract

B

Contract for the sale of
goods (tiles)

Suppliers

Fig. 6.9 *Young & Martin Ltd.* v. *McManus, Childs Ltd.* 1969

dealing with implied terms as to the work and labour element is dealt
with in Ch. 4 on contract.

Passing of property and risk

Contracts for the supply of building materials must be read in
conjunction with the main contract, so that insurance is maintained to
cover risk of loss, whether the materials are on site or off and whether
property has passed or not (*see* p. 179).

Transfer of possession of chattels

Like land, physical things can be in someone else's possession. This can
be for a variety of reasons. The possessor may have hired the thing, or
borrowed it, or be doing something to it, such as mending it, or may
be holding it as security for a loan. This temporary transfer of
possession is called a **bailment**. The transferor is called the **bailor** and
the transferee the **bailee**. After the particular purpose has ended, the
goods are transferred back. It should be noted, that the bailor need **not**
be the owner of the goods. He may be a mere possessor such as an
employee with a company car who bails the car to his garage for
repair. This sort of bailment is probably the most common. The bailee
is under a duty to look after the goods in his care, and must hand
them back to the owner or his agent unless payment has not been
made, in which case he has a **lien** i.e. a right to hold the goods pending
payment.

If someone finds goods, and keeps them in his possession, he will become a bailee of those goods, pending their return to the owner.

Types of bailment

Hire

For example, television, ships, telephones, video recorders, motor cars, lorries, JCB's etc. Hire agreements are also called leases or rental agreements or even finance leasing. Legally, however, they are treated as contracts of hire. The important element is that there is a complete transfer of possession to the hirer.

Obviously, the hirer, as bailee, must look after the goods during the hire period, but he is not responsible for damage or loss to them, unless caused by his own negligence. If the bailee tries to sell the goods, then the hire agreement, automatically comes to an end, and the bailor can seek repossession.

If the hire agreement could last for more than 3 months for a rental of less than £5,000 then, this is a consumer hire agreement under the Consumer Credit Act 1974 and statutory formalities have to be complied with. The person hiring the goods should nevertheless make sure that they are aware of the contents of the agreement.

Hirers have also been given greater protection in the Supply of Goods and Services Act 1982.

Under this Act, special terms are now implied into the contract of hire. This means, that without having to mention them, important duties are imposed on the owner of equipment, who lends goods for a consideration. The relevant sections are Ss. 6–10.

These sections closely follow the implied terms contained in the Sale of Goods Act 1979 (see pp. 171–3).

By S.7 there is an implied condition that the bailor has the right to transfer possession to the bailee. Thus, the bailor must either own the goods or he must have lawful possession. There is also an implied warranty that the bailee will enjoy quiet possession except so far as possession may be disturbed by the owner of any charge or encumbrance disclosed to the bailee prior to the contract. By S.7(3) the previous sections do not affect the right of the bailor to repossess the goods under an express or implied term of the contract e.g. if the hirer does not pay the rental.

If the property has been hired by description, then by S.8, there is an implied condition that the goods comply with that description. This can be very important in car fleet hiring agreements.

Section 9 follows closely S.14 of the Sale of Goods Act 1979. Thus, S.9(1) states that the hirer must beware. Section 9 only applies to goods bailed in the course of a business whereas Ss. 7, 8 and 10 apply to all contracts of hire. Section 9(2) imposes an implied condition that the goods supplied must be of merchantable quality. This is defined in S.9(9) as 'fit for the purpose or purposes for which goods of that kind are commonly supplied as is reasonable to expect, having regard to any description applied to them, the consideration ... and all other relevant circumstances.'

Thus, the goods must not only be fit from the beginning of the contract, but they must remain so for a reasonable time. However, the Act does not impose an implied condition that the goods must be of merchantable quality for the duration of the contract of hire. This is usually because the owner expressly contracts to service and maintain the goods. The inclusion of such a clause should therefore be checked. There is no implied right to have unlimited maintenance throughout the contractual period.

Note, that S.9(3) does not apply to goods examined by the bailee **before** contract or to defects which were specifically drawn to the bailee's attention prior to contract.

By S9(4) and S.9(5) there is an implied condition that where goods are bailed for a particular purpose which was made known to the bailor either expressly or impliedly, then those goods must be suitable for that particular purpose. This will be so unless circumstances show that the bailee did not rely on the skill or judgment of the bailor.

Note that S.9 also applies if the goods are hired from a finance house although supplied by the retailer who sold the goods to the finance house before hire. Section 9(4) and (5) will also apply even if a particular purpose was made known only to the 'credit broker' i.e. the retailer who arranged for the goods to be sold to the finance house before hire.

Loan

A loan may be gratuitous i.e. with no payment, or it may arise from a contract, in which case, there must be some sort of consideration.

Here the borrower must use the goods loaned, provided he complies with the conditions of the loan e.g. he must not drive the motor car in the dark at night.

During the bailment, the borrower is responsible for the goods and must take reasonable care of them, but he is not responsible for 'fair wear and tear' i.e. the normal wear associated with normal use. He is liable for his own negligence and dishonesty as well as that of his employees, particularly if he did not use reasonable care when employing them. He is never liable for Acts of God or war or robbery with violence.

At the end of the loan, the goods must be returned, to comply with the terms of the contract, 'give it to me back next week'. If there is no contract, because the borrower is giving no consideration to the lender, his duties will be determined by torts which deal with the unlawful keeping of or interference with chattels. Such torts are beyond the scope of this book.

Pledge or pawn

Chattels may be pledged or pawned (the words are almost interchangeable) as a method of raising money. The goods are transferred into the possession of the lender (pawnee) by the owner (pawnor), where they act as security for a loan made to the pawnor.

The owner of the goods is then entitled to have the goods returned to him, provided he repays the loan with interest within a specified period. The lender of the money becomes a bailee of the goods and must make sure that the goods are not damaged or lost during the bailment through his negligence. Until the loan is repaid, the lender retains a **lien** over the property, and after a specified time, can then sell the goods to recover his loss. If there is any money over he must then pay the pawnor the balance.

Professional pawnees are called **pawnbrokers** and must be licensed under the Consumer Credit Act 1974. They usually have a symbol of three balls outside their windows.

Goods being prepared or otherwise worked on

As stated before, bailments are very commonly made when getting property repaired. Often this involves incorporating new parts or equipment into the property. For example, if my garage repairs my car, I will expect to pay for all the goods and materials used in the repair such as spark plugs, fan belts etc.

Under the Supply of Goods and Services Act 1982 statutory terms are now implied into contracts for the supply of work and materials (*see* p. 182).

Carriage of goods

Goods carried by owner. Such goods are carried at his own risk and he should therefore have sufficient insurance cover. If goods are being carried by a builder's own lorries, then the driver's duties and the builder's liability depends on the instructions given, the driver's contract of employment, the state of the lorry and the goods and statutory limitations e.g. under the Road Traffic Acts. Thus, if equipment is damaged in transit and there was no fault, then the builder must claim for his loss from his insurance company. If the driver was at fault, then this may be grounds for dismissing or even suing him. If someone else was at fault, then they could be sued in tort.

Goods carried by seller or agent.   In this case the Sale of Goods Act 1979 applies (*see* p. 171).

Goods carried by an independant carrier.   The law depends on whether or not the carrier is a **private carrier** (which is more usual) or a

common carrier. Private carriers are simple bailees, whereas common carriers have greater duties. The law is now supplemented by the Supply of Goods and Services Act 1982 (*see* above).

1. Common carriers. A common carrier is in business to transport anybody or anything by land, sea or air, subject to a few exceptions. He must therefore carry anything for a reasonable sum. If he refuses to do so, he can be sued or even prosecuted.

Furthermore, a common carrier must ensure the safety of the goods entrusted to him, unless the damage was caused by an Act of God, enemy action, because of an inherent defect in the goods, or the fault of the consignor. For this reason he must insure the goods, and he will be liable to the consignor for any loss. This is strict liability and he will not be able to rely on these exceptions if he was negligent. However, the common carrier may exclude this liability by inserting an exemption clause, restricting or excluding his strict liability, subject of course to the Unfair Contract Terms Act 1977.

Obviously as a result of the harsh liability imposed on a common carrier, there are virtually no common carriers left, and most carriers have in their conditions that they are not holding themselves out to be common carriers. Nationalised industries such as British Rail and the National Freight Corporation are not common carriers either. However, private bus companies and parcel delivery services could be.

2. Private carriers. They are bailees and are therefore liable only for negligence. If they wish to exclude their liability they can, within the confines of the Unfair Contract Terms Act 1977.

The following is a summary of the main rights and duties of a private carrier (in addition to those implied by the Supply of Goods & Services Act 1982).

- He must deliver the goods to the consignee or some other specified person at the correct address in accordance with his instructions.
- He must obey any change in instructions given.
- He may act as an **agent of necessity** and sell the goods he is carrying, if the goods are in danger of perishing. In such cases, it must be impossible for him to contact the owner of the goods, and this is unusual nowadays with modern forms of communication.
- He does not hold out that his vehicles are safe to carry the goods.

Choses in action

For example debts, shares, goodwill, negotiable instruments, patents, designs, trademarks, copyrights, life insurance policies and legacies.

Transfer of ownership

Because they are not physical things, it is impossible to transfer possession of choses in action.

To transfer ownership, this must be done by **assignment**, either in accordance with S.136 Law of Property Act 1925 or by the rules in equity, unless there are special rules appropriate for that type e.g. negotiable instruments and shares.

Why would anyone wish to transfer a chose in action? As you can see from the above examples, all have the potential to provide possibly large sums of money and therefore buying power. So whilst a debt, for example, seems to be a strange sort of property, banks and finance houses make their money by owning debts. Should a creditor be short of money then he can sell his debt to someone else to get immediate cash to solve his financial problems.

Example

Creditor is owed £10,000 by debtor payable one year from now with interest from todays date. Creditor needs his money, but cannot call on debtor to pay it yet. He therefore wishes to sell his debt to X to realise some, but not all, of the money. Obviously, X is not going to pay the full amount as there would be no financial benefit to be gained when debtor pays the debt on the due date.

How does he transfer the debt?

1. Transfer under S.136 LPA 1925. The transfer must be in writing and must be of the whole amount, not part only. The transfer document must be signed by the transferor and express notice must be given of the transfer to the debtor. Thus, creditor must transfer, in writing, the whole debt to X and notify debtor, that on the due date, he must pay the sum owed to X and not creditor.

Because the transfer has been done properly, if debtor defaults, then X can sue debtor, without needing to get creditor to join in the action as co-plaintiff (*see* Fig. 6.10).

2. Transfer in equity. If the transfer did not meet the requirements of S.136, e.g. because it was not in writing, then there *must* still be an intention to transfer the debt for it to be valid in **equity**. Notice will still be necessary, but this need not be express, for otherwise, debtor will not be aware that his debt has been taken over by X and may pay creditor instead (creditor may keep the money and X would then have to sue him).

If debtor defaults, X must ask creditor to join him as co-plaintiff in the action to recover the money.

Intellectual property

Patents, registered designs, copyright and trade marks, come within a category of personal property now called **intellectual property**, as they are all concerned with ideas or creative work. They are all choses in

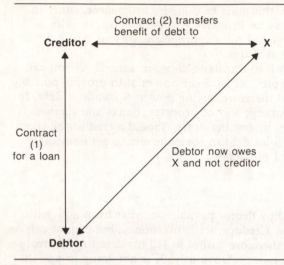

Fig. 6.10 Transfer of a debt

action. Because of their potential value and because of the difficulties of protecting such intangible forms of property, the law has evolved complex rules to enable the creator or owner of the property to safeguard their rights. In particular, they need to be able to stop other people from copying their work or using or manufacturing their inventions without permission. Some protection requires the registration of the invention or design. Nearly all the law is now found in statute law. Because of the international implications, if protection is required in other countries, then international conventions may have to be complied with and legal action would also have to be started within those countries to enforce property rights. This is one area of the law which will eventually benefit from the United Kingdom's membership of the EEC and protection may then be granted in all member states.

The builder will mostly be concerned with copyright, in particular the copyright of plans and possibly patents. Registered designs protected under the Registered Design Act 1949 are more concerned with articles which have an artistic design applied to them, such as a dinner service pattern or a drinking glass design. In certain cases, a design may be covered by both copyright protection and protection under the Registered Design Act 1949. Trade mark protection is more the concern of manufacturers of goods, and this is an area which is giving many problems at present with foreign manufacturers making cheap copies of manufactured goods and then applying a forged registered trademark to the copy.

Copyright

Relevant law

The law is found primarily in the Copyright Act 1956 and the
Copyright Act 1956 (Amendment) Act 1982.

What property rights are owned

The owner of a copyright has the exclusive right to copy, publish,
broadcast or in any way reproduce copies of the copyright material. He
may give permission called a **licence**, to others to reproduce the
material and if a fee is paid this is called a **royalty**. By S.19, the licence
must be signed by the owner or his agent.

What material may be the subject of copyright?

The main Act is in two sections. Both are of relevance for the builder.
Part I deals with: literary, dramatic, musical and artistic work. Part II
deals with: sound recordings, cinematograph films, television and
sound broadcasts and published editions of works.

There are lengthy definitions of the above words and in general,
their meanings are far wider than a laymen would expect. However the
builder will deal with original literary (written) work, as well as
published editions of works. He will also deal with artistic work. This
is defined by S.3 as covering drawings (including architectural
drawings), works of architecture, and artistic craftsmanship. Drawings
do not have to have any artistic quality (unlike a registered design for
example). As a drawing is defined by the Act as covering any diagram,
map, chart or plan, one can see that the builder is mainly concerned
with 'artistic' work for the purposes of this Act.

Artistic works have an additional protection under the Design
Copyright Act 1968 (*see* below).

The builder may also be concerned with the copyright of films, video
tapes, sound recordings for example, when presenting safety lectures to
employees.

What acts are prohibited by the Copyright Act?

Each type of copyright, e.g. literary or artistic, has protection against
certain **'restricted acts'** which are specified within the Act. Such acts are
known as piracy.

Thus, artistic work should not be published, broadcast on television,
or reproduced in any way. Methods of reproduction would include
photocopying. Each set of restricted acts have exceptions which are
strictly applied. For example, literary work may be reproduced for
research or private study, but this exception does *not* apply to
published work.

For how long does the copyright last?

Copyright lasts for the life of the author/designer/maker plus 50 years. If the work is a published work, then copyright is for only 25 years from the end of the year in which it was first published.

How do you create a copyright?

It is created automatically on creation of the copyright work, e.g. on finishing a book or the designs for a house. Nothing need be done or registered with any one. Readers will, however, be familiar with the symbol © which appears in many publications. This is not necessary for legal protection in the United Kingdom, but it is necessary to gain protection in the USA. This is because the USA is party to only one international convention on copyright, the Universal Copyright Convention. That convention requires that all publications should have the copyright symbol ©, together with the name of the copyright owner and year of first publication. Countries such as the United Kingdom who are parties to another convention, the Berne Convention, do not require this. Of course, the protection afforded by other countries, will only be as good as that given to one of their own nationals, no more and no less.

Anyone in breach of the copyright may be sued for damages or an injunction and any profits made from use of the copyright may be ordered to be paid to the owner. In the case of breaches of copyright of building designs or plans however, S.17(4) of the Copyright Act 1956 provides that where a breach of copyright action is being pursued 'in respect of the construction of a building, no injunction shall be made (*a*) after construction of the building has been begun, so as to prevent it from being completed, or (*b*) so as to require the building insofar as it has been constructed, to be demolished'. This may thus leave the architect or builder who prepared the plans with only damages as a remedy.

Who owns the copyright?

Unless varied by agreement, as say, in a contract to write a book for a publisher, the copyright will normally belong to the creator of the material. However under S.4, there are exceptions to this. For our purposes, the most important is where someone is employed to produce designs, in which case, the employer will own the copyright. A person commissioning artistic work, will also own the copyright. So, if you are asked to draw up plans or designs for someone, you should agree on the ownership of the copyright, as otherwise it will belong to the commissioner. It should be noted that the copyright material, e.g. a tape or plan may actually be owned by someone else by agreement, and the copyright could belong to another.

Transfer

Section 36 requires that any transfer should be in writing, signed by the owner or his agent. The transferee will then have full rights to the copyright. All or part of the copyright may be assigned. For example, nowadays, many 'best selling' authors sell the film rights separately, but retain the copyright of the published and the original literary work.

Industrial designs

As mentioned before, 'artistic' work may be given protection under the Design Copyright Act 1968. Artistic work can cover designs of a type registerable under the Registered Design Act 1949 (*see* p. 190), as well as those defined by S.3 of the Copyright Act 1956 (*see* p. 191). Whether the design is capable of registration or not, the Design Copyright Act specifically gives copyright protection for 15 years from the date the *article* is first marketed. Thus, ordinary architectural drawings or plans are not covered by this Act, but are covered by ordinary copyright.

Patents

Merely inventing something is not enough to protect it from being used or copied. So it is important to obtain a patent in order to prevent others from reaping the benefit of one's work. Owning a patent is a valuable piece of property, as those who want to use or manufacture the invention must first obtain a licence and pay a fee for the privilege.

Where are patents obtained from?

In the UK patents are applied for at the Patent Office, and if granted, will give protection in the UK only. Protection in other countries is only afforded to those who have obtained patents in those countries. There are a number of international conventions and treaties which give certain advantages to patentees who have already obtained a patent in one signatory country e.g. the Patent Co-operation Treaty 1970, the European Patent Convention and the Community Patent Convention applicable to the European Economic Community. One application need only be made to the European Patent Office, to give protection in all the EEC countries.

Relevant law

As a result of the European Patent Convention and the Community Patent Convention, British law on patents has been considerably altered. The Patents Act 1977, which codified the law on patents contains new principles of law. The procedures are governed by the Patent Rules 1978. Other applications are governed by the appropriate domestic national law or as influenced by the conventions.

What inventions may be patented

Section 1(1) Patents Act 1977
In order to be able to get a patent, an invention must:
(i) be new;
(ii) involve an inventive step;
(iii) be capable of industrial application;
(iv) *not* be concerned with a discovery, scientific theory, literary, dramatic, musical or artistic work, scheme for performing a mental act, playing a game, or doing business or a program for a computer or presentation of information.

A patent will not be granted if it would encourage offensive, immoral or anti-social behaviour or if it concerns certain biological processes.

For how long does the patent last?

A patent lasts for 20 years and is no longer renewable. The period runs from the date published in the Patent Office Official Journal.

To keep the patent alive, fees must be paid annually from the fifth year on.

How do you get a patent?

Applications may be made personally. Alternatively, patent agents or lawyers specialising in patents can register on the owner's behalf.

The application should be made in the prescribed form and filed at the Patent Office. It must contain the following:

(i) A **request** for the grant of a patent
(ii) a **specification** containing a description of the invention.
(iii) a **claim** setting out the scope of the patent. It must not be too narrow, thereby allowing others to copy the general principle involved, nor must it be too wide, so that a patent may be refused because it covers matters already known.
(iv) any **drawing** referred to in the description or claim
(v) an **abstract** giving technical information.

There follows a lengthy procedure starting with a **preliminary examination and search**. These check that the formalities have been complied with and examines **prior art** documents to discover whether the invention is truly 'new'. The results are given to the applicant. If he chooses to carry on with his application, the application, claim, preliminary search report etc. are **published**. This gives the applicant protection against anyone using this material during this stage (providing he eventually is granted a patent). A **substantive** examination is then made, and if all the requirements of the patent rules are met, a patent is then granted to whoever is entitled.

Who owns the patent?

The inventor can apply for a patent by himself or jointly with another person. But the patent will only be granted to the inventor(s) or the person entitled by law or by contract (e.g. a research scientist's employer) or to their successors-in-title, i.e. the persons entitled after the death of a person or on winding up of a company.

Transfer

A transfer is by assignment and this must be in writing, signed by the parties or their agents. All transfers or other dealings such as mortgages must be registered at the Patent Office. Failure to register will make the transaction ineffective against subsequent transferees who took a transfer without knowledge of the earlier dealing.

Infringement

This is defined by S.60 of the Patents Act 1977 and relates to persons claiming the right to manufacture or deal in a product or claiming a right to use or deal in a process. There are a number of exceptions such as the private, non-commercial manufacture of a product.

Proceedings may be brought in the Patents Court (part of the High Court) or may be referred to the Comptroller of the Patent Office, who acts as an arbitrator. He has fewer powers, and can only award damages or make a declaration. Any other remedy must be pursued in the Patents Court.

Negotiable instruments

These are another type of chose in action and include **cheques** and promissory notes, both of which are special forms of bills of exchange. Bank notes (but not coins) are also negotiable instruments (instrument – a document).

A negotiable instrument is a document which represents someone's claim to a particular amount of money and which has a special characteristic called **negotiability** (*see* below). The document itself has virtually no value, but it is the owners evidence of ownership of whatever sum is written on it. Thus, a £5 note is in itself worth about 2p. But, it is known that it can be used to buy £5's worth of goods.

Transfer of ownership of negotiable instruments

As we have already seen, most choses in action have to be transferred by written documents signed by the owner or his agent. Imagine doing this for a £5 note!

A negotiable instrument on the other hand, is transferred very simply **either** by merely handing it over to the new owner (delivery) just like a parcel **or** by endorsing **and** delivering it. Endorsing means writing one's signature on the reverse (or elsewhere) of the document. Thus, our £5 note can be transferred by mere delivery. So could a cheque. But, if the owner wishes to transfer the cheque *again* he must endorse it and then deliver it to its new owner. The new owner can then collect the money from the drawer's bank account despite the fact that the cheque was originally payable to some other person. The fact that the new owner is entitled to the money is due to the concept of **negotiability**, as the cheque was not only physically transferred to him, but he also got all the legal rights associated with ownership of the cheque.

Negotiability

Negotiability, means therefore, that on the transfer of a negotiable instrument, the transferee gets:
- all legal rights to it
- with no defect in the title (even if the transferor's title was defective)
  Provided
- he acted in good faith
- he was not aware of the defects such as if it was stolen by the transferor
- **and** provided he gave value for it.

Example (*see* **Fig. 6.11**).   Sue pays her £20 newspaper bill by cheque. The transfer of the cheque is by delivery only. It has not yet been 'negotiated'.

Mr Smith the newsagent is now the owner of the cheque. Mr Smith is short of cash and has no time to go to the bank. He goes into the butchers, endorses the reverse of Sue's cheque by writing his signature on it, and gives it to the butcher in exchange for cash. Mr Smith has thus negotiated the cheque and the butcher now has full rights to it, because he acted in good faith, had no notice of any defects in title (of which there were none) and because he gave value (the cash) for it. The butcher can now pay the cheque into his own bank account.

Advantages of negotiable instruments

What is so useful about negotiable instruments, is that they provide a relatively safe method of transferring sums of money around. Provided certain safeguards are maintained, only the persons properly entitled to the money may actually collect the money involved.

Cheques

Probably the most common type of negotiable instrument used in

Fig. 6.11 Diagram to illustrate the concept of negotiability

business and in private is the cheque, which is a type of bill of exchange. The law governing cheques is chiefly found in the Bills of Exchange Act 1882 and the Cheques Act 1957.

A bill of exchange is defined by the 1882 Act as, 'an unconditional order in writing addressed by one person to another, signed by the person giving it, requiring the person to whom it is addressed to pay on demand, or at a fixed or determinable future time, a sum certain in money, to or to the order of a specified person or to bearer'.

They are commonly used in international trade and depend on one party being owed money by another, who is then asked to pay another party a sum of money, thus avoiding two transfers of money.

In the example (*see* Fig. 6.12) Owen plc owes the Independent Minx Bank £5,500. Black Pudding Ltd owes more than this to Owen plc.

Owen plc therefore draws the bill, as drawer on Black Pudding Ltd as drawee to pay on 17 May 1984 the payee bank. If the drawee accepts the bill, then it will undertake to pay the debt on the due date

Fig. 6.12   Bill of exchange

and Black Pudding Ltd becomes primarily liable on the bill.

During the intervening two months, the payee bank will hold the bill and if it requires cash may negotiate it to others by delivery and endorsement, and whoever is the holder on 17 May, may present the bill for payment.

A cheque (*see* Fig. 6.13) is defined by S.73 as a 'bill of exchange drawn on a banker and payable on demand'.

Most cheques are never negotiated, they are merely cashed by the payee, and little can go wrong.

But, if there are insufficient funds in the drawer's bank account, the bank is under no duty to pay out to the collecting bank and the cheque will probably be returned marked 'return to drawer'. The payee now has the problem of collecting the money on the dishonoured cheque. The drawer is under a duty to pay the money owed to the payee. But, if the cheque was a mere gift and there was no consideration on the other's part, then the donee cannot sue on its dishonour.

Nobody need accept a cheque in payment of a debt. But, if it is accepted and paid by the drawee banker, then this is good evidence that the payee has received the money. For this reason it is vitally important that bank statements should be scrutinized, cross checked with completed stubs, both of which should then be filed for a sufficient period. Further checks can be made by sending covering letters containing the cheque number, and writing the cheque number on the invoice or bill and the date on which the cheque is sent.

Fig. 6.13 Cheque (This cheque is reproduced with the permission of Midland Bank plc from their booklet 'How to use a Bank Account')

Drawing the cheque

Date. The correct date is primarily important for record purposes. If the date is missing, the bank does not have to pay out on the cheque, and often, the payee will return the cheque to the drawer. Any holder of the cheque, however, may fill in the correct date, if they wish.

Once a cheque is in the hands of the payee or a holder to whom it has been negotiated, it should be paid as soon as possible into their bank account or cashed. Not only are such cheques liable to get lost, but banks will not usually pay out on a cheque if it is more than 6 months old. If left longer, the payee would have to go cap in hand to the drawer for a new cheque, as the drawer is under no duty to furnish a new one, although of course, this does not absolve his indebtedness.

Some people post-date cheques for many reasons, e.g. because their account is not yet in funds or they want to pay for goods to be delivered on a particular date, which if not done, they then have an opportunity to stop the cheque. The payee may refuse such a cheque, as strictly speaking, it does not fulfil the statutory definition, as it is not payable on demand. If he does accept the cheque, but pays it into his bank before the due date, then the paying bank should hold the cheque and pay on the correct date. If it pays before however, the bank should not debit the payer's bank account and indeed would be liable for any loss if the payer subsequently stopped the cheque.

Payee's Name. The cheque can be made payable to the payee or to his order or to 'bearer'.

The correct name should therefore be used for the payee, particularly when dealing with a company or firm, although often, the banks will still pay on a cheque where the payee's name has been misspelt.

If the words 'or order' are crossed out by the drawer, the cheque cannot be negotiated to anyone else by endorsement, and the cheque ceases to be a negotiable instrument but a mere simple chose in action. Thus, only the payee should claim payment on the cheque and if it was negotiated to anyone else by endorsement, then they would get no better rights under it than those of the endorser. Furthermore, the transferee would have to join with the payee to sue if it was dishonoured.

If the cheque says 'pay bearer' then any holder of the cheque may claim its value, and there is no need to transfer it by endorsement, delivery would be enough, like a bank note. It is for this reason that few bearer cheques are seen, because of the dangers of theft. Few people realise however, that endorsing a cheque 'in blank' i.e. by writing their signature without specifying a new payee has the same effect. Thus, if one needs to negotiate a cheque, an endorsement in blank should only be done actually at the time of transfer, or more safely, the signature should follow a direction to pay a specified transferee e.g. pay John Smith signed B T Smale. A thief would then have to pretend to be John Smith before he could be paid.

The amount of money. Part of the statutory definition of a bill of exchange, is that it must be for a sum 'certain in money'. As far as cheques are concerned, the sum is written in words first, then in figures in the right hand box. The two should always be checked to be the same. If there is a difference, then under the Act, the amount in words will be the amount payable. Most people however, would send such a cheque back for alteration.

If the drawer realises he has made a mistake in any part of the cheque, he can alter the mistake and initial the alteration.

To prevent unauthorised alterations, the drawer ought to make it as difficult as possible, by drawing a line after the words or figures, as shown in the example. No gaps should be left, preventing extra figures being inserted.

Crossings. Most people use crossed cheques without realising their significance.

A general crossing is merely two parallel lines drawn across the cheque (with or without the words '& Co' – *see* Fig. 6.14).

Fig. 6.14   General crossing of cheque

A crossed cheque may only be paid through a bank account and cannot be cashed over the counter. Thus, the holder of a crossed cheque has first to pay it into his bank account. If he has no bank account, he must negotiate it to someone who has. Their bank then collects the money from the paying bank.

Sometimes the crossing is 'special' when the name of a bank is specified. In such cases, the money must be paid through the specified bank (to be credited to the payee bank account). This is very common when collecting for charity. To save administration expenses, the charity requests that any donation cheques should be crossed and a particular bank named in the crossing (*see* Fig. 6.15).

Fig. 6.15 Special crossing

A crossing with the words 'not negotiable' written across it, means that the cheque cannot be negotiated at all. If it is attempted, the transferee gets no better right to it than the transferor. So it is good sense to refuse to accept such cheques except as the original payee.

A cheque crossed with the words 'A/c payee only' means that the collecting bank must only credit the named payee and no other. It is no longer negotiable.

Ending the bank's authority to pay cheques. Whilst the customer's account is in credit, the bank is under a duty in contract to pay out on any cheque properly drawn on it. However, unless previously agreed, the bank does not have to pay if the account is even the slightest bit overdrawn. In business, this can be not only embarrassing, but financially damaging if a company or individual appears to be unable to pay their debts. If the bank had no cause whatsoever to stop payment, the customer can claim damages in contract if he is in business. A private individual may however be able to sue for libel, if the payee is told that the customer's cheque has been returned to him through lack of funds, provided that this could be said to be a defamatory statement.

Cheques may be 'stopped' i.e. payment countermanded. This is more expensive than most people imagine, as administration charges have to be paid. Written instructions usually have to be given. If the cheque was supported by a bank guarantee card, the cheque cannot be stopped.

Other circumstances which also terminate the bank's authority to pay out include, notification of the customer's death or mental incapacity. In practice this can be very important and banks should be immediately informed of the death of a customer, otherwise, if a cheque book falls into the wrong hands, the bank may pay out on a forged cheque, leaving behind a tangle of legal liability which no-one wants to have to sort out at a time of bereavement.

If the bank is served with a garnishee order, (*see* p. 205), the bank account is frozen and no payment can be made without a court order.

If a bankruptcy petition is presented against a customer, the bank must not pay out, if notified of the petition.

Debt collection

As a debt is such a valuable type of property, it is therefore surprising how many businessmen, builders included, fail to understand the importance of efficient collection of debts. By this I mean, the prompt rendering of accounts, the issuing of reminders and the following up of unpaid bills. It is essential to have an efficient book keeping system and a trained and experienced book keeper. Computer accounting will of course maximise efficiency. Many businesses fail, particularly those of 'small' builders, because the builder tries to do all the work including that of the book keeper's. His main concern should be to maximise his time doing the job he is trained for, building. By delegating the paperwork to other appropriately qualified and experienced workers, he can relieve himself of anxiety, and can concentrate on making his business prosperous. The wages of such workers may reduce his own salary to start with, but in the long run, the firm will be more financially stable, with a steady stream of work and a steady flow of income.

In which courts does one sue?

Debts are civil liabilities which must be recovered in the civil courts, i.e. in the Queens Bench Division of the High Court, or if the debt is for less than £5,000, in the County Court.

The procedure in the High Court is quite complex despite recent reform, and when suing for large sums of money, it is advisable to seek the assistance of your solicitor. Similarly, when suing for sums over £500 in the County Court, it is better to use your solicitor. But, if suing for sums less than £500, there is a SMALL CLAIMS PROCEDURE which is an arbitration procedure designed for the layman to 'sue-it-himself'. Advisory booklets and the necessary forms are available from the local County Court Offices and the procedure is relatively simple and informal. The address of your local courts are found under COURTS in the telephone directory.

It should be noted that before actually commencing any action in court, a final letter setting out your claim, whether written by yourself or from your solicitor, will often achieve the effect of encouraging payment. The letter should state the details of the debt, e.g. the work involved, the amount required, dates and other relevant details and that if the debtor fails to pay within a specified period such as 14 days, then court action will be commenced. It may also be advantageous to point out, that if judgment is made against the debtor he will then find it extremely difficult to get credit in the future.

Course of action

Debts are **liquidated** amounts, i.e. they are either fixed or can be determined by simple arithmetic calculation. This means that in both the county court and in the Queens Bench Division, a method of action can be used where, if the defendant fails to put in a defence, then judgment can automatically be entered against him. These are called **default actions**, as judgment can be given in **default of defence.**

1. County courts. Certain documents must be filed with the county court registrar i.e. a **request note** and **particulars of claim** in duplicate, and a fee must be paid.

The registrar then arranges service of a **summons** on the defendant, together with a copy of the **particulars of claim**, so that he knows for what he is being sued. Service is usually done through the post, but it can be arranged for a **bailiff**, a court officer, to deliver the summons in person (this sometimes also encourages payment).

If, as is usual in debt cases, there is no defence, the debtor will not bother to file one, and at the expiration of 14 days from the date of service, the plaintiff i.e. the creditor, will be able to file another document, pay an additional fee to enter judgment automatically. This also applies to the **small claims procedure.**

2. Queens Bench Divison. A slightly different method is used to start the action. The plaintiff's solicitor will prepare a **writ** in duplicate and will send the writs to court for **issuing** i.e. to get the action on the court record. The writs are then sent back, duly stamped, and the solicitor then has a year in which to serve the writ on the defendant. Until a few years ago, it was common to serve writs in person, but the rules have now been changed, so that most are now served through the post (see Fig. 1.4).

The writ will either have a **statement of claim** actually written on it or there may be only a brief outline of what the claim is all about, in which case, a separate **statement of claim** has to be served on the defendant. With the writ is served a form called an **acknowledgement of service** which also contains a guide on how to complete the form and the penalties which attach, if it is ignored.

If the acknowledgement is sent back to the court indicating that the defendant does not wish to defend, or if he ignored the acknowledgement altogether, then judgment can be applied for and entered automatically.

If there is a defence.   If in either court, the defendant feels that he has a good reason for not paying the bill, then he is well advised to immediately seek legal advice, as a defence or possibly even a **counterclaim** will need to be filed and a court hearing will be necessary to settle the dispute. This is very common in building disputes, where one party has not paid another for some good reason.

Enforcing judgment. Where judgment has been awarded against the defendant, either automatically or by a judge (or registrar in a small claims case) the problem remains. How is one going to recover the money from the judgment debtor?

Before bothering to pay any more court fees to enforce judgment, it is worthwhile seeking an **oral examination** of the judgment debtor first.

The debtor is summoned to attend before a court registrar, to answer **on oath** questions concerning his assets and liabilities. If he fails to attend the court, he will be in contempt, and can be appropriately dealt with as the court thinks fit. At worst he could be committed to prison.

The advantage of this interrogation, is to find out what property belongs to the debtor, and whether he has a job, as some methods of enforcing judgment will not be appropriate. Very often, the debtor will make an offer to pay at this stage. Even if he offers only instalments, this may nevertheless be quite acceptable. It is better to make sure the money comes in, even if it is in 'drips and drops'. Occasionally, the enormity of having to attend court, will make the debtor pay the whole sum at the oral examination.

Methods of enforcing judgment

High Court – Queens Bench Division.

1. Writ of fieri facias (Fi.fa), execution against goods. This writ is obtained by the plaintiff on payment of a fee, ordering the sheriff's officers to enter the debtor's premises and to seize goods to the value of the debt plus costs. The goods are usually then sold and the creditors reimbursed. The sheriff's officers can take anything belonging to the debtor (one of the reasons for the oral examination) but not his tools of trade, clothing or bedding.

2. Garnishee order (attachment of debts). At the oral examination, the debtor will have revealed whether he is owed money. His main debtor will usually be his bank, providing his account is in credit. The garnishee order is obtained from the court and sent to the bank ordering it to pay the debt directly to the court. On receiving the order, the bank account is 'frozen' and the plaintiff can then ask for payment from the court.

3. Charging order. The plaintiff can request this order from the court which 'charges' certain property belonging to the debtor. Once the charge has been placed on the property, it acts as security for the

payment of the debt, the charge is only removed if the debt is paid. If it is not paid within a specified period, the property can then be sold to satisfy the debt. It is rather like the court ordering a house to be mortgaged.

If the charge is made against land, e.g. the debtor's house, then this should be registered as a land charge at the Land Registry (*see* p. 159).

A charging order may be made against the debtor's stocks and shares, and even his money.

4. Attachment of earnings. At the oral examination, it will have been ascertained whether or not the debtor is in employment. If he is, then the creditor can apply to the **county** court for an order to the employer to deduct money from the debtor's salary or wages in instalments.

5. Writ of sequestration. In this case, the writ directs up to four nominees, one of whom is usually the sheriff's officer, to enter the debtor's land. They then receive any rents, pensions or other income due from this property, and they may even take charge of his goods.

Their presence, and the right to continue to receive the income, continues until the debtor pays the debt.

6. Appointment of a receiver. A receiver may be appointed to take charge of the debtor's property until such time as he pays the debt. Usually, this means that the debtor's affairs are in chaos and need to be properly looked after.

County Court.

1. *Warrant of execution.*
   This is similar to writ of fieri facias (See above)
2. *Attachment of earnings.*
   (See above)
3. *Charging Order.*
   (See above)
4. *Garnishee order.*
   (See above)

Bankruptcy

This is not a true method of enforcing judgment, but it can be used to recover part (or occasionally all) of the debt owed. Also, the threat of making a person bankrupt may sometimes galvanize the debtor into action, and he may actually pay his debts.

Relevant law

The law is found principally in the Bankruptcy Act 1914 as amended and the Insolvency Act 1976 together with the bankruptcy rules and precedents made in relation thereto. Only humans may become bankrupt. Thus, in business a sole trader whose business becomes insolvent, may have insufficient personal funds to pay business debts and be forced into bankruptcy. Similarly, partners could be forced into bankruptcy if there are insufficient partnership funds to pay their debts. Registered companies on the other hand, are wound up on insolvency (insolvency means that a person is unable to pay his debts when required to do so).

What is bankruptcy?

A bankruptcy is a court procedure whereby the property of an insolvent person is administered under the authority of a court and distributed between his creditors.

During bankruptcy, the bankrupt is subject to a number of disqualifications depending on his position and status. For example, no bankrupt may be appointed to be a justice of the peace or a mayor or local authority councillor. Nor may someone be elected to parliament. If a director of a company becomes bankrupt, most articles of association provide for his disqualification from office. His bankruptcy however, protects the debtor from further legal proceedings.

The bankrupt may apply for his discharge from bankruptcy (at any time) which will release him from his obligations incurred prior to bankruptcy, and will, in most cases, restore his old position, freed from any disqualification he may have suffered.

There are roughly ten stages in bankruptcy (*see* Fig. 6.16).

The act of bankruptcy

Before anyone can be made bankrupt, he must have committed an **act of bankruptcy**.

Fig. 6.16   Ten stages of bankruptcy

The following are the most common acts of bankruptcy:

- Where the debtor himself files at court a declaration that he is unable to pay his debts, **or** files his own petition in bankruptcy.
- Where a debtor gives notice to a creditor, that he has suspended or is going to suspend payment of his debts. This may be in the form of a circular to all his creditors.
- Where a creditor has sued the debtor and obtained final judgment or order for **any amount** and has served a **bankruptcy notice** requiring the debtor to pay the debt, secure or compound for it to the satisfaction of the creditors or that of the court, and the debtor has either failed to do so or failed to satisfy the court that he has a counterclaim, set-off or cross-demand which equals or exceeds the amount of the judgment debt.

  (Note: To compound means to agree to make a composition with the creditors, *see* p. 210.)

  This method is used where a creditor has decided to use the threat of bankruptcy as an encouragement to pay. The bankruptcy notice must be in a form prescribed by the Bankruptcy Act 1914 and must be served in the prescribed manner. Bankruptcy notices are issued by the court after a request has been made by the judgment creditor.

  Failure to comply with the notice is an act of bankruptcy, and within three months of service, any creditor, not necessarily the one who served the notice, may then present a bankruptcy petition in court.
- The making of a criminal bankruptcy order. (*see* p. 49).

The petition

Bankruptcy petitions may be presented to the High Court and to certain county courts depending on certain residential factors. Before presenting a petition, a check should be made at the proposed court, to ascertain whether it has the jurisdiction to deal with the matter.

In the petition, the creditor must state:

- that the debt is more than £750. If the sum is less, then two or more creditors can join together in presenting the petition, provided their joint debt is for more than £750.
- that the debt is a liquidated sum, i.e. fixed either by the contract or on judgment.
- that the act of bankruptcy was committed during the three months prior to the presentation of the petition.
- that the debtor is domiciled in England or in other respects complies with the residence qualifications of the Bankruptcy Act 1914 as amended.
- what the act of bankruptcy was.

The petition must contain a **request** that a receiving order be made and if it is the debtor's own petition, request an adjudication of bankruptcy order.

The petition must be supported by an affidavit sworn by the creditor or someone who knows the facts. The petition is then filed at court and a copy is served on the debtor, requiring his attendance for the hearing of the petition.

The receiving order

At the hearing of the petition, if the court is satisfied as to the truth of the facts contained in the petition, then it may make a receiving order for the protection of the debtor's estate.

The receiving order makes the Official Receiver (a Department of Trade official), the receiver of the debtor's property, without whose permission (or that of the court's) no action can be taken against the debtor. The debtor, from this point has **no** control over his own property.

The court sends a copy of the order to the Official Receiver and gives notice to the Department of Trade. The Official Receiver gives notice to a local newspaper and registers the order under the Land Charges Act 1972 with the Chief Land Registrar (*see* p. 159). He also sends a copy of the order to the debtor. The Department of Trade then gives notice to the London Gazette.

The receiving order may be rescinded in a number of situations, the most obvious being, if the debts are paid in full.

It must be noted, that at this point, the Official Receiver is merely an interim receiver, having control of the debtor's property, being able to collect rents or other income of the property. He is not a trustee, unless and until, the debtor is adjudicated bankrupt.

Preliminary examination of debtor's statement of affairs by Official Receiver

Within a few days of the receiving order, the debtor must submit a **statement of affairs** to the Official Receiver, failing which he may be adjudicated bankrupt on application by a creditor or the Official Receiver.

The statement must contain details of the debtor's assets and liabilities, the creditors' names and addresses and whether they hold any security for their debts. The statement must be supported by an affidavit swearing that the statement is true.

If the debtor filed his own petition, then the Official Receiver will probably adjudge him bankrupt at this point if the statement seems to support the contentions of the petition.

Otherwise, a summary of the statement of affairs and comments on the reasons for the debtor's financial problems is sent by the Official Receiver to all the creditors, together with a notice of the first

creditors' meeting which must be held within 14 days of the receiving order. Details of the meeting must be gazetted (i.e. an advertisement must be placed with the London Gazette) and advertised in a local paper (*see* Fig. 6.17).

First creditors meeting: S.13

The creditors must prove their debts, i.e. by sending a letter to the Official Receiver or to the trustee in bankruptcy (if the debtor has already been adjudicated bankrupt) with an affidavit verifying the debts mentioned in the letter, if the Official Receiver requires an affidavit or in other cases an unsworn claim. If necessary, evidence of the debt may be required.

A debtor who has not done so is unable to vote at any creditors' meeting. Creditors may vote in person or by proxy which must be in a prescribed form.

Resolutions are normally passed by simple majority, i.e. they are ordinary resolutions. Some resolutions require a simple majority of creditors, others a 75 per cent majority in value of creditors as well, i.e. a special resolution. These are required for such matters as removing a special manager who was appointed by the Official Receiver to deal with the debtor's estate or business.

The main purpose of the first creditors' meeting is to decide whether the debtor should be adjudicated bankrupt or whether they can agree to a **composition or scheme of arrangement.** A composition is made where the creditors agree to accept a smaller sum in satisfaction of their debts.

A scheme of arrangement is a proposal by the debtor, that his assets or income should be paid proportionately between his creditors. This in effect sets out to do what actually happens on being adjudicated bankrupt **without becoming bankrupt**. This is useful as it means that a sole trader for example will be able to continue in business without the disabilities of bankruptcy. However, such schemes must have been agreed to by a 75 per cent majority in value and a majority of creditors present at the meeting and the court must give its approval at the public examination, which it is bound to refuse in certain circumstances e.g. if the proposal would not benefit the general body of creditors.

Public examination

A public examination of the debtor must be held at court as soon as possible after the expiration of the time allowed for submission of the statement of affairs.

The examination requires the attendance of the debtor unless, for example, he is too ill to attend. Failure to attend is an arrestable offence. The public examination may be dispensed with in certain circumstances.

THE BANKRUPTCY ACTS

1914 AND 1926

In the Uptown County Court

In Bankruptcy   No. 123 of 1989

RE COSMO DE'ATH carrying on business as a funeral director under the style of Cosmo Coffins from and residing at 222 Uptown Road, Uptown, Somercester. Receiving order 1st April 1989. Order of Adjudication 1st April 1989. First meeting of creditors 14th May 1989 10.00 a.m. Hanley House, High Street, Uptown UP1 3SC. Public Examination August 18th 1989. 10.30 a.m. County Court, Law Courts, Main Road, Uptown, Somercester.

Note: −   All debts due to the estate should be paid to me.

Dated 2nd May 1989.

L.M. Arkenshaw,

Official Receiver,

Hanley House,

High Street,

Uptown,

UP1 3SC.

Fig. 6.17   Notice of first creditors' meeting

The creditors or their agents, proxy holders or holders of a creditor's power of attorney may attend the examination and question the debtor about his affairs.

The debtor answers on oath and must answer the questions, even if they may incriminate him.

If there has already been a first creditors' meeting and the court is satisfied that the debtor's affairs have been properly investigated, the public examination can be ended.

The adjudication order

Such an order actually makes the debtor bankrupt **and not before** even though a receiving order has been made.

It may, of course, have been made by order of the court immediately the Official Receiver had examined the debtor's statement of affairs, if the debtor filed his own petition.

The debtor may also have been adjudicated bankrupt if he failed to submit a statement of affairs. There are various other circumstances in which the court will order the debtor's bankruptcy, e.g. if the creditor resolves that he should be made bankrupt or where the debtor has failed either to suggest a scheme of arrangement or to pay an instalment under such a scheme or composition.

Notice of the order of adjudication must be given in a local paper and in the London Gazette.

After this order has been made the debtor's property becomes vested in the trustee in bankruptcy. He is usually someone approved by the creditors, failing which the Department of Trade can appoint. The department must then grant a certificate to the trustee unless he is not fit to act as such or there are other objections to his appointment. He must also give security.

The creditors may also appoint a committee of inspection to supervise the trustee in bankruptcy: S.20 Bankruptcy Act 1914.

Realisation of assets

The trustee must then set about realising the debtor's assets with the intention of repaying the creditors, (hopefully in full). The law regards the trustee as the **owner** of the debtor's property and he must therefore act in good faith and
- may sell the property privately or by auction
- take receipt of debts owed to the debtor
- and take action to recover debts owed to the debtor: S.55.

The trustee may also take other action with the permission of the committee of inspection, e.g. refer a dispute to arbitration or carry on the debtor's business with a view to winding it up.

The property which may be used to pay the creditors obviously includes money, goods, freeholds and leaseholds in land and easements and profits belonging to the bankrupt at the commencement of the bankruptcy (i.e. the first act of bankruptcy committed in the three months prior to the presentation of the petition): S.30 Bankruptcy Act 1914.

It also includes property acquired by the bankrupt before his discharge from bankruptcy and goods in the bankrupt's **reputed ownership** at the commencement of the bankruptcy.

Reputed ownership means goods (including debts but not other choses in action) in the possession, order or disposition of the bankrupt used in his business as a sole trader, which one would assume to be his property. Such goods must have been in his possession with the permission of the true owner.

In the building industry, it is common to hire certain equipment and thus, one has to assess whether one would reasonably have assumed that the goods belonged to the bankrupt or not. If an outsider would assume not, then the goods are not in the reputed ownership of the bankrupt. Thus, it would be assumed that materials on site not yet incorporated into the building would not be in the reputed ownership of the builder. Materials at his own premises would be so presumed. Similarly, one might assume that plant and equipment in his possession actually belong to him. However, the Consumer Credit Act 1974 has made inroads into the reputed ownership of goods bought on hire purchase, under conditional sale agreements, consumer hire or regulated agreements.

To protect the parties to the JCT standard form of contract Cl. 16.2 deals with goods stored off site such as at the builder's premises, in the following manner: 'Where the value of any materials or goods intended for the works are stored off-site, has in accordance with Cl. 30.3 been included in any interim certificate under which the amount properly due to the contractor has been paid by the employer, such materials and goods shall become the property of the employer and thereafter the contractor shall not, except for use upon the works, remove or cause or permit the same to be moved or removed from the premises ... '

Thus, on payment under an interim certificate relating to unincorporated material, the ownership of such goods becomes that of the employer, even though possibly stored at the builder's own premises. As such goods may still appear to be in the builder's reputed ownership and may be seized by the trustee in bankruptcy, Cl. 16.2 continues thus: 'but the contractor shall nevertheless be responsible for any loss thereof or damage thereto and for the cost of storage, handling and insurance of the same until such time as they are delivered to and placed on or adjacent to the works ... '

Thus, if such goods are lost to the employer through the bankruptcy of the builder, he may prove for these goods as a debt.

It should be noted that under Cl.30.3: 'the amount stated as due in an interim certificate may in the discretion of the architect/supervising officer include the value of any materials or goods before delivery thereof to ... the works ... provided

30.3.1) the goods are intended for incorporation in the works
30.3.2) nothing remains to be done to the materials ...
30.3.3.) the materials have been and are set apart at the premises

where they have been manufactured, or assembled or stored and have been clearly and visible marked ... so as to identify the employer, where they are stored on the premises of the contractor and in any other case the person to whose order they are held and their destination as the works.'

Whilst such a clause does not eradicate the problem of reputed ownership, it does reduce its practical implications and gives some measure of security to the employer.

In addition to the property mentioned above, the trustee can exercise certain statutory powers and **reclaim** certain property which the bankrupt has already transferred. These include fraudulent conveyances or transfers of property. These are where the bankrupt has dishonestly transferred property intending to avoid paying his creditors or with the intention of preferring one creditor over others.

The trustee in bankruptcy may also **disclaim onerous property**: S.54. Such property must be a burden to the bankrupt and of no benefit at all to him. Thus, a lease subject to onerous covenants could be disclaimed, as could unprofitable contracts. A builder may, for example, have attempted to take on uneconomic contracts purely in an attempt to improve his cash flow situation. Disclaimer by the trustee would operate to terminate the bankrupt's rights and duties under the contract and no further work would need to be done.

The trustee in bankruptcy does not acquire rights over the following

- the bankrupt's tools of trade
- his or his family's clothes and bedding up to a value of £250.
- property given to the bankrupt **until** he became bankrupt. This will usually occur under a will or a settlement, e.g. if Blackacre Farm is given to Joe for life until he becomes bankrupt and thereafter to Mark on Joe's bankruptcy, Mark gets the farm as the bankruptcy accelerates Mark's interest.

- old age pensions and other state benefits
- property held by the bankrupt as a trustee.

The court must make an order before a bankrupt's income can be used to pay creditors and in so doing they must take into account the requirements of the bankrupt and his family.

Thus, contracts do not terminate automatically on bankruptcy, but if they are onerous, may be disclaimed by the trustee in bankruptcy.

Because the employer is particularly vulnerable if a builder goes into bankruptcy (or if a company is wound up through insolvency) most contracts should contain some clause to cover such eventualities.

Clause 27.2 in the JCT Standard Form of Contract states: 'in the event of the contractor becoming bankrupt or making a composition or arrangement with his creditors (or if a company, being wound up) ... the employment of the contractor under this contract shall be forthwith **automatically** determined but the said employment may be reinstated and continued if the employer and the contractor, his trustee in bankruptcy ... receiver ... shall so agree'.

Clause 27 continues, to allow the employer to employ other persons to complete the Works where the contract has been determined under Cl. 27.

Payment to creditors

Any creditor wishing to claim in a bankruptcy must have first proved his debt in the required form (*see* p. 210).

(*see* p. 210)

Interim payments called dividends are paid at frequent intervals pending a final dividend which is paid when all the bankrupt's property has been sold. Ideally the creditors will be paid in full. However, the very nature of insolvency indicates that there will not be enough money to be shared among the creditors. For this reason there is a statutory order of priority for the payment of debts. This does not take into account the debts of a secured creditor, who on non-payment of his debts may take his security to satisfy the debt, e.g. sell the mortgaged property. Any money surplus to the debt is paid into the estate to help pay the other creditors.

The statutory order of priority is (mnemonic A-SPOD):

  (i) administration expenses
 (ii) specially preferred debts
(iii) preferred debts
 (iv) ordinary debts
  (v) deferred debts.

Administration expenses. This includes the expenses of the Official Receiver and trustee in bankruptcy, and must be paid in full.

Specially preferred debts. These must be paid in full.

(i) Funeral & testamentary expenses of a deceased insolvent debtor
(ii) Property belonging to a friendly society or trustee savings bank in the possession of the bankrupt who was an officer of the society or bank.

Preferred debts. Provided the above have been paid in full, the following debts must be paid **pari passu**, i.e. equally without preference. If there are insufficient funds to pay all the preferential debts then they must be paid a proportion (i.e. they must be abated). These include:

1. Local rates due from the bankrupt for the twelve months next prior to the date of the receiving order.
   One year's taxes due to the Inland Revenue and class 4 contributions

due to the DHSS assessed for the period up to 5 April preceding the receiving order.

Taxes deducted out of wages by the bankrupt as employer under PAYE schemes for 12 months prior to the receiving order.

2. Wages and salaries owed to employees for 4 months prior to the receiving order not exceeding £800 per person.

By virtue of the Employment Protection (Consolidation) Act 1978 additional sums may be claimed from a bankrupt employer for such matters as paid time off, guarantee payments, pay while suspended on medical grounds (*see* p. 338) from the Redundancy Fund, if necessary (*see* p. 347).

3. All holiday pay due to an employee prior to the receiving order.
4. Social security contributions due to the DHSS from the bankrupt as employer.

Ordinary debts.   These are all the remaining unsecured debts other than deferred debts.

Mention should be made of the unusual position of landlords, who, although mere unsecured ordinary creditors are allowed to **distrain** (take possession of) upon goods of the bankrupt to cover the amount of rent owed. On discovery that the tenant is insolvent, he may seize the tenant's goods at any time whether or not a receiving order has been made. However, if he distrains after the commencement of bankruptcy, he is only entitled to claim six months' rent due prior to the date of the adjudication of bankruptcy by this method. If any further sums become due after adjudication, the landlord may then exercise his right of distress (i.e. he can distrain) for all new sums accruing.

Deferred debts.   These may only be paid after **all** the other debts have been paid in full.

1. A loan to a partnership whereby the interest is paid by reference to varying profits of the business: S.2 Partnership Act 1890.
2. Money due from the sale of goodwill of a business in the form of a share in the profits: S.3 Partnership Act 1890.
3. A loan by a husband to his wife or vice versa for the purpose of his trade or business: S.36 Bankruptcy Act 1914.
4. Interest on debts exceeding £5 per cent per annum: S.66 Bankruptcy Act 1914.

Criminal offences

Until the bankrupt is discharged there are many actions which, if committed by him, will amount to a criminal offence.

The following are examples:

Under S.154 Bankruptcy Act 1914

- Failing to disclose all of his property to the trustee or official receiver.
- Concealing or destroying or falsifying any document or making a false entry.
- Misleading the creditors by untruthful representations so as to obtain their agreement to a scheme or composition.

Under S.155 Bankruptcy Act 1914

- Obtaining credit for more than £50 without informing the lender of his bankruptcy.
- Carrying on a business or trade in a name, different to the one under which he is made bankrupt without telling clients/customers of his bankruptcy.

In addition to the above there are many other offences that may be committed regarding the bankruptcy. For example, a bankrupt may also have committed criminal offences before or after a receiving order by obtaining property by deception, obtaining a pecuniary advantage by deception under the Theft Act 1968 as amended.

Discharge

A bankrupt may apply to court for his own discharge at any time after being adjudicated bankrupt. The court will not grant the discharge in certain situations, e.g. if the bankrupt has committed an offence (*see* above): S.26 Bankruptcy Act 1914.

Under Ss. 7, 8 of the Insolvency Act 1976, the bankrupt is entitled to be either automatically discharged or to have his case automatically reviewed. Thus under S.7(1)–(3), persons who were made bankrupt after 1 October 1977 will be automatically discharged 5 years from the adjudication order provided certain conditions are met, e.g. that a public examination has been held and concluded or none was required.

Under S.8, if S.7 does not apply, e.g. no automatic discharge order was made or if it had it has been withdrawn, then there will be an automatic review of the case.

A normal application for discharge may still be made by the bankrupt, especially where five years has not yet elapsed.

Once discharged, the bankrupt is free of nearly all his debts i.e. those which could be proved in his bankruptcy. Certain debts will still be enforceable, e.g. ones incurred by fraud.

CHAPTER 7

Legal personality

The concept of legal personality

In English law, only 'legal' persons have rights and duties in law. Thus, whilst animals can benefit from our law, such as protecting them from being mistreated, no duties can be imposed on them, only their owners, for they are not legal persons.

Types of legal persons

There are only two types of legal persons (*see* Fig. 7.1), **natural** and **juristic** (or **artificial**) persons. Natural legal persons are of course human beings. Juristic or artificial are **corporations** (from corpus – a body).

Humans

Potentially they have full rights and duties, unless they become insane or bankrupt. Whilst under age, i.e. under 18, they have restricted rights and duties e.g. they cannot vote, cannot sit on juries, can only enter

Fig. 7.1   Types of legal persons

into certain contracts and cannot marry without consent, (under 16 they cannot marry at all). Bankrupts also have restricted rights (*see* p. 207).

A person operating a **business** on his own is said to be called a **sole trader**. He is self-employed and he and the business are one and the same thing. If the business does well, so will he in his private capacity. If the business should fail however, then he may become bankrupt, as his private money may have to be taken to pay his business debts.

Being self-employed, he will not enjoy as many benefits of the welfare state as would an employed person, such as sickness benefit. He should therefore take out adequate insurance cover to provide income for himself and his family should he become ill, have an accident or die.

On his death, the business will usually come to an abrupt end. This can cause great hardship for his next-of-kin, his employees, whose jobs disappear overnight, as well as persons who had entered into contracts with the deceased, and who now have little hope of the contract being performed. The deceased's will must also be very clear as to what should be done with the business. His executors have no implied rights to do more than to carry on trade for a short time with a view to selling the business as a going concern. If the deceased left no will, then as the administrator (usually the surviving spouse) cannot take out a grant of letters of administration for at least a fortnight, then a fortnight will pass by with no-one having the authority to do anything in relation to the business.

Corporations

These can be defined as **artificial legal persons**. Examples of corporations include, the monarchy, nationalised industries, such as the National Coal Board, limited companies, building societies, local authorities and the Chartered Institute of Building.

Corporations have all the general rights and duties which a sane adult would have, except, those which are impossible due to being inanimate. Thus, when entering into a contract with a limited company, even though the negotiations are made with a shop assistant, for example, the actual contract is made with the company, as *it* is the legal person.

Special characteristics of corporations

Separate entity. Corporations are thus said to have a **separate legal personality** to that of the persons who set it up or its shareholders. As it is a separate legal person, one should not talk of 'owning' a registered company as you cannot own people. A person who has a major shareholding in a company should be described as such. But of course it is common in family businesses for one shareholder to hold say 99 per cent of the shares and one can understand why it is said that he 'owns' the company. The concept that the company and the shareholders are two entirely separate entities was first put forward in the leading case, *Salomon* v. *Salomon & Co Ltd* (1897).

When does it die?   Unlike humans, a corporation does not die unless some step is taken to bring it to an end. In the case of chartered corporations this would be on revocation of the charter. In the case of registered companies, this would be on winding up, or on being struck off the company register. Statutory corporations would require the repeal of the Act that created it. (Compare this situation with sole traders on p. 219 and partnerships on p. 233).

Owns property in its corporate name.   A corporation may acquire and own all types of property in its own name, e.g. Bloggs Ltd will own land and not Mr & Mrs Bloggs, even though they may be the only shareholders in the company.

Contracts are in its own corporate name.   A corporation enters into contracts in its own name. Examine your contract of employment and you will see that your employer, if a company or local authority, is referred to by its corporate name.

Necessity for agents.   Corporations have to act through human agents because they have no physical existence.

Liability in law.   Corporations can be prosecuted and can sue or be sued in their correct corporate name. Thus, for example, prosecutions under the Health and Safety at Work etc. Act 1974, will usually be against the company and not against its personnel, unless there is an exceptional reason. It is of vital importance for legal proceedings to be undertaken using the correct corporate name and this should be ascertained before commencing legal action. In the case of registered companies, a search can be made at Companies House, (*see* p. 226). But, note the comments concerning business names on p. 226.

Seal.   A corporation must have a seal, which acts in a similar way to a human signature. The seal is used to emboss the large red seals on deeds, and must be countersigned by an officer of the corporation.

Powers of the corporation

Chartered corporations are similar to humans and have the right to enter into any sort of contract or do anything, provided it is not illegal or contrary to public policy.

On the other hand, a statutory corporation or one created under the Companies Act, can only do what it is authorised to, either by its governing Act of Parliament or the objects clause of its memorandum of association (*see* p. 226).

Anything done outside its authority is deemed **ultra vires** i.e. beyond its powers and will be **void**. A void act gives the parties **no** rights and duties in law. So, if your company contracted to do something which they had no power to do, and the other party failed to pay for this work, your company could not sue because the basic contract would be void through being ultra vires. Conversely, the other party could not force your company to perform its part of the agreement.

Thus, before dealing with a corporation, it is imperative to find out the scope of its authority, to ensure that any contracts made are valid. Fortunately, this rule is less important nowadays, as most of the authority given to corporations is drawn in the widest terms, to ensure that all their acts are valid. Also, in relation to registered companies, under the European Communities Act 1972 S.9(1), if a person is ' ... dealing with a company, **in good faith**, any transaction decided on by the directors shall be deemed to be one which ... is within the capacity of the company to enter into ... and a party to a transaction ... shall not be bound to inquire as to the capacity of the company to enter into it ... '

It should be noted that the outside party must be acting in good faith to gain the benefit of S.9, otherwise the ultra vires rule stands. Knowledge of a company's memorandum of association can be gained by a search at Companies House. The register is recorded on microfiche and a small sum has to be paid. Otherwise, a company search agent can be employed to do the search for you.

Methods of creating modern corporations

This process is called **incorporation**. There are three methods, by Royal Charter, an individual Act of Parliament or by registering under an appropriate Act.

Royal charter

These may be granted by the Crown, after a petition has been made requesting incorporation by charter. This method is now used for educational and professional bodies such as the Chartered Institute of Building, Royal Institute of British Architects, the British Broadcasting Corporation, the Bank of England, universities, local authorities who have borough status etc (*see* Fig. 7.2).

Special Act of Parliament

Obviously, for a proposed corporation to have its own Act of Parliament, it must be of great public importance to warrant the time spent in Parliament debating the Bill. The normal rules relating to

Fig. 7.2 Royal Charter of Chartered Institute of Building (photographer Kingsley Jones, courtesy of the CIOB)

direct legislation apply. Examples of corporations created in this way include all the nationalised industries as well as most local authorities. Thus, the National Coal Board was created by the Coal Industry Nationalisation Act 1947, and local authorities were created by virtue of the Local Government Act 1972. These types of corporations are sometimes referred to as public corporations.

Note. The present government has a **privatisation** policy and corporations such as British Telecom have been taken out of the public sector and made a registered company in the private sector. An Act of Parliament was necessary. Because of its size and importance and because the shares were offered to the public, it became a **public limited company**. Thus, a public **limited company** *is* a corporation, but not a **public** corporation.

Economists use the expression public and private sectors to indicate the difference between nationalised industries and local authorities, which are controlled in some measure by the government, and are therefore deemed to be in the Public Sector, and every other sort of organization of an economic nature which are not controlled by the state and which are therefore in the Private Sector.

Registration under Acts

The most common sort of corporation created by registration is the registered **company**. The relevant Act is the Companies Act of 1985. Building Societies are created by registration under the Building Societies Act 1962.

As 'ordinary' people can set up registered companies, and these are the most important sort of business organization, we shall examine these in more detail.

Types of registered company

It should be noted that the word company does not in itself indicate more than a collection of people gathered together for a common purpose. Indeed, the word used in a name of a business is misleading e.g. Jones & Company Builders, or Jones & Co. Builders. Both of these examples are *not* limited companies, see below. They will probably be either sole traders or partnerships (although they could also be unlimited companies, but these are unusual).

Companies registered under the Companies Act may be either unlimited liability or limited liability companies. The liability is that of the members (shareholders) and refers to whether or not they have to pay the company's debts if the company is unable to do so.

Unlimited liability

Here, the members have to pay the debts of the company if its assets are insufficient. There is **no** limit on the amount they have to contribute until all the debts are satisfied. The company has the ordinary characteristics of a corporation however. Also, there are a number of other special advantages. For example, there is no necessity to publish accounts annually.

Limited liability by shares

Here, the members or shareholder's liability is limited to the amount they have left unpaid on their shares. This is best illustrated by an example.

Tiny Construction Company Ltd has been set up with a share capital of 1,000 divided into £1 ordinary shares. There are four members holding a quarter of the shares each. Three of them have paid for their shares immediately, the fourth, just out of college, has been allowed by the others to pay only half.

Nominal Share Capital	– £1,000 in £1 shares			
Issued Share Capital	– £1,000 –	Tom	250	shares
		Dick	250	shares
		Harry	250	shares
		Ringo	250	shares
			1000	
Paid-up Share Capital	– £875 –	Tom	250	
		Dick	250	
		Harry	250	
		Ringo	125	
			875	
Uncalled Share Capital	– £125			

The company never becomes profitable and ceases trading owing substantial amounts to many creditors.

Tom, Dick and Harry lose all the value of their shareholding, but **no** more, as their liability was limited by shares. Ringo, on the other hand, is called upon to pay the extra £125, on top of losing the value of the £125 he has already paid. But, he still benefits from the limited liability in that he need contribute no more than £125.

It should be remembered that the company **must** pay its debts – if it can. But, if it can not, the members will *not* have to put their hands in their pockets, unless they have not paid for their shares.

For this reason, all 'limited' companies must warn potential clients and creditors of the members' limited liability, by incorporating the word limited into its name. Public limited companies, must under the Act, go further. They must incorporate the words public limited company or plc or the Welsh equivalent into their names. Certain companies can seek permission from the Department of Trade to be allowed to drop the word limited, provided the objects of the company are for scientific, commercial, artistic, religious or charitable purposes.

Limited liability is of great advantage to the shareholder. He will not necessarily go bankrupt if the company in which he has invested has gone into liquidation.

If he has invested a small amount in a large public limited company, then he will have to face the loss of that money. However, if he has set up his own company with, say his wife, as the other shareholder, when it comes to borrowing money in practice, banks or other financial institutions will usually insist on personal guarantees or second mortgages on his personal property to overcome the limited liability. Thus, because of this private security, he could still go bankrupt if the company failed.

Liability limited by guarantee

Here, the members guarantee that if the company cannot pay its debts at a particular time, such as winding up, then they will pay a guaranteed amount each. Their liability is thus limited to the amount guaranteed and they need pay no more. They are often used to form clubs, charities, etc, as no business capital is required.

Registered companies classified as public limited companies or private companies

Under the Act, registered companies must now be classified in a way which is more akin to company law in the EEC.

Public limited companies

A public company is a company:

- limited by shares or guarantee but with a share capital
- that must state in its memorandum of association that it is a public company
- whose nominal value of the company's issued shares must be at least £50,000 (at present) a quarter of which must be paid up
- having the words **public limited company** or plc or in Welsh **cwmni cyfenedig cyhoeddus** or CCC in the company name
- with a minimum of two members
- quoted on the Stock Exchange so that the public can buy its shares
- which starts business on issue of a registrar's trading certificate.

Private companies

A private company is **not** a public company. Therefore it follows that it may be:

- an unlimited company, *or*
- a company with a share capital of less than £50,000. *or*
- a company in whose memorandum there is no statement that it is a public company.

It is an offence to directly offer a private company's shares to the public. Thus, such companies are never quoted on the Stock Exchange. Nevertheless, in 1982–83 an **over the counter** market has developed in London, to which, people wishing to purchase shares in private companies may apply. Obviously, only those companies wishing to sell will place their shares in this way.

Family run companies, which are probably in the majority of private companies, usually restrict the sale of shares by inserting a clause in the articles of association (*see* p. 226). Such a restriction may require the seller to offer the shares first to members of the family or to the directors. This method prevents strangers being able to take control of a family business.

Like public companies, there must be a minimum of two shareholders.

If it is a limited company, it must have **Limited** or **Ltd** or its Welsh equivalent in its name.

Unlike a public company, it can start trading immediately on issue of its certificate of incorporation.

Formalities of registering a company

A registered company can be set up quite easily using a company agent who will supply the necessary documents and seal for a relatively small fee. He can even supply an 'off the shelf' company which is already in existence. If the name is not suitable, it can be changed to one that is. More complex requirements should be dealt with by a solicitor specializing in company matters.

The documents are registered at the Companies Registration Office, Crown Way, Maindy, Cardiff CF4 342. If the requirements of the Act are complied with, the registrar of companies issues a certificate of incorporation. This is the company's 'birth certificate' as it becomes a legal person from that day. If it is a public company, it also requires a trading certificate in order to start business (most businesses will have already been trading as private companies or partnerships).

The most important of the documents required on registration is the memorandum of association which deals with the external affairs of the company and the articles of association which deals with internal affairs, such as meetings, shares etc (*see* Fig. 7.3). The memorandum has certain compulsory clauses concerning the company name, domicile of office (England or Scotland, as it affects the relevant law); objects i.e. the acts a company may perform; liability (limited or not); whether public or private; and the number, type and value of shares.

One important aspect of forming a company is the choice of name. The rule relating to company names is found in the Business Names Act 1985. A company cannot register a name which is identical to that of an existing company. The name chosen must not be offensive, nor must it mislead people to think that it is connected with the government, a local authority, royalty etc. If the name is similar to that of another, whilst it may still be registered, the first company may still start a **passing-off** action and sue the new company. The company registrar can require a company to change its name if it is too like that of another or if the name is so misleading as to be harmful to the interests of the public.

Often, companies (or any sort of business) trade under a different name for some reason. In such cases, all business stationery **must** carry the true names and addresses e.g. if Paul Smith and Andrew Long are in partnership with the title Brickbuilders and Co. then their letters,

Example of a memorandum of association for a private
limited company

The name of the company is "Thom and Jerry Limited".

The registered office of the company will be situate
in England.

The objects for which the company is established are
"to act as buyers, sellers, agents, managers and
converters of real and personal property and
businesses of all kinds, including the building
and/or conversion of houses, flats, offices,
warehouses, factories and the like and the letting
thereof at such places as the company may from time
to time determine, and the doing of all such other
things as are incidental or conducive to the
attainment of the above objects".

The liability of the members is limited.

The share capital of the company is two thousand
pounds divided into two thousand shares of one pound
each.

WE, the several persons whose names and addresses
are subscribed are desirous of being formed into a
company, in pursuance of this memorandum of
association, and we respectively agree to take the
number of shares in the capital of the company set
opposite our respective names

NAMES ADDRESSES AND DESCRIPTIONS OF SUBSCRIBERS	Number of shares taken by each subscriber

Fig. 7.3   Example of memorandum of association

```
┌─────────────────────────────────────────────────┐
│ NAMES ADDRESSES AND DESCRIPTIONS OF SUBSCRIBERS   │
│                                                   │
│                              Number of shares     │
│                              taken by each        │
│                              subscriber           │
│                                                   │
│ Obadiah Thom                 One                  │
│ 123, The Street,                                  │
│ Splott,                                           │
│ Surrey.                                           │
│                                                   │
│ Builder                                           │
│                                                   │
│                                                   │
│ Cosmo Jerry,                 One                  │
│ The Nook,                                         │
│ Knotty Ash,                                       │
│ Surrey,                                           │
│                                                   │
│ Builder                                           │
│ ─────────────────────────────────────────────    │
│                                                   │
│                                                   │
│ Dated this 22nd day of May 1984.                  │
│                                                   │
│                                                   │
│ Witness to the above signatures -                 │
│                                                   │
│                  Shirley Owen,                    │
│                  63, Chemical Road,               │
│                  Trapp,                            │
│                  Surrey.                           │
└─────────────────────────────────────────────────┘
```

Fig. 7.3 cont'd.

invoices etc. must have their own names on them and the address of the partnership office.

Outsiders dealing with the business can in writing, insist on the names and addresses of the businessmen or company name and address.

If a company wishes to change its name for any reason (often where it is associated with some financial disaster) then it may do so, by the directors calling a general meeting and proposing a special resolution. If two-thirds of the shareholders entitled to vote agree, then the name can be changed.

Other aspects of forming a registered company

Taxation

Registered companies are subject to corporation tax. The directors of the company however, will pay normal income tax. It may be better therefore to set up business as a sole trader or as a partnership, as there are certain tax advantages to be gained for new businesses formed in this way, in which trading losses can be offset against income for, at present, the first four years of business. This income includes salaries paid for the previous three years.

Financial advice is thus absolutely necessary at the time of business formation.

Accounts

Annual accounts must be filed with the company registrar. These must be properly audited in accordance with the Companies Act. They are available to the public for inspection.

While this may seem to be onerous, it is one way of concentrating the mind on the necessity for proper account keeping, the absence of which is so often the reason for a business failure.

Winding up of a registered company

A registered company may be wound up in three ways:
- by the court
- by a voluntary winding up which may be either a members' or a creditors' winding up

By the court. A petition may be presented to the Companies Court (part of the High Court) or to a county court having jurisdiction in bankruptcy for companies with a paid up share capital of less than £120,000.

There are six grounds on which such a petition may be based:

(i) the company has passed a special resolution to wind it up.
(ii) the company, being a public company has not received a trading certificate and has been registered for more than a year.
(iii) the company has not commenced business within the year after incorporation or has suspended business for a year.
(iv) the membership has fallen below two.
(v) the company cannot pay its debts.
(vi) the court thinks that it is just and equitable to wind it up.

Inability to pay its debts.   A company is deemed to be unable to pay its debts in similar circumstances to those of an individual or partnership in bankruptcy (*see* p. 206).

The procedure is extremely similar to that of a bankruptcy. Thus there is a petition; hearing in court; winding-up order; statement of affairs to Official Receiver; Official Receiver's report; creditors' meeting; appointment of liquidator; committee of inspection; vesting of control or possession (but not ownership) in liquidator and payment of debts.

Voluntary winding up.   These types of winding up are desirable as there are fewer formalities.

By S.572 of the Companies Act 1985, a company may be voluntarily wound up if:

● the articles specified a date or event in which the company should be dissolved and the company in general meeting passes an ordinary resolution to be wound up voluntarily.
● if the company resolves by special resolution to be wound up voluntarily (no reason need be given for such a resolution).
● if the company passes an extraordinary resolution that because of the company's liabilities, it cannot continue in business and that it should be wound up.

Thus, if a company is insolvent, it does not have to be wound up through the courts.

The course of a voluntary winding up, however, depends on whether the company is solvent or not. If it is solvent, the company is wound up by a **members' voluntary winding up**. No-one, other than the members and a liquidator appointed by them is involved. A **declaration of solvency** must be filed with the registrar of companies within a certain number of days of passing the resolution to wind up the company. Any director making such a declaration without good reason may be imprisoned for six months and/or fined. The declaration is not necessarily to the effect that the debts will be paid immediately but that the company will be able to do so, in full, within a period, being not less than 12 months from the beginning of the winding up.

From the time of the resolution to wind up, the company must cease business unless it is necessary to be able to sell the business as a going

231

concern, the company remains in existence however, until actual dissolution, (*see* below). Share dealings must of course cease as must the powers of the directors.

The liquidator holds regular general meetings, annually, giving details of the course of the liquidation. On finally settling the company's affairs, a final general meeting must be called, gazetted and notice must be given of the accounts and the decision of the meeting to the registrar of companies.

The company is then automatically dissolved three months after the registration of the returns of the final meeting.

If no declaration of solvency has been filed, then the winding up is a **creditors' voluntary winding up**. A creditors' meeting is called and gazetted and advertised in local newspapers (*see* Fig. 7.4).

At the meeting a liquidator and a committee of inspection are appointed. Statements of the company's affairs, a list of creditors and the amount of their debts are presented. If the company had already appointed a liquidator, the creditors' appointment takes precedence although an application may be made to court for a decision if there is a dispute.

The course of liquidation is much the same as under a members' voluntary winding up above.

IN the matter of Splodge Limited and in the matter of the Companies Act 1948 Creditors Voluntary Winding Up.

Notice IS Hereby Given that a meeting of the creditors in the above matter, in pursuance of Section 293 of the above Act, will be held at 42, High Road, Uptown, Somercester, UP3 5AB on the 9th day of August 1985, at 12 o'clock noon or so soon thereafter as the Extraordinary General Meeting of the shareholders of the company convened for the same day and place shall have been concluded or adjourned, for the purposes set out in Section 294 and 295 of the above Act.

Dated this fifth day of July 1985. By Order of the Board, C. Regan, Secretary. Registered Office: 42, High Road, Uptown, Somercester, UP3 5AB.

Fig. 7.4 Notice of creditors' meeting

232

Winding up under the supervision of the court. These have been abolished by the Insolvency Act 1985.

The Crown

Before concluding corporations, a mention should be made of the special position of the Crown or monarchy, which is a type of corporation represented by one person only, the reigning monarch.

Traditionally, the monarch is outside or above the common law. Even today in her private capacity, the Queen cannot be sued.

However in the twentieth century, the monarch in its public capacity, responsible not only for royal households but also government ministers, their departments, the civil service, the armed forces and the police, is no longer immune from action.

The Crown Proceedings Act 1947 brought in a limited amount of liability in law for the Crown. The Crown can now be sued on its contracts and for torts committed by its employees or agents, e.g. nurses, police, government department employees etc. The correct department has to be sued, or failing this, the Attorney-General (the chief law officer of the Crown and head of the Bar).

Crown premises do not have to pay rates. This is derived from the fact that an Act or statute is said not to be applicable to the Crown unless it is specifically stated in the relevant legislation. The original Statute of Elizabeth imposing rates did not do so and this position has been followed ever since.

The Health and Safety at Work etc Act 1974 for example, specifically mentions the Crown, but limits the enforcement powers.

Therefore, whilst hospitals, army barracks etc. have to follow the requirements of the Act and may be inspected, they cannot be forced to comply like ordinary people.

The armed forces are in a special position because of the nature of their work. Whether or not they are liable for something, will depend on relevant legislation.

Unincorporated associations

These are associations of individuals from two upwards, who get together for a common purpose. They may be simple unincorporated associations such as clubs and societies who have not formed companies, or they may be special types, such as partnerships and trade unions, governed by special Acts of Parliament. An association of the above type is **not** a corporation and is **not** a separate legal entity. Thus, the club *is* the membership, the partners are the partnership etc.

Nevertheless, because one is dealing with a collection of people, the law has modified its approach towards unincorporated associations in a number of ways.

Simple unincorporated associations e.g. The Trubshaw Hamster Appreciation Society

Builders are most likely to meet these as clients, or they may belong to one socially. These are not partnerships, because they are not in business, nor are they companies because they have not incorporated themselves under the Companies Act.

The members of the society **are** the club. It has **no** separate legal personality from its members. Thus, should a civil wrong be committed by the club or a member on its behalf, all the club members are liable. Similarly, if the club enters into a contract, then strictly speaking, all are liable on the contract.

However, the chances of tracing all the members at a particular time, in order to sue them, is extremely difficult and undesirable. Thus, the courts allow the club to be sued (or to sue) in a **representative action**. This means that the plaintiff may trace a few members, who he then sues as **representatives** of the club. Judgment against them is judgment against the club, and if there is no club property to satisfy judgment, then the property of the representatives may be taken. The representatives of course, can then claim back from the other club members a contribution to their loss. But, this is easier said than done in practice.

Most clubs will have a **committee**. If they should do or authorize something on behalf of a club, then they will be primarily liable as if they were representatives above.

Property of the club belongs to all the members. But in most cases, if there is more than a few hundred pounds worth, then trustees should be appointed to deal with it properly on behalf of the club.

Anyone signing or otherwise making a contract on behalf of a club, make themselves primarily liable for that contract, with a right of contribution and indemnity from the other members.

Thus, one can see that membership of a club has its drawbacks. For the builder, when undertaking work for a club, it is probably sensible to make sure that he has a sufficient advance payment before starting the job. This can also be said of small registered companies as clients, and the builder ought to check on their credit worthiness. There are firms (business organizations) which undertake enquiries into financial status, and these can be very useful in business, when dealing with an unknown client.

Partnership

Definition. A partnership is defined by S.1 Partnership Act 1890 as 'the relation which subsists between persons carrying on a business with a *view of profit*'.

So any business relationship between two or more people which falls within the definition will be a partnership. There must be a business, at least two people and an agreement to share profits. Thus, if you and a friend agree to buy a dilapidated house, do it up and split the profits, then that is a partnership. Partnerships may be set up for a particular project (a consortium), or for a particular length of time or they may carry on for an unspecified period.

Not legal entities.   A partnership is **not** a corporation and thus the partners are the business. If the business does not do well, then the partner's own private assets can be taken to pay the business debts. If the partnership is sued, then the individual partners must be sued (*see* the Civil Liability (Contribution) Act 1978 on p. 240). However, the courts allow actions to be brought or defended by the partnership in the partnership name: RSC Ord. 81 r.1.

The partners are self-employed for tax and social security purposes, and once again, adequate insurance should be taken out by each of the partners to cover not only their own life and health but also those of the other partners.

Formalities.   The essence of a partnership is contractual. Thus, a partnership can be created very informally as in the example above. A verbal agreement may be sufficient or the partnership may be inferred from the parties' conduct. A person may even be estopped from denying that he is not a partner of someone else, if that is how he has been behaving.

Most sensible and businesslike people however enter into a written agreement which will form the basis of their working relationship. The best type of written agreement would be a proper partnership agreement which would contain terms covering all the sorts of matters which could create problems in the future (*see* Fig. 7.5).

A partnership agreement is particularly important because in the absence of any agreement between the parties, the terms of the Partnership Act 1890 apply and this can cause individual hardship.

Partnership Act 1890. Rights and duties in the absence of contrary agreement either verbal or written.   Under the Act, partners are entitled to share profits and losses equally, and must make equal contributions to capital. In practice, most people make unequal capital contributions and therefore **must** make a contrary agreement to make sure their share of the profits is in proportion to their contribution or work-load.

Each partner is entitled to share in the management of the firm. Once again, a sensible partnership will have partners of different ages and experience to make sure of the continuity of the firm. By agreement, new young partners being taken on, will usually not be allowed to take part in running the business.

The Act makes no allowances for a salary to be paid pending profit sharing at the end of the year. The partnership agreement should therefore alter this position: S.24.

If the partnership has no time limit, then any partner may give

Parties	AN AGREEMENT made the thirtieth day of January one thousand nine hundred and eighty four BETWEEN BIGGLES SMITH of 9 Splott Lane Ewell in the County of Surrey of the one part and COSMO BLOGGS of 37 Coronation Street Ewell aforesaid of the other part
Formation	WHEREBY IT IS AGREED that the parties hereto (hereinafter together called the partners) shall be partners in the business of builders upon the terms hereinafter contained namely
Name	1. The partnership business shall be carried on under the firm name of
Address	Bloggs, Smith & Co. at 86 Drain Drive Ewell aforesaid and at such other places or place as the partners may from time to time approve
Duration	2. The partnership shall continue until determined as hereinafter provided
Capital	The partners shall immediately after the signing of this agreement pay into an account to be opened in the name of the partnership at Cashwell Bank Ewell Branch the following sums namely the said Biggles Smith the sum of five thousand pounds and the said Cosmo Bloggs the sum of three thousand pounds
Shares capital profits	4. The capital and profits of the partners shall belong as to five-eighths to the said Biggles Smith and as to three-eighths to the said Cosomo Bloggs and they shall bear all losses in the same proportions

Fig. 7.5   Partnership agreement

236

Accounts	5. The usual books of account shall be kept properly posted up
Half-yearly accts	6. On the first day of April and on each succeeding first day of September an account shall be taken of all assets and liabilities of the partnership and a balance sheet and profit and loss account showing what is due to each partner in respect of capital and share of profits shall be prepared and shall be signed by each partner who shall be bound thereby unless some manifest error shall be found therein within three months in which case such error shall be rectified
Drawings	7. The partners shall be entitled to draw out of the partnership bank accounts on account of their respective shares of profits the following weekly sums namely the said Biggles Smith the sum of eighty pounds and the said Cosmo Bloggs the sum of sixty pounds but if when the next following half yearly account is taken it appears that either partner has drawn any sum in excess of his share of profits he shall forthwith repay such excess
Duties	8. Each partner shall be just and faithful to the other and shall diligently attend to the partnership business and devote his whole time and attention thereto. Each partner shall be entitled to four weeks holiday in each year

Fig. 7.5 cont'd.

Acts not to be done without consent

9. Neither partner shall without the consent of the other engage in any business other than that of the partnership or engage or dismiss any employee of the partnership or become bail or surety for any person or lend any partnership property release any debt due to the partnership or except in the ordinary course of business draw accept or endorse any bill of exchange

Determination

10. The partnership may be determined by either partner giving to the other not less than three month's notice in writing expiring on the 1st day of April or the 1st day of September in any year

Rts on determination or dissolution

11. (i) if the partnership shall be determined by notice pursuant to the last preceding clause or dissolved by the death or bankruptcy of either partner or by order of the court the partner to whom notice is given or the surviving or solvent partner or the partner to whose application such order was made as the case may be may within twenty-one days from the giving of such notice or within twenty-one days from such death or bankruptcy or the making of such order as the case may be by notice in writing to the other partner or his personal representatives trustee in bankruptcy or receiver elect either to have the partnership wound up pursuant to the provisions of the Partnership Act 1890 or to purchase the share of the other partner at the net value thereof as agreed between the partner giving

Fig. 7.5 cont'd.

notice (hereinafter called the
purchaser) and the other partner or
his personal representatives trustee
in bankruptcy or receiver elect as the
case may be (hereinafter called the
vendor) or in default of such
agreement as assessed by a valuer to
be nominated by the purchaser and the
vendor jointly in writing or in
default of such nomination to be
appointed by the president for the
time being of the Royal Institution of
Chartered Surveyors and in agreeing or
assessing the net value of such share
the goodwill of the partnership shall
be taken into account.

(ii) Any valuer so nominated or
appointed shall act as an expert and
not as an arbitrator and his
professional charges shall be borne by
the vendor and purchaser in equal
shares

**Payment of
purchase
price**

12. On the purchase by one partner of
the share of the other partner
pursuant to the last preceding clause
hereof the purchase money shall be
paid with interest thereon at the rate
of £14 per cent from the date of
determination or dissolution of the
partnership within one year from such
date

**Restriction
on
competition**

13. The partner whose share is
purchased shall not for three years
from the date of determination or
dissolution of directly or indirectly
carry on or be concerned or interested
in the business of building within a
radius of two miles from Ewell either

Fig. 7.5 cont'd.

```
                    alone or jointly with or as director
                    manager agent or employee of any other
                    person firm or corporation

AS WITNESS our hands the day and year first before
written



SIGNED BY THE SAID BIGGLES SMITH
in the presence of:-




SIGNED BY THE SAID COSMO BLOGGS
in the presence of:-
```

Fig. 7.5 cont'd.

notice to dissolve the partnership **at any time**. It is important therefore to enter into a fixed term partnership which will then end only at the expiration of the period: S.26.

The death or bankruptcy of a partner will bring a partnership automatically to an end. This position should be altered by agreement, to allow the other partners to carry on the business. No allowance is given in the Act for retirement.

Liability of partnership.   Each partner acts as an agent for the firm and binds the firm by any acts made on its behalf.

The old rule that only one action can be brought for a claim in contract is now altered by the Civil Liability (Contribution) Act 1978 (*see* p. 243). Thus, at common law, liability in contract is joint and only one action could be brought necessitating knowing all the partners names to make sure of getting judgment against all of the firm (and thus being able to enforce the judgment against all of them). Now, judgment against one partner if not satisfied, will allow the continuance of the action or the starting of another action against the other partners. In practice however, a representative action can be used and judgment can then be given against all the partners.

Other aspects of forming a partnership.   Certain types of businesses can **only** operate as partnerships e.g. solicitors, accountants, architects, as incorporation is not allowed by the Companies Act 1985.

Partnership names.   *See* Business names on p. 226. Where a partnership has more than 20 partners, the names of *all* need not be included on their documentation. But, a list of names must be kept at the principal place of business.

Taxation.   As they are businesses, partnerships have to prepare annual accounts and submit these to the Inland Revenue. However, each partner is then separately taxed on his partnership income.

CHAPTER 8

The law of torts

Types of wrongs

Crimes

There are many things which people should not do, because they are crimes, i.e. wrongs which are so bad, that the commission of them may lead to **prosecution** by the State, and possibly, some sort of punishment (*see* Ch. 1). Punishments may take the form of fines, imprisonment, suspended sentences, community service orders, driving bans etc (*see* p. 49).

The most serious crimes, such as murder, were developed by the common law, and for this reason, the Crown prosecutes the offender on behalf of the State. Such criminal cases are referred to in the law reports as '*R* v. ?', the title *R* being short for Rex (King) or Regina (Queen) and v. short for versus (against). Less serious cases are usually prosecuted by the police, and the name of the chief constable for the area, will be used in the title of the case. Prosecutions by private citizens are possible but these are less common.

Before such prosecutions can be dealt with in the criminal courts (magistrates' or Crown Courts), the offender will usually have to be apprehended by the police. The case for the prosecution will then be prepared, either by the Crown Prosecution Service which is being introduced by the Prosecution of Offences Act 1985, which employs barristers and solicitors, or by the police themselves, in less serious cases.

There are many other types of offences which are dealt with in the criminal courts which, perhaps do not strictly fall within our own concept of what is criminal, e.g. traffic offences, hygiene regulation breaches, breaches of the Health and Safety at Work etc. Act 1974, breaches of the Construction Regulations, Town and Country Planning Act etc. These offences have been created by statute, and are designed to improve society in general. As they are statutory creations, many are not the responsibility of the police, and other agents of the state have to apprehend offenders and **prosecute**. Who does what, depends on the enabling Act, and reference should always be made to the appropriate Act, to see that any prosecutions are **intra vires** i.e. within the powers, given to them by the Act. Thus local authorities will prosecute people making a statutory noise nuisance, under the Control of Pollution Act

1974, or for breaching building regulations. The Inspectorate of the Health and Safety Executive will prosecute under the Health and Safety at Work etc Act 1974.

Torts

There is another category of wrongs however, which does not fall within the public legal sphere. These are torts which are **private** or **civil wrongs**. Whether or not someone has the right to **sue** another for such a wrong, depends on the individual tort and the circumstances. Generally, torts are a product of the Common Law, and not of statute (although there are some exceptions). Torts are not treated in the same way as crimes, because the tort is usually offensive only to one person, or a small section of society, and not to society in general. If someone walks across my lawn, or calls me a thief, or spits on me, it will only be upsetting to me, unless their behaviour crosses the thin dividing line between 'pure torts' and becomes a **crime**. Thus, torts are in the province of private law, and are dealt with in the civil courts, (county or Queens Bench Division). But, some behaviour can be **both** a **tort** and a **crime**. For example, if a workman is injured on site, and there was a breach of the Construction Regulations by his employer, his employer may be **prosecuted** for that breach, as it was a crime. **Also**, he may be sued in the civil courts, either for the tort of breach of statutory duty, or for breaking his employer's duty to take care of his employees, i.e. a sort of negligence.

In tort, there is no 'punishment' for the tortfeasor. If he is found to have committed the tort, then he will be made to pay compensation or damages to the other, there are alternative remedies, such as injunctions. The following are torts: negligence; defamation (libel and slander); trespass to land; trespass to the person (assault and battery); trespass to chattels; malicious prosecution; false imprisonment; breach of statutory duty; *Rylands* v. *Fletcher* liability; nuisance (private).

Breaches of contract

If someone does something which is against the terms of their contract with another, then liability is once again civil (private). Generally, the state is unconcerned with contract disputes and rights and duties stem from the agreement made between the parties (the contract). Thus, only the contractual parties have rights and duties, and no-one else. These presuppose that there was a valid, binding contract to start with, and the rules of contract law must be applied. On the whole, contract law has been formulated by the common law. But in the nineteenth and twentieth centuries, consumerism has led to Acts of Parliament being passed, to give greater protection to certain types of contracting parties, such as a buyer of goods.

If there is a dispute, then the parties generally **sue** in the civil courts (county or Queen's Bench Division).

Some breaches of contract would amount to torts or even crimes, e.g. if a builder builds so badly, that the house is unsafe and kills people, he could be in breach of his contract, to build in a workmanlike manner. Therefore, he could be prosecuted for breaching building or construction regulations, and could be sued for negligence or breach of statutory duty.

Whether a plaintiff sues for breach of contract or a tort, the causes of action are dealt with using the separate principles of law.

Breach of contract, if proved, generally leads to a claim for damages, although there are other remedies, e.g. a decree of specific performance, or an injunction.

The torts which we will examine, are those which are more likely to be committed in construction work. Each one will be dealt with separately. However, there are some common aspects to each tort. But, before we look at each tort, let us first examine, the different types of liability in tort (*see* Fig. 8.1).

Types of liability for torts

Personal liability

Here, the person who actually committed the tort (the **tortfeasor**) is sued and will have to pay **all** the damages.

If other people are involved in committing the **same** tort, then they will be **jointly** liable, i.e. they are both personally responsible for the **same** tort. In such cases, they may both be sued, or either may be sued. They are both liable for all the damage.

Sometimes, the resulting damage may have been caused by different torts. For example, a drunken driver may have caused an accident which is made worse by the fact that his car was negligently repaired by his garage. The sufferer can sue both parties for two separate tortious acts (both negligence). They are **concurrently** liable, and both are personally liable for the victim's injuries.

By S.3 of the Civil Liability (Contribution) Act 1978, where judgment for a debt or damages has been awarded against a person who is jointly liable with another, then this, is no **bar** to another action or the continuation of the same action against that other person. Thus, if Arthur, Bill and Charlie (a building partnership) are sued for a tort or a debt, for which they are jointly liable, and Arthur admits that he is liable, and judgment is entered against him, the action against Bill and Charlie can continue. Before this Act, judgment against one tortfeasor could have prevented further actions in certain cases.

On being held liable in an action or on settling a claim made against him a defendant may recover a contribution from any other person who is responsible, for the same damage. The responsibility of such other persons may be by virtue of liability in tort, in contract, breach

Public Law	Private Law	
Crimes	**Torts**	**Contracts**
State prosecutes offenders in criminal courts.	Individuals sue tort-feasors in civil courts	One contracting party sues the other in the civil courts.
Criminal law for the benefit of the state	Tort for benefit of citizens as individuals depending on each type of tort.	Contract usually only for benefit of parties to contract.
Everyone has rights and duties.	Rights and duties belong only to those to whom they are owed under each type of tort.	Only the parties have rights and duties. There must therefore be a **valid** contract.
Generally liability is personal.	Liability can be personal and vicarious.	Liability is personal.
If found guilty, offender is punished	If liable in tort either pays damages or subject to an injunction.	If in breach must pay damages or sometimes subject to injunction or decree of specific performance.
Limitation periods – none.	Personal injury claims – 3 years Others – 6 years	Simple contracts – 6 years Specialty contracts (Under seal) – 12 years

Fig. 8.1 Characteristics of crimes, torts and contracts

of trust or in any other way.

In claiming such a contribution, the defendant must do this within **two** years of the date on which the right to recover contributions arises: S.1 Civil Liability (Contribution) Act 1978. However most contribution proceedings are part of the main action. Thus, if the plaintiff fails to join all possible co-defendants, the defendant, himself, may serve a third party notice on other persons who are jointly or concurrently responsible for the damage.

The amount that must be contributed by others will be assessed by the court in much the same way as under contributory negligence (*see* p. 274).

Thus, in a building contract, if a contractor is sued for a tort and he regards the employer as partly to blame for the resultant damage, he may serve a third party notice on the employer and join him as a co-defendant in the action. Alternatively, if he settles the claim out of court, he may then seek a contribution from the employer within two years of the date of the cause of action.

Vicarious liability

Where someone authorizes another, either expressly or impliedly to do something, and that person in so doing, commits a tort, then the person authorizing the behaviour will be **vicariously** (Vicar. – Latin, a delegate), i.e. indirectly, liable for that tort.

Thus, employers may be vicariously liable for their employees. Vicarious liability is **additional** to personal liability. So, for example, an employer may be personally negligent for failing to warn his operatives of a dangerous substance used on site. He may be vicariously liable if one of his foremen inadequately supervises workmen dealing with that substance, so that an accident occurs, injuring those workmen.

Vicarious liability is joint, and the injured person can sue one or the other, or both the employer and the foreman. If only the employer is sued, he may then try to recover **all** the damages paid, back from the employee, as an employee owes a right of **indemnity** to his employer (but, *see* page 387). If the employer partly contributed to the commission of the tort, then he can only claim a contribution (i.e. **part**) from the employee. If the employee alone is sued, the employer can claim nothing from the employee, as he has lost nothing, nor can he claim anything from his employee (unless, the employer was partly to blame in which case, the employee can bring in the employer as a co-defendant in the course of the action).

Obviously, the employer is not always vicariously liable for his employee's torts. The following must therefore be noted.

The tort must have been committed 'in the course of his employment'

An employer is never responsible in tort for the private behaviour of his employees. Thus, a quantity surveyor who runs someone over on a Sunday outing will be solely and personally liable for that act, even if he was driving a company car.

How wide is 'in the course of the employment'?

Obviously, vicarious liability is an additional problem for the employer. Not only is he responsible for his **own** torts, but he may also be responsible for the torts of his many employees. To minimise his liability, he will therefore, try to restrain the behaviour of his employees. He will, for example, lay down terms and conditions of employment in the employee's contract of employment. He may specify forbidden acts, and these may be backed up by written warnings or notices to the employees.

Unfortunately, while these restrictions are designed to avoid vicarious liability, the courts are reluctant to protect the employers in such situations. Thus, often, where an outsider would have presumed that the employee had the authority to do the forbidden act, which amounted to the tort, then in all likelihood, the employer will still be liable.

If the employee is doing something totally outside the scope of his employment, or as it is known 'on a frolic' of his own, such as leaving work without permission, then, any tort committed is his sole responsibility. For example, in *Hilton* v. *Thomas Burton (Rhodes) Ltd* 1961, some demolition workers were allowed the use of their employer's van. After working some time, they decided to travel seven miles to a cafe for tea. When they were almost there, they changed their minds, and started back to the demolition site. One was killed in an accident, caused by the other's negligent driving. The employer was held **not** to be vicariously liable, as they were on 'a frolic'.

Employers, must, by law, have insurance cover, to cover claims by injured workmen. Building contractors, usually have greater insurance cover than most. Thus, if they are sued for vicarious liability, the claim will (if proved) be met by the insurance company. But, if the workman was on 'a frolic', then he alone will have to shoulder the claim. If he is insured, e.g. under a third party motor insurance policy, which is compulsory when driving, then he is also protected from severe financial loss. But, if he was driving without insurance, or the tort was committed in an uninsured situation, then he will have to bear the cost, possibly, for the rest of his life.

It is clear therefore, that employees are wise to obey their employer's instructions, to make sure of the existence of vicarious liability, and thus share the financial burden.

Furthermore, failure to insure for third party claims, whilst driving, is foolhardiness of the utmost degree. Being prosecuted for driving whilst uninsured, is nothing, compared to a lifetime of weekly payments to an injured victim.

What is meant by 'employment'

There can be no vicarious liability on the part of an employer, for someone who is not an employee, (unless he was authorised in some other way, e.g. as an agent).

Thus, one must distinguish between employees who have a contract **of** employment or a contract **of** service with their employer from independent contractors, who are employed under a contract **for** services.

This seems simple enough, but modern practices, especially in the construction industry, very often combine elements of both types of contract, and the result, legally, can be confusing. The following example indicates the probable legal situation.

A builder is vicariously liable for his own workmen's torts (*see* Fig. 8.2). If the builder sub-contracts the roofing work to another company, the builder will not necessarily be responsible for the torts of the sub-contractor's employees. The roofing company, will, of course, be responsible for the torts of their workers.

The trouble is, that, it is often difficult to decide, whether, someone is an employee or an independent contractor. Remember, we are concerned with the tort situation, and not with the contractual.

There are many factors to be taken into account. Someone is more likely to be an 'employee' in tort:

- if he is described as such in his contract (but, *see* below).
- if he is paid by an 'employer' who pays his national insurance contributions and taxes.
- if his 'employer' has the right to dismiss him, and to tell him what to do (but, not necessarily how to do it) (the control test).

Even if the contract describes the worker as an **employee**, the court will decide on the true nature of the relationship. A similar problem was faced in *Ferguson* v. *John Dawson and Partners (Contractors) Ltd* 1976. A labourer was taken on the 'lump' system, to be paid at an

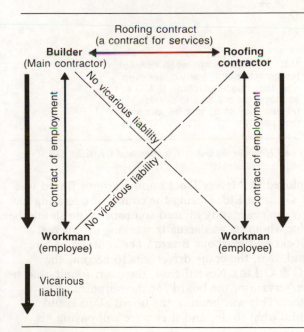

Fig. 8.2 Diagram to illustrate the concept of vicarious liability

hourly rate. As he was on the 'lump', **no** tax was deducted from his wages, nor did he receive national insurance cards, or a written statement of his contract terms. He was injured when he fell from a roof, and claimed damages for breach of statutory duty, laid down by the construction regulation. Thus, he had to prove that he was an employee. On examining **all** the relevant circumstances, the court found him to be an employee.

Sometimes, an employee of another, may become the responsibility of the person, for whom he is actually working. This can happen, where, a workman is lent or hired to another company. The leading case on this is *Mersey Docks and Harbour Board* v. *Coggins and Griffiths Ltd* 1947 (*see* Fig. 8.3).

Fig. 8.3 *Mersey Docks and Harbour Board* v. *Coggins and Griffiths Ltd.*

A crane driver employed by Mersey Docks and Harbour Board was hired to Coggins and Griffiths Ltd. During the course of operating his crane for the company, he negligently injured someone. Who should be sued? The company for whom he was **actually** working or, his real employers, Mersey Docks and Harbour Board? The contract of hire between them, had said, that, the crane driver was to become the servant of the hirer (C & G Ltd). Nevertheless, the court found, that he was still the employee/servant of the board for the purposes of vicarious liability in tort. This was because the board alone could dismiss him and tell him what to do, and they were still paying his wages.

Thus, applying these criteria described previously labour only subcontract workmen, would probably, in tort, be the employees of the main contractor, for the purposes of vicarious liability. But, of course each case is decided on its merits.

Liability for independent contractors – exceptions

As stated above, generally, an employer is **not** vicariously liable for the acts of an independent contractor, but this all depends on the circumstances of each case.

Employer's personal negligence in choosing or instructing independent contractors   However, even if he may not be vicariously liable, he may nevertheless be held responsible for the acts of an independent contractor. This is because, there may be a breach of his own **personal duty of care.** Thus, he will be personally liable, if he chose an incompetent contractor.

In building work, therefore, a main contractor, should exercise reasonable care in choosing sub-contractors. There is less room for such error in the case of nominated sub-contractors, where the employer will have played his part in the choice. But, remember this is tort, and we are concerned with the liability of the main contractor.

Thus, the standard of care will be approached in the usual way (*see* p. 262). If the work is of a specialist nature, then the contractor should see that the job is given to a competent sub-contractor. He would be negligent, if he failed to check that the sub-contractor was competent, or if he failed to instruct him properly on what was required.

In *Kealey* v. *Heard* 1983, an owner of adjoining houses, contracted with a number of different specialists, to convert the houses into flats. One of these specialists was a plasterer, who was injured on scaffolding erected by another unknown workman. The plasterer sued the owner for, among other things, negligence. The Queen's Bench Division held that he was liable. He owed a duty to take care and control of the building work on his property. He had not discharged this duty by appointing an independent contractor who he thought to be competent. He should have supervised the work properly.

(Note: the occupier's duty to his lawful visitors under the Occupiers' Liability Act 1957, *see* p. 275 is discharged by S.2(4)b if the damage caused is due to faulty workmanship of construction, maintenance or repair done by an independent contractor, and the occupier had, in all the circumstances, acted reasonably in choosing or supervising that contractor.)

The employer's absolute or strict personal duty, to see that the independent contractor, takes care.   If a tort or statute, imposes a strict duty on someone, such as an employer then there can be **no** defence, to say that the independent contractor actually committed the dangerous act.

1. Under the Factories Act 1961. Certain machines must be properly fenced, and that is the end of the matter. If they are not, it is the factory owner who is responsible.

2. Rule in *Rylands* v. *Fletcher. (see* p. 285). The employer, as the occupier, is responsible for independent contractors.

3. Public nuisance. Employers are responsible for independent contractors' torts committed on a highway which amount to a public nuisance.

4. Private nuisance. An occupier is responsible for independent contractors (being within their control), for nuisances they commit on a highway, or interference with rights of support, and probably for other types of nuisances.

5. Employer's Liability (Defective Equipment) Act 1969. If damage is caused by a faulty piece of equipment, then, under the Act, the **employer** is liable for injury to his employee, *provided* the equipment was faulty through the fault of another (e.g. the manufacturer).

6. Liability for a negligent act, which is an essential element of the delegated task. If a person contracts with another, to do something, which is, in itself, completely negligent, or partly negligent, or, which will necessitate some negligent act, then that person, will be liable for the independent contractor's act.

Strict liability

Usually, in tort, there has to be some element of fault on the part of the tortfeasor. In other words, he should have taken greater care than he did when he committed the tort.

Examples of strict liability

There are some exceptions to this rule however, when a person will be strictly liable, even though there was **no** fault or intention on his part. Merely by doing certain things is enough to give rise to an action in torts.

Defamation. Thus, writing something libellous about another which is not true, is grounds for an action for defamation. This is so, even if the maker of the statement meant no harm, or thought the statement to be true. Such a tort is said to be actionable per se (in itself).

Trespass. This is also a tort actionable per se. Merely entering on another's land, is sufficient to give grounds for an action in trespass. **No** damage need be shown, nor intention, and mistake is no excuse.

Rule in *Rylands* v. *Fletcher*. There is strict liability for people allowing dangerous things to escape from their land (*see* p. 285).

Vicarious liability. Also, vicarious liability is strict liability. This means, that provided the elements of the tort are proved against the tortfeasor, then the employer/authorizer will be liable, even though there was no fault on his part.

Statutory breaches. In the case of statutory duties, there may be strict liability, for failure to abide by the statute, e.g. certain breaches of the Factory Act 1961.

Liability for independent contractors. See also the examples given under the preceding heading, where persons are strictly liable for the torts of independent contractors.

Premises close to highways. There is also strict liability for dangerous premises situated close to a highway which, through disrepair, injure passers-by (*see* p. 289).

Specific torts

Negligence

This is probably the most well known and certainly the most important of all the torts. Most people know of someone who has sued for damages following a car accident, an accident at work or a hospital operation that went wrong. In each case, the most likely cause of action was negligence, although they might have been able to sue for breach of statutory duty as an alternative (*see* p. 304).

In order to be able to sue successfully for negligence, three essential elements must be proved. The lack of any one of these elements will make the action fail.

The vital elements

1. The defendant must have owed the plaintiff a 'duty of care' at the time of the alleged negligent behaviour, *and*
2. There must have been a breach of the duty of care, *and*
3. Actual damage must have been caused as a result of the breach.

However, the presence of the vital elements can only be determined **after** the event. Thus, whilst one can recommend an ideal pattern of behaviour in a given situation, this may still not prevent there being negligence at a later date.

This is because the tort of negligence is not a set of fixed rigid rules like the construction regulations. It is very fluid and can change and adapt to meet society's needs. Of course, if there is a case of negligence proved in circumstances similar to those in which you are operating, then obviously you should examine your procedures before someone gets injured.

The duty of care

For many years before 1932, many successful cases of negligence were taken to court – but these were usually based entirely on there having been a precedent covering the special circumstances of the case. For example, perhaps in 1850 someone was injured by a stagecoach being driven negligently. If that man was able to sue, then a victim injured at a later date in similar circumstances would also have been able to recover damages in negligence.

Thus, despite the existence of liability for negligence, what did not exist was a standardized way of deciding whether in **any** given factual situation, a legal duty to take care existed, giving someone the right to sue for the tort of negligence. Remember, no law can exist without there being a duty and a corresponding right.

Donoghue v. *Stevenson – formulation of a test 'the neighbour principle'*

So until 1932, no such test to find whether a duty relating to negligence existed. Fortunately, the famous Scottish case of *Donoghue* v. *Stevenson* was taken to the House of Lords, purely on a preliminary point of law.

What Mrs Donoghue's lawyers wanted to know was, could a ginger beer manufacturer owe a consumer of his ginger beer, a duty vis-á-vis the ginger beer to take care of that consumer, so that he would not suffer injury by drinking it?

What happened was this. Mrs Donoghue had gone to a park cafe with a friend. The friend bought her a bottle of ginger beer, which unbeknown to all contained a decomposed snail, the bottle being of the old opaque type. As a result of drinking the ginger beer and being shocked at the sight of the snail, she was absent from work with gastro-enteritis and shock.

Before her lawyers would risk pursuing the case on the facts, they asked the court to rule on whether, if they proved those facts, the case would be successful. This of course would depend on whether the manufacturer was under **any** legal duty to the consumer.

If we look at Fig. 8.4 we can see what the judges were trying to do. They knew of the other legal relationships (of contract) between manufacturer/cafe proprietor and cafe proprietor/friend. But, these were of little help to Mrs Donoghue who had no contract with anyone. Also, even if the friend had been the one to suffer and had sued in contract, the damages that he would have received would have been based on normal contractual rules (*see* p. 120) and not on the more

Fig. 8.4 *Donoghue* v. *Stevenson* – the legal position in contract and tort

true reflection of what was suffered as in negligence.

The House of Lords finally decided by a bare majority, that if the case proceeded and the facts were proved, Mrs Donoghue would succeed, (subsequently the case was never tried on the facts and Mrs Donoghue never recovered any compensation).

In the Lords' judgment, a very important principle emerged. This was described in Lord Atkin's speech and is usually referred to as the 'neighbour principle'.

He said that 'You must take reasonable care to avoid acts or omissions which you can reasonably foresee would be likely to injure your neighbour.

Who, then, in law is my neighbour? ... Persons ... so closely and directly affected by my act that I ought reasonably to have them in contemplation as being so affected when I am directing my mind to the acts or omissions which are called in question'.

The first part of the quotation is Lord Atkin's requirements for the tort of negligence. The second part shows that neighbours may only be people who are in a close legal relationship with the defendant. This is Lord Atkin's attempt to define 'proximity', a word used in cases prior to *Donoghue* v. *Stevenson* which had proved a stumbling block through lack of a suitable definitive test. Indeed, it seems from recent cases that 'proximity', this closeness of relationship in law, is the paramount determinant for the existence of a duty of care.

Lord Wilberforce in the important building negligence case *Anns* v.

Merton London Borough Council 1978 restated the principle in a more modern way. He said, that whether a duty of care exists can be 'approached in two stages. *First*, one has to ask whether as between the alleged wrongdoer and the person who has suffered damage, there is sufficient relationship of *proximity* or *neighbourhood* such that in the reasonable contemplation of the former, carelessness on his part may be likely to cause damage to the latter, in which case a prima facie duty of care arises.

Secondly, if the first question is answered affirmatively, it is necessary to consider whether there are any considerations which ought to negative or to reduce or limit the scope of the duty or the class of person to whom it is owed or the damages to which a breach of it may give rise.'

The proximity requirement

'Persons so **closely** and **directly** affected by my act' per Lord Atkin in *Donoghue* v. *Stevenson*. 'A sufficient relationship of proximity or neighbourhood' per Lord Wilberforce in *Anns* v. *Merton LBC*.

The courts therefore require that there should be a sufficient closeness of relationship (proximity) between the wrongdoer and the plaintiff. In some cases, the proximity aspect is sufficient to override any other objections (such as those of policy) to there being a duty of care in existence. It may even override the objection that in normal circumstances, damages for pure monetary loss cannot be claimed in negligence (*see* p. 261). For example in *Junior Books Ltd* v. *Veitchi Ltd* 1982, (another Scottish case of immense importance), specialist flooring sub-contractors negligently laid a floor in the plaintiff's factory. The floor required replacing and the plaintiff asked for damages to cover that cost as well as for removing the machinery and loss of company profits during the period of relaying. It should be remembered that as they were sub-contractors, there was no privity of contract between them and the employer, and thus no chance of suing them in contract. (For some reason not mentioned, the employers chose not to sue the main contractors in contract or delict (Scottish tort)).

However, the House of Lords decided that the parties were in a sufficiently proximate position to allow a duty of care to exist, as the sub-contractors should have known the consequences of negligently laying the floor.

As Lord Roskill said 'Why is it conceded that the appellants owed a duty of care to others **not** to construct the flooring so that those others were in peril of suffering loss of damage to their persons or their property, (but) that a duty of care should not be equally owed to the respondents who though not in direct contractual relationship with the appellants, were as nominated sub-contractors **in almost as close a commercial relationship** with the appellants as it is possible to envisage short of privity of contract; so as not to expose the respondents to a possible financial loss for repairing the flooring should it prove that the flooring had been negligently constructed.'

Similarly in *Ross* v. *Caunters* 1980 a firm of solicitors drew up a will. They failed to warn the testator that the will should not be witnessed by the husband of one of the beneficiaries (which nullifies the gift). When the testator died, the beneficiary sued the solicitors for the loss of her legacy. Although the solicitors agreed that they had been negligent, they said their only duty was owed to the testator. Applying the proximity test however, there was a sufficient degree of neighbourhood or proximity between the parties because, beneficiaries in such a position should be owed a duty of care as they would have been contemplated as being affected by the lack of advice to the testator. Thus, this was another example of pure monetary loss and professional negligence for which there are more restricted duties of care (*see* p. 260-1).

In *Anns* v. *Merton LBC*, the case which re-evaluated the neighbour principle, the council's building control inspector allegedly either failed to carry out an inspection of the foundations of a block of maisonettes, which were not deep enough to conform with the approved plans, or if they did, they did so negligently. The plaintiffs, the owners of the maisonettes, had suffered damage to their homes because the defective foundations caused structural movements. The building bye-laws did not impose a **duty** to inspect in such circumstances. The council had a mere **discretionary right** to do so if they wished. But, the court said that this discretion should have been exercised with care, and this gave rise to the close proximity between the plaintiffs and the council. As Lord Wilberforce said 'It must be in the reasonable contemplation, not only of the builder, but also of the local authority, that failure to comply with the bye-laws' requirements as to foundations, may give rise to a hidden defect, which in the future may cause damage to the building

---

Junior Books v. *Veitchi* 1983

Employer

Main contractor   ? Did the sub-contractors owe a duty to the employer. Yes. Close proximity.

Sub-contractor

Fig. 8.5 *Junior Books* v. *Veitchi*

Solicitors

Testator

?

Specified beneficiary in testator's will

Q. Was a duty owed when making the will to warn the testator not to have the will witnessed by a beneficiary or the spouse of a beneficiary, thereby showing that a duty was owed to such named beneficiaries.

A. Yes. The solicitors should have contemplated the problem, therefore proximity proven.

Fig. 8.6 *Ross* v. *Caunters*

affecting the safety and health of owners and occupiers. And as the building is intended to last, the class of owners and occupiers likely to be affected cannot be limited to those who go in immediately after construction.'

It should be noted that the judges also considered the position of the builder, which was not an issue in the appeal. They confirmed dicta in previous decisions about a local authority failing to inspect foundations properly, (*Dutton* v. *Bognor Regis UDC* 1972). Thus, builders of houses whether they own the land on which they are building or not, should owe duties of care to purchasers and subsequent purchasers, should the houses be defective. Lord Wilberforce also said, obiter, that in his opinion, the builder could be sued for breach of statutory duty for failing to comply with building regulations, by those people for whose

Anns v. *London Borough of Merton* 1978

Builder

Merton LBC

lessees

Subsequent Purchasers

? —————— ? Did the Council owe them a duty to inspect properly? **YES**

Fig. 8.7 *Anns* v. *Mertin L B C*

protection the regulations were made. Liability for breach of a duty under the Building Regulations is also imposed by S.38 Building Act 1984 a section yet to come into force. Thus, the builder is not immune from liability.

To sum up the proximity aspect therefore, we find that a duty of care will definitely have existed in relationships which were contractual or just short of contractual, or so close that no one else could have been contemplated as being affected, e.g. solicitor/client, builder/client, doctor/patient, dentist/patient, teacher/pupil, instructor/student situations and in the examples given previously. Perhaps you could make another list. Such relationships were so close that a duty of care should exist in negligence. As one moves away from such close proximity to the defendant (see Fig. 8.8) where there is no contractual or near contractual link, the possibility of there being a duty of care gets less certain and the reasonable foresight aspect comes into its own.

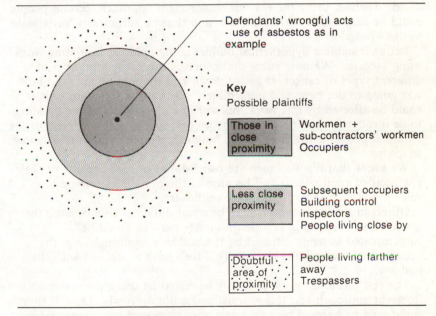

Defendants' wrongful acts
- use of asbestos as in example

Key
Possible plaintiffs

Those in close proximity	Workmen + sub-contractors' workmen Occupiers
Less close proximity	Subsequent occupiers Building control inspectors People living close by
Doubtful area of proximity	People living farther away Trespassers

Fig. 8.8 Illustration of proximity

The reasonable foresight aspect

'You must take care to avoid acts or omissions which you can reasonably foresee would be likely to injure your neighbours'; 'that I ought reasonably to have them in contemplation' Lord Atkin in *Donoghue* v. *Stevenson*; 'such that in the reasonable contemplation of the (wrongdoer) carelessness on his part may be likely to cause damage to the (plaintiff) in which case a prima facie duty of care arises' Lord Wilberforce in *Anns* v. *Merton LBC*.

In cases such as *Ross* v. *Caunters; Junior Books Ltd* v. *Veitchi Ltd*, the required degree of proximity between the parties is so clear, that it is obvious that the defendant should have owed the plaintiffs a duty of care. The consequences of their negligent actions should have been plain.

In less obvious situations, where the relationships between the parties do not appear to be so clear cut, the plaintiff's solicitors will have to examine all the circumstances, and try to prove to the court, that the defendant placed in the situation of the case **ought** to have contemplated his client as being someone who would be affected by the defendant's negligent actions. If they can prove this to the court's satisfaction, then they will have proved the required proximity between the parties, and thus shown the existence of the duty of care.

Expert and other evidence and common sense should be applied to decide whether, using the reasonable foresight approach, certain people could be neighbours within the law, and thus be sufficiently 'proximate to the wrongdoer'.

Let us imagine a hypothetical builder contemplating insulating work using asbestos. We now know that asbestos can cause a number of different types of cancer. If he sat down and thought about what he was going to do, he would immediately see that the following people could be affected by this work: his workmen; occupiers of the building to be insulated; building control inspectors; subsequent occupiers of the building; people living close to the building; people living further away; trespassers.

We know that his workmen are owed duties of care because of their contracts of employment and because of the pre-1932 common law rules which impose such duties on employers.

Others in the list however, may be owed duties of care because they are so closely related in law that no other persons could be contemplated as being affected by the builder's negligence, e.g. the occupiers of the building (especially if they have a contract with the builder).

The rest of the list must probably be tested by using the reasonable foresight approach and this is construed quite narrowly. Thus, if they could only be harmed by a fantastic possibility and not a reasonable probability, then they will not be neighbours within the law (and thus not sufficiently 'proximate'). It is at this end, that policy decisions may preclude the existence of a duty of care, and they will have no remedy in negligence.

Are there 'any considerations which ought to negative, or to reduce or limit the scope of the duty or the class of person to whom it is owed or the damages to which a breach of it may give rise'? (Lord Wilberforce, Anns v. Merton LBC 1978)

There are certain alleged cases of negligence in which, although it appears that there are all the elements for a successful case of negligence, the courts either refuse to find that a duty of care is owed or they impose stricter pre-conditions on finding the existence of such a duty.

Thus, certain people cannot be sued for negligence **at all**. Lawyers for example, when conducting court cases are immune from legal action (but not, for pre-trial work). Judges cannot be sued for negligence in conducting a court case, nor can arbitrators when making an award in an arbitration. A valuer is not an arbitrator however, if he is merely carrying out a valuation, and thus has no immunity.

Matters of public policy also enter into this question e.g. *Ashton* v. *Turner & another* 1980, partners in a crime should not be allowed to sue for negligence when it goes wrong (*see* p. 273).

Other important categories are concerned with liability for negligent statements and liability for pure monetary (pecuniary or economic) loss. With the emphasis on the proximity approach however, it may be that we are now moving to a situation where people suffering loss of any kind caused by negligent acts or statements will be able to recover damages, provided there was a sufficiently close relationship between the tortfeasor and the injured party.

Negligent statements – liability for words

Is it possible for someone who gives wrong advice or gives incorrect information to be sued for negligence? The answer, as always, is that it all depends.

Lord Atkin in *Donoghue* v. *Stevenson* 1932, probably never contemplated there being liability for negligent words, unless they resulted in damage to person or property.

For example, in *Clay* v. *A.J. Crump* 1963, an architect allowed a wall to remain standing on a demolition site. This lack of advice was held to amount to negligence when the wall fell and injured a workman.

Nevertheless, through this century, and in some cases, even before, there was a certain degree of liability for bad advice.

Thus, people in contract with each other, such as solicitor and client could sue for breach of contract. If the solicitor gave negligent advice, he could be sued. Similarly, if someone in a fiduciary (of good faith) relationship to another, such as a doctor and patient, gave bad advice, then he could be sued.

If the maker of a false statement is trying to induce someone to enter into a contract with him, then a number of courses of action are open to the other party. If the maker of the statement is telling downright lies, he can be sued for the tort of deceit, also called fraud. Certain requirements of the tort must be complied with. As the statement is a misrepresentation, the misled party can proceed under the

Misrepresentation Act 1967 (*see* p. 109) if the representation is made negligently or even innocently.

The above causes of action, however, are and were only available to contracting parties, parties in a fiduciary relationship, or people who had been deceived by a liar.

The leading case of *Hedley Byrne & Co Ltd* v. *Heller & Partners Ltd* 1964, has extended liability for the making of negligent statements to people who are not in such relationship.

H B & Co advertising agents were preparing an advertising campaign on behalf of a client, Easipower Ltd. They therefore booked advertising space in newspapers and time on radio and television in their own name, and thus, they would have to pay for this and recover their costs from Easipower.

In order to check whether Easipower would be able to pay the bill, H B & Co asked their bankers to find out from Easipower's bank (Heller & Partners Ltd) if they were financially sound. Initially, they confirmed by telephone that the company was sound. After a further request as to their creditworthiness, Hellers wrote that the company was 'good for its ordinary business engagements'. However, the letter contained an exclusion clause, so that the statement was made 'without responsibility on the part of this bank'. Easipower Ltd then went into liquidation and H B & Co Ltd lost a lot of money.

The question asked in this case was, did Hellers owe Hedley Byrne & Co a duty of care in the tort of negligence? The case went to the House of Lords.

The Lords in differing speeches agreed that the 'reasonable foresight' approach to the neighbour principle would not be enough to establish a duty of care. A sufficiently close relationship would be required. This was termed a 'special relationship'. How this relationship was decided

Fig. 8.9 *Hedley Byrne & Co. Ltd* v. *Heller & Partners Ltd.* 1964

upon, they failed to agree. But, in the present case they felt one did exist.

Unfortunately, because of the exemption clause, H B & Co lost their case.

So, the important aspect of this case, is that it allowed negligence cases to be brought for negligent words, be it advice or representations in a wider range of situations than the courts had previously allowed.

Thus, solicitors can be sued in negligence or in contract by their clients for their advice.

Architects when giving certificates in building contracts, can be sued in negligence by the employer if they negligently perform this task: *Sutcliffe* v. *Thackrah* 1974.

Liability can of course be excluded as it was in the Hedley Byrne case itself. However, such exclusion clauses must now be read in the light of the Unfair Contract Terms Act 1977 (*see* pp. 93–4).

Liability for economic loss (monetary or pecuniary loss)

Until recently, persons suffering from negligence which resulted in economic loss only, with no attendant physical damage to property or person, could not recover damages in negligence. Thus, if there was **only** economic loss, they could not sue in negligence at all unless the principles in *Hedley Byrne & Co Ltd* v. *Heller and Partners Ltd* 1964 could be applied.
(Note: shoddy workmanship will result in immediate economic loss if the work has to be redone e.g. wallpaper applied upside down. If actual damage is caused to the property, then there is no problem about suing in negligence.)

It now appears from *Junior Books Ltd* v. *Veitchi Ltd* 1982 (*see* pp. 254–5) however, that where there is a sufficiently close degree of proximity between the parties, damages for economic loss only, can be recovered. To quote Lord Roskill: 'The appellants must be taken to have known that if they did the work negligently (as it must be assumed that they did) the resulting defects would at some time require remedying by the respondents expending money upon the remedial measures, as a consequence of which, the respondents would suffer financial or economic loss.'

Lord Roskill, thus, has encouraged 'the next logical step forward in the development of this branch of the law. I see no reason why what was called 'damage to the pocket' simpliciter should be disallowed, when 'damage to the pocket' coupled with physical damage has hitherto always been allowed'.

Thus, in *Junior Books* v. *Veitchi Ltd* the argument by the sub-contractors that their duty of care was limited only to 'exercise reasonable care, so as to mix and lay the flooring as to ensure that it is not a danger to persons or property, excluding … the flooring itself', was rejected.

To conclude therefore by pointing out some anomalies. If someone buys a bottle of ginger beer with a snail in it and suffers no injury, he cannot sue in negligence, probably because, whilst there is a close enough relationship of proximity for injury to the person, there isn't for economic loss, as reasoned in *Junior Books Ltd* v. *Veitchi*. The injured consumer has two courses of action however. He can go back to the shop and ask for his money back under the Sale of Goods Act 1979, *see* p. 171, and he can complain to the local authority who may prosecute whoever is responsible, be it manufacturer or shop owner under various regulations.

When is the duty owed?

A person can only be owed a duty of care **at the time the damage occurs**. This seems obvious if one thinks in simple terms of a car accident, for example. Only the person who has been run over is owed a duty of care. Such a person may be one of a class, e.g. members of a bus queue, who are hit by an out of control bus.

This is less easy to understand in relation to damage to buildings, because, if one is only owed a duty when damage **actually** occurs (and not when the damage is discovered) subsequent purchasers of houses could be excluded from having a right of action. *Pirelli General Cable Works Ltd* v. *Oscar Faber & Partners* 1983 however confirms this point of view. Thus, the date on which the cause of action is founded in an action for damages caused by negligent construction or building design, is the *date of the damage*. Purchasers of such property known as successors-in-title would still be able to sue, (but subject to the limitation periods) (*see* p. 307).

Breaching the duty of care – the second element

Having established that a duty of care was owed in the circumstances, the plaintiff must then prove to the court that there was a breach of that duty i.e. that he was negligent in fact.

This is done in two stages. **First** taking the circumstances of the case, the court decides on the **standard of care** i.e. what should have been done by the defendant. **Secondly**, the defendant's actual behaviour is measured against the established standard. If it falls short, he is negligent, if it matches or is above the standard, then there is no breach.

The standard of care

The standard of care is not that of 'superbuilder' nor that of a fool. The court 'fixes' the standard by examining evidence which would show what the **average reasonable** person placed in the circumstances of the case should have done. Experts may be called to give evidence of trade practice.

So, the average bricklayer building a wall, has the standard of care of the average bricklayer, i.e. to build carefully and safely in a workmanlike manner. The same bricklayer driving his car home has the standard of care of an average driver. If he decides to repair his television set, his standard of care is that of the average layman. Whether he is extremely intelligent or not, or normally lazy or careless is not important, because this introduces a further subjective element, which has been rejected by the courts.

Furthermore, the knowledge which one is supposed to possess, depends on the current state of knowledge. So, at present, we are probably doing many things which in years to come will prove to have been dangerous. Once we have that knowledge available (even if the actual defendant is ignorant of it) then ignoring it could amount to negligence.

Other factors which may raise or lower the basic standard of care

Is the risk reasonably likely?   The courts are not going to be impressed with a defendant who failed to avoid an obvious risk. Once again the reasonable foresight test is used. Thus, failure to see that safety helmets are being worn where necessary on building sites will amount to negligence because of the extreme likelihood of injuries caused by falling materials.

Even if the risk is not likely but is reasonably foreseeable then, when determining the standard of care this should be taken into account. This follows dicta in the *Wagon Mound No 2* 1967, a Privy Council shipping case which involved an unusual chain of events. For example, in *Haley* v. *London Electricity Board* 1965, the electricity board's employees had dug a hole in a pavement, and although they erected adequate barriers to prevent a sighted person from falling down the hole, they were inadequate for a blind person. So, although the risk of harm being caused by their action was slight, the fact that a blind person could have fallen down it was reasonably foreseeable.

If the risk is a 'fantastic possibility' then probably there would be no need to do more than take the usual precautions.

Are the plaintiffs at particular risk?   If having decided that certain categories of people are owed a duty of care, then if they would be at particular risk because of age, infirmity, or other special reason such as being women of child bearing age, then the standard of care is much higher than normal. So, school teachers owe a high standard of care towards their pupils. Employers of handicapped people must see that such people are safe, e.g. by making sure that fire exits can cope with wheelchairs etc. In the building industry, apprentices, or even people doing a new job are at particular risk, and their work should be adequately supervised, and warnings and advice should be given and seen to be understood.

In *Paris* v. *Stepney Borough Council* 1957, the employing council was held to be negligent in failing to give goggles to a one-eyed workman, although it would not have been negligent had he been fully sighted. This seems an odd decision, but the court specifically mentioned the high degree of risk to a partially sighted person. By analogy, it is possible that failure to see that ear muffs are worn by a partially deaf person working in relatively noisy circumstances would amount to negligence, but not if he were of good hearing.

Could the risk of injury or harm have been eradicated by a small outlay? Of course, no court will be impressed with the defendant arguing that he could only have avoided the risk of harm at great expense, (unless this was coupled with the argument that the risk was a fantastic possibility). But, if the harm could have been avoided at a small cost, and the defendant failed to take avoiding action, then the courts are more likely to find that the standard of care was higher than normal, and there would be a case of negligence.

Is the defendant an expert? If I fall down a pot hole smashing my leg, and the only way to free it is by amputation, then the standard of care to be shown by an unqualified rescuer, is that of the average rescuer in an emergency. But if my leg is to be amputated in hospital, then the surgeon is expected to show such skill and expertise as is appropriate to his position, qualifications and experience.

Thus, in the first case, the standard is quite low and in the second, the standard is extremely high.

Similarly, a builder is expected to perform construction work safely and of a high quality.

Amateurs doing work which could better be done by experts, should show reasonable care, as their standard of care would be that of the average amateur doing a particular job. In determining such a standard, the courts assume that all people have a certain degree of common knowledge, such as, water is a good conductor of electricity.

Are there regulations, codes of practice, etc. to follow? If there are statutory regulations laying down conditions to be observed, then these should be complied with, and in many cases, it will probably be more appropriate to sue for breach of statutory duty (*see* p. 304). If for some reason, it is impossible to sue in this way, due to a lack of one of the essential pre-conditions, then in the alternative, the plaintiff can sue in negligence and plead that the regulations established a particular standard of care which was not met.

Similarly, if there are statutory codes of practice, which, whilst they do not constitute absolute legal requirements, they will in most cases establish a set standard of care.

If there are house or company rules or regulations, then this will indicate a certain level of care, which may or may not be what would have been acceptable in the circumstances. For example, some company rules may be far too stringent, and whilst a breach would perhaps be grounds for dismissal, it would not amount to negligence in tort.

Is the defendant handicapped in some way? If the defendant has some handicap such as extreme old age, infirmity, or is very young, then this does not necessarily establish a very low standard of care. The reasonable man test is still applied, but of course, the average reasonable man would have the handicap of the defendant placed in the circumstances involved.

Very old people often have impaired faculties and should not perhaps drive or be expected to look after children. Their age however, does not excuse them if their alleged negligent act could in no way have been attributable to their longevity. Foolishness is not the prerogative of the young. Similarly, physically handicapped people could still, for example, telephone for help in many situations, even if they could not be expected to run for help. Mentally handicapped people would not generally be expected to be responsible for their acts, but this all depends on the degree of handicap and the circumstances involved.

What about the otherwise normal average man, who causes an accident as a result of having a heart attack or a fit?

If the attack was reasonably foreseeable because he had been warned by his doctor, or he had suffered one before, then his standard of care would be high, and ignoring the likelihood could amount to negligence. If on the other hand, he had no inkling of the impending attack, then he could never be found to be negligent. This could have important consequences for an employer who is of course vicariously liable for an employee's torts. Should an employee work whilst ill and unfit and thereby cause injury to another, then the employer will be liable as well. Thus, it is possible that more stringent supervision or regular medical examinations should be given in potentially dangerous work.

Was there an emergency? Whether this lowers the standard of care depends on the circumstances of each case. If for example, there is a fire, there should be rules laid down to follow to avoid worsening the situation. If these are not followed, then there may be a case of negligence. But if there are no regulations and the defendant does the best one could in the circumstances, then he will have acted as the average reasonable man should have done in the circumstances, and there can be no negligence.

Is the plaintiff an expert? If the defendant is working with a plaintiff who is an expert, then this may reduce the standard of care, so as to negative any claim of negligence against the defendant, provided that the expert knew what was being done. If negligence is proved however, the defendant could claim that the plaintiff was contributorily negligent, or even that there was consent (*see* p. 272).

What did the defendant do?

Having determined the standard of care which should have been exercised in the given situation, the plaintiff must then prove, that the defendant did not conform with that standard. So, if car drivers should normally be sober, then a defendant causing an accident whilst inebriated, will be found to be negligent.

Normally, the burden of proving the breach will fall on the plaintiff's shoulders. It is not for the defendant to prove that he was not negligent. Evidence must be produced to satisfy the court that on a **balance of probabilities** the defendant was negligent in the circumstances. For this reason, all evidence must be properly produced and preserved. Obviously, the types of evidence will be different in each situation, but they could include photographs, pieces of equipment or machines, medical evidence, witnesses accounts, experts evidence, accident reports, letters, accounts, contracts, drawings and plans. The more evidence the plaintiff produces of a persuasive nature, the more likely the court will agree that the defendant was negligent.

A conviction in criminal proceedings may now be used as evidence in civil proceedings when establishing the existence of a tort.

If the evidence is overwhelmingly in favour of the plaintiff from the start, then it is highly unlikely that the case would ever actually go to a court hearing. The lawyers would then 'settle out of court'. Sometimes however, despite the fact that the defendants have admitted their liability, the amount of damages, known as the quantum is disputed. This is particularly so in relation to personal injuries or fatalities, as there is a highly complex approach by the courts to arrive at a final global amount. In such situations, the case will go to court, but merely for the judge to decide on the amount of damages to be awarded, and no evidence need be produced.

A special rule of evidence – res ipsa loquitur, 'The facts speak for themselves'. Occasionally, the facts of a particular situation point immediately to the existence of negligence. Decided cases have included, barrels of flour falling out of warehouse windows and hitting someone, surgical swabs being left in a patient's body after an operation, and dangerous chemicals being used to 'finish' underpants.

In such cases, the plaintiff has the right, to shift the burden of proof from his own shoulders on to the shoulders of the defendant, who then has either to admit liability or prove that there was no negligence. The plea of res ipsa loquitur is thus only a rule of evidence allowing the plaintiff to sit back, whilst the defendant tries to extricate himself from the action brought against him.

RES IPSA LOQUITUR

('The facts speak for themselves')
People do not usually get hit by
falling barrels of flour unless there
has been negligence of some sort.

Fig. 8.10 *Res ipsa loquitur*

Of course, such a rule is not as simple as that. There are a few conditions attached to its use.

First, the victim's injury must be one that would not actually have happened without there having been some sort of negligence. Discovering surgical instruments lodged in one's body after an operation is probably the best example of this. Negligence, is the **only** explanation of their presence.

Secondly, there must be no explanation for the occurrence other than, one of negligence. Thus, if you are alleging that someone was drunk when he caused the accident, then *res ipsa loquitur* cannot be successfully pleaded, and the plaintiff must use the evidence available to prove negligence.

Thirdly, the facts (res) must indicate negligence on the part of the defendant. For example, a plaster found in the middle of a cake, can only indicate that the bakery was responsible, as it must have been lodged before baking. No one else could be responsible. However, in the case of motor accidents, the plea of res ipsa loquitur can be used to indicate equal personal liability, if it is unknown in which proportion each driver was to blame.

In *Kealey* v. *Heard* 1983, *res ipsa loquitur* was successfully pleaded against the owner of two adjoining houses which were being converted. Scaffolding erected by an independent contractor collapsed, injuring another independent contractor, a plasterer. He sued the owner of the houses for negligence and was successful. The court took the view that the house owner was in overall control, despite having instructed competent (or so he thought) contractors. As scaffolding does not collapse, unless negligently erected, res ipsa loquitur applied.

Damage must result from the breach – the third element

Damage must be caused

First, there must be damage caused. If there is no damage, there can be no action, even if one can prove the first two elements of the tort. This is because negligence is *not* actionable per se as is, for example, trespass.

Damage can take any form

Secondly, damage can be either physical, i.e. damage to person or property, or it can be purely economic (monetary). However, to sue for pure economic loss, one has to prove a sufficiently proximate relationship between the parties as shown in *Ross* v. *Caunters* 1980 and *Junior Books Ltd* v. *Veitchi* 1982.

The damage must not be too remote from the negligent act in fact

If there is damage, then it must not be too far removed from the negligent act in fact. So, if I fall over on a slippery floor suffering no apparent injury, and a year later suffer backache, which may or may not be due to the fall, it would be extremely difficult to sue successfully for the resultant damage. There has to be a **causal** link between cause and effect. If there is none, an action will fail.

A good example of a case failing through lack of causal factual connection between negligence and injury is found in *Barnett* v. *Chelsea Hospital Management Committee* 1961. Here, nightwatchmen drank tea containing arsenic which someone had malevolently slipped into the pot. They visited the local hospital, where the casualty officer, who was rather off-colour, was in bed. The duty sister telephoned the doctor, describing their symptoms of vomiting and diarrhoea. The doctor told her to send them home and if they were no better in the morning, to see their own doctors. At no time did he examine them. The next day, one of them died. There had undoubtedly been a duty of care owed to these men and a breach of that duty. But it was proved that even if they had been examined, no test could possibly have given a result quickly enough to save the man's life. Thus, the widow's claim against the hospital committee failed.

Occasionally, the courts take a more liberal view of this aspect if it is difficult to say whether or not the defendant's negligence caused the injury to the plaintiff. In *McGhee* v. *National Coal Board* 1975, for example, a workman contracted dermatitis, probably as a result of not being able to shower after working in the defendant's brick kilns. Current medical knowledge made it impossible to determine whether the provision of showers could have prevented the dermatitis. Despite this, the House of Lords found for the plaintiff. It seems a very generous decision (for the plaintiff) as the plaintiff's dermatitis may have been caused in another way, totally unconnected with the lack of showers.

The damage must not be too remote in law – the reasonable foresight approach again

In order to limit the liability for **all** the direct **factual** consequences of negligence, the courts now recognize that one should only be liable for those consequences which could have been **reasonably foreseen** at the time of the negligence. This test was approved by the Privy Council in another *Wagon Mound* case, the *Wagon Mound No 1* 1967.

Because greater strides are always being made in science, it is this element which could defeat a claim by a worker for damages caused by cancer for example, if the employer could not have known that what he was doing, which otherwise amounted to negligence, would cause cancer. Similarly, there would probably be no responsibility for the deterioration in a building material, if at the time of its use, the industry thought it was safe (provided of course, that the damage was only created by the deterioration and not by negligent building work).

It is **never** a defence in law to claim that you did not realize that what you were doing was legally wrong. Ignorance is no defence. Thus, employers or anyone in business have a particularly difficult task in taking note of all modern developments affecting their work. Very important problems are usually the subject of government department circulars which are sent around to all appropriate bodies or industries, and these are ignored at peril.

Injury caused by a number of different sets of circumstances

It often happens that a person suffers injury, not from **one** act. but from a chain of events, which started with the defendant's negligence. Should the defendant be responsible for **all** the final damage?

The factors considered previously still apply, i.e. first, is the injury a factual result of the negligence, and secondly, was the first injury reasonably foreseeable at the outset.

Novus actus interveniens – a new intervening act. If however, a new happening occurs which breaks the chain of causation completely, then the defendant ceases to be responsible for any other injury. The new intervening act will only do this, if the act or event was **not** reasonably foreseeable by the defendant.

So, if I fall on the proverbial slippery floor caused by negligent cleaning and am then hit on the head by a door being opened, this second event will probably not break the chain of causation. This is because the second occurrence is a likely and reasonably foreseeable consequence of the initial negligence. Nor will the person opening the door be liable in any way, because he would not expect to find lecturers lying around on floors behind closed doors.

In *Knightly* v. *Johns* 1982 for example, the plaintiff, a police motor cyclist, sued a number of defendants. The first crashed his car in a tunnel. The fourth, a police inspector, went to the scene of the accident instead of immediately closing the tunnel, as was more sensible and was required by standing orders. The inspector then ordered the cyclist to go into the tunnel in order to close it. Whilst travelling against the traffic, he collided with the second defendant. At first instance, the judge gave judgment against the first defendant only. In the Court of Appeal, an appeal by the first defendant was upheld and the judge gave judgment against the fourth and third defendant (who was the chief constable and therefore vicariously liable for the police inspector's negligence). This was done because, although the first defendant's negligence had created a situation which required a rescue of some sort, he should have only been liable for reasonably foreseeable consequences. As the inspector's behaviour was not reasonably foreseeable, this amounted to a break in the chain of causation, i.e. it was a novus actus interveniens which completely relieved the first defendant from liability.

What sort of later events will not break the chain of causation from the original negligence?   It all depends on whether these later events are reasonably foreseeable or not. The following are examples which could occur in the building industry.

Acting in the agony of the moment.   Occasionally, the plaintiff in 'the agony of the moment' caused by the defendant's negligence chooses to do something which in fact worsens the situation e.g. he may grab something for support, which collapses and falls onto him causing him severe injury. This will not amount to contributory negligence (*see* p. 270). In fact, it is a reasonably foreseeable deliberate act on the part of the plaintiff which will not break the chain of causation between the original negligence and final injury. If the defendant had thought about the negligent act which caused the plaintiff to fall in the first place, then it is reasonable to expect him to try and save himself. The fact that this effort worsened the situation does not alter the defendant's blameworthiness for all the resultant injury.

Rescue by plaintiffs.   Here the defendant behaves negligently and the plaintiff attempts to rescue him from harm.

In the *Knightly* v. *Johns* 1982 situation, it is clear that a rescue would have been and should have been mounted. Thus, the first defendant would have realized that his negligence would require a rescue of some sort. However, the plaintiff was not injured as a result of the rescue attempt in itself. Had he been, he may have been able to sue the first defendant successfully as it would have been a reasonably foreseeable result of the negligence.

Similarly in *Harrison* v. *British Railways Board and another* 1981, the defendant passenger tried to get on a moving train. The plaintiff who was a guard gave an incorrect signal to the train driver in order to stop the train. At the same time he pulled the defendant on to the train which had not stopped and was now accelerating. Both fell from the train, the plaintiff badly injuring himself. Could the plaintiff sue the defendant for negligence?

The court ruled yes. If someone puts himself into a position which is dangerous and from which one could expect to be rescued then, such people do owe duties of care to their rescuers.

Without such liability, no-one would be keen on mounting rescues where there was negligence, as they would not be able to recover damages for any injuries. However, the rescue must fulfill three pre-conditions, otherwise the rescuer might be thought to be consenting to run the risk of the negligence and the defendant may successfully plead the defence *volenti non fit injuria* (see p. 272).

The three pre-conditions

1. The rescue must be reasonably foreseeable. This is self evident.

2. The rescue must be necessary. The classic example of an unnecessary rescue is in the case of the runaway milk float horse *Cutler* v. *United Dairies* 1933. The horse had bolted into a field, where his milkman master was trying to calm him down. The milkman called for assistance to a passer-by. During his attempts to pacify the horse, the passer-by was kicked, and he sued the dairy. The dairy was found to have been negligent in using the horse, as it was known to have bolted on more than one occasion, and was not the ideal beast to pull a milk float. But the Court of Appeal stated that the rescue was unnecessary and the plaintiff lost his case.

Necessary acts of rescue have been found where there was a risk to life and limb, and even in some cases, a risk to property, e.g. where a house is on fire.

3. The rescue must be reasonable. What is reasonable would depend on the circumstances, but the courts take a very wide view of this and seldom make decisions like *Cutler* v. *United Dairies* 1933.

Miscellaneous actions taken by the plaintiff. If a plaintiff commits suicide as a direct result of depression caused by the defendant's negligence, then his widow will probably be successful, as in *Pigney* v. *Pointer's Transport* 1957. The plaintiff had suffered head injuries which caused his depression. As the injuries were thus still existing in the form of the depression, the suicide was therefore reasonably foreseeable.

In a similar case however, *McKew* v. *Holland Hannen & Cubitts* 1969, the plaintiff aggravated the situation by attempting to go down some stairs without a handrail, whilst still suffering from a leg injury caused by the defendant's negligence. This was held to be so unreasonable on the part of the plaintiff as to break the chain of causation vis à vis the final injury, but not for the original injury. Of course it could have been argued, that he was not deliberately being silly, but rather he was being contributorily negligent (*see* p. 274.).

In the above situations, the second event which worsened, or even caused the final injury, was perpetrated by the plaintiff. But often the second act or event is caused by someone else, or even is a chance happening. The same rules apply. Is the final injury a factual result of the initial negligence, and if so, was it reasonably foreseeable? If the answers to both questions are, yes, the defendant will be liable for all the resultant loss.

Defences

The defendant in a court action does not sit back and cross his fingers, hoping that the plaintiff will not be able to prove his case. He will attempt to raise appropriate defences which could cancel out any negligence.

The burden of proving a defence obviously falls on the defendant and he must produce his own evidence in support.

Necessity

It is vaguely possible that the defendant may claim that the tort was committed necessarily to prevent another greater harm occurring. However, most of the cases involving necessity as a defence are concerned with other torts where the act was deliberate.

A more likely effect of doing something negligently to reduce a greater injury, is that, it will lower the standard of care required in the circumstances, so that a case of negligence will not be substantiated.

Volenti non fit injuria – consent or 'there is no injury to a willing person'

This is an absolute defence, and if proved, cancels out the negligence, thus defeating the plaintiff's claim. It arises where the plaintiff:

- knew that the defendant was being negligent
- knew of the risk
- continued to co-operate with the defendant
- and suffered injury of the type one would expect would result from such negligence.

Nowadays the courts are very reluctant to find a case of consent existing in all but the most open and shut cases. For this reason, strict guidelines are adhered to for its application.

The plaintiff must know that the defendant is being negligent   There can be no valid consent if the plaintiff did not know there was any negligence. Thus, the defendant must prove there was either express or implied consent *to the negligence*. Express consent will be either verbal, (and therefore witnessed to stand up in court) or written, which may be witnessed (but *see* the effects of the Unfair Contract Terms Act 1977 p. 274). Consent may be implied where the plaintiff continues to co-operate despite the negligence.

(Note: consent concerns the negligence and not mere hazards of the job. People who do dangerous work may be paid danger money and they consent to run the risk of the ordinary hazards of the work (and possibly sign an agreement to that effect) but they are *not* consenting to actual negligence.)

The plaintiff must have known of the risks which could be caused by the negligence.   Someone who consents to run the risk of a negligent act will not lose his action for negligence if he was injured in some other way.

Consent must be freely given.   Sometimes, a worker is put under pressure to continue to work, knowing of the presence of danger caused by negligence. This usually takes the form of a threat of dismissal. In such cases, the defence will fail, as the consent was brought about under duress.

Because this is a complete defence which would cancel out all liability on the part of the defendant, the courts are more likely to agree to there being contributory negligence on the part of the plaintiff, see below.

However, the following case is a classic example in which volenti (consent) was successfully pleaded.

In *Ashton* v. *Turner and another* 1980, the plaintiff and the two defendants went on a drinking session, during which it was planned that the plaintiff and the first defendant would commit a burglary, using the second defendant's car.

The plaintiff was injured in a chase following the burglary. He sued both defendants for negligence. The first, for dangerous and drunken driving (for which he had already been convicted in the criminal courts), the second for allowing the driver to drive without insurance.

The High Court was asked whether the plaintiff was owed a duty of care. The judge decided that he was owed no duty of care as a matter of public policy, and also stated that the first defendant would be able to plead volenti successfully.

Exclusion of liability

Can the defendant plead consent if he puts up notices such as 'the public enter this property at their own risk?'

This sort of notice is an example of how people seek to exclude their liability (whether or not there has been any negligence). They may also seek to do this by excluding their liability in clauses in their contracts with other people (*see* p. 93).

Until a few years ago, these exclusion clauses worked well in the defendant's favour. In contract, such clauses were pleaded to nullify liability as in *Hedley Byrne Ltd* v. *Heller & Partners* 1964 (*see* p. 260). In negligence, the notices gave plaintiffs the opportunity of not using the premises, and if ignored, the defendant could have tried to plead volenti as a defence (and could possibly succeed if the elements of the defence were proved).

In 1977 however, the Unfair Contract Terms Act was passed, severely limiting the scope of such exclusions. Under the Act, liability for what amounts to negligence which causes death or personal injury cannot be excluded by contract or notice **at all** in the course of a **business**. Where negligence results in economic loss only, such an exclusion of liability is valid, but only if it is **reasonable**, taking into account all the circumstances, such as the balance of bargaining power between the parties.

It should be noted that, exclusions between parties **not in a business relationship** are still valid. Also, the Act does not cover unenforceable contracts with minors (*see* p. 101) and effective exclusions could be inserted into these.

Employers cannot exclude their liability for vicarious liability for employee's torts causing injury or loss to fellow employees under the Law Reform (Personal Injuries) Act 1948. Nor can car drivers exclude their liability in tort towards passengers under the Road Traffic Act 1972. Thus, notices which were common at one time when hitch hiking was less hazardous, such as 'the driver takes no responsibility for any damage or loss done to passenger's property or person' are no longer valid, nor can they be used to prove volenti, e.g. if the driver is drunk. The circumstances of the case must therefore be examined to find whether the elements of the defence can be found.

Contributory negligence

This is not a complete defence, but it acknowledges the fact, that whilst negligence may have been proved against the defendant, the plaintiff may, at the same time, by his own fault have contributed to his injuries or loss, e.g. by failing to wear his safety helmet or harness.

The Law Reform (Contributory Negligence) Act 1945 introduced this defence and by S.1(1) in such cases, 'the damages recoverable ... shall be reduced to such extent as the court thinks fit and equitable, having regard to the claimants' share in the responsibility for the damage'.

The wording of the Act allows the defendant to plead this, without having to prove *negligence* on the part of the plaintiff. All he needs to do is to show that the plaintiff was at fault in some way, which contributed to the damage. The plaintiff should have reasonably foreseen that his behaviour would contribute to his injury, otherwise the defence will fail.

As a result of this, the court will work out the damages in the usual way, and then reduce them proportionately, taking account of the blameworthiness of the plaintiff, e.g. that the plaintiff by failing to wear his seat belt was 50 per cent to blame, and therefore gets only 50 per cent damages.
(Note: there is no set amount attributed to the non-wearing of seat belts, it will all depend on the circumstances.)

Once again it is clear, that it is in the worker's own interests to do all he can to prevent greater injury to himself by complying with all safety requirements, such as wearing safety clothing.

Liability for dangerous premises

This can be dealt with under 3 separate heads: 1. liability of the occupier to lawful visitors; 2. liability of the occupier to other people and 3. liability of non-occupiers for premises in a dangerous state.

An occupier's liability for the state of his premises – Occupiers' Liability Act 1957

The duty towards lawful visitors

As far as liability for premises is concerned, the tort of negligence is only applicable to **activities being** carried on there, and is probably not applicable to premises being dangerous **because of their state**. Thus, if someone is injured on site by a brick being dropped on his head, then the proper course, is to sue either for negligence or for breach of a statutory duty, such as under the construction regulations.

If on the other hand, the brick had become dislodged in a storm from an improperly maintained wall, then, the injured man could sue under the Occupiers' Liability Act 1957.

In some cases, an injured person would probably sue for both negligence and breach of the Act, just to be on the safe side if one or the other causes of action failed, e.g. as in *Wheeler* v. *Copas* 1981 on p. 278.

The 1957 Act was introduced to improve the common law situation, where occupiers of premises owed varying degrees of responsibility towards entrants. What it did not change however, was the concept that as the occupier is the person in control of the premises, he can therefore make sure that the premises are safe to entrants. This area of the law pre-dated *Donoghue* v. *Stevenson*, and therefore the two areas have developed slightly differently.

Fig. 8.11 Warnings like these may absolve an occupier of liability under the Acts

The common duty of care owed under the 1957 Act

All **lawful visitors** to premises are now owed a **common duty of care** by the occupier. This is defined by S.2 as a duty to take such care as in all the circumstances of the case is reasonable to see that the visitor will be reasonably safe when using the premises for all the purposes for which he is visiting.

This is a significant difference from negligence. In negligence, the plaintiff must first prove he *was* owed a duty of care by applying the proximity or neighbourhood tests. Under the Act, the plaintiff merely has to prove that he was a **lawful visitor** in order for a statutory duty to be automatically owed to him.

Who are lawful visitors?

Before the 1957 Act, there were a number of different types of visitors, who were each owed a differing degree of care by the occupier. The categories are worth noting for two reasons. First, they indicate the types of visitor who may enter premises and secondly, certain visitors, who whilst entering the land quite lawfully, are **not** owed the statutory duty and would have to rely on the Occupiers' Liability Act 1984, ordinary negligence or the old pre-1957 law (*see* below).

The categories of visitors were as follows:

Category 1 – Invitees, i.e. people who have been allowed to enter for a special purpose, and whose presence is in the interest of the occupier, such as a private guest or customer in a public house.

Category 2 – Licensees were people who merely had permission to enter the premises, but who held no interest for the occupier, e.g. neighbours' children allowed to enter to recover a ball.

Category 3 – Contractors were people who had entered the land by virtue of a contract, e.g. a window cleaner or builder.

Category 4 – Persons entering under a statutory or common law right, e.g. health and safety inspectors, policemen, building control inspectors.

Category 5 – People in general exercising a public or private right such as a right of way.

Category 6 – Trespassers.

Under the 1957 Act, the common duty of care is only owed to lawful visitors, being those in categories 1–4.

Unless the 1984 Act applies category 5 entrants are still owed only a duty not to **actively** do things which could make the entry dangerous, e.g. to dig up the road without warning. This is so if they could not be regarded as licensees. Thus, in a recent case *Holden* v. *White & another* 1982, a milkman fell over a manhole cover which was in a state of disrepair in the defendant's pathway. At the time of the incident, he was in fact, delivering milk to a third party, who merely had the right of access over the pathway. The Court of Appeal agreed that the defendant was an occupier but did **not** owe a duty to the milkman **under the 1957 Act**. So to sue the defendant, he would have had to sue in negligence and prove fault on her part. Since May 1984, however, such situations may now be covered by the 1984 Act.

Category 6, i.e. trespassers are not owed any duty under the Act, but they may be owed duties under the 1984 Act (*see* p. 281).

Who are occupiers?

There is no statutory definition of occupier, although most authorities use Lord Denning's concept of the occupier, being the one in **control** of the premises: *Wheat* v. *Lacon & Co Ltd* 1966.

There is no need for the occupier to have a legal or equitable interest in the property. So a contractor by virtue of clause 23 of the JCT form of contract has a **legal** licence to be in possession of the site. But, in other situations, a building contractor may be an occupier by virtue of his contract to build say, a garage or extension, which otherwise gives him no legal or equitable interest in the land. Nor is there a need for the occupier to have **exclusive** possession of the property. Thus, the owner of a building site and the building contractor may both be in occupation of the site. Such people may still be in occupation or control even if there are independent contractors working there. Thus, the building contractor may be in occupation and so may a roofing sub-contractor. Each separate set of circumstances may give a different result.

By S.2(4)b, the occupier may in certain situations delegate his responsibility for technical aspects of his occupancy, by employing an independent contractor to deal with that particular aspect. For example, it is common to entrust building maintenance to outside contractors. If such contractors fail to maintain part of the building properly, then the contractors cannot be sued under the Act as they are not occupiers. The plaintiff will have to sue the contractors in negligence. However, the transfer of responsibility is only sound, if the occupier appointed properly qualified or experienced contractors to do the work. An occupier may still therefore find himself liable (*see* p. 279).

What are premises?

The word premises includes land, buildings, ships, diving boards, cranes, ladders, scaffolding, boarding, grandstands, platforms, sea promenades etc. The list is not closed. In *Wheeler* v. *Copas* 1981, a farmer contracted with a bricklayer to help him build a house. At one point, the bricklayer required a long ladder. When he used it, it broke under his weight. Expert witnesses gave evidence that the ladder was unsuitable for building work, although it was suitable for farm work. The bricklayer successfully sued for injuries caused, either by the farmer being negligent in lending the ladder, or as an occupier failing to discharge the common duty of care towards his lawful visitor. Because of the bricklayer's expertise however, his damages were reduced by 50 per cent due to contributory negligence (*see* p. 274).

The common duty of care – what levels of care must be attained

The levels of care to be taken are really the same as those found in negligence, and reference should be made to p. 262.

Children: S.2(3)(a). However, the 1957 Act specifically mentions the special duties owed to children, in that they are expected to behave less carefully than grown-ups. The standard of care owed to child visitors is very high, and gets higher as the child is younger. Nevertheless, in certain cases, the occupier will be excused liability, because it would be reasonable to expect a very young child to be accompanied by an older person as in *Phipps* v. *Rochester Corporation* 1955, where a boy aged five fell into a trench when accompanied by his seven year old sister. The occupier was held not to be liable.

Also, the occupier should not have any **allurements** on his land which attract children. Despite the fact that the Act does not apply to trespassers, if something is kept on the land which is tempting and dangerous, i.e. an allurement, then the occupier may nevertheless be liable for injury. Presumably, this is because the child probably would not have gone on the land, but for the allurement. 'Allurements' thus, in this context have included poisonous berries (such as on laburnam) and railway trucks. Building sites may inadvertently provide allurements to children.

It is also possible that a child trespasser may become a licensee to enter land if the occupiers know of their presence and do nothing to stop them from entering, nor forbid them from doing so. If a child trespasser crosses the thin 'dividing line' between trespasser and becoming a licensee, then he is owed the statutory common duty of care. If he remains a trespasser, then he may be owed duties under the 1984 Act or at common law (*see* p. 284).

Specialists: S.2(3)(b).

The 1957 Act, furthermore recognizes also that the occupier's standard of care will be lower in the case of visitors who are carrying out their normal work. Such visitors should take care to protect themselves from injury caused by the normal risks of their work, and therefore, should not be the responsibility of the occupier. Thus, if demolition contractors are carrying out demolition work of an old house, they should take all reasonable steps to prevent injury to themselves, and cannot sue the occupier under the Act for failing to maintain the house properly, as they should have inspected to view the state of disrepair.

Delegation to a competent independent contractor: S.2(4)b.

If the occupier delegates certain duties of a specialist nature to a competent contractor, then he also discharges his liability towards persons injured through the fault of the contractor. The injured party would then have to sue the contractor for negligence or breach of statutory duty (*see* p. 304).

Extent of duties owed to contractual visitors.

Contractual visitors may either be those entering by virtue of a contract **with** the occupier e.g. a building contractor and a sub-contractor (where the contractor has possession of the site), or those entering by virtue of a contract, but not made with the occupier e.g. a consulting engineer or architect, who is in contract with the employer out of occupation, and is permitted to be there because of the main contract. The first situation is governed by S.5, the second by S.3.

Extent of duty owed to visitor in contract with occupier: S.5.

For example window cleaner, maintenance worker, sub-contractor. Where there is a contract, its terms may regulate behaviour between parties, and obviously, the contract must first be examined to see the extent of liability owed to the contracting visitor.

But, if there is no term in the contract, then by S.5(1) the **common duty of care** will be owed. Because there is a contract, the law of contract is primarily the basis of an action. But, if the common duty of care is implied (because of the lack of an express term) then, the plaintiff can choose to sue for breach of contract or for breach of the Act (see fig. 8.12).

Extent of duty owed to a visitor who is empowered by a contract to enter the occupier's land: S.3. Section 3 entrants are visitors under the 1957 Act, and are thus owed the common duty of care by the occupier. They are not in contract with the occupier, and thus have no choice of action. They can only proceed in tort under the Act.

Excluding or restricting Liability S.2

Pre-1977

The occupier was free to exclude or restrict his liability under the 1957 Act under S.2(1) by 'agreement or otherwise'. Thus, until the Unfair Contract Terms Act 1977, occupiers of property frequently put up notices or inserted clauses in contracts, excluding their liability altogether. This **was** perfectly legal and often rendered the 1957 Act of little use to the injured visitor.
(Note: such notices were valid to exclude liability for negligence as well, *see* p. 273).

After 1977

Occupiers of **business** premises however, are now subject to the 1977 Act which makes such notices or contractual terms **void**, if they try to exclude liability for **death** or **personal injury** caused by the occupier's breach of any duties, including the common duty of care. By an amendment under the 1984 Act, recreational or educational reasons for entry are not to come within the definition of business purposes, unless the business is concerned with providing education or recreation.

It should also be noted, that people occupying premises for non-business purposes e.g., a private house, can still exclude or restrict their liability.

Business occupants may exclude their liability for damage to property providing the exclusion is reasonable in the circumstances.

The 1977 Act does not apply to trespassers, so exclusions of liability or notices excluding liability will be valid against such entrants.

Defences

Warnings: S.2(4), a special defence

If a warning is given of the danger which, if observed by the visitor, would make him safe, then this will absolve the occupier from liability. The examples in Fig. 8.11 would be perfectly sound, provided that they would protect the type of visitor expected. So a written warning is useless if blind people are to be expected at a hospital for example (*see* p. 263).

Volenti non fit injuria S.2(5) consent and willingness to run the risk

This should be read in conjunction with the rules relating to warnings above. A warning, plus the defendant's proven willingness to enter the dangerous premises would therefore be a good defence. Knowledge of the danger or risk from another source however, may or may not be grounds for a good defence if the visitor then enters the dangerous premises. The plaintiff would have to prove that the visitor knew of the danger, e.g. because he had visited the site on a previous occasion. Consent can then be pleaded as a defence, but the court would ask the question, why was not there a warning if the occupier knew of the danger to visitors? The duty to warn seems to be implicit in the Act. What is more likely, is that the court will use the partial defence of contributory negligence e.g. *Wheeler* v. *Copas* 1982 (*see* p. 278). Contributory negligence may occasionally cancel out damages altogether. But, this will only be so if the knowledge of the danger would have made the visitor absolutely safe.

Liability of an occupier to 'non-visitors' to his property

The Occupiers' Liability Act 1957 does not apply to trespassers. However, the Occupiers' Liability Act 1984 may, as it imposes a duty of care on an occupier in relation to other people, not being visitors under the 1957 Act. If neither of the Acts apply, then the rules of common law must be used.

The Occupiers' Liability Act 1984

The 1984 Act replaces the common law rules in determining:

- whether any duty is owed by an occupier of premises to persons who are not his visitors in respect of any risk of their suffering injury by reason of any danger due to the state of the premises or to things done or omitted to be done on them.
- if such a duty exists, what that duty is.

The words 'occupier' and 'visitor' are used in the sense as under the 1957 Act.

To whom is the duty owed?

By S.1(3) of the 1984 Act, an occupier owes a duty to **another** (not

Fig. 8.12 Diagrams to show the application of S.3 and S.5 of the Occupiers' Liability Act 1957

being his visitor), in respect of the risks mentioned above if:

1. he is **aware** of the danger or has **reasonable** grounds to believe that it exists.
2. he **knows** or has **reasonable** grounds to believe that the other is in the vicinity of the danger or that he may come into the vicinity. This is so, whether or not the other person had lawful authority to be there, *and*
3. the risk is one against which, in **all** the circumstances of the case, he may be reasonably expected to offer the other some protection.

Thus, in *Pannett* v. *Mcguinness & Co* 1972 a child was injured on a demolition site. The demolition contractors had been burning rubbish and knowing of the allurement of bonfires, had employed a watchman to chase the children away. The watchman went absent one day and a child got burnt. The contractors were held vicariously liable for the workman's tort. The children's presence would have been reasonably foreseeable, and they should have made sure that they were kept out.

Similarly in *Herrington* v. *British Railways Board* 1972, a child was electrocuted on the live rail on British Railway property. Evidence was brought to show that the fence through which the child had crawled, was in a bad state of repair. Also, it was clear from the path worn in the ground, that there was a well-used 'short cut' to a park used by local children. British Railways Board was held liable.

In both those cases, the result would have been the same had they been dealt with under the 1984 Act. In each case, the occupier was aware or had reasonable grounds to believe that a danger existed; they knew or had reasonable grounds to realize that people were in the vicinity of the danger; and lastly, the risk was of the kind which they could have guarded against and protected those people. Such a duty may also have been owed in *Holden* v. *White and another* 1982, had the new Act been enacted earlier.

The extent of the duty

If a duty exists under the 1984 Act, by virtue of applying the pre-conditions, then the duty is 'to take such care as is reasonable in all the circumstances of the case to see that (the other person) does not suffer injury on the premises by reason of the danger concerned'.

It must, therefore, be noted that the 1984 Act does **not** impose the same duty as under the 1957 Act. The 1984 Act only requires protection from 'the danger concerned'. The 1957 Act requires that the visitor be reasonably safe when using the premises for **all** purposes for which he is visiting. The 1957 duty is thus considerably wider than the 1984.

Warnings

By S.1(5) of the 1984 Act, any duty owed under the Act may **in an appropriate case**, be discharged by taking such steps as are reasonable in all the circumstances, to give warning of the danger concerned or to **discourage** persons from incurring the risk.

It will be interesting to see how the courts interpret this section in the future.

Acceptance of risk

By S.1(6) no duty will be owed to someone who willingly accepted the risks of a dangerous situation (*see* p. 281).

Not applicable to highways

The 1984 Act does not apply to highways. The common law rules are therefore applied.

Finally, it should be noted, that the 1984 Act does not extend the duty to cover damage to property as does the 1957 Act.

At common law

In situations in which neither of the Acts apply, then only minimal duties are owed at common law to persons entering premises occupied by another.

Persons who enter premises by reason of exercising a public or private right of way, are only owed a duty in tort not to actively make the exercise of that right dangerous. This would probably also cover highways. However, there are many other duties owed under the Highways Act 1980 which impose much more stringent duties on many categories of people, not just occupiers.

As far as other situations are concerned, it is possible that we have now returned to the old pre-Herrington situation based on a House of Lords decision of the twenties, *Addie & Sons* v. *Dumbreck* 1929. That case said that an occupier should not intentionally injure uninvited entrants nor should they recklessly disregard their presence on land. Herrington's case in 1972 however, regarded that decision as socially unacceptable in the twentieth century and substituted a test of humanity. Whether this test has survived the 1984 Act is open to conjecture. In the writer's opinion, it probably has, as there are bound to be cases which are unable to satisfy the preconditions of S.1 of the 1984 Act.

The test of humanity takes into account the likelihood of the presence of the non-visitor; the type of entrant (children obviously being more favoured than vandals and burglars); and also whether an occupier has the finances to eradicate a source of harm. Fortunately, with the passing of the 1984 Act, few cases will fall into this category.

Non-occupiers responsibility for dangerous premises

On the basis of the ordinary duty of care in negligence, people who create dangers should guard against injury. So a builder who is not in either sole or joint occupation of a site, but perhaps is doing some repair or maintenance work, must still discharge his duty of care by preventing accidents.

He can do this by warnings, guarding dangerous premises or preventing people from entering. In *Billings (AC) & Sons Ltd* v. *Riden* 1958, such a duty of care was said to be owed by a building contractor to persons he could reasonably foresee would be affected by his work. A warning may be insufficient if this does not make the premises safe.

Non-occupiers who create reasonably foreseeable risks may also be liable to **trespassers** if there was a likelihood of a trespasser being injured.

The above situations are concerned with people who are working on the property, even if not in technical occupation.

Amazingly however, before the 1970s, people who sold or leased premises which turned out to be unsafe, were virtually immune from action, as they were no longer occupiers. It is a true case of caveat emptor i.e. let the buyer/lessee beware. This was so unless there was some other basis for a claim, such as a breach of contract. This is still the case where someone merely sells premises and fails to point out dangerous defects in the property. It is only where they tell lies or actively do something to make the place unsafe, or misrepresent facts to induce a contract, that the misled buyer has any course of action.

Thus, builders who owned the land on which they built, were in a strong protected position compared with builders who built for other people. Land owner/builders were immune from actions in **negligence**, (but not in contract) and so were lessor/builders. Non-owner or non-lessor builders were not immune. The law was obviously wrong and inequitable and two things occurred to change this position.

Firstly, the Defective Premises Act 1972 imposes liability on land owner/builders to build in a workmanlike manner with proper materials, and to make a dwelling fit for habitation. Houses covered by the National House Building Council Scheme are excluded from the provisions of the Act, however.

Perhaps, more importantly, dicta in *Anns* v. *Merton LBC* 1978 (*see* p. 253) which has been confirmed in subsequent cases such as *Batty & another* v. *Metropolitan Property Realizations Ltd & others* 1978, show that builders who own the land on which they build, owe a duty of care in negligence to subsequent purchasers and not just in contract. If there has been a breach of the Building Regulations, then there is also statutory liability for damage caused under S.38 Building Act 1984 (*see* p. 257).

As far as lessors are concerned, the Defective Premises Act 1972 imposes liability in negligence on lessors under a statutory obligation to repair, or where the lease or tenancy agreement contains a lessor's repairing covenant, and provided the lessor is aware of the defect or should be aware of it. Thus, lessor/builders are now covered by the Act. But, the Act is not all embracing, and there are some areas which are still uncertain, and liability may not be imposed.

The rule in *Rylands* v. *Fletcher* 1868. Occupier's liability for dangerous things escaping

This is an example of a case creating a new area of liability in tort. Once again it was formulated before *Donoghue* v. *Stevenson* 1932 and thus has developed in a different direction to that of negligence. It is so restricted in its application that it would be an unusual occurrence in the building industry. Nevertheless, it is of importance because it is a tort of strict liability. The defendant is strictly liable for damage caused in circumstances covered by the rule, whether or not there has been negligence or whether or not a nuisance has been committed. The harm and the escape thus caused does not have to be foreseeable. The case concerned a mineowner and a millowner. The mineowner plaintiff had leased land for mining purposes which were adjacent to the defendant millowner's land under which there were some disused mineshafts (*see* Fig. 8.13). The millowner needed more water for his mill and contracted with independent contractors to excavate a reservoir on this land to increase the water supply. The contractors failed to seal up the disused mine shafts which they did not realize connected with the mines next door. On filling the reservoir the plaintiff's mine became flooded causing severe damage. The plaintiff sued and won the case in the House of Lords, thereby establishing a new area of liability. Previous cases of a similar nature had been based entirely on precedent. The dicta in *Rylands* v. *Fletcher* established requirements for liability which could be found in certain situations. Thus the defendant must take on to land in his occupation, something which is not naturally there for his own use, which is likely to cause mischief and then escapes. If this occurs then the defendant is

Fig. 8.13 *Rylands* v. *Fletcher* 1868

responsible for all the natural consequences of the escape, even if there is no negligence.

The elements of the rule

Occupation of land

The rule applies to persons in ordinary occupation of land. They do not need to actually own it. Thus, a building contractor in possession of a site will come within the scope of the rule.

The 'thing' must not be naturally present on the land

Otherwise, the defendant could not have taken it there in the first place. But if he fails to control natural occurrences such as rainwater or wild rats, then he may be liable for nuisance or negligence.

The 'thing' does not have to benefit the defendant

He merely has to bring it there for his own use. It does not have to be for his own good. Thus, it has been suggested that local authorities could possibly be responsible for the escape of sewage from their sewage works without proof of negligence.

The 'thing' must be dangerous if it escapes

This does not mean that the thing itself must be inherently dangerous, only that it will cause mischief if it escapes, as in the facts of the case. The water was inherently harmless. It was only when the water flooded the mineshaft that it caused the damage.

There must be an escape of the 'thing'

In *Read* v. *J Lyons & Co* 1947 a ministry factory inspector was injured in the defendant's shell-filling shop. She sued under *Rylands* v. *Fletcher*. As there was no escape from the defendant's property, the plaintiff lost her case.

Examples of the rule being applied

The rule has been applied to the following: water – *Rylands* v. *Fletcher* 1868; petrol in car tank causing a fire which spreads – *Musgrove* v. *Pandelis* 1919; explosives – *Rainham Chemical Works* v. *Belvedere Fish Guanoco Ltd* 1921; poisonous tree planted whose leaves fall elsewhere – *Crowhurst* v. *Amersham Burial Board* 1878; gas escaping – *Batcheller* v. *Tunbridge Wells Gas Co* 1901; electricity – *National Telephone Co* v. *Baker* 1893.

The defendants must use the land in a non-natural way

This is defined quite normally and means that a special use which increases the possibility of harm to others must be shown. So ordinary use is *not* 'non-natural'. Nor must the use be for the general benefit of the community. It appears therefore that *Rylands* v. *Fletcher* 1868 will thus be applied in exceptional circumstances.

Remedies

The plaintiff may recover damages for physical damage to person or property but probably not for mere pecuniary loss.

Defences

Act of God

This covers uncontrollable events such as earthquakes.

Plaintiff's consent

Consent to the thing being taken on to the defendant's land may be expressed or implied. If express consent has been given there will definitely be a good defence. Even if it is only implied from acquiescent behaviour this may well be a good defence.

Statutory authority

Where bodies such as nationalized industries act under statutory **duties** to supply gas, electricity, water etc., the rule is excluded and the plaintiff would have to prove negligence. If the organization only has a statutory power to do something, i.e. they may do something if they wish, then they can be sued under the rule.

Unforeseeable act of a stranger

The rule only imposes strict liability for things within the occupier's control. An unforeseeable event which is caused by a stranger is a good defence. Note, a stranger is someone such as a trespasser who was not reasonably expected to be there e.g., a vandal.

Nuisance

There are three types of nuisance. **Public** nuisance is a crime created by the common law. **Private** nuisance is a tort, and **statutory** nuisance is nuisance created by Acts of Parliament. All three types may possibly be committed during building work.

Public nuisance

A public nuisance has been defined as 'an act or omission which materially affects the reasonable comfort and convenience of life of a class of Her Majesty's subjects': *AG* v. *PYA Quarries Ltd* 1957.

Thus, for a nuisance to be public, it must affect a large enough class of people, such as a village. Because of its ancient beginnings, it has embraced different types of behaviour, which one would not normally consider to be nuisances. Thus, obstructing a highway, or making a highway dangerous are public nuisances, as is keeping a brothel and polluting a public water supply.

Public nuisances are indictable offences, and therefore they can be tried in the Crown Court in the usual way. They can also be dealt with in a civil **relator** action by the Attorney General or the local authority under S.222 of the Local Government Act 1972, who act on behalf of the affected public.

Once the criminal or relator case has been proved, if an individual member of the public particularly suffers as a result of the nuisance, then that individual can then sue in tort and get damages, even for personal injury, e.g. *Halsey* v. *Esso Petroleum Co Ltd* 1961, where there was an excess of noise, smell and acid smuts caused by the defendant's business.

It should be noted that as public nuisances are essentially crimes, it is **no** defence to say that there has been consent to the nuisance, as one can never consent to a crime. But one can always consent to a tort being committed.

There does not have to be any invasion of private land, as there has to be in private nuisance.

Public nuisance on highways

The special dangers that users of highways face are reflected in this aspect of public nuisance.

A public nuisance on a highway may be committed by someone obstructing the highway. The obstruction must either be permanent, such as a wall, or be of sufficient duration to be a nuisance. Thus, an obstruction for a reasonably short period may not necessarily be a nuisance.

A public nuisance may also be committed by someone who occupies premises close to a highway. If he fails to keep them in proper repair and if they then collapse and injure someone, then that person will be able to sue, whether or not the owner or occupier knew of the danger. *Wringe* v. *Cohen* 1940. This is another example of strict liability (*see* p. 250).

It should be noted that such liability is only concerned with damage caused by disrepair, and not by natural causes or dangers caused by trespassers. This, of course, is of great concern to builders, who should maintain property close to highways, not just to avoid prosecution under the Health and Safety at Work etc Act 1974, nor to avoid claims for negligence (which requires proof of a degree of carelessness) but to avoid **strict** liability, which needs no intention or negligence.

Private nuisance – a tort

Definition

A private nuisance has been defined as an interference for a substantial length of time by owners or occupiers of land, with the use or enjoyment of the neighbouring land.

Such interferences may be caused by noise, smoke, smell, water, gas, fumes, roots or any type of behaviour which causes the neighbour to be unable to use or enjoy his property. The courts agree that the list of nuisances is by no means closed. Thus, it can be seen that the building site operator is always in danger of committing a nuisance. It must be noted that this tort protects interest in **land** only, such interests includes interference with easements (*see* p. 147).

Criteria for suing in nuisance

Unlike negligence, there is only one essential element to be found. But many other factors have to be taken into account when deciding whether a nuisance has, or has not, been committed.

Damage or harm must have been caused – the essential element. Nuisance is like negligence. There *must* be some damage or harm suffered on the part of the plaintiff in relation to his land.

This may take the form of physical damage to the property which could be caused by vibrations or roots undermining walls or water. If there is physical damage, the court looks no further at whether damage has been caused and is less likely to investigate its triviality.

If, on the other hand, the damage is an interference with the use of land or its enjoyment, then it must not be trivial. For the courts take the view that there should be 'give and take' between neighbours. So an occasional smoky, smelly fire or a noisy do-it-yourself session would not be actionable. But, weekly bonfires or continuous noisy drilling and sawing probably would amount to a nuisance. The damage that results in these situations would be that the plaintiff is unable to use a room or his garden in the normal way because of the nuisance.

The behaviour must be unusual, excessive, unreasonable. This follows on from the previous section. Normal, reasonable and moderate use of property cannot be actionable. Building work, which has to be done almost continuously for a particular period could thus amount to being excessive and possibly unreasonable.

In *Andreae* v. *Selfridge & Co Ltd* 1938, demolition contractors caused an unreasonable amount of dust and noise, which affected the plaintiff's hotel trade to its detriment.

The behaviour must have gone on for some time. Generally, an isolated act will not be actionable. But, the isolated incident arising out of a continuing state of affairs may indicate an interference with the use of the property. Thus, if builders habitually throw down materials close to another's land, causing the occupier to fear being hit, then the one occasion that e.g. a tool lands on that property, may amount to evidence of the existence of the nuisance.

The nuisance must be caused by another person on neighbouring property and not on the plaintiff's own premises.

Character of the neighbourhood. If the plaintiff's land is in a built up area, the defendant is not allowed to claim that his behaviour causes no nuisance, merely because of that. But it is reasonable to expect less personal comfort in towns and industrial areas compared with, say, the tranquillity of the Hebrides. It will thus affect the question 'is the damage trivial?'

Is it necessary to prove that the defendant behaved maliciously? No. Malice is not an element of the tort. It is in torts such as malicious prosecution. But malicious behaviour may sometimes tip the balance in favour of the plaintiff.

Could the nuisance have been prevented easily? If it could have been prevented for a relatively small cost, then the nuisance should have been stopped, and the court will take this into account.

This is important when considering nuisances caused by natural things on land. In *Leakey* v. *National Trust* 1980, houseowners, close to the defendants' land, in which there was a large natural mound called 'Burrow Mump', were caused annoyance by earth and rubble which fell naturally from the 'Mump' on to their land. After adverse weather conditions, a large crack appeared in the mound. The houseowners reported this to the defendants, who said they were not liable for natural earth movements. Later, earth and tree stumps fell against a house. The houseowners sued the defendants in nuisance. In the Court of Appeal, the judges said that the defendants were under a duty to remove or eradicate the nuisance, even if it was naturally caused.

Abnormally sensitive plaintiffs. The tort only protects normal use of property. If however the plaintiff proves that there is a nuisance anyway, the plaintiff with a special use of the property or an abnormal sensitivity to such nuisances, can claim greater damages than the average plaintiff.

What sort of plaintiff may sue?

As the tort only protects interests in land, the plaintiff must prove that he has a right to enjoy the land itself or an easement over that land. Thus, he must normally be in possession, unless the damage is physical and affects the property in some permanent way, in which case, persons out of possession may sue.

So, owner/occupiers, tenants in possession, licensees in possession and lessors (if their reversion has been damaged) can sue.

Who can be sued?

The occupier.   Obviously he should be primarily liable as he is in control of the premises. He will be responsible for his own and his family's acts, those of his employees, independent contractors (possibly, depending on the degree of control), his invited guests and persons who have licenses to enter his property.

If one looks at the building contractor who is in prime control of his site, this is a heavy burden.

The occupier is even responsible for nuisances which were created before he came to the property, e.g. by previous owners blocking the neighbour's light, which the new owner fails to remedy. If he makes use of something which is a nuisance, he is said to adopt the nuisance, and he is more likely to be liable, than if he merely failed to remedy the nuisance.

Creator of the nuisance.   He is always responsible for a nuisance, even if he has left the land on which he created the nuisance and can no longer abate the nuisance.

Persons authorizing a nuisance.   If a person lets land for a purpose, which by its very nature entails the commission of a nuisance, then that person may be liable in tort. This applies even if it is only foreseeable that the nuisance may be committed by the occupiers. By including a clause in the letting agreement prohibiting behaviour which could amount to a nuisance, the lessor cannot be said to authorise the nuisance.

Defences

Consent.   *See* p. 272. Even if there has been consent, the courts may still take the view, that the complainants did not know to what extent they had consented and may still allow them to proceed in nuisance.

Prescription.   *See* p. 150. In order to gain the legal right to continue to commit a nuisance by prescription, the owner of the land must prove that he has been committing the nuisance for 20 years at least. He must not have done this with the other landowner's permission, nor must he have done it secretly, nor used force to exercise it (*nec vi, nec clam, nec precario* – without force, secrecy or permission). But, the behaviour amounting to a nuisance should be capable of existing as an easement (*see* p. 147). So, in practice, prescription may be of little use, especially for builders, who are generally not going to be in occupation of land for 20 years.

Statutory authority. If an Act of Parliament or a relevant rule or regulation imposes a duty on someone or somebody, to do something which inevitably will cause a nuisance, then the authority will be a defence, provided that there was no negligence, e.g. *Allen* v. *Gulf Oil Refinery Ltd* 1981. Here, under powers given by the Gulf Oil Refinery Act 1965, an oil refinery was built. Local villagers complained about noxious odours, vibrations and excessive noise. The House of Lords held that the section of the Act relied on gave the company immunity from any action for nuisance which might be the inevitable result of building such a refinery.

Remedies

At common law.

Damages. On proving his case, the plaintiff is entitled to compensation for the damage caused to his land, such as depreciation or loss of business. The court will take into account and offset the loss caused by reasonable behaviour, when the job which caused the nuisance was necessary. For example, in *Andreae* v. *Selfridge & Co Ltd* 1938, there would have been loss of custom due to the work anyway, but not as much as was actually caused.

Where the nuisance is a continuing nuisance, the plaintiff can recover damages for remedying it, even though he has acquired the interest in the property after the nuisance had commenced. For example, in *Master* v. *Brent LBC* 1978, the council planted trees outside a house, whose roots caused subsidence, thereby undermining the foundations. The plaintiff purchased the house later and was able to sue and recover the cost of remedying the damage.

In equity.

1. Injunction. An injunction may be awarded at the discretion of the court, if damages would be an inadequate remedy. The injunction may be permanent or it may request modification of behaviour e.g. operations to be carried out during specified hours only. An injunction may also be granted but suspended in order to give the defendant the opportunity of modifying his behaviour.

2. Abatement of nuisance. This amounts to self help and is not usually advisable. The complainant gives notice and enters the land of the person committing the nuisance and does whatever is necessary to

remove it. Unnecessary damage must not be caused.

Abatement would be a defence to an action for trespass. Once exercised however, the complainant cannot then sue for damages.

Statutory nuisances

There are various pieces of legislation which make some behaviour statutory nuisances. It would appear, that even where the Act or regulation defines the behaviour which is a nuisance, that it should also amount to a nuisance at common law. Thus, the criteria used previously should be applied when considering whether something is a nuisance, albeit statutory. The main legislation affecting builders is the Control of Pollution Act 1974 and the Public Health Acts 1936 and 1961. The following is merely an outline of some statutory nuisances which could be committed during building work.

Noise control

Under S.57 Control of Pollution Act 1974, the local authority must inspect its area from time to time in order to detect whether a noise nuisance exists. If a local authority is satisfied that a noise amounting to a nuisance exists or is likely to occur or recur in the area, then it shall serve a notice imposing all or any of the following requirements:

- it may require the nuisance to be abated;
- it may prohibit or restrict the occurrence or recurrence of the nuisance;
- the notice may specify the execution of such works and the taking of such steps as may be necessary to give effect to the requirements or as may be specified within the notice: S.58.

The notice must specify the period in which the requirements must be carried out. It must be served on the person responsible for the nuisance. If he cannot be found, it must be served on the owner or the occupier of the premises from which the noise is being or would be emitted: S.58(2). Thus, the notice can be served on landlords even though it is the tenant who is creating the nuisance.

Section 58 thus gives the local authority wide-ranging powers. Not only may it give notice to stop or reduce existing noise, but it may also restrict the emission during certain parts of the day or week. Furthermore, a notice may be served where a noise amounting to a nuisance is *likely* to occur, but has not yet started, e.g. where site work is going to commence. The carrying out of works, necessary to give effect to the notice, is a newer concept and may entail modifying machinery, making a building 'soundproof' or even moving the cause of the noise to a place where it is less likely to create a nuisance.

Should the work not be carried out as requested, the local authority can execute the works and recover the cost from the recipient of the notice.

Appeals. Appeals against the notice may be made to the magistrates' court within 21 days of receiving the notice. There are various grounds for appeals. Perhaps the most important for builders is where the noise to which the notice relates is noise caused in the course of a trade or business, that the best practicable means have been used for preventing, or for counteracting the effect of the noise.

On hearing the appeal, the court may quash the notice, vary it in favour of the appellant or dismiss the appeal.

Furthermore, the regulations specify two situations in which a notice will be suspended:

- when the notice requires expenditure on works before the appeal has been heard; and
- when the noise to which the notice relates is caused in the course of the performance of a legal duty, e.g. by a statutory undertaker.

But the notice shall not be suspended in the above situations if the noise is injurious to health or is of such limited duration that suspension would render the notice of no practical effect or the expenditure incurred on the works before the hearing would not be disproportionate to the public benefit. In such cases the notice must include a statement that it shall not be suspended pending appeal. Such a statement was included in the leading case, *Hammersmith LBC* v. *Magnum Automated Forecourts Ltd* 1978 (*see* below).

Breach of notice. By S.58(4) if the recipient of a notice contravenes any requirement contained in the notice without reasonable excuse then he commits an offence against this part of the Act. In other words, by ignoring the notice, the recipient commits an automatic offence, rather like parking on double yellow lines. Summary proceedings will then proceed in the magistrates' court.

Defences. There are a number of defences. First, it is a defence if the recipient had 'reasonable excuse' to commit the nuisance. This will depend on the facts of the situation.

Secondly, if the noise was caused in the course of a trade or business, then it is a defence to prove that the 'best practicable means' have been used for preventing or counteracting the effect of the noise. Section 72 defines 'best practicable means': 'practicable' means reasonably practicable, having regard amongst other things to local conditions and circumstances, to the current state of technical knowledge and to the financial implications. It is possible therefore that a factory, vital to the community, may have the sympathy of the court, if vast sums of money are required to eradicate the nuisance. 'The means to be employed' include the design, installation, maintenance and manner of operation of plant and machinery and the design, construction and maintenance of buildings and acoustic structures.

In addition to the 'best practicable means' defence, which *only* may be used in relation to trade or business circumstances, S.58(6) sets out other possible defences.

It will be a defence if the alleged offence was in relation to a notice served under S.60 or consent had been granted under S.61. These sections relate to construction sites (*see* below).

Section 58(8). The right to take High Court action.   This section allows the local authority to take proceedings in the High Court, if it feels that proceedings for an offence under S.58 would be an inadequate remedy. In this way nuisance may by injunction be restricted, abated or prohibited. This occurred in *Hammersmith LBC* v. *Magnum Automated Forecourts Ltd* 1978. In 1976, the defendant company erected a new building in a quiet street and used it for a 'taxi care centre'. This provided 24-hour service for taxis selling fuel, washing facilities and vending machines. People living nearby complained about the noise, particularly in the early hours of the morning. On being satisfied that a noise amounting to a nuisance existed, the local authority served notice under S.58(1) requiring Magnum Ltd to stop all activities on the premises between 11 pm and 7 am. In the notice, the authority had stated that the expenditure necessary to comply with the notice was not disproportionate to the public benefit. Thus, the notice was not suspended pending any appeal. The defendants continued to operate as before. They also appealed against the notice. The local authority therefore decided to apply to the High Court for an injunction. When the appeal came before the magistrates' court, the magistrates said that the High Court must now deal with the matter. When the case was heard in the High Court, it decided that the magistrates should determine the case. Before the magistrates' appeal was heard, the appeal from the High Court was heard by the Court of Appeal. It decided that the present situation was adequately covered by S.58(8) and that recourse to the High Court for civil remedies was thus available. The notice had specifically stated, as required, that it would not be suspended pending an appeal. When the nuisance continued in contravention of the notice, action had to be taken and if the authority was of the opinion that proceedings under S.58(4) would be inadequate, then there could be no alternative but to seek an injunction. The Court of Appeal thus granted an interlocutory (i.e. pending the outcome of the action) injunction, pending determination of the matter in the magistrates' court.

Occupier's rights: S.59.   An occupier of premises may make a complaint to the magistrates' court if he is suffering from noise amounting to a nuisance. The bench may, if satisfied that a noise nuisance exists or even if it has abated but is likely to recur, order:

- the abatement of the nuisance within a specified time and to do any work necessary for its abatement; and/or
- prohibit the recurrence of the nuisance and order the defendant to do any work necessary to prevent its recurrence: S.59(2).

The order may be brought against the same people as in Ss.58–59(3).

It must be noted that proceedings under this section cannot be brought where the noise is 'likely to occur' as under S.58. By contravening the above orders, the defendant will commit an automatic offence unless there is 'reasonable excuse'. The 'best practicable means' defence is available to persons committing the offence whilst operating a trade or business.

The bench may direct the local authority to carry out any work that the convicted person had been ordered to do and the authority has the opportunity of being heard on the matter.

Construction sites. One of the most difficult areas involving noise control is that relating to construction sites, which by virtue of the type of work involved, often create noise nuisance. The Act has therefore formulated special rules peculiar to construction site work. Such work is defined by S.60(1) as works for erecting, constructing, altering, repairing and maintaining buildings, structures or roads; and the breaking up, opening or boring under any road or adjacent land in connection with building, demolition or dredging work and any work of engineering construction.

Section 60 notices. If it appears to a local authority that any of the above work is to be carried out or is being carried out, then it may serve a notice imposing requirements as to the way the work is to be carried out and, if necessary, publish the notice of the requirements in such a way as the authority thinks appropriate.

Such a notice may specify:

- plant or machinery which is or isn't to be used
- times of operation
- levels of noise for:
(i) emission from the premises
(ii) emission from any particular part of the premises during specified hours.

It may also provide for any change in circumstances.

The local authority must have regard to the Control of Noise (Code of Practice for Construction and Open Sites) 1984. They must also ensure that the 'best practicable means' are employed to minimize noise, including suggestions for alternative machinery.

The local authority must have regard to the need to protect persons from the effects of noise in the locality in which the premises are situated.

The notice must be served on the person who is going to carry out the works and on such persons as have control over the operations, as the local authority thinks fit.

Appeals may be made to the magistrates' court within 21 days and the Control of Noise (Appeals) Regulations 1975 apply. The following are the grounds of appeal:

- that the notice is not justified by the terms of S.60;
- that there has been some informality, defect or error in, or in connection with, the notice;
- that the authority has refused unreasonably to accept compliance with alternative requirements, or that the requirements of the notice are otherwise unreasonable in character or extent, or are unnecessary;
- that the time, or, where more than one time is specified, any of the times, within which the requirements of the notice are to be complied with is not reasonably sufficient for the purpose;
- that the notice should have been served on some person instead of the appellant, being a person who is carrying out, or going to carry out, the works, or is responsible for, or has control over, the carrying out of the works;
- that the notice might lawfully have been served on some person in addition to the appellant, being a person who is carrying out, or going to carry out, the works, or is responsible for, or has control over, the carrying out of the works, and that it would have been equitable for it to have been so served;
- that the authority have not had regard to some or all of the provisions of S.60(4).

If the person served with a notice fails to do anything required within the specified time and without reasonable excuse, then he commits an automatic offence. But, if consent has been given under S.61 it will be a defence.

Prior consent on construction sites: S.61. This section gives those people responsible for construction work, and the local authorities, an opportunity to settle any problems relating to the potential noise, before the work starts. Indeed, the Department of the Environment circular suggests that there might be some sort of 'early warning system' by the local planning authority giving attention to work with potentially serious noise problems. Furthermore, advice is given in the Codes of Practice that the noise requirements of a local authority should be ascertained *before* the tender documents are sent out, so that they can be incorporated into those documents.

Application may be made before the work begins and consent may be given to the applicant. It has been suggested that the consent should be sought before the tender is made in order to take account of any requirements made by the local authority.

If building regulation approval is required, then the application must be made at the same time as the request for approval. Perhaps greater use of the consent procedure would reduce the number of S.58 notices or High Court injunctions served on builders, which can contribute to the lowering of profits on a contract. The application must contain the following particulars: (i) the works and the method by which they are to be carried out; (ii) noise minimization steps.

If the local authority considers that sufficient information has been given and that if the works were carried out in accordance with the application it would not serve a notice under the preceding section in respect of those works, then the authority shall grant its consent within 28 days and must not serve a notice under S.60, but in doing so may:

- attach conditions;
- limit consent where there is a change in circumstances;
- limit duration of consent.

If there is a contravention of any of these, then there will be an offence. The consent may be published if the authority thinks fit. Where the local authority does not give its consent or gives its consent but subject to conditions, then the applicant may appeal to a magistrates' court within 21 days. Should proceedings be brought under S.60(8), then it would be a good defence to prove that the alleged contravention amounted to the carrying out of the works in accordance with consent given under this section.

Any consent given does not in itself constitute a defence to proceedings under S.59. Where consent has been obtained by someone other than the site worker, e.g. employer/architect/consulting engineer, then those people *must* bring the consent to the notice of the site worker, otherwise the applicant will be guilty of an offence.

Smoke

Building work may be affected by smoke control laws in various ways.

First, ordinary smoke which amounts to a nuisance to the neighbourhood is a statutory nuisance under the Public Health Act 1936 and the local authority may serve an abatement notice on the person responsible such as the demolition contractor. Where it appears that there may be a recurrence, then a prohibition order may be applied for from the magistrates' court. Ignoring such orders will amount to an offence. These provisions do not apply to smoke from private dwellings, which may nevertheless be covered by bye-laws. Thus, builders should ensure that any burning of rubbish is done without causing a nuisance and without it becoming a hazard which could cause accidents and thereby liability and negligence.

Secondly, under the building regulations, there is strict building control on the height of industrial chimneys so that they prevent smoke, gases etc from becoming prejudicial to health, or a nuisance.

Thirdly, under the Clean Air Acts of 1956 and 1968 the emission of 'dark' smoke (which is defined by reference to a special chart) from industrial or trade premises is an offence, for which **no nuisance** need be proved. This is a form of strict liability and allowing dark smoke to occur on only one occasion can result in prosecution.

Fourthly, there is local authority control of the building of new non-domestic furnaces.

Builders may of course also be affected when building in smoke control areas, in which only smokeless fuel can be used and **no** smoke may be emitted from buildings.

Generally as the occasional bonfire is not a nuisance, most builders will be able to burn waste material providing they do so in a controlled and reasonable way.

Miscellaneous

The Public Health Act 1936 makes certain behaviour statutory nuisances. Some are deliberately vague and interpretation is left to the courts. Two common factors are, that most have to be either prejudicial to health or be a nuisance, e.g. keeping premises in a state as to be prejudicial to health or a nuisance; an accumulation or deposit which is prejudicial to health or a nuisance, dust or effluvia caused by any trade, business manufacture or process and which is prejudicial to the health of, or a nuisance to, the cohabitants of the neighbourhood: S.92; using a tent, van, shed or similar structure for habitation which is so overcrowded and so deficient in sanitary accommodation as to be a nuisance or prejudicial to health: S.268(2). It can be seen therefore that building work could easily cause these types of nuisances and the site operator could then be subject to delay through prosecution.

As under the Control of Pollution Act 1974 noise abatement procedures, abatement notices may be served and if necessary will specify the works required to remedy the nuisances. Should the nuisance be likely to recur (or occur if it is not already in existence) a prohibition notice can be served. If the notices are ignored, a nuisance order may be applied for from the magistrates' court. The magistrates can at the same time impose a fine. If the person served ignores the order, he will be guilty of an offence and can be fined a fixed sum plus a fine for each day after conviction that the nuisance has not been remedied.

Under the Public Health Act 1961, a quicker abatement procedure is available in circumstances in which the local authority feels that the 1936 Act procedure is too slow. In this, notice is given of the remedial work necessary, and if after 9 days, the notice has been ignored, the authority may carry out the work and recover its expenses. The Act does not oust the jurisdiction of the High Court. The authority can still start proceedings (as in *Hammersmith LBC* v. *Magnum Automated Forecourts* 1978). This of course can give rise to much greater penalties, e.g. an injunction, which if it stops work being carried on altogether, will put the building contractor in an extremely difficult position.

It should be noted that private individuals can complain to a magistrate if they are suffering from a statutory nuisance and the magistrates have similar powers as before.

Trespass to Land

Definition

Trespass to land, is committed by someone who intentionally goes on to the land in the possession of another, or, having been asked to leave, remains on that land after permission to be there has ceased. Putting something on to the land would also amount to trespass.

Examples

Thus, a person merely crossing another's land is committing trespass. Building contractors could commit trespass by dumping rubbish or materials, or digging a tunnel on another's piece of land, erecting a sign in another's air space, or swinging a crane through that air space, as in *Woollerton & Wilson Ltd* v. *Richard Costain Ltd* 1970. When working very closely to the boundary of the land, it is quite easy to commit a trespass, and therefore prior consent should be obtained to

Trespassers will be prosecuted

Wrong

As trespass is a **tort** the occupier can only sue the trespasser unless there is an Act of Parliament or other legislation making the trespass a crime, e.g. as on railways.

Fig. 8.14   Typical signs erected to deter trespassers

site scaffolding and ladders, e.g. *Westripp* v. *Baldock* 1939.

It should be noted, that trespass is a **direct** interference. Thus, roots and branches of a tree spreading into another's land is a nuisance, and not trespass: *Lemmon* v. *Webb* 1894.

No damage necessary

There is no need to prove that the trespasser did any real damage, because the tort is **actionable per se** (for itself). Merely committing the tort is enough, and ignorance is no defence.

If damage is committed however, compensation will be awarded, to reflect that damage.

If the damage is serious, then the matter may best be dealt with in criminal law, under the Criminal Damage Act 1971, and the police called. In criminal law, however, the first priority is to punish the offender, and not compensate the sufferer. Thus, a civil action may still be necessary to recover full damages.

Trespass protects **possessory** rights to land

As we have already seen, English law often protects possession of property. Thus, if a plaintiff wishes to sue someone successfully for trespass, he must show, that he was in actual possession of the land at the time of the alleged trespass. The owner, if out of possession would not therefore be able to sue for trespass, (although, if necessary he has another remedy called **ejectment**, *see* p. 304). So, those building contractors who are in possession of a site would be the proper persons to sue for an injunction to prevent trespassers repeating their trespass, and not the site owner. Similarly, lessees can sue for trespass where they, and not the lessors, are in possession of the leased premises.

Trespass actions used for boundary disputes

It should be noted, that an action for trespass, is often used for the court to decide who actually owns or possesses a particular piece of land. Whilst, in such cases, the damages would be very low, the end result is that the legal position of the owners and the person in dispute will have been sorted out. Also, many such disputes do not concern large tracts, but may be mere boundary disputes. For this reason, when marking out sites, the boundaries should be clearly shown to correspond exactly with the plans and the plans on the title deeds. Also, if a description of the land is used, this should be accurate.

What amounts to land

See p. 133, but note, land includes the surface of the ground, fixtures, buildings, rooms, growing plants, the earth below and the airspace above, subject to modern limitations. Merely flying over someone's land is not a trespass: *Bernstein* v. *Skyviews Ltd* 1977.

The trespass must be intentional

This means, that the trespasser must have meant to enter on the land, *even if he was mistaken* about some aspect, e.g. because he thought he was allowed to enter the land, or he did not realize he was on private land but not if he had been thrown onto the land by another.

Defences

Consent. If the occupier has given permission for the 'trespasser' to be on his land, then this would be a good defence. Written permission is preferable as this is better evidence in any court proceedings at a later date.

Statutory rights to enter. Certain public officials have the right to enter another's land, e.g. police, electricity board, and tax officials (*see* p. 136).

Public rights of way. If land is subject to a **public** right of way, then those exercising that right are not trespassers. But, they must not do anything beyond the exercise of that right, otherwise, it could amount to trespass.

Easements. These are private rights e.g. a right of way or of light. The owner of an easement, has the right to enter the land to exercise that easement.

Necessity. It may be, that the defendant committed the tort of trespass, in order to prevent a greater wrong occurring, e.g. entering land to put out a fire. If this is so, then it could be a defence.

Abatement of nuisance. *See* p. 293.

Recaption of chattels. Here, the owner of chattels enters another's land, to recover them. He can only do this if the occupier of the land, or someone else, wrongfully took them there in the first place, or they got there by accident. This is an unusual right, and may prove a defence to an action for trespass.

Re-entering land by person entitled to have possession. It must be remembered, that, if the person entitled to possess the land, is out of possession, then he has **no** remedy in trespass. He can, of course take other types of action, as set out in the note on p. 304. Does this mean, that, if he re-enters the land, to regain possession, that he could be sued for trespass?

The answer is, yes, but he can raise a number of different defences, provided he used only reasonable force to eject the trespassers, and provided the occupiers were not, or had not been, tenants, in which case he would need a court order to evict them.

Remedies

Damages. Once the plaintiff has proved his case, he is entitled to damages **as of right**, as this is a legal remedy. Because the tort is actionable per se, no actual damage is needed, and damages must be awarded, to compensate for the reduction in the value of the land. But, if the trespasser, did no more than tip-toe across your front lawn, the damages awarded could be **nominal** (from latin, nomen-nominis-name) e.g. 1p, because the judge may be unimpressed with your case and feel it was wasting the court's time. If the defendant actually occupied the land, by living there, or leaving rubbish behind, then the plaintiff is entitled to ask for rent.

Injunction. This is an equitable, and therefore, discretionary remedy. It will only be awarded, where it is 'just and convenient'. A prohibitory injunction is awarded, to stop the defendant from continuing the trespass. If the injunction is ignored, the plaintiff can ask for the defendant to be committed to prison.

Declaration by the judge. A declaration may be made by the judge, concerning the rights of the disputing parties, and may be used in boundary disputes, especially, if there has been no actual trespass proved.
(Note: if the owner of the land wishes to remove people in unlawful possession of his land, then trespass is not the appropriate action to take. He must, therefore, bring an action of **ejectment** to get possession, and may claim damages for the period of occupation by the trespassers. Such damages are called **mesne** (pronounced mean) **profits.**)

Repossession only, can be claimed by more modern methods under RSC (Rules of the Supreme Court) Ord 113 (White Book) or in the CCR Ord 26 (Green Book). Here, an originating summons (and not a writ) can be issued, supported by an affidavit, setting out a claim against the persons in possession. This is useful when recovering land from 'squatters' and can be used even if the names of the squatters are unknown.

Breach of a statutory duty – a tort

Certain Acts of Parliament and regulations impose duties on many people, but especially employers and employees to do or not to do specific things, e.g. the Construction (Working Places) Regulations 1966.

A breach of such duties is primarily punished by criminal proceedings.

Whether the relevant Act or regulations allow someone to be able to sue in **civil** law for damages caused as a result of the breach of statutory duty, depends first, on what is intended by the criminal Act (*see* p. 25). Having said that, in the majority of cases, it is perfectly valid to sue, following a breach of a statutory duty, whether or not there has been a successful prosecution.

Probably in the absence of an express bar, such a civil action will be permitted as under S.38 Building Act 1984 when it comes into effect. Thus there is **no** right to sue for breach of the general duties laid down by the Health & Safety at Work etc Act 1974, as this is specifically stated in the Act. But, if there has been a breach of one of the regulations or relevant Acts which come under the umbrella of the Act, then there can be a civil action.

The most common examples of breaches of statutory duty are, for our purpose, found in the sphere of health and safety at work.

What must be proved to be able to sue

There are five things which must be proved:

1. That the regulation or act imposes a duty to do something.
2. That the particular regulation or Act has been broken.
3. That the plaintiff is within the class the regulation was designed to protect. Thus visitors to a site are probably not owed statutory duties under the Construction Regulations (but, of course, they are owed duties in negligence and under the Occupiers' Liability Act 1957).
4. That the Act or regulation conferred a right to sue on the plaintiff.
5. That the plaintiff is suffering from an injury which the regulation was designed to protect against even if the injury did not occur in the precise way anticipated. Thus in *Donaghey* v. *Boulton & Paul Ltd* 1968 a man fell through a hole in a roof and not through fragile roof material as anticipated by the Construction Regulations designed to protect people from falls from roofs. He was able to recover damages.

Some of the statutory duties are absolute. Thus, failing to do the precise act required amounts to a breach. In other cases, the duty is not specified and principles of the same sort found in negligence will be used to determine criminal (and civil) liability. The existence of phrases such as 'by the best practical means' or 'so far as is reasonably practicable' will indicate a 'reasonable man' approach as in negligence. There are, of course, statutory definitions of such phrases in some Acts.

Contributory negligence. *See* p. 274.

Volenti non fit injuria. *See* p. 272. An employer cannot plead this as a defence in a claim by his employee against him for his own personal liability. It may be pleaded, however, in a claim for vicarious liability. But note a plea of volenti is not often successful.

A claim based on a delegation of the statutory duty by the employer to the plaintiff. Where the plaintiff clearly knew of the statutory obligations which had been validly transferred to himself, this may be raised as a proper defence. There is, of course, a duty imposed on the employer to see that the employee understands the extent of this duty and the consequences of failing to carry out its requirements properly.

Specified under the Act. By S.38 Building Act 1984, for example, a prescribed defence may be provided for under the Building Regulations.

Liability for spread of fire

Historically, this has always been treated in a separate way from other branches of tort. However, it now seems to have been absorbed into the main stream of tort except in some areas mentioned below.

Strict liability in *Rylands* v. *Fletcher*

See p. 285.

Strict liability in public nuisance

See p. 289.

Strict liability for breach of statutory duty

See p. 304. It should be noted that by S.71 of the Health & Safety at Work etc. Act 1974, there can be civil liability for a breach of a statutory duty imposed under the Building Regulations. Part B of the regulations is concerned with safety in fire of buildings and it is possible that someone could be sued for breach of such regulations. Such liability was expressly referred to in *Anns* v. *London Borough of Merton* 1977 and confirmed by S.38 Building Act 1984 in a section yet to come into effect.

Negligence

The tort of negligence will, of course, apply to the spread of fire, despite the existence of the Fire Prevention (Metropolis) Act 1774 which toned down an earlier type of liability for the spread of fire, which amounted to almost strict liability. The Act says that it is a defence for an occupier, if the fire began 'accidentally' on his land. Of course, this is now in line with modern thinking in negligence, that where there is no fault, there can be no liability. Nevertheless, if a fire is started and spreads and negligence is proved, the occupier is responsible not only for his own actions but also for those of his employees or independent contractors. This is of particular importance in demolition work, where burning rubbish is an essential and continuous part of the job. In *H & N Emanuel* v. *GLC* 1971 the council gave permission to the Ministry of Works to clear a GLC site of houses. The Ministry contracted with a demolition contractor who negligently allowed a fire to spread and cause damage. The GLC was found to be liable, as an occupier, for the contractor's negligence.

Limitation Act 1980

It is unfair that plaintiffs do not take advantage of their right to sue within a reasonable period. The 1980 Act which consolidated previous legislation, lays down various periods in which the action must be brought. For most torts this is a period of six years with the exception of actions brought for damages for negligence, nuisance or breach of duty, when the damages claimed include damages for personal injuries, when the period is three years. The limitation period begins to run from the date on which the cause of action accrued. This can be a problem in cases concerning personal injury and thus in such cases the time runs from either the injury or the plaintiff's knowledge of the injury. This knowledge is that the injury is significant, that the injury is due to the alleged negligence of the defendant and that the plaintiff knows of the identity of the defendant. In any event the courts have the discretionary right to override the time limits where this is fair subject to certain statutory criteria.

Because of the difficulties concerning latent damage in the case of building claims (see p. 262) the Law Commission has suggested that reforms be made in this area. The Bill should be enacted in 1986.

CHAPTER 9

The law relating to highways

Introduction

The word highway has a rather old-fashioned ring to it, conjuring up visions of Dick Turpin on Black Bess, galloping furiously to York.

In fact, highway is an all-embracing word used to cover many different types of routes which may be used by the **public** in general, without permission or limitation, except perhaps as to the manner of use. Thus, a highway may be a road, footpath, street, bridlepath, metalled or a mere track. But, it must be used by the public, as of right.

Builders are affected by the laws relating to highways, as they travel across them to transport materials to site, they construct roads, they deposit things such as skips there, they park vehicles on them and erect hoardings and scaffolding close by.

Relevant law

The law is found principally in the Highways Act 1980, which consolidated previous Highways Acts, and at common law, particularly in tort.

Definition

A highway may be defined as a particular route across a piece of land which is open to the public, over which they may pass or repass **AS OF RIGHT**. Section 328 of the Highways Act 1980, specifically includes bridges and tunnels if they form part of a highway, but excludes ferries and waterways.

1. They must be open to the public in general. Otherwise, if a right of way exists over a piece of land, it may only be an easement, for which there must be a dominant and servient tenement (*see* p. 148) or it will be a private right of way for the benefit of a small community such as a village, which may be created by custom.

2. There must be a definite route, which may be shown on a map. Thus, a right to cross a field in any direction can not be a highway.

Whilst the public must be allowed to pass and repass over the land, it is not necessary for the highway to be a thoroughfare (i.e. a through road or path).

3. If a road or any other purported highway can only be used by special permission, e.g. by licence, as on a toll road, or if the landowner merely puts up with the public using the land, then the public will not have the use **as of right**.

4. The route will still be a highway if its use is restricted in some way. For example, it may be restricted to horse riders or pedestrians. Highways are usually maintained at public expense by the highway authorities and appropriate government departments. In exceptional circumstances, highways may be maintained privately by the owner of the land over which the highway passes. Other routes exist which are not the liability of anyone, known as **private streets** (*see* p. 329).

It should be noted, that private streets may also be highways, but if the right of the public to use them is restricted, then they will not be highways. Thus, 'private roads' on exclusive housing estates are usually private streets in legal terms.

As a highway is a route over land, all the usual rules relating to land are applicable (*see* Ch. 5).

Types of highway – Part II Highways Act 1980 Ss. 10–23

The following types of highway are roads maintainable at public expense.

Trunk roads

These are main roads which form the basis of the national system of routes for through traffic in England and Wales. Local roads may be designated trunk roads. The Department of Transport is the highway authority for trunk roads, but county councils may become agents for the department and either they, or even district councils, may carry out work for them.

Principal or classified roads: S.12

This is an outdated classification used when road grants were awarded for important route-ways.

By S.13, the minister may by order, give another (more meaningful) description.

Metropolitan roads: S.15

These are important roads in London. Those that were metropolitan before the Act, continue to be so, and under S.10, certain trunk roads may become metropolitan by order of the minister.

Special roads: S.16

These are roads reserved for particular classes of traffic, most of which are motorways.

Any other publicly maintained roads

Generally the responsibility of the county council. Publicly maintained roads are those roads which:
(i) were publicly maintained before the Highways Act 1835, *or*
(ii) have been **adopted** for maintenance at public expense under statutory rules contained in the various provisions of the Highways Act. This may be under the following sections.

Section 37 Highways Act

Where someone dedicates part of his land for use as a highway by the public, it will become publicly maintainable if the highway authority certifies to its dedication and to the fact that the road has been made up to their satisfaction.

Section 38

A highway authority may adopt an existing highway by agreement.

Section 53

The owner of a privately maintained highway, may deposit a requisite sum with the highway authority, who will then adopt it for public maintenance.

Sections 54, 116

Where a privately maintained highway is diverted by order of the magistrates, the new highway is maintainable at public expense.

Section 228

A private street may become publicly maintained if private street works have been executed (*see* p. 330).

Section 229

A private new street must become publicly maintained if payment has been made under the Advance Payment Code S.229 (*see* p. 330).

Creating a highway

A highway may be created in two ways, either at common law by dedication and acceptance or by statute.

Dedication and acceptance

1. Dedication by landowner. A landowner may dedicate, i.e. set aside for a special purpose, a right over his land to the public, allowing them to pass and repass. He can do this **expressly** by executing a deed. This may occur when a builder buys a piece of land, builds a housing estate on it with new roads, intending those roads to be used by the householders and the public. The fact that the new road may be used by the public will be written into the deeds transferring the land to the new owners.

The landowner can also dedicate the highway in an **implied** way. This would mean that the dedication is obvious from the landowner's actions. This may occur where he allows the public to pass over a particular road without restriction.

Whether express or implied, the dedication must have been **intended** by the landowner. There can be no dedication either if the landowner restricts the right in some way, e.g. so that only certain people such as the local villagers, can use the path. To prevent dedication, many landowners close the route by a gate or chain every now and then to show that they have no intention of allowing it to become a highway.

A landowner who does not own the fee simple cannot dedicate the land for the public's use, as he will only have a restricted interest himself.

There can be no dedication if the public pay for permission to use the highway, e.g. on a toll road.

As we know that bridlepaths and footpaths can also be highways, any restriction as to the **type** of use, will not alter the fact that it is a highway, provided all the other requirements are fulfilled.

2. Acceptance by the public. In addition to dedication there must **also** be acceptance of the dedication by the public. This is indicated by the public's use of the highway **as of right**.

Acceptance may be examined by the courts in much the same way as other customary rights in terms of how long it has been going on etc (*see* p. 150).

But in most cases S.31(a) of the Highways Act 1980 provides a simpler method of declaring whether there has been a valid dedication and acceptance. This states that 'where a way over any land ... has been actually enjoyed by the public, as of right and without interruption for a full period of 20 years, the way shall be deemed to have been dedicated as a highway unless there is sufficient evidence that there was no intention during that period to dedicate it'.

By S.31(2) the period of 20 years is calculated retrospectively from the date the highway's dedication is first called into question.

In order to negative the landowner's apparent intention to dedicate the way as a highway, the landowner may erect a notice declaring this to be so, and this is sufficient to prevent the dedication: S.31(3).

If the land is leased, the person owning the freehold reversion may exhibit such a notice on the land: S.31(4). Such a notice must be visible to the highway users. But, if the notice is torn down or defaced, e.g. by hostile road users, the owner can give notice to the appropriate highway authority, informing them of the fate of the notice, and that he has not dedicated the way as a highway: S.31(5).

In order to clarify his position, e.g. if there seems to be a dispute brewing, a landowner may deposit a map with the authority and a statement indicating which routes (if any) have been dedicated and those which are not. These are available for public inspection.

So to give an example of how the dedication and acceptance test can be used in practice, imagine that Big C Construction plc have started to build houses on Lord Avarice's estate. Lord Avarice told the builders that the highway through the estate was not a public highway, as he had always maintained a notice stating this fact as required by the Act. When the company started to rip up the road, a lobby of motorists from the surrounding area, forced them to stop work by obtaining an injunction. From this date, the 20 years' period will be calculated retrospectively. Thus, if in the ensuing court case, the motorist's lawyers can prove that there has been 20 years' use of the road without interruption, as of right and there has never been a notice or plans deposited, then the road will be declared a highway.
(Note: if Lord Avarice had barred the way occasionally, and this can be proved, this will still indicate there was no use **as of right** and that there never had been an **intention** to dedicate.)

Creation by statute

Highways can be created by Acts in various ways. There may be a local Act covering a particular area or roadway or a general Act such as the Enclosure Acts of the past. But the most important Act is the Highways Act 1980 Part III Ss. 24–35.

The Act makes provision for the highway authorities and the minister to create new highways in general such as motorways and to provide road ferries as well as new footpaths and bridleways. Highways created in this way will be maintained at public expense. They can also create walkways, now popular in shopping precincts, which have certain characteristics of highways, but whose use is regulated by byelaws and departmental regulations. The land on which the highways are to be constructed may be bought by agreement or by compulsory purchase. Landowners who are affected by the new highways may be granted compensation under the Land Compensation Act 1973 as amended, for the depreciation in the value of their property. The Act also provides for acquiring rights over someone's land, but not buying the land itself.

Under S.34 a new private street, say on a housing estate, may be declared to be a highway by the highway authority. This also applies to a road which has been designated on a development plan under planning legislation.

Under S.35, walkways may be created by **dedication agreement** between the owner of the land and the local highway authority or district council. The agreement will contain strict provisions as to the walkway's use and maintenance.

Ownership of highways

As has already been shown, a highway does not have to belong to the highway authority, even if it is maintainable at public expense.

But, if the road is maintained at public expense, the Act vests a sufficient proportion of the road surface in the highway authority, so as to allow it to carry out required maintenance: S.263. The underlying subsoil thus remains the property of the landowner, but subject to such restrictions on use as are contained in the Act and other legislation, e.g. the Town and Country Planning Act 1971 (*see* Fig. 9.1).

The rights of the public over the highway

It is always important to differentiate between a highway and private property, as certain acts may be quite legal on private land, but may amount to an offence if committed on a highway, e.g. driving a motor vehicle without a licence.

The extent of the rights of the public over a particular highway depend on what was specified by dedication and acceptance or in any legislation. Thus, for example, a motorist has no right to drive his motor car along a bridlepath. Parking may be permitted on roads, provided it is not prohibited and that no obstruction is caused. At common law, obstruction of a highway may amount to a public nuisance (*see* p. 289), as may allowing hedges to encroach on to the highway, depositing rubbish or dumping something on the highway, or allowing the road to fall into disrepair. Direct interferences with the highway may amount to trespass (*see* p. 301) even if the behaviour merely exceeds the normal and reasonable use expected of a member of the public.

Protection of public rights: S.130 Highways Act 1980

It is the **duty** of the highway authority to assert and protect the rights

Highway

Highway authority is
vested with sufficient
depth to maintain road.

Privately owned sub-soil

Highway over private land but publicly maintained

Highway

All sub-soil privately owned

Highway over private land not publicly maintained

Fig. 9.1 Ownership of highways

of the public in relation to their use and enjoyment of any highway for
which it is responsible.

Any local authority has a **power** to protect the rights of the public in
their use and enjoyment of any highway within their area, but for
which they are not responsible as highway authority.

Highway authorities must prevent as far as possible the **stopping up**
or **obstruction** of highways as well as the unlawful encroachment of any
roadside waste. To this end, they may take or defend legal proceedings
and take such steps as they think expedient.

Stopping up and diverting highways and stopping up of means of access to highways

As we have seen in conveyancing (*see* pp. 158–67), it is not enough to buy land on which to build. Searches and enquiries must be made to check that the land is not adversely affected by matters which will prevent building or restrict the use of the land in some way. One particular aspect is important in relation to highways. If there is a public (or private) right of way over the land, the builder must respect this right or face the consequences. If he builds on a public right of way, he will commit a criminal offence. If he builds on a private right of way, he faces civil action by those benefitting from the right (such as the owner of an easement).

What he must therefore do, is to arrange for the diversion or the stopping up of the highway **before** the work is started.

However, in *Ashby* v. *Secretary of State for the Environment* 1980, the Court of Appeal ruled that the Secretary of State could confirm a diversion order made under the Town and Country Planning Act 1971 *after* the work had begun. Reliance on such a possibility is not good commercial practice, especially in relation to breaches of the Town and Country Planning Act 1971 under which orders may be made to demolish houses built in contravention of planning permission.

Part VIII Highways Act, Ss. 116–130

Section 116: the magistrates' power to stop up or divert highways

If the magistrates, after viewing the highway in question, are of the opinion that the highway is unnecessary or can be diverted so as to make it **nearer** or more **commodious** to the public, then the court may, on application by a highway authority, authorize its stopping up or diversion. Their consent must not be unreasonably withheld. The section does not apply to trunk roads or special roads (as they are usually by definition necessary and beneficial).

By S.117, a person who wishes to have the highway stopped up or diverted, such as an estate developer may request the highway authority to make an application on his behalf. He may be required to pay for the application, but he has no right of appeal against a refusal. He may need to make such an application if he wishes to build on a particular piece of land which is affected by the presence of a highway. It must be noted, that the highway will only be diverted if it is no longer needed or would be commodious to the public.

If such an order is made, it only extinguishes public rights over the highway. Private rights of way remain (and could thus still be a problem in practice).

Section 116 is not the only statutory means of closing or diverting highways. The following are also important.

Acquisition of Land Act 1981

S.32 authorizes the Secretary of State for the Environment to make an order **extinguishing** a non-vehicular public right of way over land that

316

has been compulsorily purchased or acquired by agreement as an
alternative to compulsory purchase.

Housing Act 1957

By S.4 the Secretary of State may give his approval to a local authority
to make an order **extinguishing** a public right of way over land
purchased by the authority as part of a clearance area.

Town and Country Planning Act 1971

By S.209, the Secretary of State may, by order, authorize the **stopping
up** or **diversion** of a highway, if he is satisfied that it is necessary to
enable development to be carried out in accordance with any planning
permission or by a government department. The order thus made may
also require the provision or improvement of other highways to
compensate for the loss of the highway.

Also, by S.214, the Secretary of State may make an order
extinguishing any public right of way acquired by a local authority for
planning reasons.

In practice therefore, the builder will use Ss.116, 117 of the
Highways Act 1980 or S.209 of the Town and Country Planning Act
1971.

Section 118: stopping up of footpaths or bridleways

Public path extinguishment order. A council may by order confirmed
by the Secretary of State extinguish a public right of way over a
footpath or bridleway if the way is not needed for **public use**.

Section 119: diversion of footpaths and bridleways

Public path diversion orders. If an owner, lessee or occupier of land
which is crossed by a footpath or bridleway satisfies the council that to
enable his land to be used efficiently or to provide a shorter or more
commodious path or way, the footpath or bridleway should be
diverted, then the council may make an order to be confirmed by the
Secretary of State for the Environment. The order may,

- **Create**, from a particular date, a **new** footpath or bridleway, so as
  to effect the diversion **and**
- **Extinguish** the public right of way over all or part of the path as
  seems necessary to the council

The land owner/lessee/occupier who requested the diversion order
may be required to defray or make a contribution towards the cost of
compensation which may be awarded to someone whose land has
depreciated in value or who has been disturbed in his enjoyment of the

land or who has suffered damage as a result of the creation of a new footpath: Ss.28, 119(5). Also, a contribution to expenses may be required.

Section 122: power to make temporary diversions where highway is about to be repaired or widened

Where a highway authority or a person who is liable to maintain a highway is about to repair or widen a highway, they may construct on adjoining land, a temporary highway for use while the work is in progress. The owner or occupier of the land on which the temporary highway is constructed may recover compensation from the highway authority or other person constructing the road, if he sustains any damage as a consequence of the work.

The section does not authorise interference with land which is part of a house-site, garden, lawn, yard, court, part, paddock, plantation, planted walk, or tree nursery.

Stopping up of means of access to highways

Under Ss.124 to 129 of the Highways Act 1980, there are provisions for the stopping of private accesses to highways by order, S.124; private accesses to premises, S.125 and agreements to stop up private accesses, S.127.

Building and improvement lines: Ss.72–75 Highways Act 1980

Improvement lines: S.73

A highway authority may wish to widen certain streets, and therefore the appropriate local authority may prescribe a line to which the street may be widened called an **improvement line**. This is a local land charge and must therefore be registered on the register of local land charges (*see* p. 162).

Once an improvement line has been made **no new building** may be erected and **no permanent** excavations below street level shall be made beyond the line, without first obtaining consent.

Breach of this amounts to an offence and a fine is levied for each day the contravention continues.

Building lines: S.74

The highway authority may also prescribe a building line similar to the improvement lines. Once prescribed, no new buildings (or permanent excavations) other than boundary walls or fences may be erected without consent beyond the building line, which is a specified distance from the centre-line of the highway. It is thus a frontage line beyond which no building may project. Contravention of this amounts to an offence.

It should be noted that statutory undertakers such as water or electricity boards are not affected by the above.

General restrictions on damaging highways

Penalty for damaging highways

By S.131, anyone without lawful authority who causes damage to a highway, by digging a ditch, excavating, removing soil or turf, depositing anything or lighting a fire on the highway is guilty of a criminal offence.

It is also an offence to remove road signs, milestones or direction posts.

Unauthorised marks on highways (graffiti)

Under S.132, anyone painting or fixing a picture, letter or sign upon a highway without the highway authority's consent is guilty of an offence. The authority is empowered to remove the offending mark.

Damage to footways of streets by excavations

Under S.133, if a street footway (pavement or similar) is damaged by a person excavating on land adjoining the street, the highway authority may make good the damage and **recover** the **expense** from either the landowner or the person causing the damage.

Obstructing highways and streets

Section 137: obstruction

If someone without lawful authority or excuse in **any way** obstructs the free passage along a highway, then he is guilty of an offence and may be arrested on site without the necessity of obtaining a warrant.

In addition to this section under the Highways Act 1980, there are a number of other legal methods of restricting similar behaviour, e.g., by Reg. 122 Motor Vehicles (Construction & Use) Regulations 1978, trailers must not be allowed to stand on roads so as to cause unnecessary obstruction. Also, the rules relating to public nuisance apply (*see* p. 289).

Section 138: offences for erecting buildings in carriageways

Anyone erecting a building, fence, plant or hedge on a carriageway, without lawful authority, is guilty of an offence. A carriageway is part of a highway used by vehicles: S.329.

Sections 139, 149: builders skips

Skips must not be left on highways without the consent of the highway authority. Such consent may be granted unconditionally or subject to conditions. Conditions may include restricting the dimensions of the skip, determining its siting, lighting, guarding, care and disposal of contents, and removal at the end of the period.

Anyone depositing a skip without permission is guilty of an offence.

Once permission has been granted, the owner must clearly mark details of his name, address and telephone number on the skip. He must keep it properly lighted at night, so that it is visible to traffic and pedestrians. After it has been filled, it must be moved as soon as is practicable. All conditions of the consent must be complied with. Even if permission has been given, the skip may be removed or repositioned at the wish of the highway authority or a uniformed police constable: S.140.

It is a defence to prove that the offence was due to the act or default of another person and that the person charged took all reasonable precautions and exercised all due diligence to avoid the commission of such an offence by himself or anyone under his control. Such a defence can only be relied on, if, within seven days before the hearing, the defendant serves a notice on the prosecution giving such information, identifying or assisting in the identification of that other person, e.g. a sub-contractor.

Section 139 does not authorize the creation of a nuisance or of a danger to users of the highway. Nor does it impose liability on the highway authority for any injury or damage caused to someone, resulting from the presence of a permitted skip.

Section 141: restrictions on planting of trees etc. in or near a carriageway

It is an offence to plant trees or shrubs in a carriageway or within 15 ft from the centre of a carriageway.

However, under S.142, the highway authority may grant a licence to the occupier or owner of premises adjoining a highway to plant and maintain or to retain and maintain, trees, shrubs, plants or grass in such parts of a highway as may be specified in the licence.

Section 143: structures erected on a highway

Anyone erecting a structure, which includes anything capable of causing an obstruction, without permission or statutory authority, (*see* p. 293) may be required by notice, to remove it within a specified period.

'Structure' includes any machine, pump, post or other object, capable of causing obstruction and it may nevertheless be a structure if it has wheels.

Section 148: penalty for depositing things on a highway

It is an offence to deposit on a made-up carriageway dung, compost, material or rubbish on or within 15 ft from the centre of the carriageway, or by such deposit **interrupt** the use of the highway without lawful authority or excuse.

Section 149: removal of things so deposited as to be a nuisance.

Anything deposited on a highway which is a nuisance, may be required to be removed by the highway authority by notice to the person who deposited it there. If he then fails to remove it, the authority may make a complaint to the magistrates and ask for a **disposal order**.

If the authority considers that the unlawful deposit constitutes a danger (even by merely obstructing the view), and that the deposit ought to be removed without the delay involved in the above procedure, the authority may remove it forthwith and charge the cost to the person who made the deposit.

Section 150: duty to remove snow, soil or other obstructions from highways

A highway authority is under a duty to remove obstructions on highways caused by an accumulation of snow, falling down of banks on the side of the highway **or from any other cause**. If the authority fails to remove the obstruction, **any person** may make a complaint to the magistrates court, who may then order the removal of the obstruction within a specified period.

The authority may take any reasonable steps to warn highway users of the obstruction, recover the cost and if necessary, **sell** the obstruction.

The sort of obstruction that comes within this section, must be construed to be in the same categories as snow and falling banks, i.e. natural obstructions which occurred suddenly, such as falling trees and not lorries which are dealt with elsewhere in the Act.

Section 151: prevention of soil being washed on to the street

A local or highway authority may, by notice to the owner or occupier of any land adjoining a street maintainable at public expense, require him to execute such works as will prevent soil or refuse from that land falling, being washed or carried on to the street or into any sewer or gully, so as to obstruct the street or choke the sewer or gully.

Failure to comply amounts to an offence, and if convicted, fines are incurred for each day the offence continues.

Scaffoldings and hoardings and other projections

At common law

Public nuisance

The principles of *Wringe* v. *Cohen* (*see* pp. 289–90) will also apply to building constructions which project across highways. Liability is strict, but only in relation to **disrepair**. Also, these rules only appear to apply to **artificial** projections and not to things such as trees, in which case **negligence** would have to be proved.

Private nuisance

See pp. 290–94.

Statute

Section 152: Highways Act 1980: powers as to removal of projections from buildings

A highway or local authority may by notice to the occupier of any building, require him to **remove** or **alter** any porch, shed, projecting window, step, cellar, cellar door, cellar window, sign, signpost, showboard, window, shelter, wall gate, fence or other obstruction or projection which has been erected or placed against or in front of the building **and** is an obstruction to safe or convenient passage along a street. If the recipient of the notice fails to remove the obstruction, he is guilty of an offence.

Section 153: doors etc not to open outwards

Doors opening outwards into the street are prohibited unless the highway authority gives its consent for a public building. A notice to alter the door may be served on the occupier and failure to do so amounts to an offence.

Section 154: cutting or felling etc. trees that overhang, or are a danger to roads or footpaths

A local or highway authority may serve a notice on the occupier on whose land is growing a hedge, tree or shrub overhanging a highway, so as to endanger or obstruct the view of drivers of vehicles or the light from public street lamps. The notice may require the lopping or cutting of the obstruction.

If it appears that the tree etc is diseased or dead, and is likely to cause a danger, a notice may be served to require its removal.

Section 169: control of scaffolding on highways – licences

No person is permitted in relation to any building, demolition, alteration, repair, cleaning etc works, to **erect** or **retain** on or over a highway, any scaffolding or other structure which obstructs the highway, without a **licence** issued by the highway authority. The terms of the licence must be complied with.

Provided an applicant for a licence furnishes the authority with such particulars as are required, the authority must issue a licence in respect of the structure, unless:

- the structure would cause unreasonable obstruction of a highway, or
- an alternative structure could be erected to that proposed by the applicant, which would cause less obstruction and could be used for the work in question.

An appeal against a refusal to grant a licence or particular terms contained in a licence, may be made to a magistrates court. Once a licence is granted, subject to exceptions, a licensee must ensure that the structure is lit at all times between half an hour after sunset and half an hour before sunrise. He must also comply with all written directions concerning the erection and maintenance of traffic signs.

However, if no part of the structure is less than 18 inches horizontally from a carriageway and no part is less than eight feet above a footway, then these two provisions do not have to be complied with (*see* Fig. 9.2).
He must give access to any apparatus belonging to or used by statutory undertakers, e.g. the electricity boards.
Failure to comply with the above amounts to an offence.

Civil and criminal immunity under S.169(7)

Provided there is a licence granted for the structure and the terms of the licence are complied with, then **no civil** or **criminal** proceedings lie in respect of any **obstruction** of a highway, either in relation to the licensee or the highway authority.

Danger or annoyance to users of highways and streets

Section 161: deposits on highways endangering or injuring users

A person who without lawful authority, deposits **anything** on a highway which causes injury or endangers a user commits an offence: S.161(1).

Work being carried out over 8 feet above footpath

8 feet

In such cases no precautions regarding lighting and traffic signs referred to in the text do not have to be complied with (under the Act).

18 inches

Carriageway

Work being carried on more than 18 inches horizontally from carriageway.

Fig. 9.2 The exception to the requirements regarding lighting and maintenance

A person lighting a fire within 50 feet of the centre of a carriageway of a highway, which injures or endangers a user or interrupts the use of the highway without lawful authority is guilty of an offence: S.161(2).

A person is also guilty of an offence if he allows any filth, dirt, lime or other offensive matter to run on to a highway from any adjoining premises without lawful authority: S.161(4).

Section 162: placing ropes etc. across highways

The placing of a rope, wire or other apparatus across a highway, so as to be a likely cause of danger to users, is an offence, unless adequate warnings were given of the danger.

Section 163: prevention of water falling on or flowing on to a highway

A local or highway authority can require steps to be taken by the

324

occupier to prevent water from his premises falling upon users of a highway or so far as is reasonably practicable, surface water from flowing on to or over the footway of the highway.

Section 164: removal of barbed wire

Similarly, an authority may require the occupier of land adjoining a highway on which there is a fence made with barbed wire and which amounts to a nuisance to the highway, to abate the nuisance within a specified time. By S.164(1)b, such barbed wire is deemed to be a nuisance, if it is likely to be injurious to persons or animals **lawfully** using the highway. Thus, barbed wire used to discourage entry to a site, would generally not fall under this section.

Section 165: dangerous land adjoining a street

A local authority may serve a notice on the owner or occupier of land which adjoins a street, if in or on such land, there is an **unfenced or inadequately fenced source of danger** to persons using the street. The notice may require work to be carried out, to repair, protect, remove or enclose the land, to obviate the danger.

Section 167: retaining walls near streets

This section imposes conditions on the construction and maintenance of retaining walls which are within 4 yards of a street and over 4 ft 6 ins high. It requires that their erection shall be in accordance with plans, sections and specifications approved by the local authority.

Precautions to be taken when doing work on or near streets or highways

Section 168: building operations affecting public safety

If in the course of carrying out building work in or near a street, an accident occurs which:

- gives rise to the **risk** of serious bodily injury to a person in the street or
- would have done so if the local authority or highway authority had not prevented this happening,

then the land or building owner on which the operation is being carried out is guilty of an offence.

It is a defence to prove that the person charged, took all reasonable precautions to avoid endangering passers-by, or that the offence was committed by some other person and that he took all reasonable precautions to avoid committing the offence by himself or any person under his control.

'Building operation' includes, inter alia, construction, repair, maintenance etc. demolition, laying foundations and erecting or dismantling cranes or scaffolding.

Scaffolding

See pp. 321–2.

Section 170: control of mixing of mortar etc on highway

It is an offence to mix or deposit on a highway, any **mortar** or **cement** or any other substance which is likely to stick to the surface of the highway or to solidify in drains or sewers.

Section 170(2) allows the mixing of such substances in receptacles or on plates, thereby preventing it from touching the highway. The section does not apply to highway authorities, statutory undertakers and certain other persons.

Section 171: control of deposit of building materials and the making of excavations in streets

Permission may be given by a highway authority to someone to **temporarily** deposit building materials, rubbish etc or make a temporary excavation in a street.

Such consent may be subject to conditions. Appeals against the refusal of consent may be made to the magistrates' court.

The deposit or excavation shall be properly fenced and lighted in the dark. It must not remain there longer than necessary.

Failure to comply with any of the above, amounts to an offence.

Section 172: hoardings to be set up during building

Before a building is erected or demolished, its outside repaired or altered, in a street or court, then **prior** to the commencement of the work, a close boarded hoarding or fence must be erected to the county authority's satisfaction, so as to separate the building from the street or court.

This obligation may be dispensed with by the consent of the authority. Once erected, it must be properly maintained, lighted if necessary, and be removed when required. Contravention amounts to an offence.

Section 173: hoardings to be securely erected

A hoarding adjoining a street, must be securely fixed, to the council's satisfaction, otherwise an offence is committed.

Section 174: precautions to be taken by persons executing work in streets

Any person executing work in a street must:

- erect such barriers and traffic signs to prevent danger to traffic, regulate and warn traffic, and remove them when no longer necessary.
- light and guard the works in the hours of darkness.
- when the work so requires, shall cause any building adjoining the street to be shored up, or otherwise protected.

Failure to do so amounts to an offence. Any person removing any such warning sign, barriers etc or extinguishing a light, is also guilty of an offence.

Section 175: liability of servants of highway authorities or of persons responsible for maintenance of highway

If a servant of a highway authority or district council or a person who is himself responsible for the maintenance of a highway, **causes** any object or heap of material to be put on to a highway, so as to become a danger to traffic, without taking all reasonable precautions, he is guilty of an offence.
(Note: this is a statutory duty, which could lay an *individual* open to civil action for breach of statutory duty or negligence.)

Restrictions on construction of bridges or buildings or placing of rails, beams etc over highways

Section 176: restriction of construction of bridges over highways

No bridge may be built across a highway without a licence from the highway authority.

Section 177: restriction on buildings over highways

No building may be constructed over a highway maintainable at public expense, unless it is in the exercise of statutory powers and a licence has been obtained from the highway authority.

Section 178: restriction on placing rails etc over highways

No overhead beam, rail, pipe, cable, wire or similar, shall be placed over, along or across a highway, without the consent of the highway authority. Contravention amounts to an offence.

Cellars. Construction under streets or carriageways

Section 179: cellars

Consent must be obtained from the appropriate authority, before constructing a vault, arch or cellar under a Greater London street or under a carriageway outside Greater London.

Section 180: openings into cellars etc under streets

Consent must be obtained before making an opening in the footway of a street, as an entrance to a cellar or vault. Such consent may be given with conditions attached, as to the manner of construction of the door or covering.

Section 181: breaking open highways

Anyone who without lawful authority or excuse places apparatus, e.g. pipes, cables etc. in or under a highway, or breaks open a highway in order to place or repair such an apparatus, is guilty of an offence. A licence may be granted by the highway authority for the purposes of such a work.

Part X Highways Act 1980 Ss.186–202

New streets

Every county council, London borough council and the Common Council of the City of London **may** make byelaws concerning **new streets**. The Secretary of State may order such byelaws to be made.

Any byelaws made must regulate:

- the level and construction of new streets in the authority's area
- the provision of sewerage of such streets.

Byelaws made may also require a person constructing a new street to provide separate sewers for foul water and surface water drainage respectively. They may also provide for:

- the filing of notices and the deposit of plans
- the inspection of work, the testing of sewers and the taking of samples of the materials to be used in the execution of the works.

Finally, any byelaws made under this section expire 10 years from the date on which it was made (subject to extension by the Secretary of State): S.186.

Thus, a builder who is developing land or building houses which abut onto what is to become a street (even if he himself does not make up the street) must comply with any 'new street' byelaws in existence.

What is a 'new street' is a question of fact in each case. Indeed the street may be an old highway, such as a country lane or path. It may also only be intended for private use.
(Note: the expression is new *street* not new highway.)

It is probable that a 'street', for the purposes of the new street byelaws, is what most people would call a road (*see* adoption of streets under private streets on p. 330). Thus, if a builder constructs new buildings on each, or even one side, of an existing highway, formerly only a lane, then it would come under the byelaws and the builder must then comply with them or face criminal penalties.

It should be noted that because of the problems associated with applying new street byelaws, especially when their requirements are more onerous than is absolutely necessary for the benefit of the community, then under S.190, the councils may, relax the requirements of a byelaw or even dispense with compliance in particular cases, with the consent of the Secretary of State.

Plans

Plans of proposed work must be deposited with the appropriate council, which must:

- pass them unless they are defective or would contravene a byelaw in which case they must,
- reject the plans: S.191.

By S.192 where plans have been deposited and been rejected or passed but the work has not been started within 3 years from the date of deposit, then the council may by notice declare that the deposit of the plans is to be of no effect.

Main thoroughfares: S.193

If a new street appears to be a main thoroughfare, a main approach or a means of communication between such places, then the council may require that the new street be of a particular width. If it must be more than 20 feet wider than is normal then the council will pay compensation for any loss or injury sustained as a result. Any extra expense over and above normal expenditure caused as a result of this section must be defrayed by the council.

Enforcement

Removal or alteration of street not in conformity with byelaws: S.197

Where work has been executed which is subject to but has contravened the new street byelaws then the council may serve a notice:

- requiring the removal of the work or

the carrying out of such work as necessary to comply with the byelaws. If the work is not carried out then the council may do it and remove the offending work and recover their expenses from the person responsible.

It should be noted that a council may **not serve a notice after twelve months** have expired after the completion of the works. However, this does not affect the right of the council or the Attorney-General to apply for an injunction for the removal or alteration of the work before or after the twelve month period unless the council had passed the plans and the work was carried out in accordance therewith. If such is the case the council would then have to pay compensation.

Fines

The byelaws may impose fines for breach. If there has been a breach of a condition attached to the passing of plans under S.193 then a fine may be imposed for such breach: S.198.

Infringement of conditions against owner of land: S.199

Conditions attached to the passing of plans may be enforced against the owner of the land to which the conditions relate. 'Owner' for the purpose of this section is the owner of a fee simple (in possession or in reversion) or a lease of more than 8 years left to run.

In some areas, new street regulations are contained in local Acts of Parliament. In such cases certain parts of the Highways Act apply to such local Acts.

Part XI Highways Act 1980: Ss.203–237

Private streets

The Act defines a street as any 'highway, road, lane, footpath, square, court, alley or passage' whether a thoroughfare or not and which may be a part of a street.

A private street is not maintainable at public expense, but it may become so if the relevant statutory requirements are complied with.

Generally, no-one can be forced to maintain such streets. However, the frontagers (the people abutting onto the private street) may be forced by the highway authority to carry out emergency repairs, say for example, to a hole in the road. If they refuse to do the repairs, the authority may execute the works and recover the costs from them.

Adoption procedures

No-one unless they are very wealthy, really wishes to maintain a private street for their own convenience, especially as they cannot be forced to do so. Builders developing a housing estate will, of course, be in this category. Neither they nor the prospective purchasers would wish to pay for road maintenance. Adoption by the highway authority is therefore necessary and it can be achieved in two main ways. (Note: the general outline for adoption is on p. 310).

1. The Private Street Works Code: Ss.204–218. This is concerned with **existing** private streets, which are not made up to the satisfaction of the highway authority. The authority may therefore pass a resolution to that effect and make up the street, bearing the whole of the cost itself or sharing the cost with the frontagers. The work required may cover total making up or it may merely be some aspect, e.g. lighting or sewerage.

Notice of the job specification and estimated cost and apportionment of costs between frontagers must be displayed in a local newspaper or in the relevant street for certain specified periods. A copy of the notice must also be served on those frontagers who are to share the costs. Copies of all the documents must be available for inspection at the highway authority's offices (district & county).

The affected frontagers may object against the charge. The local authority must then take the matter for a decision before the magistrates.

Once the work is finished, a final apportionment is made of the costs and notice is served on the frontagers who may appeal. They may be allowed to pay in instalments. If they fail to pay, the costs may be recovered as a civil debt in the magistrates' court (*see* p. 37). They can also recover the money in the county court or High Court.

Alternatively the authority may charge the premises with a **local land charge** (*see* p. 161). This gives the authority the powers of a mortgagee and the property could be sold by them to cover their costs.

Once the work has been completed, the street may then be adopted for maintenance at public expense under S.228. The frontagers may object to this and if the objections are in the majority, the street may remain a private street, now made up, but not maintainable at public expense, and not maintainable by the frontagers, except for emergency repairs.

2. Advance Payments Code: S.204, Ss.219–225. This is more familiar to builders who are developing a new estate with new roads and who **at the outset** intend that the roads should be maintainable at public expense.

Within six weeks of the builder's plans having received building regulation approval, the authority gives the builder 6 weeks' notice of the required sum needed by the authority to make up the road. This must either be paid to the authority or security must be given for it.

No such deposit need be paid if the builder builds the road at his own expense or if the new buildings are being built abutting onto an existing publicly maintained highway.

After the work is completed, the sum is adjusted and more money may be required or some may be repaid. Failure to pay is punishable by a fine.

If the builder has merely secured the payment of the sums (and not passed on the making up costs as an element of the sale price), the new houseowner must pay the proportionate sum required. Even if only one houseowner has paid the sum, provided at least half the street/road is built up, then the frontagers may call on the council to require the making up of the road under the Private Street Works Code and then adopt it as maintainable at public expense under S.228 (*see* p. 330).

CHAPTER 10

Employment law

The contract of employment

Like all other areas of contract law, the basic principles apply. Thus, without the essential elements of a contract, the contract would be void and there would be no binding rights and duties. In addition to the rules of common law, there are a wide ranging number of Acts of Parliament which govern different aspects of employment.

For many of these statutory rights, and indeed, for much of the common law, it is important that the contract of employment between the employer and the employee is one of **service** and not **for services**, as **only** employees have protection under these Acts (*see* pp. 246–7). It must be remembered that whatever the parties call the relationship existing between them, in a dispute, all aspects must be examined to discover its true nature.

Form of contract

Like most contracts, the contract may be in any form. Thus, it may be verbal, in writing, or implied from the parties behaviour, or by reference to trade union agreements or practice within a trade or to employer's working rules or a combination of any form. Terms may also be implied by the common law or by statute.

For many people, the contract will be verbal. For example, if a person goes to an interview for a job, he may be offered the job at the interview. If he accepts, the contract will be verbal. If he accepts by letter, it is a combination of a written and an oral agreement. If he was offered the job by letter, which he accepts by letter, then it will be in writing. He may be given a formal contract to sign and this is usually desirable where there are unusual terms. If he is not supplied with all the terms in a written contract, then the employer must supply written particulars of the terms of employment (*see* below).

Employer's duties towards employees

The employer's duties are a combination of both common law and statute. Any unusual duty should be an express term of the contract.

The parties may make such terms as they wish, provided they comply with basic contract rules and statutory restrictions.

He must provide written particulars of the terms of employment

This is a statutory duty under S.1 Employment Protection (Consolidation) Act 1978. Because of the problems associated with verbal contracts which may have been made when the employee was in no fit state to take in the terms of his new employment, the Employment Protection (Consolidation) Act 1978 as amended by the Employment Act 1982 requires employers to provide written particulars of the terms of the employment, or a proper written contract containing the details required under the Act. These particulars must be given to the employee within 13 weeks from commencing the job, provided he works for 16 hours or more per week.

The particulars must give details of the following:

- Names of parties to the contract (N.B. companies, partnerships and sole traders often trade under different names to their true ones).
- Job title.
- Date employment commenced.
- Whether previous employment counts as part of the employees continuous employment.
- Amount of pay or method of calculating this.
- Whether pay is weekly or monthly if applicable.
- Hours of work and conditions relating to them.
- Holiday entitlement.
- Details of sick pay and incapacity for work.
- Details of pension (if any) and whether the employee is contracted in or out of the state pension scheme.
- Length of notice for employees to give and receive on terminating employment.
- If the job is for a fixed period, the date on which it ends.
- Disciplinary and grievance procedures. (There is an ACAS code of practice dealing with disciplinary procedures – Disciplinary Practices and Procedures in Employment. The person to whom the employee should complain about a grievance should be clearly stated (*see* p. 342).

Particulars provided for information only, if given after the job has started, cannot form the contract, and reference, for other purposes, would have to be made to the contractual terms contained in the (possibly verbal) contract made earlier.

But, if the particulars are given *before* the contract was entered into, then they could form part of the contract. Once the particulars have been delivered to the employee, generally neither can then deny that any of the particulars do not form part of the working conditions.

If preferred, the written particulars may refer the employee to an agreement such as a collective agreement, e.g. the Working Rules Agreement in the construction industry, which is issued by the Building and Allied Trades Joint Industrial Council.

Alternatively, the agreement referred to, could be a company master document. Access to copies of such agreements must be freely available.

Changes in the terms of employment

Should any change be made, these must be notified within **one** month. They should then be attached to the original document or written particulars, or reference may be made to an amended document to which access is available. However changes must have been approved by both parties unless the contract contains a clause allowing one party to change terms such as those relating to working conditions.

Breach of this duty

If the employer fails to provide the particulars, the employee may go to an industrial tribunal (*see* p. 353). The tribunal may then decide on any terms of employment which might reasonably have been imposed.

To provide statements of pay

This is a statutory duty under S.8 Employment Protection (Consolidation) Act 1978. Under the Act, every employee is entitled to a proper statement of pay, setting out his gross wages, all the appropriate deductions and net wages.

Anyone not receiving such a statement can apply to an industrial tribunal. The tribunal can then declare the employee's rights. It cannot order the employer to repay money which was underpaid. Action would have to be taken in the county court or Queens Bench Division. But, if the deductions were not mentioned at all, the tribunal can award compensation for the 13 weeks prior to application.

To make guarantee payments

This is a statutory duty under Ss.12–13 Employment Act 1980 and Schedules 2,3 of Employment Act 1982. If the employer has no work for the employee, then the employee is entitled to a guarantee payment, unless, the lack of work is due to an industrial dispute involving another employee or another employer, or if he refuses an alternative reasonable offer of work. This provides protection for those laid off without pay. There is a maximum of five days payment during each quarter (i.e. a maximum of 20 days per annum, with a maximum wage of £10.50 per day in 1985).

If the contract states that he will be paid for workless days in any case, then any money paid, discharges the employer's duty to make guarantee payments.

In many cases, if employees are paid weekly or monthly, then the employer has **no right** in law to lay off staff without pay, unless this is **expressly** incorporated into the contract of employment, or if the employee agrees to be laid off.

Failure to pay any of the guarantee payments, gives the employee the right to complain within three months to an industrial tribunal.

Should there be a **collective agreement** which deals with guarantee payments, then the particular body responsible for the agreement can apply for an exemption order from the Secretary of State for Employment, if such payments would be inappropriate in the circumstances. In the building industry, the Guarantee Payments (Exemption) No 20 Order, S.I 1980/1715 excludes from S.12 all employees who work under the Working Rule Agreement of the Builders & Allied Trades Joint Industrial Council.

Duty to provide work at common law

There is no definite duty to provide work for the employees, unless by failing to do so, it would lead to loss of earnings. Also, it might indicate that the employer is trying to avoid the contract and thus there should be some remedy for the employee, e.g. for breach of contract.

Duty to pay workers at common law

If the employee does any work, then he must be paid. Details of the *method* of calculation should be inserted in the written particulars. If there is no **express** agreement as to the amount, then reference may be made to a collective agreement or as may be fixed by one of the wages councils. There are no wages councils for the construction industry.

There is no duty imposed to provide references for an employee

If he does provide them however, he should make sure that they are true as he may face a court action in tort for deceit or perhaps in negligence for a negligent misstatement by a prospective employer of his former employee or a libel action if the references are defamatory.

Duty to see that the employee is safe at work under common law and statute

This duty has a number of different bases. First, at common law in tort, an employer owes a personal duty of care to his employees to provide safe plant and equipment, a safe place of work, a safe system of work and competent staff. This duty pre-dated *Donoghue* v. *Stevenson* 1932, but is really the same as the duty of care in the tort of negligence.

Secondly, it could be a breach of contract, if he failed to provide the above.

Thirdly, under the Employers' Liability (Defective Equipment) Act 1969, an employer is strictly liable to employees who are injured in the course of their employment, by equipment provided by the employer, providing that the fault in the equipment is that of a third party such as the manufacturer. No fault has to be proved on the part of the employer in such cases. But, if the equipment was unsafe because of poor maintenance, then the employer will have to be sued under the first head above, and fault would have to be proved.

Fourthly, an employer is vicariously liable for torts committed by his employees in the course of their employment, and this would cover acts which cause harm to fellow employees.

Fifthly, the Health & Safety at Work etc Act 1974, encompasses a number of different Acts which cover the employee's safety and health whilst at work. Regulations such as the Construction Regulations, are now under the ambit of this Act (*see* Ch. 11).

Duty to pay statutory sick pay – statute

Under the Social Security & Housing Benefits Act 1982, it is the duty of the employer to pay statutory sick pay to an employee for the first 8 weeks of incapacity to work, caused by sickness or injury. It is an offence to avoid paying it.

In many jobs, the employer pays a greater amount in sick pay than the statutory minimum. But, he is entitled to claim back the statutory sick pay element from the Department of Health and Social Security, by deducting it from the national insurance contributions, which the employer must deduct from the employee's wages on behalf of the DHSS.

Sex and race discrimination

Under the Race Relations Act 1976 and Sex Discrimination Act 1975, it is prohibited to discriminate against persons on racial or sexual grounds, or because of their marital status.

Discrimination can take various forms, e.g. restricting recruitment, giving less favourable conditions of employment, or dismissal.

Complaints about racial discrimination may be made to an industrial tribunal within three months of the alleged discriminatory act, where up to £8,000 (in 1985) can be awarded for loss, (including injury to feelings).

The Commission for Racial Equality can investigate allegations of discrimination in companies and serve non-discrimination notices, which can be backed by a county court injunction.

Complaints about sex discrimination or discrimination against married people, may be made to industrial tribunals, where compensation may be awarded as above.

The Equal Opportunities Commission can investigate allegations of sex discrimination and serve non-discrimination notices.

Duty of the employee

Duty of good faith towards employer – implied by common law

This is an all embracing duty and covers such matters as being honest, not accepting bribes or secret profits, not competing with the employer for business or soliciting the employer's clients, nor divulging confidential information learned during his employment and disclosing information which could affect his ability to do his job, such as a bad heart.

In some cases, certain aspects of this general duty will be specifically expressed in the contract. For example, it is very common to include in contracts, a term restricting the employee from working within a certain distance of the employer, on leaving that employment. Such terms must not be so restrictive as to prevent the employee from working at all and they can be reviewed by the courts if necessary (*see* p. 104).

Obedience – implied by common law

The employer can expect that his employees should obey all reasonable instructions. What is reasonable will depend on the circumstances and it is unlikely that the isolated refusal would be grounds for lawful dismissal. But of course, the degree of refusal is important. The use of obscene language when refusing to do the work (or at any time) could constitute grounds for dismissal.

Often, refusal to do work, stems from lack of clarity in explaining the scope of the job in the first place. Only the title of the job is necessarily included in the written particulars. Perhaps, a job description would be more useful. Trade unions, of course, often intervene in demarcation disputes, and this, sometimes in the end, leads to clarification of working conditions.

Duty to exercise skill and care and be generally competent for the job – implied by the common law

Obviously, the employee should be able to perform his job properly in accordance with the qualifications he holds, and his experience doing the job. The degree of competence will depend on what type of job he holds and there is a certain responsibility on the part of the employer to check that the employee is up to the job and that his qualifications are genuine. If they were not genuine or if he did not have the experience he professed to have, then this would undoubtedly be grounds for dismissing him. Where an employee has an easily testable skill, such as being able to do calculations or lay bricks, then it is wise to check this before offering him the job. If the skill is not easily testable, then probably a probationary period is a good idea. In either case, the hazards of sacking someone are lessened in such circumstances.

What is far more difficult, is to dismiss someone who becomes incompetent at a later date, i.e. he was competent to start with, but has grown lazy or careless.

Rights of the employee

Right to pay while suspended on medical grounds – statute

Under Ss.19, 20 Employment Protection (Consolidation) Act 1978 (as amended by Schedule 2 Employment Act 1982), an employee is entitled to be paid for up to 26 weeks if he has been suspended on medical grounds under any statutory requirement or under recommended codes of practice issued by the Health and Safety Commission.

At present, such a suspension will have been for a good reason, to protect the health of the worker in relation to specific regulations concerning dangerous chemicals, radioactive substances or lead.

He is only entitled if he is still able to do the work and is not physically or mentally ill. He will lose this right if he refuses a reasonable offer of alternative work.

Right not to have action taken against him for trade union activity or membership

Under Ss.23(1),(2),(6) Employment Protection (Consolidation) Act 1978 (amended by S.15 Employment Act 1980 and S.10 Employment Act 1982), an employee may not be prevented from or penalized for becoming a trade unionist or taking part in trade union activities, **nor** may he be forced to become a trade unionist or a member of a particular union or category of trade union.

If a closed shop exists, an employee can not be forced to belong to a trade union. Should pressure be brought on him, which led to his dismissal because he did not want to join the union, then this would amount to a case of **unfair dismissal** under S.58(3A) or S.58(3C) of the 1978 Act (*see* p. 350). Nor can he be forced to make a payment e.g. to charity, instead of joining the union.

Examples of penalties against an employee could be blocking his promotion, pay rise, or bonus.

Should there be an agreement whereby the employees **must** belong to a trade union, then their rights are reduced to cover union activities only.

If there is a **closed shop agreement** whereby the employees must belong to a **particular** trade union as for example, in the newspaper industry, then the employee has no rights to prevent action being taken against him to compel him to join one. This is so **unless** he had not been a member before the agreement took effect and he has not joined since the agreement. Where the agreement took effect after 15 August 1980, the closed shop must have been approved by at least 80 per cent of employees entitled to vote by secret ballot, and if it was so agreed, the employee must never have joined since the agreement was so approved.

The following would also be unfairly dismissed despite closed shop agreements: employees who genuinely object on grounds of conscience or personal conviction to being a trade union member; employees who are unreasonably excluded or expelled from trade unions and who have complained under S.4 EA 1982; or employees who are subject to written codes of conduct and who have refused to join a trade union or have been expelled from one for failing to strike or take part in industrial action, which action *would* be contrary to that code of conduct.

If the action taken was dismissal, then this would be unfair and he can take remedial action (*see* p. 351).

The Department of Employment has issued a Code of Practice on Closed Shop Agreements and Arrangements.
(Note: in certain exceptional circumstances, trade union membership can be banned by government action, usually for security reasons.)

Right to have time off work: S.27 Employment Protection (Consolidation) Act 1978

For trade union officials

Employees who are trade union **officials** are entitled to **paid** time off work in order to carry out their union duties concerned with industrial relations between the employer, associated employers and their employees. Also, time off is given for them to undergo industrial relations training. Such matters are dealt with by an ACAS code of practice, Code 3 Time off for Trade Union Activities.

For trade union members: S.28 Employment Protection (Consolidation) Act 1978

This differs slightly to the above. Here, a member of an **independent** trade union is entitled to time off in order to take part in his own trade union activities or to activities where he is acting as the union's representative. Such activities do **not** cover industrial action. He is not entitled to, (although he may receive) any remuneration. The union must be one recognised by the employers.

Safety representatives: Health and Safety at Work etc Act 1974

Under the Safety Representatives and Safety Committee Regulations 1977, safety representatives properly appointed, are entitled to **paid** time off work for such duties.

Right to have time off to perform public duties

Under section 29 Employment Protection (Consolidation) Act 1978 certain employees are entitled to time off work to perform certain public duties, e.g. justices of the peace, local councillors, members of tribunals, members of a health authority, members of a governing body of an educational institution or a water authority. They are not necessarily entitled to payment unless their contracts of employment specifically provide for this. Of course, in some cases such as justices of the peace, expenses may be claimed.

Under the Juries Act 1974, anyone employed or otherwise is under a **duty** to attend court for jury service and expenses will be paid.

Right to have 'equal pay' – Equal Pay Act 1970

Men and women in full or part-time employment have the right to be treated on equal terms as far as their pay and conditions of work are concerned. They must either be in work which is of a similar nature, or if the business they work for operates a job evaluation scheme, they must have jobs with a similar grade.

Termination of contracts of employment – common law

Contracts of employment may be terminated in the same way as other contracts (*see* p. 112). However, there is now a great deal of statutory law which gives the employee protection against summary dismissal without good reason or dismissal without the correct period of notice. Such statutory law is in addition to the usual common law remedies for breach of contract. This is still important, however, as statutory protection depends on the employee having worked for the employer for a particular length of time.

Methods of termination

Performance

Where the contract was for a particular task, the contract will end automatically on its completion.

Effluxion of time

If a contract is made for a fixed term then this ends automatically on the due date, without either party having to give notice.

Frustration

Its application in employment law has been shown in cases involving the death of an employee, an employee's serious illness, or injury or conscription. The frustrating event or circumstances must be outside the employee's control and thus imprisonment due to the employee's conviction after a trial is not a frustrating event (but would be grounds for the employer to repudiate the contract and dismiss the employee for misconduct). (*See* p. 342).

Agreement

As in all contracts, the parties may agree to end the contract either by virtue of a contractual term or by agreement at a later stage (*see* p. 116). If consideration is paid by the employer for the employee's agreement to terminate, it is colloquially known as a 'golden handshake'.

Death of an employer (as a sole trader)

This will again terminate the employment unless there is a transfer of the business as a going concern (*see* below).

Liquidation of a registered company

This automatically ends the contract if the liquidation is as a result of a compulsory winding-up order.

If on the other hand the company is being wound up voluntarily, this does not necessarily terminate the contract unless the company is insolvent. Under the Transfer of Undertakings (Protection of Employment) Regulations 1981, SI No 1794 contracts of employment will **not** be terminated if the employees have been transferred from one company to another as a result of the transfer of the business as a going concern, even if the original company has been dissolved. The employee's rights are thus, protected and preserved and the length of his employment will date back to the beginning of the original contract.

If the employee is dismissed by reason only of such a transfer, he will be regarded as having been unfairly dismissed (*see* p. 348). However, if there was an **economic, technical or organizational** reason' for a change in the workforce affecting the employee, then he may be fairly dismissed. It is up to the employer to prove that he acted reasonably in dismissing the employee: Reg. 8.

Dissolution of partnership

The rules above will more or less apply to an employee of a partnership. If the partnership ceases trading through insolvency, the employment will cease. If there is a transfer of business as a going concern, the regulations above will apply.

Bankruptcy of a sole trader

This will usually terminate the employee's contract, unless the trustee in bankruptcy or receiver obtains permission to continue the business (*see* p. 212).

Breach of contract

Only a serious breach will allow a party to repudiate the contract. However, if the wronged party affirms the contract, then after the elapse of a reasonable time, he will be unable to rely on the breach as a ground for terminating the contract.

Dismissal

Some contracts end by operation of law, e.g. on the liquidation of a registered company (*see* above). The rest will be summary dismissals, i.e. dismissal without notice or dismissals with notice.

Summary dismissal

The contract itself may contain terms giving either party the right to terminate without the giving of notice.

Furthermore, the law recognizes that there will be certain situations which allow the parties to terminate where there has been either a serious breach of contract or where a party has committed some act which amounts to repudiation of the contract. In both cases no notice need be given but, of course, the employer should be able to justify the dismissal, otherwise he may be sued for wrongful dismissal at common law or an action may be brought for unfair dismissal in an industrial tribunal. The employee could be sued for breach of contract.

Thus, the reasons for such a dismissal must be of a very serious nature. Most of the existing cases have concerned behaviour such as gross misconduct, serious dishonesty, immorality during working hours, serious disobedience, assault on the employer, competing for business with the employer and disclosing trade secrets.

Of course, the employer may be guilty of some serious breach or repudiating action and the employee may then regard the contract as terminated. This may amount to constructive dismissal, i.e. by virtue of the employer's behaviour, the employee regards himself as dismissed.

The ACAS Code of Practice No 1 (Disciplinary Practice and

Procedures in Employment) sets out guidelines for the proper organization of a disciplinary procedure. It emphasizes that fair discipline means good industrial relations. Workers are entitled to know what standards of conduct are expected of them and the management, whose prime responsibility it is to maintain discipline, must operate within their system and operate fairly otherwise they may face an unfair dismissal claim in an industrial tribunal.

The disciplinary machinery should be explained to employees in writing. It should set out the people who have power to discipline (and to dismiss).

An employee should be informed of the types of breaches of contract which would be grounds for summary dismissal.

Opportunities of answering complaints should be afforded to the employee and information of the complaint should be given. Unless there is a case of gross misconduct, no-one should be summarily dismissed for a first 'offence'. An appeal procedure should be operated.

The code suggests that normally a formal **oral** warning should be given first concerning the matter of complaint, unless the matter is very serious in which case a **written** warning may be given. If the worker fails to mend his ways, a **final** written warning should be given, informing him that dismissal or suspension or other penalty will be imposed. Only after ignoring the final warning should the employee be dismissed.

It should be noted that if the worker commits a crime outside his employment, this should not be a reason for his automatic dismissal. His whole position should be looked at to see whether he is now unsuitable for the job.

Records of the warning system should be kept (including, perhaps, written evidence of the oral warning), to provide the employer with a possible defence to a claim for unfair dismissal.

Dismissal with notice

Most cases, however, are concerned with the employee being given notice of his dismissal. Nevertheless, employees should comply with their contract and give the correct length of notice before leaving. If there is no such clause, they should give such notice as would be implied at common law.

It is unlikely that they would be sued for breach of contract if they gave too short a period of notice, unless their presence is vital to the employer. Whether the employee is dismissed by notice, without notice or as a result of the expiry of his fixed term contract, he is entitled to request a written statement giving the reasons for his dismissal. S.53 Employment Protection (Consolidation) Act 1978.

Fixed term contracts.   As these are usually intended to end on a particular date, no notice is required to end the contract.

344

But, the contract may contain a clause allowing termination **before the contract date** by a period of notice. If there is no such clause, then there is no such right.

Contracts for indefinite periods.

1. *At common law – implied terms of notice.* If the employee is working less than 16 hours a week, he is not entitled to the statutory protection in (2) and (3) below and must rely on his rights at common law.

Thus, if no period of notice is expressed in the contract, be it written or oral, then 'reasonable notice' must be given by either party. What is reasonable depends on the circumstances such as previous cases, the facts involved and even trade custom. The greater the responsibility the employee has, the longer the period of notice. Similarly, the length of service will usually result in an expectation of longer periods of notice. Also, the calculation of pay period may influence the period of notice.

If a period of notice is specified, whether in writing or not, then that will be the length required (and it may be less than the statutory minimum in 3.).

2. *Express terms of notice required by statute: S.1 Employment Protection (Consolidation) Act 1978.* Provided the employee works for 16 hours or more a week, then he is covered by the provisions of the Act requiring written particulars of the employment to be given to the employee. One such particular is concerned with the length of notice required (*see* p. 333).

3. *Statutory minimum lengths of notice under S.49 EP(C)A 1978.* Provided the employee has worked for **one** month and works for more than 16 hours a week, he is entitled to the following minimum periods of notice (in practice, he may get more under his contract).

Length of employment	Length of notice
4 weeks – 2 years	1 week
2 years – 12 years	1 week × years of employment
12 years +	Not less than 12 weeks

Redundancy

The law is found principally in the Employment Protection (Consolidation) Act 1978.

An employee may be paid a redundancy payment if:

- his employer dismisses him by reason of redundancy **or**
- his employer lays him off or keeps the employee on short time in such a manner as is specified by the Act: S.81.

By S.81(2) an employee is dismissed by reason of redundancy:

- if the employer has stopped or intends to stop carrying on the business for the purposes of which the employee was employed, e.g. where a business is wound up.

- If the employer has stopped or intends to stop carrying on business in the place where the employee was employed.
- If the business no longer requires work of a particular kind which the employee was doing or such work would be stopping or diminishing, e.g. where mechanisation eliminates the need for manual labour such as riveting in the car industry.

Dismissal

For the purposes of S.81, an employee is treated as having been dismissed if:

- his contract is terminated by the employer, with or without notice, *or*
- his fixed term contract has expired without being renewed under that contract, *or*
- he terminates the contract with or without notice in circumstances such that he is entitled to terminate it without notice by reason of the employer's conduct (constructive dismissal *see* p. 349): S.83.

Where there has been no actual dismissal under S.83

The above section applies if the employee has actually been dismissed (summarily or with notice). Often, however, an employee may be made redundant by force of circumstances and not by dismissal.

Thus by S.93, if an employee has his employment terminated by reason of:

- any act on the part of an employer (e.g. a 'moonlight flit'), *or*
- any event affecting an employer, e.g. death or frustration of contract, then such acts or events are treated as if the employee has been made redundant, provided such matters would not otherwise have terminated the contract. Thus, if an employer goes bankrupt or the company is compulsorily wound up, which is treated as the fault of the employer, then S.93 does not apply (S.81 may however).

Consultation

Before contemplating redundancy an employer should consult with the relevant unions to determine who should be selected for redundancy and for what reason the redundancies are required. Also, the Secretary of State for Employment should be notified in certain circumstances.

Time limits for redundancy payments

Within six months of the relevant date, the employee must have:

- claimed a redundancy payment by written notice to his employer;
- referred a question to the industrial tribunal concerning his right to

346

- a payment or amount of payment;
- presented a claim for unfair dismissal to an industrial tribunal; *or*
- agreed or accepted a payment.

The tribunal may, in certain circumstances, allow an additional 6 month period in which to claim, if there are good reasons why the employee failed to take such action. The relevant date is the date notice expires, expiration of the fixed term contract or when termination actually takes effect.

Qualifications for redundancy payments

Compensation for redundancy will only be paid to employees who have been *continuously employed for at least two years* and who are *over 18*. It will not be paid to employees over the normal retirement age. They must have been dismissed by reason of redundancy and voluntary redundancies will count for payment. But, if the employees resign because of the threat of redundancies, then they have *not* been dismissed and will not get compensation.

An employee may be offered alternative employment by the employer. This must be 'suitable', i.e. comparable with the job he already held. If he unreasonably refuses the offer then he will probably lose his entitlement to a redundancy payment because he will not have been dismissed by reason of redundancy. However, there is a statutory trial period under which the employee can decide whether he would like the new job or not. Provided he terminates his job reasonably within that period, then he will still be entitled to a redundancy payment.

Compensation for redundancy

A worker must have worked for the employer for at least 2 years prior to redundancy. Pay is calculated by reference to the number of complete years of employment with the same employer (sometimes previous employment counts) up to a maximum of 20 multiplied by a weeks basic pay. The years worked before 18 do not count (*see* Fig. 10.1).

Lay-off and short-time: Ss.87–89 EP(C)A 1978

It should be noted that this is not concerned with the right to guarantee payments (*see* p. 334).

If an employee

- has been laid off or kept on short-time for four consecutive weeks or more or for six weeks during a period of 13 weeks (three of which were consecutive), *and*
- has within four weeks following such a period of lay-off or short-

Age	Compensation
18–21	1/2 weeks pay for each year in band
22–40	1 weeks pay for each year in band
41–64	1½ weeks pay for each year in band.

Example
Thus, a 36-year-old person who has worked for the same employer since he left school at 16 will get:

For the years   16–18 - nothing
                       18–21 - 3 × ½ a weeks pay
                       21–36 - 15 × a weeks pay.

(A week's pay is calculated by reference to the salary paid when made redundant and does not include overtime or other extra payments, up to a statutory maximum.)

Fig. 10.1   Calculation of redundancy payment

time served a notice of intention to claim a redundancy payment on his employer, *and*

- has terminated his contract by giving the contractual length of notice within a specified period,

then he may claim a redundancy payment.

The employer may respond by actually dismissing the employee (who is then effectively dismissed by reasons of redundancy anyway) or by serving a counter notice giving details of work coming up, in which case a claim for a redundancy payment under these sections may be defeated. (If that is the case, however, he may be able to claim a guarantee payment).

The redundancy fund

Compensation should be paid by the employer directly. However, he is entitled to claim back 35 per cent from the redundancy fund which is funded by contributions from all employers' national insurance contributions.

Should the employer not pay for some reason, the employee can make a claim to an industrial tribunal within 6 months of ending that employment (*see* p. 353).

If the employer cannot pay because of insolvency, the Department of Employment will pay the total amount from the redundancy fund.

Remedies for dismissal of employee without good reason or insufficient notice

At common law – wrongful dismissal

As employment is a branch of contract law, the employee is always entitled to sue his employer (and vice versa) for breach of contract, if the other has breached his duties in any way.

If the breach is to dismiss the employee without good reason, or by giving too short a period of notice, the common law has developed a breach of contract action called **wrongful dismissal**.

Like all contractual breaches, the main remedy is for damages. It should be remembered that contractual damages are governed by the Rule in *Hadley* v. *Baxendale* (*see* p. 120). Thus, damages awarded will not exceed the amount the employee should have been paid had he been given a proper period of notice before his dismissal. Also, because of the personal nature of the contract, no court will grant a decree of specific performance, as this would force the parties to enter into an employment situation again (cf. reinstatement and reengagement below).

Despite the introduction of proceedings for unfair dismissal, wrongful dismissal is still important for those who have not the requisite length of service and for those who wish to sue for sums higher than permitted under legislation.

By statute – unfair dismissal

The law relating to unfair dismissal is found primarily under the EP(C)A 1978 as amended by the Employment Acts 1980 and 1982 (EAs).

An employee who is dismissed with notice or without, may take his employer to an industrial tribunal in a claim for **unfair dismissal** on various grounds.

The claim must be made within three months of the date of termination of the contract.

Exceptions

By S.54 EP(C)A 1978 every employee has the right not to be unfairly dismissed **except** in the following situations:

1. where the employee has not been in continuous employment for at least **one** year: S.64.
2. where the employer is a small company with less than 20 employees, the relevant period of employment is *two* years.
3. where the 'employee' has got a contract for services, i.e. he is **not** an employee: S.55 (*see* p. 246).
4. if the employee has reached the normal retiring age for that job or if not, 60 in the case of women and 65 in the case of men: S64(1).
5. if there is a procedure agreed between the employer and trade union which deals with dismissals. However, such an agreement must be 'designated' by the Secretary of State for Employment: S.65.

6. where the employee normally works outside Great Britain: S.141(2)b.
7. where the employee has a fixed term contract of more than one year and the dismissal merely consists of the expiry of the contract without it being renewed *and* the employee has agreed *in writing* not to pursue a claim for unfair dismissal. (Thus contracts for fixed terms ought to be carefully checked before signing, otherwise the remedies for unfair dismissal will be lost, even if all that has happened is that the normal contractual date has been reached): S.142(1).
(Note: This is the only type of contract in which an employer can exclude his liability for unfair dismissal.)
8. where employees are share fishermen, registered dock workers, policemen but not Crown employees unless in the services: S.144(2).
9. if the contract is illegal either at its inception or in its performance (rule of common law), e.g. in *Tomlinson* v. *Dick Evans U Drive Ltd* 1978 an employee was paid without deduction of tax. The employer and employee had deliberately defrauded the Inland Revenue. The Employment Appeal Tribunal confirmed the industrial tribunal's decision that the contract was unenforceable and thus no rights accrued and the employee could not complain of unfair dismissal.

There must be a 'dismissal'

The employee must prove that he has been dismissed in fact and in law.

Section 55 EP(C)A 1978 states the three circumstances in which there will be a dismissal.

1. Where the employer terminates the contract with or without notice. Thus, resignations or mutual agreements terminating the contract are **not** dismissals. Invitations to resign, which are often used to 'save face' may amount to a dismissal, if it is implicit that if the employee does not resign then he will be dismissed.
Where the words of dismissal are couched in the vernacular e.g. '---- off' the industrial tribunal will have to determine the true intention of the employer.
2. Expiry of a fixed term contract without it being renewed under the terms of that contract. A fixed term contract may be for a particular period or may, as in some building contracts of employment, be for the duration of a project, provided it has a fixed date of completion. As a result of *Dixon* v. *BBC* 1978, a fixed term contract is still one even if either party can terminate by notice before the due date.
3. Where the employee terminates the contract with or without notice in circumstances such that he is entitled to terminate it without notice by reason of the employer's conduct. This is known as **constructive dismissal** and is concerned with circumstances in which

the employer has behaved in such a way that the employee has decided to resign rather than continue to suffer the employer's behaviour. In *Western Excavating (ECC) Ltd* v. *Sharp* 1978 the Court of Appeal found that deciding whether or not someone has been constructively dismissed, depends on whether the employer has committed a serious breach of contract or not. If he has not then there can be no grounds for the employee repudiating the contract.

What sort of dismissal is fair

It is up to the employer to prove that the dismissal was fair. The following are grounds for dismissal to which the tribunal would agree with the employer, as being capable of being fair: S.57 EP(C)A 1978:

- Redundancy (*see* p. 344).
- Misconduct (*see* p. 342). Potentially fair.
- Incapability to do the work, whether through lack of qualification, experience or physical or mental incapacity (*see* p. 337). Potentially fair.
- If the employment is in contravention of statute law. Potentially fair.
- Any other substantial reason for justifying the dismissal of an employee in his position. Potentially fair.

Having proved that the dismissal was for one of the above reasons, the tribunal then has to decide whether the ground was a **reasonable** one for dismissing the employee in the particular circumstances.

Each case is then judged on its special merits. Whether the ACAS Code of Practice on Disciplinary Practice and Procedures and the Industrial Relations Code of Practice on redundancy has been followed will also be taken into account (*see* pp. 342, 351).

The following are definitely **unfair** grounds for dismissal: S.58(1) EP(C)A 1978 (as amended by EA 1982):

- where the employee was or intended to become a member of an independent trade union, *or*
- has taken or intended to take part in independent trade union activities, *or*
- was not a member of a trade union or a particular union or who had refused to join or remain a member of a union (*see* p. 338).

The legislation thus provides protection for trade union members, activists and those who do not wish to become trade union members.

Closed shop agreements: S.58(3) EP(C)A (as amended by S.7 EA 1980 and S.3 EA 1982)

However, where there is a closed shop agreement, then provided the statutory requirements for such agreements are complied with (*see* p. 339) then the dismissal of someone who refuses to join or remain a member will not be unfair per se.

There are a number of situations in which an employee would be deemed to be unfairly dismissed in relation to closed shop agreements (*see* p. 339).

Strikes or other industrial action: S.62 EP(C)A 1978 (amended by S.9 EA 1982)

If an employee is dismissed during a lockout or whilst on strike, an industrial tribunal shall not consider whether the dismissal was unfair or not **unless**

- One or more fellow employees have *not* been dismissed (implying that the employee had been victimised)
- One or more fellow employees have been offered re-employment and the claimant employee has not. (This is subject to a three-month time limit from the date of dismissal).

This piece of legislation is designed to prevent discrimination in industrial action but no more. The tribunal is not concerned with the reasons or the merits of industrial action.

It should be remembered that whilst there is a right to withdraw one's labour, this immediately makes the employee in breach of contract which is a ground for terminating his contract at common law. No statutory protection is available to such a person unless he has been victimised and the above sections apply.

Sex and race discrimination

(*See* p. 336). Anyone dismissed on grounds of sex or race discrimination is deemed to have been unfairly dismissed (even within the first year of employment).

Redundancy: S.59 EP(C)A 1978

If only a particular employee is made redundant, yet the surrounding circumstances for other employees are the same and they have not been dismissed by reason of redundancy, then if the main or only reason for selecting that worker for redundancy is inadmissible or if he had been selected in a way that was against a customary arrangement or agreed procedure, then the dismissal shall be regarded as unfair.

Employers are under a statutory duty to consult with trade unions and in certain cases to inform the Department of Employment before making people redundant. Also the Industrial Relations Code of Practice, Paras. 44 & 45 gives advice on dealing with redundancy and if this advice is not followed, it may influence a tribunal's decision that the dismissal was unfair.

352

Remedies of industrial tribunals

Re-instatement and re-engagement orders under the Employment Protection (Consolidation) Act Ss.68 & 69

Where the employee has been unfairly dismissed, the tribunal can, if asked, order his re-instatement or re-engagement.

Re-instatement means that on return to work, the employee is treated as if nothing had happened. Thus, he will get his back pay and will lose none of his pension rights. If he would have been upgraded or got better conditions had he still been working there, then these must be awarded to him.

Re-engagement means that the employee returns to work for the employer or his successor in a job similar to that from which he was dismissed.

These orders are discretionary as in many cases, they would be totally inappropriate and in some cases impracticable.

Compensation under Ss.72–76 EP(C)A and Employment Act 1982

There are three types of compensation awards, the basic award, the compensatory award and the special award.

1. The basic award: S.4 EA 1982. The basic award is calculated in much the same way as under awards for redundancy (*see* Fig. 10.1).

The basic award for unfair dismissal under Ss.58 or 59 of the 1978 Act, i.e. dismissal for an inadmissible reason is at least £2,100.

2. Compensatory award. Subject to a maximum of £8,000 (in 1985) a compensatory award is paid such as the tribunal thinks is just and equitable in all the circumstances to compensate for loss directly attributable to the employer's behaviour.

This parallels the rule in *Hadley* v. *Baxendale* in basic contract (*see* p. 120). Thus, compensation may be awarded for such varied losses as loss of pension rights, future loss of earnings, loss of pay in lieu of notice, etc.

3. Special award: Ss.72, 75A EP(C)A 1978 and S.5 EA 1982. Those employees who have been unfairly dismissed because of their trade union membership, or activities, refusal to join a union or unfair selection for redundancy can ask for an additional **special award** provided they had asked for re-instatement or re-engagement.

If no such order to reinstate or re-engage is made by the tribunal then the employee receives 104 weeks pay or £10,500 whichever is the highest amount subject to a limit of £21,000.

If an order for reinstatement **was** made by the tribunal but the employer failed to comply then the award will be 156 weeks pay or £15,000, whichever is the highest amount.

Industrial tribunals

Origins

These were originally set up by the Industrial Training Act 1964. They are independent bodies which make decisions on questions or claims concerning aspects of employment under a number of Acts.

Relevant Acts

The most important relevant Acts are: Industrial Training Act 1982; Employment Act 1982; Employment Act 1980; Employment Protection (Consolidation) Act 1978; Race Relations Act 1976; Employment Protection Act 1975; Sex Discrimination Act 1975; Health & Safety at Work etc Act 1974; Equal Pay Act 1970.

Application

Forms of application (IT1) are obtained from the tribunal offices which are found in most big towns or from the Department of Employment. On completion, the form must be sent to the Central Office of the Industrial Tribunals in London or to a regional office. The address of the Central Office of Industrial Tribunals (England & Wales) is 93 Ebury Bridge Road, London, SW1 8RB.

The application is scrutinized to see whether it asks for relief which the tribunals are capable of giving under the relevant Acts. On registration of the application, a hearing at a local tribunal is arranged. Copies of the claim are sent to the respondent who is asked to file an answer and a defence, if any.

Conciliation

In some cases, copies of all relevant documents are sent to a **conciliation officer** from ACAS i.e. the Advisory, Conciliation & Arbitration Service, whose head office is at 11–12 St. James' Square, London, SW17 4LA. The officer attempts to come to some agreement between the parties before the hearing. This is designed to save time and money and a more harmonious relationship, especially if reinstatement to the job itself is sought. It is interesting to note that because of conciliation, approximately 50 per cent of all cases never actually reach a hearing by the industrial tribunal.

Composition of tribunals

As the word tribunal indicates, each tribunal consists of three people, the chairman who is a lawyer and the other two lay members who are chosen from employer's and employee's associations. All have relevant experience but the lay members are not intended to represent a particular point of view.

Preliminary hearing

In order to reduce costs, a preliminary hearing is often held in which the case is scrutinized to see whether the applicant has a good case to go before the tribunal.

The hearing

They are less formal than court hearings and legal representation is not necessary. (It may be advisable however.) Most trade unions have officers who will present a member's case for him. The applicant must provide sufficient evidence to support his allegations. Witnesses can be compelled to attend and the production of documents can be ordered. In such cases, this is best ordered at the preliminary hearing (if any). Otherwise, an adjournment may be required.

Despite the informality of the proceedings, evidence of a cogent nature must be presented, i.e. it must be believable and support the claims made. The burden of proof is the normal civil 'balance of probabilities' and hearsay evidence may be accepted.

Previous conduct, whilst not acceptable in criminal cases, can be used in tribunal cases. For example, if the employee was dismissed for dishonesty, evidence of earlier dishonesty would be accepted. The hearing is in public.

Reviews (not appeals)

Where either party thinks the decision made was **wrong** they can make an application to the industrial tribunal for a **review** of the proceedings within **14** days of the decision (or at the hearing).

A review may be requested where:

- the decision was made through an **error** on the part of staff at the tribunal.
- where a party received **no notice** of the proceedings. (This may occur through not sending a notice to a company's registered office where all official letters should be sent.)
- where a decision was made in the absence of one of the parties. This will usually have arisen through illness.
- where new evidence has been found since the decision whose existence would not have been known or not reasonably foreseen. Such evidence should be important, relevant to the case, not have been available before and must be believable.
- *where it is in the interests of justice.* This is a 'catch all' for the tribunal and can cover many types of situations.

The procedure is simple and cheaper than applying for an appeal on a point of law (if there is one involved) to the Employment Appeals Tribunal. The application can be made by mere letter setting out a request for review giving the reasons for the application and his reasons why the decision was wrong.

Appeals

Appeals on points of law only are taken to the Employment Appeals Tribunal (EAT). This is presided over by High Court judges assisted by members appointed by the Lord Chancellor and the Secretary of State for Employment, who have specialist knowledge of industrial relations. Like the industrial tribunals, the lay members are appointed by the Trades Union Congress and the Confederation of British Industry.

Each hearing is heard by a judge plus either two or four members. The numbers must, of course, remain equal so that there can be no bias towards workers or employers. The judge has no greater power than the lay members and thus, it is possible for him to be outvoted.

Most appellants, if employees, are represented by counsel, some by solicitors and a small minority represent themselves or get a friend or trade union representative to do this. Employers are usually represented by counsel. It should be noted that at present there is **no** legal aid for applications to tribunals of any sort, except mental health tribunals.

Especially difficult cases are heard by the President of the Employment Appeals Tribunal in a special procedure list who first listens to agreements for approximately thirty minutes before deciding whether to allow the appeal to be made to the full tribunal.

The Construction Industry Training Board (CITB)

Industrial training boards are governed by the Industrial Training Act 1982 and the Secretary of State for Employment after consulting with the Manpower Services Commission. There has been a Construction Industry Training Board since 1964 authorized under previous legislation. Its present address is Radnor House, London Road, Norbury, London SW16 4EL.

Training boards are designed to:

- provide or arrange training courses for entrants into an industry;
- act as a watchdog over such courses;
- provide advice for those involved in training and encourage research;
- make recommendations and public reports vis-à-vis standards to be achieved as a result of training and whether they are being achieved.

In achieving the above ends, the boards may provide financial assistance for persons undergoing training or to employers whose personnel are going to undergo training courses.

In order to be able to monitor an industry an ITB can require employers to provide such information as may be necessary and to keep certain records for examination. An employer who fails to comply with these requirements is guilty of an offence.

To pay for the training system, levies are imposed on employers based on the number of their employees. At present the levy rates vary from £18 per head to £85 per head subject to exemptions for trainers and certain other staff. A maximum ceiling of 1 per cent of the total cost of remuneration to employees is levied. 'Small' builders whose total payroll plus 'lump' payments did not exceed £15,000 pa for the financial year up to 5 April 1983 are exempt.

If an employer arranges his own approved training courses, e.g. through a further education establishment, he can apply for exemption. The exemption certificate can be made subject to many conditions and shall not exceed three years from its issue. If the application is turned down by the CITB an appeal can be made to referees appointed under the Act.

The board also operates a training centre specializing in certain aspects of construction work.

Trade unions

Reasons for setting up

These are groups of workers who gather together on a formal basis with the intention of improving their pay and other working conditions. In the nineteenth century they were illegal, classed as unlawful conspiracies e.g. the Tolpuddle Martyrs, the centenary of whose trial was celebrated in 1984.

Nowadays, they are governed by the Trade Union Act 1984, Trade Union and Labour Relations Act 1974 (TULRA) the Employment Protection Act 1975, and the Employment Acts of 1980 and 1982.

Not corporations

Generally trade unions do not have corporate status. However, a series of statutes have given them some of the outward characteristics of a corporation. For example, they can sue and be sued and make contracts in their own name. Their property however, cannot be vested in the union itself like a normal corporation. It must be transferred to trustees to hold for the benefit of the union.

Also the members can be prosecuted in the union's name and the union's property can be taken to satisfy any judgment made against it in court.

Possible causes of action against trade unions or unionists in common law

A union or a member of a union could possibly be sued for the torts of inducing a breach of contract, intimidation and unlawful interference with trade or employment contracts. Under S.10 Trade Union Act 1984, a trade union may be liable for inducing a person to break his contract of employment or a commercial contract if no secret ballot was first taken which supports industrial action. A ballot need not be taken but if so, statutory immunity under S.13 below would be lost. Furthermore, a number of unionists could be prosecuted for criminal conspiracy if they had conspired to perform a criminal act or could be sued for civil conspiracy if they conspired to commit a tort.

Statutory immunity of individuals: S.13 TULRA 1974

Whilst no protection should be given to unions or unionists to enable them to commit crimes, a limited amount of protection has been given to individuals in situations in which they try to pursue their legitimate interests. Thus, by S.13, an act committed by a person **in contemplation or furtherance of a trade dispute** shall not be actionable in tort if it only:

- induces another to breach a contract
- or induces any other person to interfere with its performance, *or*
- consists of threatening that a contract (to which he may or may not be a party) will be broken or its performance interfered with, *or*
- that he will induce another person to break a contract or interfere with its performance.

As these actions are the direct result of a strike call, S.13 protects the right of an **individual** to be able to strike or encourage others to do so, in that they cannot be sued for such action. It should be noted that striking is still a breach of contract and would be a ground for dismissal (*see* p. 351).

However additional protections contained in S.13 have been repealed by the Employment Act 1980 and it appears that the immunities falling within the categories above may be narrowly interpreted in the future.

The possibility of being sued for civil conspiracy has also been restricted provided that the agreement between two or more persons to do or procure the doing of an act in contemplation of a trade dispute, would **not be actionable** if done by **one person**. It should be noted that such immunity only applies to torts. There is no immunity against criminal conspiracy.

Statutory immunities of trade unions

Probably this will be dealt with by applying S.13 to the larger

membership as union immunity per se was repealed by the
Employment Act 1982.

Thus, a trade union can be liable in tort but only if the act which
resulted in the tort being committed was authorized by a 'responsible
person' e.g. employed officials or executive committee. S.10 Trade
Union Act 1984 deprives a union of such immunity if it failed to gain
the support of a secret ballot of its members.

Any damages recovered are limited in proportion to the size of the
membership of the union. The damages are restricted to each claim
and not per dispute and there are no restrictions in personal injury
claims.

Permitted peaceful picketing: S.16 Employment Act 1980

Peaceful picketing which is in contemplation or furtherance of a trade
dispute is permitted:

- by a person at or near his **own** place of work, *or*
- by an official of a trade union, at or near the place of work of a
  member of that union, whom he is supporting or for whom he
  represents.

Secondary action: S.17 Employment Act 1980

Nowadays, unions seek to increase the effect of their industrial action
by taking action against companies and individuals who are not in
direct contact with the dispute.

Section 17 defines secondary action as consisting of inducing or
threatening to break or interfere with a contract of employment where
the employer in that contract is **not** a party to the dispute. Such actions
are now no longer protected under S.13 TULRA unless it is protected
under S.17 EA 1980. Section 17(3) restores protection if the main
purpose of such action is to prevent or disrupt supplies to employer
(A) in the dispute by taking secondary action to encourage others to
breach their contracts of employment with another employer (B) who
is supplying goods and services to A.

Secondary action taken against 'associated' employers is also
permitted. Associated employers are probably companies, one of which
is controlled by the other either directly or indirectly.

Secondary action outside the above permitted areas is not protected
and thus civil action could be taken against persons or unions
participating.

CHAPTER 11

Safety law

Introduction

Obviously unsafe work situations are affected by the common law rule relating to negligence and nuisance, and statutes such as the Occupiers Liability Act 1957 and the Defective Premises Act 1974. However, the main object of these rules is to **compensate** victims of incompetence rather than to prevent accidents happening in the first place. It has therefore been left to Parliament to introduce legislation to encourage safe working conditions.

Unfortunately, whilst the majority of accidents occur in the home, it would be impossible to monitor domestic safety conditions. For this reason, legislation has concentrated on trying to control accidents at **work**.

Originally, legislation was introduced in a piecemeal way covering at first, only the most dangerous of occupations and later the most common, such as factories, offices and shops. In the building industry, the multiplicity of processes and varied places of work have meant that building work was (and still is) covered by a number of different Acts and regulations. For example, a site office may come under the Offices, Shops and Railway Premises Act 1963, as would the contractor's permanent office, but the building work itself is covered by the current Factories Act 1961 and the Construction Regulations made under it and earlier Factories Acts. (Note the Building Regulations are more concerned with the quality of the work, whereas the Construction Regulations are designed to protect the worker whilst doing the job.)

This piecemeal approach to legislation has now been 'tied' together by the Health and Safety at Work etc Act 1974, which covers all work situations. It takes under its 'umbrella' all the old Acts and regulations which continue in force until replaced by new regulations made under the Act (*see* Fig. 11.1).

As stated before, the Act does **not** set out to enable compensation to be recovered from wrongdoers, although compensation may be awarded if there is a breach of a **specific** duty under the Act (*see* p. 364). The Act's prime responsibility is to impose **criminal** liability on those breaching the Act or regulations made under it.

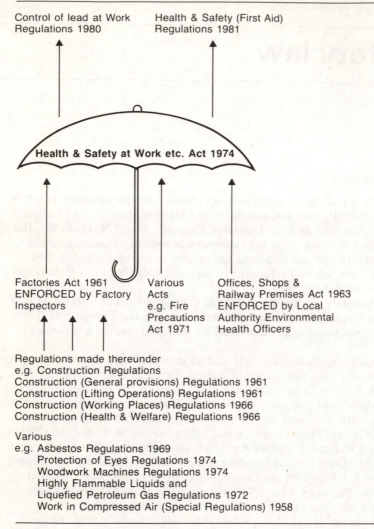

Control of lead at Work
Regulations 1980

Health & Safety (First Aid)
Regulations 1981

Health & Safety at Work etc. Act 1974

Factories Act 1961
ENFORCED by Factory
Inspectors

Various
Acts
e.g. Fire
Precautions
Act 1971

Offices, Shops &
Railway Premises Act 1963
ENFORCED by Local
Authority Environmental
Health Officers

Regulations made thereunder
e.g. Construction Regulations
Construction (General provisions) Regulations 1961
Construction (Lifting Operations) Regulations 1961
Construction (Working Places) Regulations 1966
Construction (Health & Welfare) Regulations 1966

Various
e.g. Asbestos Regulations 1969
Protection of Eyes Regulations 1974
Woodwork Machines Regulations 1974
Highly Flammable Liquids and
Liquefied Petroleum Gas Regulations 1972
Work in Compressed Air (Special Regulations) 1958

Fig. 11.1 The Health and Safety at Work etc. Act 1974 'umbrella'

Reasons for enactment

This came into effect in 1975 and was designed to provide for the first
time, safety, health and welfare protection for **all** people at work
(except domestic servants) **and** also for people **affected** by the dangers
of work.

The Act thus provides a framework on which complex technical and
scientific regulations can be formulated to cover all work processes, but
which will be administered and enforced in a standardized way.

The Health and Safety Commission

This is a body having corporate status (*see* p. 219) which was set up by
the Act, with the purpose of achieving better health and safety of
working people, by undertaking research and training, formulating
policy, providing advice and information and acting in close liaison
with appropriate government departments. Its present address is
Baynards House, 1 Chepstow Place, Westbourne Grove, London W2
4TF. The commission may also issue codes of practice which, whilst
not actually forming part of the legislation or general law, provide
good evidence in court if any recommended practice has not been
followed, e.g. the Code of Practice on Safety Representatives 1978.

The commission may also approve existing codes of practice issued
by other specialist bodies or government departments. It must have the
consent of the Secretary of State before approving a code and must
first consult appropriate bodies.

The commission may also hold informal investigations and formal
inquiries into accidents or situations when it thinks necessary.

The Health and Safety Executive

Prior to the 1974 Act, there were a number of different inspectorates
having similar responsibilities, but whose authority stemmed from their
controlling Act, e.g. the factory inspector was empowered by the
Factories Act 1961. All the inspectorates have now been brought under
the control of the executive, which is the health and safety law
enforcement agency. Within the executive, they still retain their old
titles however, e.g. inspectors of nuclear installations, alkali and clean
air inspectors, inspectors of mines and quarries, inspectors of factories
and inspectors of pipelines.

Some of the inspector's powers may be transferred to other
enforcement agencies. For example, activities involving catering,
offices, the sale or storage of goods in shops and warehouses and
launderettes are dealt with by the local authorities' environmental
health departments. They have exactly the same powers (under the Act)
as the other health and safety inspectorates.

The Act is an enabling Act

Therefore, no new Acts need be passed covering health and safety at
work (although it is of course possible). New regulations containing
new laws will be made by the appropriate Minister of State in liaison
with the Health and Safety Commission.

Powers of the inspectorate

Investigative powers

An inspector may, at any reasonable times, (or at any time, if it is believed that there is something dangerous going on) enter premises and may take a police constable with him to prevent being obstructed in the course of his duty. Once on the premises, he may, inter alia:

- examine and investigate
- take samples
- take photographs
- make measurements
- dismantle or remove something dangerous
- take possession of something to prevent it being tampered with
- inspect documents
- and require **anyone** to give such information as he requires.

The above powers are of an investigative nature. If he finds that there has been a breach of the Act or regulations he may take the following enforcement steps.

Enforcement powers (mnemonic PIPS)

Issue of improvement notice: S.21

Such a notice informs the recipient of the breach, and requires that the situation be remedied within a specified period.

The measures required to remedy may be specified. However in the case of an improvement notice served in relation to a building, then any requirements made cannot be greater than those imposed under the Building Regulations.

Issue a prohibition notice: S.22

If there has been a breach of a statutory provision and the inspector is of the opinion that if the situation continues, there will be a risk of **serious personal injury**, then he may serve a **prohibition notice**. This prohibits the behaviour amounting to the breach, either immediately if the risk appears imminent or it may be suspended until the expiry of a specified period. Prohibition notices can thus be used to stop a particular practice, e.g. a worker who fails to use protective clothing or it can be used to close a whole workplace e.g. where toxic fumes are not being effectively removed from a factory. The service of a prohibition notice in building work is to be avoided at all costs, as the responsibility for any delay would invariably fall on the shoulders of the building contractor unless the liability for the notice was due to the fault of someone else, e.g. the employer.

(Note: Improvement and prohibition notices cannot be enforced against the Crown. Nevertheless, the commission allows a **Crown notice** to be served on government departments, hospitals etc which specifies the breach and imposes a moral duty to comply.)

Seizing, rendering harmless or destroying articles or substances: S.25

Sometimes the inspector may find articles or substances which he believes could cause imminent personal injury, e.g. gelignite which has deteriorated and has become unstable. In such cases, the inspector may remove the goods in order to destroy them or to have them made safe.

Prosecution: S.33

A person who contravenes a relevant statutory provision, including ignoring prohibition or improvement notices can be prosecuted in the magistrates' court and in certain specified cases in the Crown Court. Fines and even imprisonment can be imposed. Furthermore, if a notice is ignored, the court can order that work should be carried out or some step be taken which if also ignored will amount to contempt of court. If a recipient of a notice fails to carry out the requirements contained in any notice or order, then each day he continues to be in contravention, he will be fined a further fixed sum.

Anyone, including a corporation such as a company, may be prosecuted if in breach of the Act. However, it is interesting to note, that under S.37 where it appears that an offence committed by a corporation (an inanimate person) has been committed with the consent or connivance of or through the neglect of a director, manager or other officer, then he may also be prosecuted, *Armour* v. *Skeen* 1977. Remember, ignorance of the law is **no** defence. It is interesting to note that although the Crown cannot be prosecuted (*see* p. 362) the inspectorates have informed government departments and other Crown departments such as health authorities that they are still entitled to use Ss.7 & 8 (*see* p. 365) against individuals.

These sections concern an employee's duty to take care of himself and others and the duty of anyone not to intentionally or recklessly interfere with anything provided to comply with health, safety and welfare provision.

Appeals against notices: S.24. Of course, the recipient of a **notice** may think he has grounds for an appeal and he may do so to an **industrial tribunal**. The grounds include insufficient time being given to remedy the situation. Also, the alleged breach may in fact not be a breach of a statutory duty. These rules and regulations must therefore be scrutinised to check whether there has been a breach and it is generally no defence to say that there have been no accidents in the past despite the breach. That might have been pure luck. The degree of likely risk is also a ground for appeal. If the risk is likely then all steps must be taken to remedy the situation. But if the risk is less likely, then the tribunal may be satisfied with fewer safeguards than are required by the notice. This also affects the financial aspects which may influence a tribunal to lessen the requirements of a notice. Thus, a firm may successfully argue that the requirements will prove financially ruinous, especially as the risk is not reasonably likely. Should the risk be likely however, no-one will relieve anyone of their duty to guard against that risk.

The tribunal may at its discretion award costs against a party who is unsuccessful in bringing an appeal.

An inspector has only those powers set out in a document given to him on his appointment, and this should be produced at any time he chooses to exercise his rights. Should he overstep those powers, he can be sued by the person suffering as a result. Under S.26 of the Act, the employers have a power (not a duty) to indemnify him for any claims made against him.

In the case of a building site, the inspector will be a member of the factory inspectorate as the Factories Act 1961 S.127 applied much of that Act to work involving building operations and engineering construction work by way of trade or business or for industrial or commercial purposes. Environmental health officers however will be responsible for site offices as well as the contractors permanent offices.

Civil actions for breaches of the Act. By S.47, a breach of the **general** duties under the Act does **not** give rise to civil action in tort for a breach of a statutory duty (*see* p. 304). Thus, if there is a breach of a general duty, only criminal proceedings may be taken **vis à vis the Act.** However, this does not prevent civil action being taken in negligence, but all the requirements of that tort will have to be met.

On the other hand, if there is a breach of one of the **particular** Acts, e.g. the Factories Act 1961 or one of the regulations made thereunder, a civil action for breach of a statutory duty may be taken in addition to (or instead of) criminal proceedings **unless** the Act/regulation specifically forbids this.

Should someone wish to sue as a result of a dangerous occurrence which has been investigated by an inspector, then a party in the action may require the inspector to provide a written statement concerning the occurrence.

The general duties under the Act

Under S.2 an employer is under a duty to ensure, so far as is reasonably practicable, the health, safety and welfare at work of his employees. This duty is expanded by S.2(2) which specifies five areas of responsibility.

1. The employer must provide and maintain plant and systems of work which are as far as is reasonably practicable, safe and without risks to health.
2. He must ensure the safety and absence of risks to health in the use, storage, handling and transport of substances and articles.
3. He must provide sufficient information, instruction, training and supervision in order to ensure the health and safety of his employees.
4. He must maintain the place of work in a condition which is safe and without risk to health and ensure safe access and egress to it.
5. He must provide a safe working environment with adequate welfare facilities.

Furthermore by S.3 every employer and every self-employed person is under a duty to ensure so far as is reasonably practicable that persons not in his employment are not exposed to risks to their health or safety by the conduct of the business. Thus passersby and visitors to a site would be owed a duty under S.3.

By S.4, a person in control of non-domestic premises which are used by people who are not in his employment, is under a duty to ensure so far as is reasonably practicable, that the premises, the means of access and egress and any plant or substance used there are safe and without risks to health. This section would cover places such as launderettes or self-service petrol stations.

By S.7 an employee is under a general duty to take reasonable care at work for the health and safety of himself and others such as his workmates and he must co-operate with his employer and others in complying with any relevant statutory provision.

Finally, under S.8 a person who wilfully or recklessly interferes or misuses anything provided in pursuance of a relevant statutory provision, such as safety apparatus, is guilty of an offence.

The Construction Regulations

Construction (General Provisions) Regulations 1961.

These were made under the Factories Acts 1937 and 1948.

Applications under R.2

The regulations apply to building and engineering work undertaken by way of trade or business or in connection with industrial or commercial undertakings or by or on behalf of the Crown, or municipal or public authorities, or for lines or sidings connected therewith.

The chief inspector may grant exemption from compliance certificates for any particular plant or equipment or class of plant or any particular work or type of work, if he is satisfied that the

366

regulation requirements are **not** necessary for the protection of persons employed or are **not reasonably practicable**.

Duties imposed under R.3

The duties under the regulations are imposed on:

- **every contractor** and
- **every employer of workmen**.

A contractor includes labour-only sub-contractors.

However, the requirements are not deemed to affect any workmen, if they are present at the workplace, but **not** in the course of their employment and have not expressly or impliedly been authorized or permitted to be there, by their employer.

Thus, the construction regulations only affect (and therefore protect) workmen who are present at work in the course of their employment, with the express or implied permission of their employer. If they are there for some other reason (e.g. picketing) the regulations do not apply, but they would be affected by S.3 of the Health and Safety at Work etc Act 1974.

Apart from the duties imposed on the contractors and employers by R.3(2), every person employed is under a duty to comply with the requirements of the regulations, to co-operate in the carrying out of the regulations, and if he discovers defects in the plant or equipment, to report such defects to his employer or foreman, or to a safety supervisor appointed under Part II of the Regulations.

Part II

Supervision of safe conduct of work

Appointment of safety supervisors: R.5

Every contractor and employer of workmen undertaking building or engineering work, who employ **more** than 20 persons at one time (but not necessarily on one site) must **expressly** appoint in writing an experienced operative as a safety supervisor, in order to:
(i) advise the contractor or employer on the observance of safety rules under the Factories Act;
(ii) supervise observance of such rules and encourage safe working habits.

The safety supervisor's name must be entered by the contractor or employer on the abstract of the regulations of the Factories Act, which must be displayed.

Other duties and joint appointments: R.6

Whilst this need not be a full-time appointment, the safety supervisor must **not** be given other duties which would make it impossible for him to carry out his duties as safety supervisor.

A supervisor may be appointed for a group of sites, or two or more contractors or employers working on one site may make a joint appointment of one or more people as safety supervisors.

Part IV

Excavations, shafts and tunnels

Supply and use of timber: R.8

An adequate supply of timber or other suitable support must be provided and used to prevent, so far as is reasonably practicable, danger to employees from a fall or dislodgement of earth, rock or other material forming a side or roof of any excavation, shaft, earthwork or tunnel. If the fall would be less than 4 ft then timbering is not required, nor is it required if physical conditions make it unreasonable.

Inspection and examination of excavations: R.9

Such places should be inspected by a competent person, at least once a day, whilst work is carried on in them.

However, where the working end of a trench or face of a tunnel is more than 6 ft 6 ins, then the base or crown must be inspected at the start of each shift. A report in Form 91 (Part 1 Section B) should be completed and signed by the examiner at each examination.

Supervision and execution of timbering and other work: R.10

Timbering or supports for excavations etc work, must not be erected or substantially added to or dismantled unless under the direction of a competent person, and by suitably experienced workmen.

Means of egress in case of flooding: R.11

Should there be apprehension of danger from rising water or an irruption of water, then a means of getting to safety must be provided.

Excavations etc likely to reduce security of a structure: R.12

Should excavation etc work be likely to reduce the security or stability of any part of the structure, whether permanent or temporary, then it should not be started or continued, unless steps are taken to prevent danger to any employee from a collapse or fall of the structure.

Fencing of excavations etc: R.13

Should there be a possibility of an employee falling more than 6 ft 6 ins into an excavation etc then a suitable barrier should be provided, or the hole should be securely covered, unless it is not yet practicable to provide such protection.

Safeguarding edges of excavations: R.14

Materials should not be placed close to the edge of any excavation etc so as to endanger employees working below. Nor should plant or equipment be placed or moved close to such excavations where it is likely to cause the sides to collapse.

Part V

Cofferdams and caissons

Construction and maintenance: R.15

They must be of good construction, of suitable and sound material, free from obvious defect, of adequate strength and must be properly maintained.

Means of egress in case of flooding: R.16

Suitable means of escape must be provided in the case of inrushing water, unless physical conditions make this impracticable.

Supervision of work and inspection of material: R.17

No part of the work must be constructed, placed in position or added to, altered or dismantled, except under the supervision of a competent person or be done by experienced and competent workmen. All materials used should be inspected by a competent person before use and unsuitable or defective material should not be used.

Inspections and examinations: R.18

No-one must be employed in a cofferdam or caisson unless it has been inspected by a competent person, at least once on the same or preceding day. Also, if explosives have been used which may have affected the strength or stability of the cofferdam or caisson or if it has been damaged, it must be thoroughly examined, and in any event, a thorough examination must be carried out once a week.

Reports of such examinations must be made in the prescribed form (Form 91).

This regulation does not apply to people actually constructing or repairing or altering the cofferdam or caisson, provided proper safety precautions are taken.

Part VI: R.19
Explosives

These must not be handled other than by or under the control of a knowledgeable, competent person. When a charge is fired, employees must not be exposed to risk from the explosion or flying material.

Part VII
Dangerous and unhealthy atmospheres

Inhalation of dust and fumes to be prevented: R.20. All reasonably practicable measures must be taken to prevent inhalation of dust or fumes which may be injurious to health, during grinding, cleaning, spraying or manipulation of any material. Such measures may either be by ventilation or by providing respirators.

Ventilation of excavations etc: R.21. Effective steps must be taken to adequately ventilate such places so as to maintain an atmosphere in which it is fit to breathe, to make all dangerous or injurious fumes, dusts or impurities harmless, so far as is reasonably practicable.

Should it be believed that the atmosphere of such a place is poisonous or asphyxiating, then no-one can be employed or allowed to enter, until the atmosphere has been tested, or the place is supervised by a competent person, who is satisfied that the place is then free from danger.

Internal combustion engines: R.22. These must not be used in an enclosed space, unless there are safety precautions whereby there is either adequate ventilation or a means of conducting the gases into the open air.

Part VIII. Work on, or adjacent to water
Transport by water: R.23

Persons should be transported by water, where necessary, in suitably constructed, properly maintained vessels, which are not overloaded and which are manned by a competent person.

Prevention of drowning: R.26

Where work is close to water, suitable rescue equipment should be provided and prompt rescue procedures must be taken. Secure fencing should also be provided where there is a risk of falling into water.

Part IX. Transport

This part is concerned with the provision of and maintenance of rails and rail tracks: R.25; locomotives: R.26; clearance: R.27; gantries: R.28; brakes, sprags and scotches: R.29; replacement of derailed locomotives: R.30; warning of movement of locomotives, trucks or wagons: R.31; competent persons to drive locomotives etc: R.32; precautions regarding capstans and haulage winches: R.33.

Mechanically propelled vehicles and trailers: R.34

These must:

- be in an efficient state, in working order and in good repair,
- not be used in an improper manner,
- not be loaded in such a manner as to interfere with the safe driving or operation of the vehicle whether carrying workmen, goods or material, subject to certain exceptions.

Riding in insecure positions on vehicles etc: R.35

No-one must ride on the buffer, running board or in an insecure position on a vehicle to which R.34 applies, or on any locomotive truck or wagon.

Remaining on vehicles during loading: R.36

This is not permitted if this would endanger someone.

Vehicles near edge of excavations etc: R.37

These should be prevented from overrunning the edge.

Part X. Demolition

Application: R.38

Part X applies to the demolition of the whole or any part of a building or other structure.

Supervision: R.39

Demolition contractors must appoint an experienced, competent supervisor, and where more than one demolition contractor takes part in the work, each contractor shall appoint a supervisor or a joint appointment must be made. No operation must be undertaken without consultation between the supervisors.

Fire and flooding: R.40

All practicable steps shall be taken to prevent danger to employees from fire, explosion through leakage, gas, vapours or flooding.

Precautions: R.41

No part of a building shall be so overloaded with debris or materials as to render it unsafe to employees.

Certain demolition operations shall only be carried out under the immediate supervision of a competent foreman, chargehand or by experienced workmen and under the direction of a competent foreman or chargehand. These are inter alia, the cutting of reinforced concrete, steelwork or ironwork forming part of the building being demolished.

Before demolition is started and during the work, precautions shall, where necessary, be taken by adequate shoring or otherwise, to prevent so far as is practicable, the accidental collapse of any part of the building or structure, or of any adjoining building, which may endanger someone.

Part XI. Miscellaneous

These concern the fencing of machinery, R.42; and fencing of new machinery, R.43.

Electricity: R.44

Before any operations are commenced, and during their progress, all practicable steps shall be taken to prevent danger to employees from any live electric cable or apparatus.

Generation of steam, smoke and vapour: R.45

This should be prevented so far as is practicable from obscuring any work or machinery, plant or equipment where people work.

Protection from falling materials: R.46

Steps must be taken to prevent workers from being hit by falling material. The method is probably to be left to the person responsible.

Materials should not normally be thrown but should be lowered where practicable. Otherwise, precautions should be taken to prevent injury.

Lighting of working places: R.47

These should be adequately lit.

Projecting nails and loose material: R.48

Projecting nails shall not be left so as to cause danger. Loose materials, when not required, should be properly stacked away, so as to leave unobstructed passage. Nor should it be insecurely stacked, so as to overload any floor or building.

Construction of temporary structures: R.49

These must be of good construction and properly maintained.

Avoidance of danger from collapse of structure: R.50

All practicable precautions should be taken to prevent the collapse of buildings not yet completed, e.g. by guys, stays, supports etc.

Wet paint or cement wash on ironwork or steelwork: R.51

Such work should not be moved or walked upon whilst wet.

Helmets or crowns for pile driving: R.53

These must be of good construction, of sound material, of adequate strength and free from patent defect.

Lifting excessive weights: R.55

No-one must be employed to lift or move a load likely to injure him.

Keeping of records: R.56

Required records must be kept on site or at the contractor's office. These must be available for inspection by any factory inspector at all reasonable times.

Construction (Lifting Operations) Regulations 1961

These apply to building operations and works of engineering construction, and to the same people as before. Exemptions may be granted by the chief inspector of factories in certain specified situations: R.5. Also, certain appliances are specifically exempted in the regulations: Rr.6, 7, 8 & 9.

Part III: lifting appliances

A lifting appliance is defined in R.4 as a crab, winch, pulley, block or gin-wheel used for raising or lowering, and a hoist, crane, sheer legs

excavator, dragline, piling frame, aerial cableway, aerial ropeway or
overhead runway.
These should be properly:

- Constructed, maintained and inspected: R.10.
- They should be supported, anchored, fixed and erected: R.11
- Precautions should be taken where the lifting appliance has a
  travelling or slewing motion: R.12
- Platforms should be provided for crane drivers and signallers: R.13
- Cabins should be provided for drivers: R.14
- Drums and pulleys should be of suitable diameter and construction:
  R.15
- Brakes, controls and safety devices should be provided, to prevent
  the load falling or accidentally moving: R.16
- A safe means of access should be provided: R.17.

The regulations also concern:

- Poles or beams supporting pulley blocks or gin wheels: R.18
- Stability of lifting appliances: R.19
- Rail mounted cranes: R.20
- Mounting of cranes: R.21
- Cranes with derricking jibs: R.22
- Restriction on use of cranes: R.23
- Use of cranes with timber structural member prohibited: R.24
- Erection of cranes under supervision: R.25
- Competent persons to operate lifting appliances and give signals:
  R.26
- Giving of signals: R.27
- Testing and examination of cranes: R.28
- Marking of safe working loads: R.29
- Indication of safe working load of jib cranes: R.30
- Load not to exceed safe working load: R.31
- Precautions on raising or lowering loads: R.32
- Scotch and guy derrick cranes: R.33

Part IV: chains, ropes and lifting gear

These regulations concern:

- Construction, testing, examination and safe working load: R.34
- Testing rings etc altered or repaired by welding: R.35
- Hooks: R.36
- Slings: R.37
- Edges of load not to come into contact with sling etc: R.38
- Knotted chains etc: R.39
- Examination of chains, ropes and lifting gear: R.40
- Annealing of chains and lifting gear: R.41

Part V: special provisions as to hoists

These concern:

- Safety of hoistways, platforms, cages: R.42
- Operation of hoists: R.43
- Winches: R.44
- Safe working load and marking of hoists: R.45
- Test and examination of hoists: R.46

Part VI: carriage of persons and secureness of loads

These concern:

- Carrying persons by means of lifting appliances: R.47
- Hoists carrying persons: R.48
- Secureness of loads: R.49

Part VII: keeping of records

Under the regulations, certain reports must be kept and these shall be kept, either at the site or at the contractor's or employer's office, depending on whether the work is carried out on site or not. If the work is to take less than six weeks, then they can be kept at the contractor's office. They shall be available for inspection by the factories inspectors.

The reports are the following:

Form 91 Part I Inspection report of lifting appliances.
         Part II Testing of crane and load, radius of jib anchorage.
         Part IV Results of tests of hoists for carrying persons.

Construction (Working Places) Regulations 1966

These were made by the authority of the Factories Act 1961. They apply to building operations and to the same people as before. Exemptions may be granted in certain specified situations.

Part III: safety of working places and access and egress

General: R.6. So far as is reasonably practicable, suitable and sufficient safe access and egress shall be provided from every place at which any person at any time works and this shall be properly maintained.

Also, every place shall be made and kept safe for any person working there so far as is reasonably practicable.

Provision of scaffolds: R.7. Where work cannot be safely done on or from the ground or from a building or other permanent structure, then suitable scaffolding, ladders or other means of support shall be provided.

Supervision of work and inspection of material: R.8. Scaffolding should not be added to or altered or dismantled without competent supervision and by competent experienced workmen. The material used should be inspected before use.

Material used should be suitable and sound and in sufficient quantity: R.9.

No defective material should be used: R.10.

Scaffolds should be properly maintained and prevented from accidental displacement: R.11.

Safe use of scaffolds. Scaffolds shall not be left partly erected or dismantled so that they could be used unless the regulations are complied with or a warning notice is displayed or access to them is blocked: R.12
  The regulations also deal with the following:

- Manner of fixing standards or uprights, ledgers and putlogs: R.13
- Type of ladders to be used: R.14
- Stability of scaffolds: R.15
- Requirements regarding slung scaffolds: R.16
- Cantilever, jib, figure and bracket scaffolds: R.17
- Support for scaffolds, ladders, folding step-ladders or crawling ladders, must be sound and sufficiently stable: R.18
- Suspended Scaffolds (Not power operated): R.19
- Boatswains' chairs, cages, skips etc (Not power operated): R.20
- Trestle scaffolds: R.21
- Inspection of scaffolds, boatswains' chairs etc: R.22
- Scaffolds used by workmen of different employers: R.23

Construction of working platforms, gangways and runs.

- If a person would fall more than 6 ft 6 ins, then these should be closely boarded, planked or plated: R.24
- Boards and planks used on working platforms, gangways and runs should be of required thickness and width: R.25
- Width of working platforms: R.26
- Width of gangways and runs: R.27
- Guard-rails and toe boards at working platforms and places: R.28
- Guard-rails etc for gangways, runs and stairs: R.29
- Platforms, gangways, runs and stairs to afford safe foothold: R.30
- Construction and maintenance of ladders and folding step-ladders: R.31
- Use of ladders and folding step-ladders: R.32

- Openings, corners, breaks, edges and open joisting subject to exemptions under R.34: R.33
- Sloping roofs: R.35
- Work on, or near fragile materials: R.36
- Loads on scaffolds: R.37
- Prevention of falls and provision of safety nets and belts: R.38

Part IV. Keeping of records.

Regulation 22 requires the keeping of records regarding scaffold inspections. This is Form F 91 (pt. 1)

Construction (Health and Welfare) Regulations 1966

These were made by virtue of the Factories Act 1961. They apply in the same circumstances and to the same people as before.

Shelter and accommodation for clothing and taking meals: R.11

The following shall be provided at or near every site:

(i) Adequate and suitable accommodation for taking shelter during interruptions of work caused by bad weather and for leaving clothing.

- If more than five people are employed, the place should be suitable to gain warmth and to dry wet clothes.
- If less than five people are employed, the same should be provided. but only so far as is reasonably practicable.

(ii) Accommodation for deposit of protective clothing and arrangements as are reasonably practicable to dry them.

(iii) Accommodation affording protection from weather, including tables and seats/benches for taking of meals, facilities for boiling water, and if more than 10 employees on site, and if heated food is not otherwise available (as for example in a canteen) facilities to heat food.

(iv) An adequate supply of wholesome drinking water, marked as such.

Washing facilities: R.12

Where one or more persons are employed on site for more than four consecutive hours, adequate and suitable facilities shall be available for washing.

If 20 or more employees are to be on site for six weeks or more, suitable washing facilities must be provided, including:

(i) adequate troughs, basins or buckets.
(ii) An adequate means of cleaning and drying, being soap and towels or other means.
(iii) Sufficient supply of hot and cold water.

If 100 or more employees are to be on site for 12 months or more, then the contractor must provide as above: plus, an additional four washbasins, plus, one for each 35 persons over 100 employed.

The washing facilities must be kept conveniently accessible to eating places and must be kept clean and orderly.

Sanitary Conveniences: R.13

1 W.C. (not a urinal) for every 25 employees on site. If over 100 are employed on site and there are sufficient urinals provided there must be one W.C. for every 25 persons employed up to the first 100 and one for every 35 thereafter.

Protective clothing: R.15

Every contractor shall provide adequate and suitable protective clothing for any person so employed, who by reason of the nature of his work is required to continue working in the open air during rain, snow, sleet or hail.

Safe access to places where facilities are provided: R.16.

Provisions of the Offices, Shops and Railway Premises Act 1963 relating to the building industry

Of course, not all building work will be covered by the Factories Act 1961 and the Construction Regulations. Any offices (or railway premises) will be covered by the Offices, Shops and Railway Premises Act 1963 (OSRPA). Thus, site offices, though temporary, will be covered, but only if they are in use as such for more than six weeks, if a fixed structure or more than six months if a moveable structure: S.86. A contractor's main office will of course be subject to the Act at all times.

Definition of office: S.1

An office is a building or part of a building, used solely or principally for office purposes, i.e. administration, clerical work, handling money, telephone and telegraph operating. Thus, whilst the rest of the premises might not be covered by this Act, the office will be. Premises occupied with the office for office purposes are also covered, such as storerooms or canteens.
(Note: For definitions of shops and railway premises, see the Act itself.)

Exclusion of Act: Ss.2 & 3

The Act does not apply to offices where only the employer's relatives work. Nor does it apply to workers working from their homes: S.2.

Also, by S.3 if fewer than 21 man hours are worked at that office, then the Act does not apply.

Notification of employment: S.49

Before a person begins to employ people at premises to which the Act applies, he must serve on the local authority two copies of Notice No. O.S.R.1 informing them that such persons will be employed, and giving details of the employer, trading name, postal address of the office, telephone number, nature of business, number of employees, type of work-places, number of employees on floors higher than ground floor level or in separate buildings, whether the employer is owner of the workplace, and if not, the name of the lessor.

Should the employer fail to notify the authority, then he commits an offence.

Health, safety and welfare of employees (general provisions)

Cleanliness: S.4.   Office premises, furniture and fittings must be kept clean. Dirt and refuse should not be allowed to accumulate there, and the floors and steps should be washed or swept, if suitable, at least once a week.

Overcrowding: S.5.   No office room must be so overcrowded as to cause injury to health, taking account of the number of persons expected to be working there at one time, and the space occupied by furniture, machinery etc.

Each person must have at least 3.7 square metres of floor space and 11 cubic metres of breathing space.

Temperature: S.6.   An office room should be kept at a reasonable temperature without the presence of injurious fumes.

Where a great proportion of the work does not involve severe physical effort, then a temperature of at least 16° Celsius shall be reasonable after one hour from commencement of work. These provisions do not apply to rooms into which members of the public are invited, such as a waiting room or to rooms in which the maintenance of a reasonable temperature is not reasonably practicable. However, anyone required to work in such places, must be given access to somewhere to warm himself.

A thermometer should be provided in a conspicuous place to check the temperature.

Exemptions relating to site offices.   Under the Offices, Shops and

Railway Premises Act 1963 (Exemption No.1) Order 1964 (S.I. 1964 No 964), offices erected at or adjacent to a place where building operations or engineering construction are being carried on, **do not** have to comply with S.6.

But, there must be provided for people working in such premises, a conveniently accessible and effective means of enabling themselves to get warm. Such people must be given the opportunity of using these means. Also, such means must not involve the escape of injurious or offensive fumes, gases or vapours.

Ventilation: S.7. Such rooms must be properly ventilated by fresh or artificially purified air. This does not mean that there is a duty to provide exhaust appliances or respirators.

See Ventilation of Buildings, Fresh Air Requirements, Guidance Note No.E.H. 22. H.S.E. 1979 HMSO.

Lighting: S.8. Offices must be effectively lighted by natural or artificial lighting which should be properly maintained. Any skylights or windows should be kept clean and free from obstruction. Should there be glare or excessive heat, such windows can be shaded however.

Sanitary conveniences: S.9. Offices should be provided, at reasonably accessible places, with suitable and sufficient sanitary conveniences, which should be clean, properly maintained, ventilated and lighted. The number of such conveniences and more detailed provisions are governed by the Sanitary Conveniences Regulations 1964 S.I. 1964 No.966.

Washing facilities: S.10. Similarly, suitable and sufficient washing facilities must be provided, with hot, warm or cold water, soap and clean towels. They must be kept clean, and properly lighted and maintained.

Note: under both S.9 and S.10, where office facilities are shared with another office or factory or some other premises, the sanitary convenience and washing facilities may be shared, provided the facilities are in accordance with the statutory requirements.

The number of washbasins and more detailed provisions are to be found in the Washing Facilities Regulations 1964 S.I. 1964 No.965.

Supply of drinking water: S.11. An adequate supply of wholesome drinking water should be supplied.

Accommodation for clothing: S.12. A place to hang or store non-working clothes should be provided. Drying facilities should also be made available.

Seats: Ss.13 & 14. If a worker has reasonable opportunities for sitting, without detrimentally affecting his work, then suitable facilities should be provided, and a worker should not be prevented from using these facilities.

Under S.14, if the job actually involves sitting, then a suitably designed and constructed seat should be provided with a footrest to support the worker's feet, if he cannot sit without one.

Floors, passages and stairs: S.16.   Floors, stairs, steps, passages and gangways in offices must be of sound construction, be properly maintained, and so far as is reasonably practicable, be kept free from obstruction and from any slippery substance. Planks have been defined as gangways. But earth surfaces in the open air are not floors.

Staircases must have handrails or handholds, and if open on one side, a rail must be provided on that side. If they are open on both sides, rails should be provided for both. Open staircases should have some means of preventing people falling through the space between the rail and the stairs.

Openings in floors should be securely fenced, unless the nature of the work makes this impracticable.

Fencing of exposed parts of machinery: S.17.   Dangerous parts of machinery used as office equipment should be securely fenced unless its position in the office makes it safe anyway. Such fencing should be soundly constructed and properly maintained, and must be kept in position whilst the machinery is being used (unless it is being examined in motion and testing conditions are complied with).

Cleaning of machinery by young persons: S.18.   People under 18 should not be allowed to clean dangerous equipment, if so doing would expose them to risk of injury from a moving part of that or any adjacent machinery.

Training people using dangerous machines: S.19.   Certain machinery prescribed by the Prescribed Dangerous Machine Order 1964 S.I. 1964 No.971 must not be used until the operative has properly been trained by an experienced supervisor. The machines in the Order are mostly to do with kitchen equipment such as potato chipping machines or upholstery equipment used in railway premises.

Prohibition of heavy work: S.23.   No-one shall be required to lift, carry or move a load likely to injure him, in the course of his work.

Recently in *Osarak* v. *Hawker Siddeley Water Engineering Ltd. The Times* 29 October 1982, it was held to be a breach of this section to require a tea-lady to lift a teapot containing 6 pints.

The section would probably also apply to typists required to lift their own typewriters.

However, refusal to employ a woman because of her inability to carry heavy weights could amount to sex discrimination.

Exemptions from the Act granted by local authorities. Local authorities may exempt all or part of the premises from Ss.5 & 6 i.e. relating to overcrowding and temperature requirements. Note, the exemption applying to site offices on page 377 anyway. Also exemption of all the premises may be granted under S.9 relating to sanitary conveniences. In such cases, the authority must be satisfied that compliance is not reasonably practicable.

Exemption from S.10 relating to running water for washing may be also given.

Such exemption may last only for two years in the case of Ss.5 & 6 in the first instance, although this may be extended. In the case of S.10 an exemption may be unlimited or for a specified period.

An application for an exemption certificate must be made by the person who would be liable for contravening the Act. The application must be made in the statutory form.

Before the application, he must display a notice to be read by his employees stating that the application is being made, the requirement from which exemption is being sought, the period of exemption required, the name and address of the local authority and informing the employees that they can make representations to the authority concerning the application.

If an exemption is granted, the certificate must be kept posted in the relevant premises.

Offences: S.63. Contravention of the Act is a criminal offence. Generally it will be the occupier who is primarily liable, unless some other person(s) is made responsible in addition to the occupier.

The penalties are those laid down under the Health and Safety at Work etc Act 1974.

Defence: S.67. If a person charged with a breach of the Act can prove he used all due diligence to secure compliance, then this is a good defence. Thus, if the Act is broken by an **employee**, then the occupier may escape liability.

Provision of information. The Information for Employees Regulations 1965 S.I. 1965 No.307 require an employer to keep posted at his premises a copy or copies of the official abstract of the Act and regulations made, or give a copy of the 'Explanatory Book for Employees' O.S.R.9A to anyone employed by him for more than four weeks.

Sufficient copies of the abstract must be posted to enable all the employees to read them (unless the employees have the explanatory book). If the abstract is posted in the open, then it must be protected from the weather.

CHAPTER 12

Insurance

Introduction

The law of insurance is found principally at common law and equity
and in some statutes mentioned in the text.

Insurance is merely another branch of contract. In this case, the
contract is between the **insured** who pays a **premium** to an **insurer** in
return for a sum of money or some other, compensating action, such
as replacing an article of property if a certain specified event occurs,
e.g. death, illness, having had judgement awarded against the insured
in a civil action, or the loss of property through theft or destruction
(*see* Fig. 12.1).

The cost of paying the insured is met by the insurer out of money
made by investing all the other premiums collected from persons
insuring through the company. Such payments may be by way of an
indemnity i.e. they make good any financial loss the insured had
suffered as a result of, for example, a fire or a court judgment.
Alternatively, the sum paid, may be a **benefit**, payable in the case of

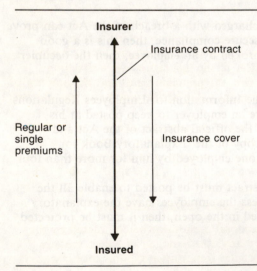

Fig. 12.1   An insurance contract

death, injury or illness, whereby, the insured pays a sum, specified in the insurance policy on the happening of such events. Benefit insurances cannot be indemnity insurances, as it is impossible to revert the insured person into the same financial position as he was prior to the accident, illness etc. In both cases, there must be an element of **uncertainty** which is beyond the control of the insured. (In the case of death, the uncertainty concerns the date of death.) Often, the first type of benefit insurance is called **assurance** as the fact of death is **assured**, and the second and third types are called **insurance** which is needed **in** case the event happens. Such terminology is not standard however, and the word insurance is perfectly acceptable at all times.

Form of contract

Insurance contracts are not like ordinary contracts in that the greater bargaining power is in the hands of the insurance companies, and a potential insurer must either accept their standard terms and conditions or go without insurance.

There is no statutory requirement for the contract to be in any particular form. Thus, it can be in writing, made orally, implied from behaviour or a combination of any form. Often, when asking for temporary cover for a new car, this is granted orally over the telephone. Normally however, contracts will be entered into by a combination of completing a **proposal form** which may or may not be accepted by the insurance company, who then send a written **policy**, which in reality is confirmation of what has already been agreed between the parties, i.e. an acceptance of the proposal form offer. A copy of the standard policy therefore, should have already been made available on request for reference by the prospective insured. Thus, all the peripheral details may not necessarily have been expressly agreed upon by the insured and his agreement to such details will be presumed. However, there must have been agreement on the main terms, such as the **subject matter** of the insurance, e.g. a dwelling house, the **risks** covered, e.g. fire, the **premium** paid, and the amount of compensation, e.g. full replacement value or the insured to pay the first £50 of loss.

On receipt of the policy, it should be minutely checked to see that it complies with what was agreed, and sent back for alteration if it is incorrect. Otherwise a claim may be prevented at a later date.

The Proposal form and the *uberrimae fidei* rule

In most cases nowadays, a proposal form must be completed by the proposer. The form contains many questions, all of which must be answered truthfully. This is of vital importance as insurance contracts are *uberrimae fidei*, i.e. of the **utmost good faith.** This is so because the insurer cannot properly assess the degree of risk involved unless he knows **all** the material facts. For example in the case of life insurance, the insurer will want to know about the health of the proposer including details of past illnesses.

Unfortunately, the concept of uberrimae fidei takes the giving of information much farther than one would expect.

It is not enough to answer all the questions on the proposal form truthfully. If there are **any other facts** which could be of **material** importance, then they must be disclosed. The consequences of failing to do this is that the contract will be **voidable** at the option of the insurer. Voidable means that, whilst the contract was previously valid, it can be set aside and treated as null and void, giving the insured no rights to payment.

This duty to provide information falls on both parties, but of course, in the majority of cases, it is the proposer who knows more of the surrounding circumstances than the insurer. Thus, there have been many unhappy cases, where someone has claimed on an insurance policy only to find, that on investigation of the events, undisclosed material facts have come to light which cause the insurer to avoid the policy.

Certain facts do not require disclosure as they are **not** material, such as where a structural survey has been made by the insurer and he fails to discover obvious facts.

The insurance contract is only uberrimae fidei at the pre-contract stage. Once the insurance contract is in being, it becomes a normal sort of contract subject only to the usual requirement of good faith. Nevertheless, most policies contain terms which require the insured to tell the insurer of any change in circumstances. Failure to do so may again lead to the contract being set aside. The agreement may also require the insured to promise (warrant) that certain facts are true at the time of making the contract and that they will continue to remain so. Such a clause in the contract must be made quite clear to the proposer if the insurer is going to be able to rely on it at a later date (*see* statement of practice post).

An ordinary householder's policy may possibly be avoided if work is being carried on at the premises which would increase the risks undertaken by the insurer (and thus be a material fact). Whilst this seems a pedantic point of view, claims are only made *after* damage or injury has been suffered, and if this was caused by building contractors working on the house, the insurer may very well try to avoid the policy because they were *not* told of the builder's presence.

In a British Insurance Association Statement of Insurance Practice, proposal forms, it is stated, should only be completed by the proposer according to his knowledge and belief. Thus, if he knows something and thinks it to be true, and signs the proposal form to that effect, then that should relieve him of the harshness of the uberrimae fidei rule.

Furthermore, facts which the insurer regards as material, should be the subject of clear questions set out in the form.

It should be noted that this statement only applies to contracts of insurance entered into by the insured in his **private capacity** and for **non-life** insurance. As much insurance is taken out to cover both a person's working life as well as his private life, this may mean that the strict uberrimae fidei rule applies to 'mixed contracts' or, it could be construed to cover only the private part of the contract. Thus, a builder's professional insurance cover, insurance of the works etc. will all be subject to the uberrimae fidei rule.

Relaxation of *uberrimae fidei* rule

As this is a very strict rule, in certain circumstances, legislation has reduced its harshness, e.g. certain inaccuracies in relation to age or physical condition of a driver are not allowed to deny compensation under a policy under the Road Traffic Acts.

Also in the British Insurance Association Statement of Insurance Practice mentioned above, it was clearly set out that, despite the fact that the Unfair Contract Terms Act 1977 does **not** apply to insurance contracts, then unless *fraud, deception or negligence is involved*, the insurer must not unreasonably refuse to indemnify a policy-holder in two situations.

(i)   Where the insured failed to disclose or misrepresented a material fact. Providing the insurer would have taken on the risk had they known of the truth of the matter, the insurer must still pay out on discovery.

(ii) Where there has been a breach of a warranty or condition in the agreement, if the loss is unconnected with such a breach, the insurer must still pay out.

(Note: The statement only covers private non-life insurance.)
(*See* above).

An insurable interest

Generally, no insurance cover may be given to anyone, unless they have an **insurable interest** in the subject matter of the contract.

An insurable interest may be in a human being, property or legal liability. The proposer must have such an interest, so that if they are destroyed or damaged, or if he has to pay because of legal liability, then he will suffer financially as a result. The requirement of having a legally recognized insurable interest was introduced by the Life Assurance Act 1774, which got rid of the old practice of insuring the lives of famous people, which really amounted to gambling (gambling, despite its contractual appearance, is unenforceable in the courts.)

386

Thus, as far as people are concerned, husbands and wives can insure each other's lives, creditors can insure their debtor's lives and so can partners for their co-partners.

Third party insurance however, is an example of one of the exceptions in which someone with no insurable interest can claim under an insurance contract.

Further points of interest in relation to insurance in general

Subrogation

We have already seen that many contracts of insurance are contracts of indemnity, i.e. the insurer pays compensation to the insured party, placing that party in the financial position he was in prior to an event, the risk of which had been covered by insurance. It follows from this right of indemnity, that the insurer may take over any rights to take legal action belonging to the insured in relation to that event. This right is called **subrogation** and it is often described as a process whereby one party (the insurer) stands in the shoes of the other party (the insured) and sues the third party who caused the loss through tort or breach of contract.

The effect of, and one of the reasons for the doctrine of subrogation is to prevent the insured from profiting from his misfortune by claiming his insurance money **and** keeping any money recovered in a court action. The insurer takes the action in the name of the insured.

In certain situations, insurers may agree to waive their right of subrogation. In particular this occurs in so-called 'knock for knock' agreements whereby motor insurers will agree to indemnify their own insured drivers and not claim damages from the other insurer's driver (*see* Fig. 12.2). It should be noted that the 'knock for knock' agreements between the insurance companies do not take away from

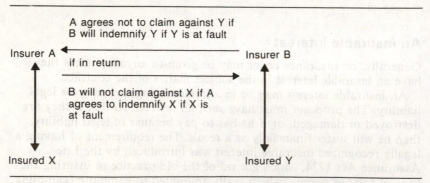

Fig. 12.2 'Knock-for-knock' agreements

the insured the right to sue the party in the wrong. Thus, action may be taken to prevent the indemnified innocent party from losing his 'no claims bonus'. However, on receipt of any damages, the insured must then reimburse the insurer for the amount previously paid to compensate him for his loss.

Insurers have also agreed not to use their rights of subrogation in employers' liability cases, where the employer is vicariously liable for a tort committed by an employee which injures another. Strictly speaking, the insurer would then be able to sue the negligent employee in order to recover the money paid in compensation. This common law right has thus been waived by agreement.

In practice, most insurance policies are extended to go beyond the common law rights of subrogation. Thus, a clause is inserted in most policies whether they are insurances of indemnity or not.

Average

A clause called an average clause is often inserted into certain insurance policies, in particular to cover fire and accident claims. Such a clause is designed to encourage the insured to insure for the full value of his property. Otherwise, if he under-insures and there is only partial damage to his property, it would be unfair (on the insurer) to expect to receive full compensation for the partial damage. Thus, if property worth £50,000 is insured for only £25,000, and a fire causes £10,000's worth of damage, then the insurer will pay only £5,000 i.e. reflecting that the property was underinsured by half.

Warranties in insurance contracts

For historical reasons, a warranty in an insurance contract is what one would normally call a condition in ordinary contract law. Thus, if there is a breach of a warranty in an insurance agreement, this will give the other party the right to repudiate the contract. Thus, all warranties must be strictly adhered to, whether or not the warranty appears to relate only to certain types of claims.

Insurance required by statute

Certain types of insurances **must** be obtained by the builder, otherwise he will be guilty of an offence.

Employers' Liability (Compulsory Insurance) Act 1969

See p. 393.

Road Traffic Act 1972 requirements

It is a criminal offence to use or allow the use of a motor vehicle, unless there is an existing policy of insurance, covering legal liability for death or injury to third parties, hospital charges, (even though we have the National Health Service, certain charges are made up to a specified limit), emergency treatment, fee for doctor, or ambulance treatment.

Cover for such liability is the minimum required by the Acts, and in most cases including the 'third party cover' policies, the insurance provided by the companies is much greater.

What sort of insurance cover is required by the builder?

(*see* Fig. 12.3.)

1. Material damage insurance. The builder should insure the building works currently under construction, his own and other people's plant and equipment, his own buildings and contents, property in transit, money and his motor vehicles, against damage, destruction or theft.

2. Liability insurance. He should insure against his liability for injury or disease suffered by his employees in the course of their employment, personal injury or damage to property suffered by members of the public and claims caused by his professional negligence.

He will also, need to insure against liability for injury, death or damage to property, caused by the use of motor vehicles.

3. Benefit insurance. If he is sensible, a builder should take out insurance to cover his own life or personal injury or illness.

4. Pecuniary loss insurance. Such insurance is used to give cover

Fig. 12.3   Insurance required by a building contractor

against pure financial loss, such as building society mortgage guarantees or loss caused by dishonest employees, non-payment of debts and loss of profits following physical damage to business premises or other property.

Composite policies

Because the work of a builder is complex and interrelated, it is usual to provide insurance cover for many different types of risks in one document. The administration involved for both the insured and insurer is easier and less likely to be overlooked.

For convenience however, the different aspects and types of insurance will be dealt with separately.

Material damage insurance

Insuring the building works

It will be remembered from the law of contract, that where someone enters into a fixed price (lump sum or entire) contract, performance of the total contract is essential. In building work, this means that the builder will not get paid at all until he substantially completes the building. If the house is accidentally or otherwise damaged, he must bear the loss, and thus, insurance is essential.

Under Cl. 22 JCT standard form of building contract with quantities

By virtue of the articles of agreement and clause 2.1, the contractor agrees to carry out and complete the works in accordance with the contract drawings and bills of quantities in consideration of a certain sum.

Article 1. For the consideration hereinafter mentioned, the contractor will upon and subject to the contract documents, carry out and complete the works shown upon, described by or referred to in those documents.

Article 2. The employer will pay to the contractor the sum of £X.

Clause 2.1. 'The contractor shall upon and subject to the conditions carry out and complete the works shown upon the contract drawings and described by or referred to in the contract bills and in the articles of agreement, the conditions and the appendix ... in compliance therewith ... '

To reduce the possibility of financial ruin for either the contractor or the employer who both stand to lose by the destruction of the works, insurance is required under Cl. 22A to cover against the most common sort of risks referred to in the contract as **Cl. 22 perils**. These are defined in Cl. 1.3 as

> 'fire, lightning, explosion, storm, tempest, flood, bursting or overflowing of water tanks, apparatus or pipes, earthquake, aircraft and other aerial devices or articles dropped therefrom, riot and civil commotion, (excluding damage caused by ionizing radiations or contamination by radioactivity from any nuclear fuel or from any nuclear waste from the combustion of nuclear fuel, radioactive, toxic, explosive or other hazardous properties of any explosive nuclear assembly or nuclear component thereof, pressure waves caused by aircraft or other aerial devices travelling at sonic or supersonic speeds).'

The cover required by the contract is not therefore 'all risks' as the damage or loss to the works must have been caused by one or more of the Cl. 22 perils.

Clause 22 A. 22 A.1 'The **contractor** shall in the joint names of the employer and contractor insure against loss or damage by the Cl. 22 perils for the **full reinstatement value** ... all works executed and all unfixed materials and goods delivered to, placed on or adjacent to the works and intended for incorporation therein but excluding (contractors or sub-contractors own or hired equipment) and shall keep such work, materials and goods so insured until the date of issue of the certificate of practical completion ... '

By Cl. 22 A.2. the insurance must be placed with insurers approved by the employer and the contractor must deposit the policy and receipts for premiums with the employer. If the contractor fails to insure or to continue to insure, the employer may then himself insure and recover the cost by deducting the appropriate sums due to the contractor under the contract.

If the contractor already maintains general insurance cover under a blanket or floater policy, which would cover the contract work in this instance, then by Cl. 22 A3.1 the obligation to insure under Cl. 22 A will be discharged on noting the employer's interest on that policy. Such policies do not, of course, have to be deposited with the employer but evidence of their existence and continued maintenance must be produced when required by the employer.

It should be noted that a policy designed to cover Cl. 22 perils does not cover, unless extended to do so, theft and vandalism, an ever present problem within the construction industry. Nor does it cover consequential loss, i.e. pure financial loss such as loss of profits through having had the works and equipment destroyed.

As an alternative to Cl. 22A, Cl. 22B allows the **employer** to bear the risk of the work and materials.

Clause 22 B.1. 'All work executed and all unfixed materials and goods delivered to, placed on or adjacent to the works and intended for incorporation therein (excluding the builders' and sub-contractors' own or hired building, or equipment) shall be at the **sole risk** of the employer as regards loss or damage by the Cl. 22 perils.'

On discovery of such loss or damage the builder must then give notice to the architect/supervising officer and the employer of the extent, nature and location. Cl. 22 B.2.

The contractor must then replace or restore the work or materials and it shall be treated as a variation of the contract. This means that he will be able to claim the extra money expended.

It should be noted that under Cl. 22B there is no contractual requirement that insurance should be taken out by the employer. Obviously, however, this is desirable to prevent serious financial loss.

Clause 22C is concerned with an existing building owned by the employer which is going to be altered in some way by the contractor. By this clause the employer bears the sole risk of loss or damage to the existing building together with the contents, contract works, unfixed materials and goods caused by the Clause 22 perils and the employer must maintain adequate insurance: Cl.22 C.1.

Notice of such loss or damage must be given immediately on discovery by the contractor to the architect/supervising officer and the employer, giving details of the extent, nature and location of the loss or damage: Cl.22C.

By Cl.22 C.2.3.3 the making good or reinstatement of such loss or damage will be treated as a variation required by the architect/supervising officer. However, by Cl.22 C.2.2.1, if it is just and equitable, either party may within 28 days of the occurrence of the loss or damage, terminate the employment of the contractor. An opportunity to go to arbitration is made in such circumstances to decide whether it would have been just and equitable.

The application of Cl.22B or Cl.22C are unusual, as it is unlikely that the employer would want to bear the risks of the building works.

As the contractor usually insures, the cost of such insurance should be reflected in the contract price and allowance must therefore be made when preparing a tender.

Insuring the builder's own plant and equipment

Generally whether a builder chooses to insure his own property is up to him as he alone suffers the loss if it is damaged or destroyed. Good sense however suggests that it is wise to insure, otherwise he might be placed in a difficult position and may be unable to complete a contract.

The cost varies depending on the type of equipment and whether cover is required merely whilst it is on site or if it is being transported. Most insurance of this type will be provided under a composite policy.

Insuring the builder's hired equipment

Most builders hire equipment using the Contractors' Plant Association Model Conditions for the hiring of plant. Whilst the conditions do not impose any duty to insure on the builder hiring the equipment, the conditions place liability on the builder in nearly all hiring situations, e.g. erecting and operating the plant. Once again it is implicit that insurance is necessary to give cover against any claims due to damage or loss of the equipment (fair wear and tear excepted) and claims for injury or death caused by operating the equipment. The conditions contain a clause indemnifying the owner against any such claims by third parties.

Insurance of building contractors' own office premises or other buildings

Once again there is no compulsion for anyone to insure their own buildings, e.g. business premises and contents. However, if the builder has borrowed money to purchase such premises and has given the lender a mortgage, it is probable that a condition of the loan will be that the property shall be fully insured and the mortgagee's interest noted on the policy (this is also true of domestic mortgages). Furthermore, if the premises are leased, it will probably be a term of the lease or tenancy agreement that the premises be insured. (If the lessor is to insure, then the lessee will have to pay towards the cost of the insurance and it will be reflected in an annual maintenance payment or ground rent).

The standard building policies cover fire, lightning and limited explosion but the policy can be extended to cover other risks such as storms, burst pipes and malicious damage.

The cover should allow for the cost of reinstatement, i.e. re-building.

Money

Money in this context does not just cover cash. It also includes inter alia bank notes, cheques, postal orders, stamps, national insurance stamps and luncheon vouchers. The loss of these must be covered on an 'all risks' basis. Thus, theft, a usual cause of loss, would be covered. However, there may be many special conditions attached to such cover, for example, that all reasonable precautions should be taken to prevent loss and there may be many exclusions. Thus, it is common to exclude the insurers duty to pay if the money was stolen by a dishonest workman in the employ of the insured. (For loss caused by dishonest employees *see* p. 399.)

Motor insurance for damage, destruction or theft

Insurance to cover such loss is not compulsory but in most cases it is sensible to obtain cover against theft or damage caused by fire and other accidents. This is known as first party cover as the cover is designed to protect only the insured and not the lives of third parties which is compulsory under the Road Traffic Acts (*see* p. 388).

Comprehensive motor insurance policies would cover not only both types of risks described above but also the injury or death of the insured (not compulsory) as well as damage to the property of third parties (which is also not compulsory). Thus, a sole trader builder would find a comprehensive policy the most desirable as it would cover all the above risks. Furthermore, most comprehensive motor insurance policies provide protection for either certain named drivers of a particular motor vehicle or anyone driving with the permission of the insured.

Building companies, if they have a large work force using company motor vehicles or even their own private vehicles, may have group or block insurance covering all or any of the risks described above.

Motor insurance is subject to many exclusions and limitations. For example, a company's block insurance policy may provide cover for a driver driving his own car whilst on company business only. Reliance must be made on the driver's own insurance when driving the rest of the time. Also, it is common for private motor insurance to be restricted to social, domestic and pleasure purposes and thus, a driver of a private car would not have cover whilst on company business.

The 'small' builder should also have cover for any business equipment carried in his motor vehicle.

Liability insurance

The concepts of liability insurance i.e. insurance against claims made as a result of legal liability, are, of course, the principles of tort (*see* pp. 241–307). It may therefore be beneficial to refresh one's memory at this point.

Employers' liability

Insurance to cover this is compulsory.

However, there are some points of interest to note. Certain categories of employers are exempt under the Employers' Liability (Compulsory Insurance) Act 1969 from having to maintain compulsory insurance, e.g. local authorities and regional health authorities. Also, there are no limitations on the insurers' right to avoid the policy for such things as non-disclosure of material facts.

Furthermore, if the employer is in breach of the Act and has **no** insurance or only insurance which does not cover his liability then there is no equivalent to the Motor Insurers Bureau to fall back on (*see* p. 397).

Liability for injury to public or their property

By Ss.68–71 of the Finance (No 2) Act 1975, building contractors must deduct income tax from the pay of sub-contractors. This is so, unless the sub-contractor can produce an exemption certificate from the Inland Revenue. One of the pre-conditions for obtaining this certificate is that the sub-contractor must have personally taken out insurance to cover his liability against claims by the public for bodily injury or disease caused by the sub-contractor or his employees for at least £250,000. Thus, in an indirect way, insurance against public liability for injury to the person has been imposed.

Requirements under the JCT standard form of contract

Under the JCT form of contract, Cl.21, the building contractor must insure against his own liability under Cl.20.

Clause 20: injury to persons and property and employers' indemnity

'The contractor shall be liable for and shall **indemnify** the employer against, any expense, liability, loss, claim or proceedings whatsoever arising under any statute or at common law in respect of *personal injury* to or the *death* of any person whomsoever *arising out of or in the course of or caused by the carrying out of the works*, unless due to any act or neglect of the employer or of any person for whom the employer is responsible.' (Clause 20.1)

Whilst this seems rather onerous on the one hand, if one applies the rules of liability in tort, this clause merely restates the contractor's tortious liability in the contract presuming there is fault on his part. However, what it does do, is to remove the possibility of being able to sue the employer as a joint tortfeasor with the contractor for vicarious liability, unless the injury or death is due to the employer himself or his agents. The burden of proving the liability of the employer or his agents probably falls on the contractor.

'Except for such loss or damage as is at the sole risk of the employer under Cl.22B or 22C (if applicable) the contractor shall be liable for and shall indemnify the employer against any expense, liability, loss, claim or proceedings in respect of **any injury or damage ... to any property** real or personal in so far as such injury or damage arises out of or in the course of or by reason of the carrying out of the **works** and provided always that the same is due to any negligence, omission or default of the contractor, his servants or agents or of any sub-contractor, his servants or agents.' (Clause 20.2)

This clause is of very wide application making the contractor liable for any damage to any property (including the works) caused by the carrying out of the works and indemnifying the employer against such claims. The clause overlaps with the duties imposed under Articles 1 &

2 and Cl.2.1 already discussed. But it is more limited in one sense, as operation of this clause (and its indemnity) only applies to claims due to the fault of the contractors or his agents (including sub-contractors). Liability under Articles 1 & 2 and Cl.2.1 is liability for loss or destruction of the works in **any** way and Cl.22A merely makes it a contractual necessity to insure against the Cl.22 perils.

It seems implicit in this clause that if the employer (or his agents) are partly or wholly responsible for the damage then, the indemnity becomes ineffective and third parties can sue the contractor (or his agents), or the employer (or his agents) or any of them together, depending on whose fault it is, e.g. *AMF International* v. *Magnet Bowling* 1968 (*See* Fig. 12.4).

Professional indemnity insurance

Professional negligence has already been discussed under negligence in Chapter 8. It is concerned with liability for the consequences of giving incorrect professional advice, which if acted upon results in either physical damage or occasionally in pure financial loss. It covers not just advice but also the making of plans, designs and suggestions of materials.

As we saw in Chapter 8 liability for physical damage or injury can be attributed to anyone who owes a duty of care, applying the neighbour principle or the proximity test: *Anns* v. *Merton LBC* 1977. Where negligent advice results in only financial loss, then a sufficient degree of proximity must be shown to exist between the giver of the advice and the injured party (*see* p. 359).

The standard of care of the professional person will depend on his qualifications and experience and in most cases proof of this will be required before an insurer will provide cover.

Separate cover is required to indemnify professionals as the public liability policy taken out by the contractor covers only the **contractor**'s liability and **not** the employers or his agents. Thus, it is essential that architects, quantity surveyors and consulting engineers take out sufficient insurance to cover their liability.

Also, it should be noted that public liability policies generally do not cover pure financial loss suffered by third parties nor damage to the contract works caused by professional negligence. Therefore, a contractor, taking on a contract in which he designs, provides plans or suggests materials, should make sure that he takes out professional indemnity insurance to cover loss occasioned by his own 'professional' negligence.

Motor insurance – third party liability

Under Ss.143 and 145 of the Road Traffic Act 1972 it is not lawful for a person to use or to cause or permit any other person to use a motor

Liabilities	Insurance Required
The Main Duty	**Clause 22A**
Under Articles 1 & 2 and clause 2.1. contractor must carry out and complete **works** etc. and carry risk of works until practical completion.	Under Clause 22A the contractor must take out insurance in joint names of employer and contractor for full re-instatement value to cover:-
	executed work and unfixed materials & goods to be incorporated into works against damage by Cl. 22 perils
	Unless
	the employer assumes risk under Cl. 22B or Cl. 22C **in which case** no insurance re. works required to be taken out *under contract* by employer, but of course desirable.

Property

Liabilities	Insurance Required
Under Clause 20.2	**Clause 21.1**
Contractor liable for loss due to injury or damage to **any property** (including the works) caused by carrying out the works **provided** his fault or his servants' or agents' fault or fault of the sub-contractors or their servants' or agents' and indemnifies the employer against such claims. (This does not cover Cl. 22B or 22C applications where employer undertakes responsibility).	Contractor must insure (and get sub-contractor to insure as well) to cover such liability

Death and personal injury

Liabilities	Insurance Required
Under Clause 20.1	**Caluse 21.1**
Contractor liable for loss, expenses etc. due to **personal injury** or **death** arising out of works **unless** employer at fault or the fault of the employer's agents', servants' etc. The contractor must indemnify the employer against such claims.	Contractor must insure and get sub-contractor to insure to cover this liability. (Insurance to cover employees must comply with employer's liability requirements.)

Fig. 12.4 Summary of liabilities and insurance requirements in relation to the JCT Standard Form of Contract

vehicle on a road unless there is a policy in force covering the required third party risks. For the third party risks *see* p. 388.

Failure to have such a policy or a security against such risks is a criminal offence for which there can be no excuse. As this is a statutory duty, anyone who suffers as a result of a breach of this can sue for breach of statutory duty.

As such insurance is a contract of indemnity it provides an exception to the usual rule of privity that only parties to the contract can derive rights and duties under it thus, if judgment is obtained against an insured, his insurance company will pay the third party by virtue of the indemnity in the policy and this could be enforced against the insurance company if they failed to pay.

As indicated on p. 388, most sensible people have cover against more risks than the mere compulsory third party risks. Indeed, even in so called 'third party policies' most are extended to cover fire and theft, which, of course, indemnify the insured directly.

The Road Traffic Act 1972 also provides additional protection for third parties by invalidating certain terms in the insurance contract which would normally give the insurer the right to avoid the policy (see p. 384). Unfortunately, the Act only renders certain specified matters as subjects of such terms, e.g. the age or physical condition of the driver or the condition of the vehicle. Thus, an insurer may still include terms limiting his right to pay out or giving him the right to avoid the policy in many other ways, e.g. limitations on the type of use to which the vehicle is put.

Another area of protection for the third party is found in the Motor Insurers' Bureau.

Motor Insurers' Bureau

If someone is injured in a road accident caused by a driver who is not insured against such risks, or insured but whose cover is avoided by the insurer for some reason, or a hit, and run driver, then they may claim directly against the bureau, membership of which is compulsory under the Road Traffic Act 1974 for all motor insurers.

Benefit insurance

Life insurance

There are various types of life insurance policies, the most common being **whole life**, i.e. the sum payable is only paid on death or an **endowment** policy whereby the sum is paid either on death or after a certain number of years have elapsed, whichever is earliest.

Life insurance policies are choses in action and can be transferred by assignment, usually to raise cash or to be used as security. The latter is often used to provide additional security for a loan when mortgaging land. For this and other more obvious reasons, life insurance is essential for a builder.

Accident insurance

Life insurance covers death in any event. Accident insurance, on the other hand, covers all or any of the following: death, personal injury, illness, disease caused by an accident. The, word 'accident' is used in a wide sense in insurance terms and its meaning is often the subject of litigation. For the purpose of first party accident insurance, i.e. the insurance of the proposer or designated persons such as employees, an accident should be an event which is unexpected or unintended. Thus deliberately inflicted injuries would take someone outside the cover of the policy.

The benefits paid may be lump sums or pensions, depending on the terms of the policy.

Thus a contractor may decide to obtain insurance against his own accidents or illness and may also insure his employees. This may be considered to be a financial inducement to employees to enter that contractors' employment, as otherwise the injured employee merely has to fall back on his own insurance (if any) or the state scheme if sick or injured at work.

Building and Civil Engineering Death Benefit Scheme

This scheme, operated by a trust company, provides death benefit for the surviving spouse or dependants of someone who dies whilst covered by the construction industry's national working rule agreement. Contributions by the workers are collected under the annual holiday with pay stamps scheme, the sum payable containing an element applicable to the death benefit scheme.

Private health insurance

The National Health Service may not always be able to cover the health requirements of an individual quickly and many companies now maintain a private health insurance scheme as part of their employees' financial package to which the employee may or may not have to contribute. The specialist companies which offer such schemes give cover for operations, examinations, etc., either privately in NHS hospitals or in their own private hospitals and clinics.

As physical fitness is generally essential in the construction industry, individuals may find all or any of the above benefit insurances desirable, if they are self-employed or if their employers do not provide such a benefit.

Pecuniary insurance

The builder may suffer pure financial loss (pecuniary or economic loss) in a number of ways. This may be due:

- to non-payment of debts;
- dishonest employees
- loss of profits or other income following physical damage to works or office or other property.

The employer may suffer in a similar way but in addition may suffer from non-performance or non-completion of a building programme undertaken by a builder.

The following insurance cover may thus be desirable.

Credit insurance

As we have seen in Chapter 6, a builders' debts (owed to him) are one of his most valuable assets. If is therefore good business sense to insure against non-payment by a debtor by taking out credit insurance.

Before cover is given, checks are made by the insurer as to the credit worthiness of the potential debtors and refusal to provide cover may be an indication to the contractor that a particular customer is not a good risk.

The insurer will also stipulate that there should be an efficient debt collecting scheme operating which, of course, will be an indirect encouragement to the contractor to improve this important part of his business.

Fidelity guarantee insurance

This can be obtained to cover the insured against his own pecuniary loss caused by his employees' dishonesty during their employment. Company fraud can be financially crippling, especially with the widespread use of computers and fidelity guarantees reduce the risk of insolvency.

Consequential loss

We have already noted that a builder should have insurance to cover loss caused by damage to his business premises and contents. The money he receives is, of course, designed to enable him to rebuild or replace the property. It can do no more. In the meantime, whilst he is rebuilding and replacing the contents, he may have to rent other premises, hire equipment and may not be able to operate as usual. He also has to pay certain continuing expenses such as ground rent, rates etc. As a result he will suffer a severe loss of income. These losses are suffered as a consequence of the main loss. A business interruption policy may therefore be desirable. This gives additional cover during a limited period following the disaster which closed down or otherwise stopped the business. Such cover will be conditional on there being a material damage policy already in existence.

400

Performance Bonds

To some extent, the employer is always at the mercy of the contractor in relation to any building work undertaken. If the contractor, for one reason or another is unable to finish the work, the employer is left with the problem of obtaining and paying new contractors to complete the job.

For this reason, the contractor may be required by the employer to obtain a performance bond from a bank or more usually an insurance company, to act as a surety. Thus, if the contractor fails to complete the work, the surety pays a sum to cover the cost of completion by other builders. The amount paid under the bond is usually sufficient only to cover the cost of actual loss and no more. Also the bond will contain a 'ceiling' on the amount that may be paid.

A bond is a contract of guarantee, but contained in a deed (under seal) and strictly speaking therefore, the surety need not require any consideration from the contractor. Obviously as this is a commercial contract, the contractor must pay consideration, usually of a single premium, for the guarantee of his work. He should therefore take this additional cost into account when tendering for work requiring a performance bond.

It is usual for the surety to require an express indemnity from the contractor, so that if the surety has to pay out under the bond, then there is an express right to recover the sums paid back from the bonded contractor. This express indemnity merely affirms the common law indemnity that already exists in contracts of this nature.

Insurance to cover employer's losses caused by a contractor's bad workmanship

Poor workmanship, bad design, the use of unsuitable materials and the desire to build quickly has, in some cases led to the existence of buildings which are now unfit for human habitation. As a result employers, usually local authorities are left with two problems, the debts left to pay for the original building work and the costs involved in rehousing tenants. It now appears that a new insurance market is beginning to open up to cover employers who may suffer similar losses in the future.

State compensation for accidents at work or diseases or conditions contracted during the course of employment

Relevant law

The law governing this area is found principally under the Social Security Acts 1975 and 1979, the Social Security and Housing Benefits

Act 1982 and the supplementary regulations made by the Department of Health and Social Security.

To whom does the law apply?

It covers anyone at work. There is usually no minimum period of employment, but the applicant must be an employee or someone holding an office with a company who pays Schedule E income tax (pay as you earn). Thus, self employed people are effectively ruled out unless they can be shown in law to have contracts of service (*see* p.   ). Contributions to the state scheme are made not only by the employee but also by the employer and state and the scheme is a sort of social insurance. However, the monies paid in are paid out the following week to claimants as there is no investment fund held as in ordinary insurance.

What benefits are available?

There are four main benefits.

Statutory sick pay – paid by the employer

This is paid by the employer for the first **eight** weeks of absence. Some employees are not entitled to statutory sick pay because of lack of service, but they will still be entitled to all or any of the following benefits.

Sickness benefit – paid by the State

This is paid for 156 working days if the applicant is unable to work as a result of an accident at work or a prescribed industrial disease contracted at work. In 1985 a single person's sickness benefit amounts to £27.25.

Disablement benefit – paid by the State

This is payable to an employee who, as a result of his injury or a prescribed industrial disease has a loss of mental or physical faculty, whether or not he is able to work.

It is paid once entitlement to sickness benefit ceases. It is based on medically assessing the person's loss of faculty as a result of his injury or disease, in comparison with another person of the same age, and sex. In 1985, 100 per cent disablement amounts to £58.40.

In addition to this pension, if the person is severely disabled or has particular difficulties, he may claim other benefits e.g., unemployment supplement, constant attendance allowance, exceptionally severe disablement allowance and special hardship allowance. There are restrictions on the total amount that an applicant may receive.

Death benefit – paid by the State

If someone dies as a result of an industrial accident or prescribed industrial illness or disease, a death benefit may be paid to the widow (occasionally the widower) for life or until the widow remarries. In 1985 the widow's pension is £50.10 for the first 26 weeks after death, thereafter £36.35 if she is supporting children or in other special circumstances. Additional child allowances are also paid.

These benefits are payable either because someone has been hurt or killed in an **industrial accident** or because they are suffering or have died from **a prescribed disease**.

Industrial accidents. The accident must have occurred:

- at work
- or in the course of the employee's employment
- as a result of no-one's fault or
- as a result of another's misconduct or act of God

providing the employee did not cause the accident himself either directly or indirectly.

Prescribed diseases. The insured must be shown to be suffering from one of the prescribed diseases or conditions set out in the Social Security (Industrial Injuries) (Prescribed Diseases) Regulations 1980. There are at present 51 specified. The claimant must in some cases also show that he has been employed in a specified occupation for a required period. For example, claimants suffering from occupational deafness must have worked in a particular job for 10 years. The regulations are divided into four categories.

Examples

Category A deals with conditions due to physical agents

Condition	Occupation
Cramp of the hand or forearm due to repetitive movements	Prolonged periods of handwriting, typing or other repetitive movements of the fingers, hand or arm.
Subcutaneous cellulitis of the hand (beat hand)	Manual labour causing severe or prolonged friction or pressure on the hand.

Condition	Occupation

Category B deals with conditions due to biological agents

Infection by leptospira	Work in places which are or are liable to be infested by rats, field mice or voles or other small mammals.

Category C deals with conditions due to chemical agents

Localised new growth of the skin, papillomatous or keratotic;	The use or handling of, or exposure to, arsenic, tar, pitch, bitumen, mineral oil (including paraffin), soot or any compound, product or residue of any of these substances, except quinone or hydroquinone.
Squamous-celled carcinoma of the skin.	

Category D – miscellaneous conditions

Diffuse mesothelioma	Any occupation involving: the working or handling of asbestos or any admixture of asbestos; ...

Claims must be made on the appropriate form obtainable from the local DHSS office. A decision is first made by the insurance officer. If the claimant is dissatisfied, he has the right of appeal to the local medical tribunal and from there to the national insurance commissioner.

Index